NEW YIDDISH LIBRARY

The New Yiddish Library is a joint project of
the Fund for the Translation of Jewish Literature
and the National Yiddish Book Center.

Additional support comes from
the Kaplen Foundation and the
Felix Posen Fund for the Translation
of Modern Yiddish Literature.

SERIES EDITOR: DAVID G. ROSKIES

THE
I.L.PERETZ
READER

NEW YIDDISH LIBRARY

THE
I. L. PERETZ
READER

Edited and with an Introduction
by Ruth R. Wisse

YALE UNIVERSITY PRESS
NEW HAVEN AND LONDON

Acknowledgment is gratefully made for permission to include the following
selections:

"Monish" from *The Penguin Book of Modern Yiddish Verse* by Irving Howe,
Ruth R. Wisse, and Khone Shmeruk, copyright © 1987 by Irving Howe,
Ruth Wisse, and Khone Shmeruk. Used by permission of Viking Penguin,
a division of Penguin Putnam Inc.

"Cabalists," by I. L. Peretz, translated by Shlomo Katz, and "If Not Higher,"
by I. L. Peretz, translated by Marie Syrkin, from *A Treasury of Yiddish Stories,* by Irving
Howe and Eliezer Greenberg, editors, copyright © 1953, 1954, 1989 by Viking
Penguin, renewed © 1981, 1982 by Irving Howe and Eva Greenberg. Used by
permission of Viking Penguin, a division of Penguin Putnam Inc.

"Venus and Shulamith" and "The Shabbes Goy" from *I. L. Peretz: Selected
Stories,* edited by Irving Howe and Eliezer Greenberg. Copyright © 1974 by
Schocken Books Inc. Reprinted by permission of Schocken Books Inc.,
published by Pantheon Books, a division of Random House, Inc., New York.

"A Chapter of the Psalms," "Stories," "All for a Pinch of Snuff," and
"Revelation; or The Story of the Billygoat" from *The Prince of the Ghetto* by
Maurice Samuel. Copyright © 1948 by Maurice Samuel. Used by
permission of Alfred A. Knopf, a division of Random House, Inc.

An earlier version of "In the Mail Coach" appeared in *Partisan Review,*
vol. 56, no. 3.

Printed in the United States of America

Library of Congress Control Number: 2001097750

ISBN 0-300-09245-8 (pbk. : alk. paper)

A catalogue record for this book is available from the British Library.

10 9 8 7 6 5 4

For Lucy S. Dawidowicz

CONTENTS

ACKNOWLEDGMENTS

This book is dedicated, with affection and gratitude, to Lucy S. Dawidowicz, who established the Fund for the Translation of Jewish Literature and served as its president until her death in 1990.

I am deeply indebted to Neal Kozodoy for his help in initiating this project, to the members of the advisory board for their counsel, and to the donors whose generosity enables us to commision translations for the New Yiddish Library. I am thankful for the talent and dedication of all the translators represented in this book.

I would also like to acknowledge the help of Zvi Kaplan, and of my former colleagues at McGill University—Lawrence Kaplan, Eugene Orenstein, Gershon Hundert, David Aberbach, Leib Tencer, and Barry Levy—in overcoming difficulties of translation and annotation; any remaining errors or oversights are mine alone. My brother David G. Roskies shared with me his knowledge, his notes, and the anxiety of the project. I hope he can also share in the pleasure of its completion. Among earlier English interpreters and editors of Peretz, I am especially grateful to the late Maurice Samuel, and to the late Irving Howe, who did much to introduce Yiddish literature to the American reading public.

The generous contributions of Martin Peretz to this project expresses the familial and cultural continuity that Isaac Leib Peretz sought but did not always find. This gift and its donor might have persuaded the Jewish writer to reconsider the idea of generational decline that he develops in a number of his works.

Introduction

▼

Isaac Leib Peretz was arguably the most important figure in the development of modern Jewish culture—and until 1939 one would not have had to argue the claim at all. Peretz dominated Jewish literary life in Warsaw almost from the moment he settled there in 1890 until his death on the fifth day of Passover, April 3, 1915, his influence radiating outward from the Polish capital to the growing centers of Jewish settlement worldwide. The estimated hundred thousand people who accompanied his remains to the Warsaw cemetery included delegates and representatives of every sector of Jewish life, testimony to his inclusive appeal at a time of increasing political factionalism. When the Yiddish writers of America formed a new literary association the year after his death, they named it for Peretz. Between the world wars, in communities from Buenos Aires to Birobidzhan, dozens of schools, libraries, streets, and organizations were named for Peretz, who had championed Jewish cultural creativity as the guarantor of modern Jewish existence.

Peretz surfaced as a Hebrew poet in the 1870s, but it was as a Yiddish writer and literary figure that he won renown. Along with Sholem Jacob Abramovitch and Sholem Rabinovitch, better known by their pen names, Mendele Mocher Sforim and Sholem Aleichem, he entered the hallowed circle of classic Yiddish masters that closed when the three men died in rapid succession (Rabinovitch in 1916; Abramovitch in 1917). Mendele, "the grandfather of Yiddish literature," and Sholem Aleichem, his self-designated "grandson," adopted the literary personae of approachable storytellers, as if wanting to maintain in literature the cohesion and security that were everywhere eroding. By contrast, Peretz was eager to expose the anxiety of a changing social order. He considered the emergence of the individual from the collectivity a necessary and encouraging mark of human progress. Toward the end of his life he became the first Yiddish literary modernist, admitting nervous doubt into his art and giving fractured expression to the tension between warring parts of his personality.

Peretz assumed that sooner or later all Jews would have to take advantage of political emancipation and scientific progress, and replace God with human reason as the determinant of their fate. This process would require supple adaptiveness on the part of individual men and women and of the people as a whole. Self-taught in European languages and literatures, law, and social and natural science, he felt that his experience and knowledge could benefit his contemporaries, even though that knowledge was partial at best, and the experience inconclusive. His lifelong program of *education*, by which he meant the striving for an integrated humanistic culture, was predicated on the assumption that the secular future of mankind would surely bring vast improvements over the religious past, if only the Jews were prepared to meet it halfway.

At least part of this optimism had to do with being a Polish Jew. Peretz was eleven years old at the time of the Polish uprising of 1863, a passionate though doomed bid for national independence that was accompanied by high hopes for mutual assistance between Poles and Jews. The pragmatic spirit of Polish positivism in the aftermath of the uprising invited all citizens to contribute to the economic and social advancement of the country, without prejudice as to religion or race. Polish artists, writers, and publicists became interested in the Jew as a colorful and occasionally sympathetic subject.

The young man aspired to become part of this anticipated liberal society. His first preserved writings, from the age of twenty-two, were Polish poems. From young manhood on, he read Polish literature and the Polish-Jewish press, and he discovered Yiddish literature in Polish translation. When he later began to edit his own Yiddish magazines and miscellanies, he included in them Yiddish translations and reviews of Polish literature.

Peretz might have wanted to be a Polish-Jewish writer, along the lines of the German-Jewish writers in Vienna, or, closer to our own time, the American-Jewish writers of New York and Chicago. But this possibility of uninhibited Jewish writing in non-Jewish languages depends on the receptivity of the host society; and the relatively welcoming atmosphere that Peretz encountered as a young man underwent very radical changes in the decades that followed. In place of the progressive toleration that the Positivists had foretold, the Jews encountered opposition and suspicion from almost all segments of the Polish population—from the church, from the peasants, from the emerging urban middle class, from political leaders who discovered in anti-Semitism a potent weapon of nationalism, and even from intellectuals. Many Poles who pressed for Jewish assimilation grew terrified of its consequences once the Jews in increasing numbers actually began to penetrate Polish culture and society.

Sufficiently confident as a Jew not to blame himself for the xenophobia of other peoples, Peretz tried to resist the enforced socioeconomic and political isolation without holding his fellow Jews responsible for their unpopularity. His belief in progress, which included the integration of Jews into European society, placed him among the reformers and alongside the radicals who encouraged acculturation. At the same time, he could neither shut his eyes to anti-Semitism, nor, finally, deny the bleak future it presaged for the Jews of Poland. For as long as he could, he tried in his writing to straddle the two worlds that were fast moving apart: then he recorded his failure.

Peretz was perfectly placed to become the figurehead of modern Polish Jewry. He was born in 1852 into a prominent, pious family of Zamość, a lovely small city in southeastern Poland that served as a hub of learning and trade for the district. The city's founder, Jan Zamoyski, who had it modeled on Padua out of a wish to capture through architecture some of the intellectual spirit of the Italian Renaissance, founded a local university as an alternative to the Catholic seminaries. Strategically situated on the shifting border between Poland, Austria, and Russia (the governing power during Peretz's lifetime), Zamość was also a walled fortress, a prized stronghold among warring nations.

The Jews of Zamość were affected by both its cultural openness and its military vulnerability. When the Ukrainian peasants under Bogdan Chmelnitski revolted against the Polish nobles and their Jewish protégés in 1648, Zamość stood directly in the line of attack, and hundreds of Jews who had sought shelter within its walls died of starvation during the protracted siege. Centuries later, during World War I, thousands of Jews fled the city that was several times overrun by the rival German and Russian occupiers. In the centuries between, the Jews of Zamość accumulated memories of local blood libels, of Jewish girls kidnapped and forcibly converted to Roman

Catholicism, of public hangings and indignities. Stories in this volume such as "Downcast Eyes" and "Three Gifts" are based on legends of martyrdom that Peretz absorbed in his youth.

The intersection of cultures also fostered a strongly cosmopolitan atmosphere. Zamość began to gain prominence as a center of Jewish Enlightenment when the city came under Austrian rule, between 1772 and 1809. It remained within the rationalist, or misnagdic, camp of Jewish religious tradition, resisting the incursion of Hasidic pietism and Hasidic courts well into the nineteenth century. In Zamość there was no necessary contradiction between the study of science or interaction with Gentiles on the one hand, and strict Jewish observance on the other. While Peretz's family took absolutely for granted the need to educate their gifted son in Talmud and commentaries, they were not opposed to the study of language or science, provided these did not conflict with his Jewish observance.

Peretz said that between them his parents provided the basis of his moral education. His mother in particular, who disallowed photographs of herself in deference to the commandment against graven images, was a model of piety. In his memoirs he recalls that once, when a guest demonstratively poured full beakers of water over his hands in the ritual washing before a meal, she said that he was "*frum oyf Ayzikl's kheshbn*"—pious at Ayzikl's expense. Ayzikl was the water carrier who for a fixed fee maintained the household's supply of well water. The distinction his mother was making between excessive ritual piety and genuine religious sensitivity became a recurrent theme of Peretz's work.

Whatever formal education Peretz received from local teachers and rabbis, and during a brief sojourn in the neighboring town of Shebreshin (Szczebrzeszyn), ended well before the bar mitzva age of thirteen. Thereafter, he read unsupervised in the study house, and discovered with great excitement Maimonides' rational approach to Jewish law. The boy's reputation for brilliance prompted a local bookdealer to give him the key to his private library. Unsystematically, and on his own, he began to read French novelists, British moral philosophers, German poets, and Polish reformers, along with the impressive Napoleonic Code of Law, which "rivaled Maimonides." This was Peretz's introduction to what he called "their *beysmedresh*," the study house of European civilization.

While many nineteenth-century biographies contain similar jolts of discovery, the typical young Jew's encounter with the new literature was complicated by the asymmetry between his native culture and the one to which he was now being exposed. Delight in the fruits of

Christian civilization had to call into question the validity of the Judaism that had persuaded him to bear its yoke and obey its commandments because of its special moral attainments. In fact, the emphasis among Jews on learning was part of that special attainment, and it was meant to prepare these youngsters for the lifelong study of Torah, the God-given Law. Once the premise of Jewish election was exposed by the more "advanced" cultures of Europe, many disillusioned youngsters turned their intelligence against the way of life to which it had been consecrated, and tried to liberate themselves simultaneously from an onerous code of behavior and from a despised people. The political handicap of the Jews meant that intellectual realignment with Christian civilization—which was in any case turning secular—also became the key to much more tangible social and economic advancement.

Peretz understood this temptation. In his own native city, along with genuine Jewish reformers, there were converts and highly assimilated Jews, like the well-to-do father of Rosa Luxemburg. When Rosa, almost twenty years Peretz's junior, helped to found the Social Democratic Party of Poland, she advertised her lack of interest in the Jews through a Marxist program strenuously opposed to Jewish peoplehood, and to any notion of a Jewish national culture. Peretz was later to write about "the paths that led away from Jewishness," which attracted those who wanted to revolutionize society as well as those who aspired to rise in it.

But Peretz remained among his own people. At about eighteen, resisting the impulse to run off to Warsaw to study, he allowed himself to be married to the girl his father had picked out for him. Later, after the marriage had failed and he became accredited as a lawyer, he once again returned to his native city, where he remarried and built up a successful law practice. He wrote and published Hebrew poetry in the Hebrew periodicals and literary miscellanies that were appearing in Galicia and Russia. He also lectured on Jewish history and Hebrew language to intensify young people's understanding of themselves as Jews. The more he distanced himself from Jewish religious observance, the more he encouraged the development of a national consciousness through a strengthened Jewish culture.

Then suddenly Peretz experienced a terrible reversal. In 1887–88, responding to anonymous and unspecified accusations against him, the tsarist government deprived him of the right to practice law. Denied explanation or right of appeal, he lost his income, his profession, and also his home, because he could find no other suitable employment in the city. Through the intervention of friends he found temporary work on a statistical expedition investigating the condition of Jews in the small towns of Poland. Then, beginning January 1, 1891, he was hired by the Jewish community council of Warsaw, a job he held until the end of his life. Unlike his earlier, fairly lucrative practice of law, this work as a Jewish functionary provided only modest financial sustenance, and a far from sufficient outlet for his energy or ambition. It did allow him to take up, in tandem with the nine-to-three workday of a Jewish public servant, the more spacious career of a Yiddish man of letters; the daily contacts it required with people from every walk of life provided inexhaustible new materials for his pen. Peretz further divided his literary life between private and public spheres, between the solitary hours spent writing and the time he devoted to generating a cultural renaissance.

Peretz's dislocation in many ways typified the move of tens of thousands of his contemporaries from small town (in his case small city) to big city, yet from the very first works that he published in Warsaw—in Yiddish, the language of the growing mass of Jewish readers—he tried to guard against the facile relegation of that small-town life to the irrelevant past. In *Impressions of a Journey Through the Tomaszow Region in 1890*, a pioneering work of Jewish reportage based on his own statistical research, a narrator very much like himself sets out to establish a reliable data base about Jews in the Polish towns that can be used to correct the false accusations of anti-Semites. Right from the start the merits of his mission are called into question by a succession of subjects who distrust his project and suspect his motives. The narrator finally succumbs to doubt himself. How will his statistics communicate the stubborn individualism of the rabbi's widow who would rather manufacture "soap" from potato peelings than become the ward of her children or the community, or the moral sweetness of the orphan who wants the Messiah to come so that the moon should regain its lost parity with the sun? The narrator, who enters these towns armed with pen, notebook, and questionnaire, learns that he cannot hope to fathom the human condition using only the instruments of social science. What is more, he begins to suspect that the modern Jew may be more knowledgeable but not necessarily any wiser than his traditional forefathers. Peretz, who had been disbarred without right of appeal, is forced to wonder whether the faith of believers in God is less reasonable than the faith of enlightened Jews in government, or his own faith in progress.

This readiness to examine the rational premises of his optimism set Peretz apart from both the older generation of Jewish enlighteners and the new generation of radicals. He certainly shared the Enlightenment's preference for science over metaphysics, and his stories take deadly aim at the excesses of Hasidic rabbis and the credulity of their flocks. But even as he exposes all the petty frauds and abuses of Jewish life with a lawyer's thoroughness, he has two bits of mitigating evidence that complicate any indictment. As long as the Jews are deprived of political rights, and subjected to economic and social discrimination, they cannot be held fully responsible for the ugliness and failure of their lives. And while the "opiate of religion" may prevent people from first analyzing, then improving, their society, it has also, in the case of the Jews, created in the face of unparalleled adversity a civilization of remarkable moral refinement. In his most sober moments Peretz concluded that the absence of any material foundation condemned the Jews of Poland to death. Pushing the metaphoric concept of "a living death" as far as it could go, he demonstrates that the moral life, dependent on meaningful moral action, is impossible for a people that lives on air and subsists on dreams. In other moods he challenges the force of his own evidence. The short story "Kabbalists" opens with a materialist's self-assured declaration that the spiritual condition of a people is determined by the degree of its prosperity: "When times are bad, even Torah—that best of merchandise—finds no takers." The main character is the last remaining student of a once-flourishing yeshiva who adds a penitential fast day to the several days he has gone without food and tries to reach the highest level of union with God before starving to death. In a sense, the narrator demonstrates his thesis: the boy dies because he didn't have, and wasn't given, enough to eat. Nevertheless, the boy's soul is so pure that it contradicts the rational prejudice of the man telling the story.

Throughout the 1890s Peretz was involved in socialist politics. His stories and publications were credited with bringing many young Jews into the ranks of the emerging socialist movement. The little fables he wrote about the pious Jewish cat who swallows the canaries, or about expensive "pike" that are prepared to urge masses of cheaper "carp" to sacrifice themselves, organized the resentment of the Jewish poor against their would-be exploiters. In particular, the character Bontshe Shvayg was held up to Jewish workers as a symbol of their passivity. Bontshe is a battered victim who never once complains or cries out, so in keeping with the scheme of Jewish folk religion, he is rewarded when he gets to heaven. Bontshe the Silent

Sufferer is greeted by an angelic chorus of praise, and after his soul is tried in the ultimate court, the Supreme Judge invites him to claim anything he wants for his heavenly reward. The scheme does not work, however, because Bontshe has never learned his worth. When he stammers out a request for a buttered roll every morning, the evil prosecuting angel has the last laugh, and readers understand that they had better learn to demand their due in this life.

Peretz was particularly eloquent in his defense of the Jewish woman who was expected to carry the financial burden of the family she was raising so that she could then sit as her scholarly husband's "footstool" in heaven. The shrewish housewife had figured prominently in earlier Yiddish writing; her ill-tempered tyranny over the household demonstrated how topsy-turvy the Jewish order had become. The reformers who wanted men to assume financial responsibility for their families set out to satirize shiftless Jewish husbands, but their comic barbs struck less at the passive males than at the overbearing wives. It was Peretz who turned this characterization inside out to show at what terrible cost to women the unwordliness and holiness of Jewish manhood was often attained. The title of his story "Bryna's Mendl" leads us to anticipate yet another portrait of a henpecked husband and his Cossack of a wife. Then, having organized these expectations, the story reveals the limits of Bryna's strength and the degree to which she has become the victim of Mendl's hypocrisy.

Despite Peretz's wholehearted sympathy for the oppressed, however, he was not satisfied by the ideological prescriptions for the reordering of society. No sooner did the Jewish political parties begin to crystallize and to turn their vague protests and aspirations into fixed party platforms than he rebelled against their materialist constraints, and in the dialectical pattern that characterized both his life and his work came to the rescue of the threatened spiritual values. Attracted as he was by some of the egalitarian and liberal aspirations of socialism, he feared that the systematic reapportionment of wealth would stifle individuality and encroach on the freedom of the creative spirit. The rule of the many could become even more oppressive than the rule of a few. He wrote to the movement after the abortive revolution of 1905 had shown the strength of the revolutionary cadres:

> I worry that as victors you may become the bureaucracy,
> apportioning to each his morsel as to inmates in a
> poorhouse, allotting work like a sentence of hard labor.

You will destroy that creator of new worlds—the human
spirit. You will plug up the purest well of human
happiness—initiative—the force that is able to pit a
single human life against thousands. You will mechanize
life . . . . you will be occupied with regulations . . . no
stomach will be empty, yet the mind will be famished.

These fears were sharpened by his concern for the creative vitality
of the Jews, because if human needs could be satisfied through the
redistribution of wealth alone, why shouldn't a Jew speed up the
process by dissolving his particular identity? Peretz was far from
persuaded by the necessity of class conflict, and unwilling to assist
in the dissolution of the Jews toward any such higher end. In 1899
he was arrested and briefly imprisoned for antitsarist activity, but at
the very moment when he was thus enshrined as a political martyr,
he used some of the time in prison to write neoromantic tales
extolling the glories of the Jewish spirit. And despite the swell of
criticism that they aroused among some of the younger revolution-
aries, these modern folktales and retold Hasidic stories became his
most popular works.

Hasidic tales were nothing new. The inspirational religious leaders
of what came to be known as the Hasidic movement had used the
miracle tale and the exemplum to inspire faith and piety in their
followers, who, in turn, traded stories about the virtues and miracles
of their respective rebbes and zaddikim. Thus, as Hasidism swept
Poland in the late eighteenth century, it generated a vast fund of
legends and music. But a century later these same Hasidim and their
charismatic leaders had come to represent for the modernizing Jews
the embodiment of everything most corrupt and reactionary in
Jewish life. Reformist writers, including Peretz himself, had mocked
the corruption that was known to infect the courts of the rabbis
and the attribution to these faith healers of supernatural powers. In
fact, in his political essays and news columns Peretz never ceased
to criticize the Hasidim for their fundamentalist beliefs and their
resistance to change.

Now, however, along with this critical view, Peretz was among the
first to recognize in the ideals of the early Hasidic masters, and in
the web of legend that had been spun around them, models of
spiritual independence that the Jews of his time were otherwise
lacking. All around him in Warsaw and in Poland he observed the
pace of linguistic adaptation to Russian and Polish at the expense of
Yiddish and Hebrew, the flight of the young to America—or to

Palestine or Argentina—and the recklessness with which a new generation was quitting what centuries of Jewish civilization had so painstakingly and at such sacrifice accumulated. Like an engineer who has tried to stoke a recalcitrant engine, only to see it hurtling down an incline out of control, Peretz tried to retard the process he had helped to set in motion, or, if not to retard it, then at least to warn against its runaway abandon.

Despite a superficial similarity to their Hasidic sources, Peretz's stories present the familiar material from a modern perspective. "If Not Higher," one of the earliest and perhaps the most famous of the neo-Hasidic stories, is told by a skeptical Jew from Lithuania who is so eager to disprove local legends about the rabbi of Nemirov that he hides under his bed to check things out for himself. The rabbi's Hasidic followers believe that when he disappears every year between Rosh Hashanah and Yom Kippur, he ascends to heaven to plead on their behalf with God. The skeptical sleuth discovers that the rabbi is assuming the disguise of a woodcutter in order to perform anonymous acts of charity. He becomes the rabbi's disciple, and thereafter, if anyone speaks of the holy man's ascent to heaven, he softly adds, "if not higher."

If faith in the Jewish God was no longer possible, Peretz expected Jews to continue to honor the exalted moral tradition that derived from faith. Somewhat like the Lithuanian in the story, he tracked the faithful, persuaded that their human values were on the one hand superior to the religious impulse that had shaped them, yet on the other hand superior to values that could be arrived at through reason alone. The pointed conclusion of the story attributes a "higher" value to earthly goodness than to its heavenly inspiration, but without repudiating the power of that inspiration. Peretz had come to the paradoxical conclusion that in order to improve the material lot of the Jews he would have to continue to nurture their spiritual-religious heritage.

The passion for folklore was already highly developed in Poland, where it also served as a kind of substitute for national autonomy. In addition to the nostalgia for folk culture that was characteristic of every industrializing society, subject minorities like the Poles or the Jews could use their folk sources to express the will to national resurgence. Inspired by the work of Polish ethnographers (some of whom appreciated the Jewish component of Polish lore), Peretz determined to gather every kind of Jewish folk expression and to instill in his followers an appreciation of their native culture. When aspiring writers came to see him with the first samples of their work, he would question them about their background, ask them to sing the songs and tell the stories of their homes, and encourage them to collect all they could. In this way he accumulated material for his own writing and directed them to where Jewish inspiration might be found.

Peretz put this material to varied use. Sometimes he retold a folktale so as to make it appear unembellished, as the Brothers Grimm and Hans Christian Andersen did in their collections. In such instances, the practiced student of literature, or the scholar who knows the original source, must hunt for the transforming hand of the modern author. Elsewhere, as in the story "Three Gifts," the author set the tales into a most ironic framework. The soul that circles the globe trying to find suitable "gifts" for heaven discovers a Jew who will die for the soil of Israel, a Jewess whose modesty is more important to her than her life, and a Jew who dies rather than dishonor his God. These are standard folk motifs, and they are selected to represent the national, moral, and religious foundations of Jewish life. But if the story values the bloody gifts these martyrs create, it is far less enthusiastic about the the heaven that invites such offerings and finds "beauty" in their martyrs' blood. Here the narrator drives a wedge between the heroism of the Jews and the metaphysical trust that occasions it.

Peretz also used Hasidic and folk settings to project the grandeur of Jewish civilization. He created mighty rabbinic personalities and an imagined golden age of the Jewish past when great yeshivas flourished simultaneously (as they never did in history) in Safed, Babylon, and Jerusalem. One thinks of Theodor Herzl, the architect of political Zionism, who insisted that all the delegates to the First Zionist Congress in Basel in 1897 wear formal attire. Herzl may have wanted to establish the credibility of his movement in the eyes of the European community, but he had also to involve the Jews in a manifestation of national dignity. A people that is forever picking away at its faults, and being impressed by neighbors with proofs of its failings, has also to be reminded of its capacity for greatness and beauty. Peretz, intent no less than Herzl on affirming Jewish national pride, dusted off the purple of the Jewish experience in dramatizations of intellectual and moral combat, of titanic struggles with God.

Peretz assumed such a major role in the development of a national Jewish literature that the personal themes of his writing are often overlooked. Part of this is due to the lingering modesty of Yiddish culture even after it broke away from its religious moorings. The kind of inquiry that is taken for granted in modern biography, into the sexual activity of the artist or writer as an indispensable key to the understanding of his art and his character, is almost completely missing in Yiddish scholarship, and there have been no such investigations of Peretz's known involvements with women. This perhaps commendable reticence need not extend to his writing, however, which accorded sex an unprecedented degree of importance as both an enhancement and a complication of human happiness.

Compared to religions that distrust the body and uphold ideals of celibacy, Judaism has a relatively liberal attitude to men and women who want to enjoy physical love as part of the fulfillment of marriage. Unfortunately, the theoretical possibility of love was often thwarted by the practical arrangement of marriages. We know that Peretz's first marriage was miserable: his father's attempt to match him up with a suitably intelligent family resulted in a real bond between Peretz and his father-in-law, but not between him and his wife. The strange and partially autobiographical little story "Uncle Shakhne and Aunt Yakhne" captures the emotional atmosphere of such a union. A writer describes the day of his marriage to a wife from whom he is long since estranged, but for whose unhappiness he continues to feel responsible. Contrasting sharply with his own misalliance, he remembers his aunt and uncle who were so alike as to be indistinguishable, less like a wedded couple than a set of twins. The uncle and aunt are sweet and kind, yet as regards romantic love or physical attraction there is not much to choose from between this fraternal couple that smothers the marital fire and the incompatible children who have been yoked together.

Peretz knew that the sexual and creative urges were closely linked. Just as communal discipline should not be allowed to throttle the individual's intellectual or artistic striving, so too domestic harmony cannot be allowed to quench erotic desire. More than once Peretz dramatized the struggle of the artist between marital fidelity and lust. All his sympathy in the story "A Musician's Death" is with the dying Mikhl, the frisky father of a band of musicians, who during his final hours has to face his wife's jealous rage. Although Mikhl tries to assure his wife that his affection for her was never compromised by his attraction to other women, neither the presence of his sons in the room nor his own impending death can persuade him to express regret for having committed adultery. Sexual freedom is no more blameworthy than the passion for life.

Elsewhere, however, this theme was also complicated for Peretz by the cautionary impulse of the filial Jew. Along with the strength of sexual desire, Peretz knew its destructive potential. As it happens, the very first work that he published in Yiddish, the poem "Monish," which he later characterized as a portrait of himself, presents the conflict between son and lover in semiplayful fashion. A pious Jewish boy is distracted from his studies by the song of a German maiden, really Lilith in disguise, and in his fierce attraction to her he betrays everything in his Jewish universe, from his sidelocks and phylacteries, through his parents and teachers, to Almighty God. The battle between passion and responsibility is often thematically linked in Peretz's writing, as it is here, to the conflict between Gentile and Jew, not only because of the proscriptions against lust in Jewish teachings (which would make a lecherous Jew feel un-Jewish), but because the sexual drive, directed often enough toward Gentile women, felt to him like an act of national betrayal. Modern man and the creative writer especially might feel they had to liberate their instincts from religiously imposed laws. But to accept the primacy of the sexual drive and to follow its instincts was to destroy any possibility of a living community.

In sum, Peretz provided Jews with the vocabulary of their experience. Focusing on problems rather than solutions, he dramatized the wrenching choices that faced young men and women who had been brought up in one way of life and now had to invent another. Was the moral discipline of the halakhic way of life possible in a secular society? How far was a Jew to go in his desire and need to feel at home among the Gentiles without sacrificing his own distinctiveness? Was the struggle for social justice compatible with the desire to preserve a unique people? How could the condition of the Jewish woman be improved without danger to the already-crumbling Jewish social structure? Was the messianic idealism of the Jew the source of his noblest striving or the fatal impediment to his progress? How could the instincts be freed from their civilizing constraints without the destruction of the civilization that was created to contain them? Throughout the centuries of dispersion, the best Jewish minds had been consecrated to precise and subtle argument over legal and moral questions. Trained in Jewish law and practiced in Russian law, Peretz adopted the courtroom as the natural venue of literature, and threw the caseload of modern doubt open to the jury of readers. People said that he was "more than a writer," by which they meant that he had achieved the status of a moral authority.

It should be noted that to some critics being "more than a writer" meant being less than a good writer. The fine Hebrew stylist David Frishman, for example, published quite a nasty parody of Peretz in 1894, and became his bitterest critic thereafter. He said that Peretz corrupted literature with polemics, that he was a careless writer, that he fawned over the reader yet failed to consummate the courtship. Sholem Aleichem had harsh things to say about Peretz's readiness to set himself up as a literary "rebbe," assuming false authority and inspiring cheap adulation. The objection to Peretz's cerebral fiction carries over to the present: though Saul Bellow included three works by Peretz in his volume *Great Jewish Short Stories*, he confessed to finding him excessively "talmudic." Even in Peretz's day, readers objected to the obscurity of his allusions—another aspect of his talmudism—and while the modern reader may be inclined to appreciate certain kinds of difficulty in fiction, he too may resent being made aware of his ignorance.

A balanced assessment of Peretz's work is made more difficult by his endless experimentation and changeability. Peretz slipped at both ends of the spectrum. Sometimes, while trying to express the restlessness and malaise of the cosmopolitan whose every new desire turns to ashes in his grasp, Peretz evokes the vagueness of his hero through an unsatisfyingly imprecise prose. And when, contrarily, he is overly determined to put the best face on an unhappy situation, he forces the triumph of his characters because he cannot convince us artistically that they do prevail. He could be alternately too misty and too dogmatic.

Curiously, Peretz produced some of his finest work when he thought he was being least profound. The stories that he designated "humoresques" stand up exceptionally well. The modern reader is likely to appreciate both their unresolved narrative tension and their moral ambiguity. The last humoresque that he wrote, "Yom Kippur in Hell," consigns the artist, in this case, a cantor, to a posture of eternal defiance within a universal scheme that demonstrates the futility of such defiance. Similarly, Peretz's satires and works of sanctification are often most successful when the unconscious hand of the author interfered with his apparent purpose. The figure of Bontshe Shvayg, mentioned earlier, was drawn by Peretz with so much residual sympathy that he defied the expectations of the story just as he had defied the expectations of heaven: the suffering saint could not be contained by the moral that was to have made a bad example of him. Peretz's contemporary audience was understandably desperate for comfort and inspiration, and many readers valued him to the extent that he was able to supply what religion no longer could. For us, the greatest works are those that betray the darker side of Peretz's doubts and fears. They are better literary works not because of their gloom, but because they allow glimpses of a deeper if more disturbing truth.

Peretz's writing was part of a broader hope that culture in the Jewish languages, Yiddish and Hebrew, would serve modern Jews as a creative substitute for both religion and politics. We have already mentioned Peretz's attempt to forge a chain of continuity by reinvigorating folktales and religious motifs. He expended much energy on translating the five Megillot of the Bible into Yiddish, and gave enthusiastic encouragement to the younger poet Yehoash (Solomon Bloomgarten), who undertook to translate the entire Hebrew Bible for modern Jews who might never learn the sacred tongue. He championed the study of Jewish history, using the analogy of a family that through genealogy and geographic contacts seeks to maintain its wholeness in time and space. As the most prominent participant in the Czernowitz Conference of 1907, which declared Yiddish to be a national language of the Jews, Peretz issued an inspirational call for the intensification of Yiddish cultural activities. He became personally involved in projects to establish Jewish choirs and a musical society, dramatic groups and a flourishing theater, informal education through an open university, and Jewish orphanages and schools.

Politically, Peretz hoped that the folk was about to replace the nation, and that in a disarmed continent of peoples, each peaceably separated from the other by a different language and culture, the Jews would live alongside the Poles, Germans, Russians, and so forth, developing their own native culture. According to this view of culture as the determinant of the national character and the guarantor of national survival, the Jews could fare very well in Europe, theirs being a particularly rich heritage and an essentially unthreatening, antiexpansionist notion of specialness or "chosenness." In the same manner that Yiddish plays could be performed in Warsaw alongside the Polish plays in a neighboring theater, Jews and their neighbors might live side by side, sharing an appreciation for one another's developing modern culture.

Unfortunately, as Peretz approached the end of his life, there was not a shred of evidence to support this idea of Europe's evolution.

Instead, anti-Semitism became an effective tool of nationalist politics, while the revolutionary movements insisted that Jews be the avant-garde of the new International. From a socialist-internationalist perspective, those nations that already occupied a place on the map would have to make a gradual transition from national to class consciousness. But because the Jews had no land, they were to dissolve themselves at once. Any attempt on the part of the Jews to regroup as a nation would be a setback to the cause of world revolution.

As for the Jews, who were the simultaneous target of both these powerful, competing political forces, they tried frantically to find a solution to their dilemma. Many emigrated, and many assimilated. Jewish political parties proliferated, and the tensions between them increased in direct proportion to the pressure against the Jews from the outside. Peretz, who stood at the center of Jewish life in Warsaw, had to confront not only the mounting hostility to the Jews on the part of his native Poland, but spreading demoralization in the Jewish community itself.

He responded in different ways to these defeats. In 1913 he began to write memoirs that seem to find—or at least to seek—solace in the remembered past. His descriptions of childhood in Zamość, free of nostalgia or bitterness, show how firmly he derives from that native locale. As an autobiographer, Peretz set himself the ambiguous task of revealing himself *as a writer*. He did not intend to provide confessional self-exposure in the manner of Rousseau, because part of the autobiographical essence he set out to reveal was the shaping influence upon him of the moral atmosphere of his childhood, emphatically including its values of modesty. At the same time, his emergence as a modern writer had been at the expense of that formative tradition. As the young boy begins to experience his uniqueness, to luxuriate in his sensations of pleasure and pain, to cultivate a critical temper, to recognize the conflict between filial devotion and the instincts of revolt, he knows that he will be forced to choose between his creative impulses and the responsible life of a Jew. The autobiography Peretz wrote is a fascinating attempt to prove (the reader will have to judge how successfully) that he had managed to keep intact the Jewish boy within the modern writer.

There is hardly an image or incident in the memoirs without its vital counterpart in Peretz's works, though the relation between the two treatments is always complex, and often ironic. The author has a habit of pointing, here and there, to motifs or characters that appear in his dramas and stories, showing the connections between memory and art on the one hand, memory and personality on the other. But the connections are often deeper where the author does not make them explicit. So, for example, the reader may want to compare Peretz's self-absorbed description of his marriage with its bittersweet transformation in the story "Uncle Shakhne and Aunt Yakhne," or the story of his forfeited first love with the ironic resolution of a youngster's philosophic doubt in "What Is the Soul?" One of the most haunting images of the memoirs is the well in the center of the marketplace that almost lures the boy to his death with its "liquid smile." This well stands at the center of the expressionistic drama *A Night in the Old Marketplace*, which he worked on during the last years of his life, only there it has already lured a band of musicians into its depths and threatens to cast its eerie spell on all the rest of the Jews in its orbit. In the memoirs Peretz tries to reimpose authorial control over the unconscious and accidental forces that shaped his development. He gives free rein to his creative will in telling how his creative powers assumed their characteristic form. This was the sunniest of his late projects, a vital counterpoint to the book of Ecclesiastes, which he was simultaneously translating into Yiddish.

Had it been possible to ensure the continuity of the Jewish people through literature in a Jewish language, or to fashion out of literature a weapon of cultural resistance sufficiently forceful to stave off those who hated the Jews, the collected works of Peretz might have secured the Jews till the end of time. When Peretz died, his most devoted biographer and interpreter, Shmuel Niger, could not bring himself to use the past tense because "Peretz was the future" and how could the future be relegated to the past? Indeed, when the American writer John Hersey set out to dramatize events in the Warsaw Ghetto during World War II in his novel *The Wall*, he described the cultural resistance of the Jews through an evening devoted to Peretz. Such commemorative gatherings had taken place not only in the Warsaw Ghetto but wherever Jews mounted a cultural resistance by trying to maintain confidence in the higher spirit of humankind.

Peretz's idea of culture as a guarantor of Jewish national survival did not prove viable. But as the Bible remains the most important book to readers who may no longer credit its divine source, so within the modern context the works of Peretz outlast the idea that inspired their creation. Arguments over what is best in the Peretz canon will

be resolved by each new generation in turn. This volume of the
Library of Yiddish Classics presents some of the finest and most
interesting of Peretz's work in the hope that a companion volume
of drama, essays, and publicistic writing will follow.

RUTH R. WISSE
Montreal, 1990

MONISH

With the poem "Monish" Peretz made his debut as a Yiddish writer in 1888. This story of a pious Jewish boy, autobiographically inspired, as Peretz tells us in his memoirs, comments on the crisis of the Jewish artist who succumbs to the powerful attraction of Christian culture. The original version contained a discursive passage about the constraints of the Yiddish language, which "has no words for sex appeal / and for such things as lovers feel." Perhaps Peretz no longer felt these constraints as sharply in later years, because he omitted this passage in the final version of 1908, on which this translation is based.

MONISH

▼

Life is like a river;
we are fish.
The water's wholesome and fresh
and we would swim forever,
but for a black figure
on the riverbank.

There Satan stands,
in his hands
a fishing rod,
and catches fish.

With a worm that eats the dust,
a little lust,
a moment's pleasure,
the line is baited.

Hardly a flick
and the pike flies in the pan
to be fried or roasted
on the flames of hell.

May his name be obliterated!
we know whose work it is—
Satan's—
and why it works so well.
The cause
is the little worm;
it draws and draws—

And so the story I'm about to tell.
Listen!

✦ ✦ ✦

There was a prodigy,
precisely when or where is hard to say,
but in Poland,
in olden days,
and he was raised
in a pious house.

Pious father,
pious mother;
the family,
one after another,
scholars all,
known and praised
everywhere,
and those who know best
say they'll all be surpassed
by our hero—Monish.

He's only
seven, eight.

Yet always at his studies
day and night.

He laps up Torah like a sponge.
His mind is lightning;
it can plunge
from the highest
to the most profound,
and can sound the *Taz*
and the ocean of *Shas*;
however stony the *Rambam*,
he finds a cleft in the rock.

And he's beautiful.
Black as night, his locks;
his lips are roses;
black arching eyebrows
and sky-blue eyes,
fire-bright.

A joy to see.
Ah, the blushes and sighs
when the maidens see Monish
go by.

The young *rebetsin* at *kheyder*
watches Monish, nothing else,
and she melts;
and the pots in the oven
spill and burn
as she sits,
her hands in her lap,
seeming to hear
how the children learn.

And the neighbor, pretty Odl,
lets her needle fall
as she listens to Monish:
her hand on her heart,
her ear to the wall,
tears rolling down her cheek.

But Monish is as good as gold;
he knows nothing of this!
What does Monish seek?

His love—Gemara,
reason and hypothesis:
shor shenoygakh es hapora[1]
"If an ox should gore a cow . . ."
He's as good as gold—

◆   ◆   ◆

And in those days
Monish was renowned.
Scholars from abroad,
rabbis near and far,
came to hear him out,
"A new star!"
say the silver beards dancing for joy—
"Happy the mother who bore him,
happy the father and the place!"
(I say only what I heard, word for word.
But is that what they would say
on Ararat?)

Those were the days
of the worthy men of old:
brass-rimmed spectacles,
tfiln housed in silver,
talis crowned in gold,
and their minds were as towers.
Other times,
other powers.

The house of study full,
and the people overflowed
to the entry and the step;
the lamp burned steady
past the middle of the night,
and judgment and Torah
abundant as the light.

◆   ◆   ◆

Now mountain peaks are plentiful,
but the Bible's Ararat
is not the average snowy

peak;
Ararat's unique,
for there when the flood waters crested
Noah's ark rested,
and the One Above Us drew the line;
and, as we've heard,
granted life forever to the earth.

"Dear people," He said, "steal, betray, and slaughter.
You will not be drowned in water,
for I avert my eyes,"
and in the sky he hung a bow
for a sign.

That was once, a pack of years ago,
but the ark is still buried deep in snow,
and there live Sammael and Lilith—man and wife—
grateful for the chill,
and to pass the time away,
far away from Gehenna,
and isn't it a pretty tête-à-tête?

One morning
as Sammael lay in bed smoking cigarettes,
and Lilith saw to her toilette
by the light of the *tsoyer*[2]
(the gem that lights the ark),
the doorbell tinkled in the foyer:
"Enter!"
and there a trembly demon stood,
teeth all a-clatter,
who flung himself flat on his face and then flatter.

"My lord and sire,
You've hidden your face
from your people.
You've heard
and seen nothing,
and now it's too late!
Your throne is going to topple!"

Satan leaped up. "Sir Baron,
what transpires?"

"In the kingdom of Poland
where the border is drawn
stands a *shtetl*
as big as a yawn.

The place doesn't matter,
it's rarely mentioned,
houses like nutshells,
prayers are their mansions!
The Jews drift around
as if these were their last days,
with nothing to eat,
living on fast days.

No business to do,
and so Torah can flourish,
and all the genius
its study can nourish.

A boy who lives there
will shame and hush
Lithuania, Poland,
Bohemia, and Prussia.
Let him mature
undiminished,
and we go under—
you're finished!
We'll be thrashed
with iron rods
and the flames of Gehenna
extinguished,
he'll pursue us
with frightening hate
to the end
and bring the Messiah,
Heaven forfend!"

The moment Satan heard these words,
the party was over; his passion stirred,
his eyes turned red,
and devil's sweat
rose like the mist
of a steaming cauldron,
and he rushed at Lilith wagging his fist.

"It's her fault, only hers!"
"The nut is hard,
good sirs," said Lilith,
"but wait.
A good set of teeth can crack it.
Victory's sweet.
Warm up the spit,
the meat
will come on its own!"
and she flew with the wind
and was gone.

♦   ♦   ♦

Tantivy-tan-ton!
What transpires?
Did somebody
see the Messiah?

When is the *shoyfer* blown?
Elul, not *Tamuz*.
Has he gone crazy,
the *shames*?

The rise and fall,
of the trumpet call,
whipcrack!
the wheels go round,
and a coach
rolls into town!
Trumpet blare
and *whipsnap!*
mouths drop open, people stare:
"What's up?"
What's up?
A German's come from Danzig.
And he's dealing in wheat, dealing in rye.
Everything's suddenly fine.
Now here's a client who knows how to pay!
The small change glitters, the dollars shine.
It's raining credit
all around,
the roads are full

of the wagon sound
of peasants coming to town,
and ah! the wheeling and dealing
of slaughterers, judges, perpetual scholars
chasing the dollars,
buying and sending things on.
God blessed the *shtetl* with luck!

Golden times and daily display
of satin and silk, whatever impresses,
weddings every day in the week,
and every tailor up to his ears
in orders for wedding dresses.
All the musicians are worn out and weary,
the *khupe* is torn, the poles are
as dull as the guests, who haven't the strength
to laugh at the *badkhn*,
and there's no wax left for *havdoles*.
Their hunger forgotten once and for all—
who eats bread or bothers to bake it?
Plum pastry, honey cake,
and liquor—a lake of it.

Now the German brought
an only daughter
with him—a jewel.
Golden hair falling to her feet,
and eyes as bright as stars,
so sweet,
to hear her voice, so sweet.
Dressed all in velvet,
and when she spoke, to tell of it,
it was a fiddle playing.
Her laugh was a cascade of joy.
The porter under his load,
the hermit fasting and praying,
laughed when she laughed, and their own music flowed
when the music of her song came thronging,
and the fiddle spoke and sang,
sweet and full of longing.

Long, long, long,
on his way to his studies at the *kloyz*

day by day,
Monish passed her house,
lingered at the gate,
and his ears drank her song
till like wine it made him drunk
(an erring mortal, dust and ashes),
and when he turns to *Rashi*,
held by its power,
he hums the tune she sang
hour after hour.
The *kloyz* listens stunned
to such musical sorrow,
neither shepherd nor folk song,
so strong it draws the marrow
from your bones.

Perplexed,
Monish sits alone,
trembling as if he'd caught
a fever, his forehead white as chalk,
gazing past the holy text
at something far away.
"What's wrong with you, Monish?" says his friend.
"Tell me."
And so it goes day after day
after day.

His mother sees him pining away:
"What's wrong, my child?
What wind put out
the light in your eyes,
my bright *havdole* candles?
Why are all the tunes you sing
lamenting?

"You used to sing other things.
My heart would laugh
When you sang with the cantor
or at the Sabbath meal,
free as a bird, clear as a bell.
And now there's something else.
What is it, child? Tell me!
It frightens me!"

"Do I know, Momma, what song
is singing in me?
It's not that I want to sing;
it sings itself.
The sounds rise like birds
from the nest,
and these are the songs they bring me."

◆ ◆ ◆

Now from olden days
there was a ruin in that place—
(I won't attempt to say
whether church or castle;
let that much remain in doubt,
I can tell you only what I've read about it.)
There are goblins in the ruin,
imps that crow and laugh for spite,
bark, meow,
and haunt at night,
hurl stones through the air
from their lair
at the houses underneath;
and on the roof
in the dark
a wild dog with tangled fell,
always on the prowl,
who never has been heard to bark,
he only grinds his teeth.
Flesh and blood tremble.
Jews and Christians both
stay well away from that street
and its tumbledown houses overgrown with weeds.

One night in the shadow of the walls
a solitary figure creeps toward the ruin;
all along the street there's no one else:
it's Monish clutching his lapels.

Two angels go with him,
one on either side;

the evil on the left,
and the good, weeping tears, on the right.

His good angel whispers in his ear,
"Have pity on yourself,
fear the Lord your God.
He created all the world,
heaven, earth,
and the seventy nations
who live by the sword.
But the essence of all people
are the Jews, whom He treasured,
and for them He weighed and measured
six hundred and thirteen commandments.
Three hundred and ten worlds
are for those who guard His Torah.
Tell me that it's worth it
to lose them for a girl!"

His evil angel sneers
in his other ear:
"When it's over, repent.
He'll forgive you. Why should *you* fear?
Reuben sinned,
David and Bathsheba sinned,
yet without stint
He gave them paradise,
because He's good by nature.
A wretched look, a tear,
fasting on a winter day;
only groan and state your
never-evers,
and He'll believe anything you say."

Monish listened to his angels
but didn't ponder long.
She appeared in a window,
he was spellbound by her song.

He had hardly seen and heard her
and he flew to her;
and his fears

he left behind him
with the angel weeping tears.

◆ ◆ ◆

Their love in the ruin, how it burns;
the bats and spiders hear
how they sing, laugh, kiss,
and how they vow.

She tells him he must swear to her
and tell her true:
I'll never choose another,
I never will forget you.

He swears by his teacher,
by his father, by his mother,
and by all of them together.

"What else?" she whispers.
"What else?"
And he swears by his earlocks,
his fringes, his *tfiln.*
And at every stage his
vow is more fevered, more outrageous.
"But what else, Monish? Tell me,"
and her smile compels.

"For a boy will mislead a girl
and leave her in the dark—"
And he swears by the curtain of the ark
that holds the Torah.

And she cries out: "Higher, higher!"
She so wants to be certain.
And her eyes are on fire,
magic as her lips are magic,
pure flowing magic,
and he barely stops to reason,
he swears by the Messiah
and his *shoyfer.*
"Higher! Higher!" The last prod—
he sinfully speaks the name of God
and is struck by the thunder of His rod.

Laughter in Gehenna,
a reek of sulfur in the room,
and fast as a bowshot
he flies through the air on a broom.

♦   ♦   ♦

Ararat goes crazy—
one hilarious, profuse
shrieking party in the ark,
all Gehenna breaking loose.

Ten Gypsy orchestras,
Gehenna's top musicians,
champagne by the bucket
while the demons do the can-can with precision.

Lamps—a thousand barrels full of pitch—
the wicked are the wicks—
and a special sexton with his scissors at the ready
goes a-trimming wicked wicks
to keep them burning steady.

Fire in her eyes,
the queen of all that place,
Lilith goes before, Sammael behind,
carrying her train of Spanish lace.

Monish stands at the side, nailed by his earlobe
to the doorway of the ark;
the fire's lit, the spit is ready,
and the rest is dark.

1888–1908 (translated by Seymour Levitan)

Impressions of a Journey through the Tomaszow Region

Impressions of a Journey through the Tomaszow Region in the Year 1890 *(the full title of the work in Yiddish) was published the next year in Peretz's miscellany* Yidishe bibliotek *(Jewish Library). He had been hired by the wealthy industrialist Jan Bloch, a Jewish convert to Christianity, to form part of a research team investigating the condition of Jews in the small towns of Poland. Bloch wanted to gather evidence to disprove anti-Semitic allegations of Jewish parasitism and draft evasion. Peretz was assigned to the area he knew best, around his native city, Zamość, where he had also practiced law for a decade. When he composed these sketches, he was able to draw not only on the materials he had collected for the Warsaw bureau administering the project, but also on childhood memories, on his experiences as a district lawyer, and on local gossip and lore.*

When the twenty-two travel impressions appeared, they bore a footnote indicating the author's intention of continuing the series at a later date. No further sketches appeared, however. The series was published in Hebrew with two additional episodes, one of which, "The Pond" (1904), is included here. Since the records of the statistical expedition appear to have been lost, Peretz's reportage remains the most complete account we have of the project.

IMPRESSIONS OF A JOURNEY THROUGH
THE TOMASZOW REGION

▼

PROLOGUE

It was toward the end of the good times and the beginning of the bad times. The sky was blackening with clouds. The wind, or spirit—the *Zeitgeist*—did not, as might be expected, dispel the clouds with ease, to pour out their hearts over some distant wilderness. In Europe's carefully tended vineyard the gardeners paid no heed while a poisonous growth took root, cracked the earth, and sent forth its thorns. The nineteenth century in its old age appeared to have caught cold and to be running a slight fever. Nobody could imagine that this marked the onset of a grave illness, a madness.

For us, then, how far away America was! Hardly a Jew even bothered to wonder how a bowl of porridge could stand right side up there, or whether the people there wore their skullcaps on their feet. European Jews were all but unaware of the two barons who dreamt of establishing Jewish colonies, de Rothschild in Palestine and de Hirsch in the New World.[1]

Psychology predicts less exactly than astronomy. Nobody foresaw that the world's soul would grow dark and its body convulsed. Even afterward few could believe what had happened. None could understand it.

In fact, people had long been uneasy, as sinister rumors multiplied on every side.

None of this detracted from the need to get to know ordinary, everyday Jewish life—to see what was going on in the shtetls. What did people hope for? How did they make a living? What did they do, how did they behave? What were the folk saying?

FAITH AND TRUST

In Tishevitz, the first stop in my travels, I boarded with my acquaintance Reb Baruch. He invited the synagogue beadle and a few of the more solid citizens to come and meet me. Waiting, I stood at the window and contemplated the marketplace.

It was a large square, hemmed in by grimy, rickety houses, some roofed with thatch but most with shingles, none more than one story high, and each with a wide porch over rotting, discolored piles. Jewish market women stood next to each other, their backs to the porches, and hovered over trays of bagels, bread, peas, beans, and fruit.

"Bad luck to you!" one cries out.

"Don't point your finger at him," another says. "He's looking."

"Shut up!" she is told.

They do not lower their voices as they tell each other that I have come to record things. I can hear them quite well.

A woman says, "That's the one!"

Another says, "Isn't it nice that we poor sheep have shepherds to care about us! But if the Shepherd above doesn't want to help, nothing will help."

A third woman is puzzled: "Can the Shepherd above really need helpers like him?" She is hinting at my trimmed beard and untraditional dress.

More broad-minded, a fourth cites doctors. "Doctors aren't proper Jews," she says, "but still and all . . ."

"That's a different case entirely. A doctor is a private individual. For something communal like this, couldn't they have found a Good Jew?"[2]

Still another opinion is voiced: "Who needs records about us? They should have sent us a couple of hundred rubles instead. Just don't register my son, and see if I care when he doesn't become a commander in chief."

At the table where I sit I can see through the window without being seen.

My host has finished his morning prayers, removed his prayer shawl and phylacteries, and drunk my health in a bit of liquor.

"Peace and good health," I answer him.

"May God send better times, so people can make a living."

How I envy him! His only need is to make a living.

He adds, very sure of himself: "It will have to come, people will have to be able to make a living! There's a God in the world. If necessary, those of our devout who excel in prayer will know how to remind Him."

I interrupt. With Reb Baruch's faith and trust, he knows that He who gives life also sustains life. Why then, I ask, is he in his own affairs so sleeplessly busy and anxious, always worrying about tomorrow, next month, next year? No sooner is a Jew finished with his wedding than he starts worrying about the clothes his grandchildren will wear at *their* weddings. Yet when it comes to the concerns of the People of Israel as a whole, the average Jew has such faith and trust that he thinks he need not bestir himself personally in the slightest.

"It's simple," Reb Baruch explains. "The People of Israel as a whole—that's the Sovereign of the Universe's concern; He bears His own in mind. If such a thing were imaginable, if forgetfulness were possible at the Throne of Glory, there are those who know how to remind Him. Besides, how long can Jewish suffering last? The Messiah *must* come, when we are all either guilty or innocent.[3] But that's not how it is with the affairs of individuals. Making a living is a different proposition."

JUST GO!

I forgot to tell you that the local rabbi wished neither to visit nor to be visited. He sent a message that my business was none of his, pitiable weakling that he was; that for some time he had been fully occupied with a knotty problem of meat suspected of contact with milk, and, most important, that he was feuding with the official community over its refusal to raise his salary by two gulden a week.

My visitors, therefore, consisted of three householders and two beadles. I start with my host.

He has no wife, he tells me, adding, without being asked and as if to apologize, "I wouldn't want you to think that it's been very long since she passed away."

In short: widower; two married sons, one married daughter, two boys and a girl at home. Without a pause he asks me to record that except for his youngest, barely four years old—the Messiah will probably make his appearance before the boy is old enough to be conscripted—all his sons are in one way or another unfit for military service.

Apart from the married sons, I have been able to meet the whole family. The married daughter has a little shop in her own house where she sells tobacco, tea, and sugar—food too—as well as grease and fuel oil, I think. Early that morning I had bought some sugar from her. She's about twenty-five, with a face like this: a long, hooked nose that seems to be counting the decayed, black teeth in her half-open mouth; a pair of bluish-grayish, cracked lips—the very image of her father. Her little sister would look like her if not for the greater attractiveness of youth: fresher, rosier face; whiter teeth— altogether, less drawn and worn. I see the two boys too, good-looking boys; they must have taken after their mother: red cheeks, appealing, bashful eyes, curly black locks. But their bearing is unattractive, with their constant shrugging and grimacing.

Obviously, their mother has been dead just long enough for their little coats to get dirty but not torn. Now that she is gone, who has time for the boys? Their older sister has four children of her own and a husband who passes his time in sacred study, besides her little shop. Her younger sister is in charge of their father's tavern, and he has no time to spare.

"What business are you in?" I ask him.

"Percentage."

" 'Percentage'? You mean moneylending."

"If that's what you want to call it."

"You know what the Gentiles call it—Jewish usury."

"You want to know something?" he says. "Here! You can have all my trash—notes, deeds, the lot. You can have it all for 25 percent of face value. Just pay cash! I'll throw in the tavern too! I would much rather go off to the Land of Israel, if only I had the money. If you want one, I'll even let you have an assurance that you will be absolved from excommunication. You think we live on moneylending? It lives on us. Debtors don't pay, so their debt grows. The more it grows, the less it's worth, and the more of a pauper I become. It's the truth!"

Before leaving to do some more writing, I witnessed a little scene. While I was gathering my things together—paper, pencil, cigarettes— Reb Baruch was buttering two slices of bread for the boys to take to school, with a scallion in the bargain.

"Now go!" says he, not wanting them in the tavern. The smaller orphan, dissatisfied, hunches his shoulders and screws up his face, preparing to cry. A bit ashamed in my presence, he tries, unsuccessfully, to hold back his tears. "Another scallion!" he sobs. "Mother used to give me two."

His sister hurries to the bin, seizes another scallion, and gives it to him.

"Now go!" she says too, only much more softly. The voice uttering the words was her mother's.

WHAT DOES A JEWISH WOMAN NEED?

We proceed from house to house, starting from Number 1. I do not need to be told where Jews and where non-Jews live. All I have to do is to look at the windows. Unwashed windows are a sign of the Chosen People, especially where gaps left by missing panes have been filled by pillows or sacking. On the other hand, flowerpots and curtains suggest strongly that the inhabitants don't have the same inherited right to poverty.

There are exceptions. Here lives not a Jew but a drunk. There, contrariwise, flowers and little curtains, but people who read the Hebrew journal of the Enlighteners, *Hatsefira*.

The worst impression is made by a peculiar wooden house. It is not only larger than the others but also darker and dirtier. The front of it, strongly tilted forward, looks down on a correspondingly darkened old ruin—namely, a wizened, stooped, unsteady old Jewish woman busy haggling with a customer. Her customer is a sallow, unkempt maidservant, and the subject of their dispute is whether she is entitled to a little extra on her purchased pound of salt.

The beadle points the old woman out to me and says, "The house belongs to her." That surprises me, I tell him, because she seems too poor to own such a house.

"In actual fact," the beadle explains, "the house isn't really hers. She owns only a sixth of it. She's a widow. Her children are the heirs, but they don't live here, so they think of her as the owner."

"How much income does the house produce?"

"No income."

"How much is it worth?"

"About fifteen hundred rubles."

"And it produces no income?"

"It's unoccupied."

I let him know I suspect the house is used for monkey business.

"No, not that house," the beadle says, smiling. "There are two other houses of that sort and they'll have to close them down eventually, but this is something different. You see, a doctor once lived in this house. Then he died, so it's unoccupied."

"Why? Did he die of a contagious disease?"

"God forbid!"

"So why doesn't anyone live there?"

"It's simply that no one would want to live there."

"What do you mean?"

"I mean that hereabouts practically everybody has his own property. Anybody who does need to rent a place to live in doesn't want the expense of having to heat an entire house. The way we do things here is that a tenant pays a few rubles a year for heat in his corner of the house. Who needs such large houses?"

"Then why did they build one like this?"

"Ah! That was in the old days. Nowadays it isn't needed."

"Poor woman!"

"Why 'poor woman'? She has her salt stand. She makes a few rubles a week, her real-estate tax is twenty-eight rubles a year, and she lives on what's left. What does a Jewish woman need? What does this one lack? Her shroud? She has hers ready."

I looked again at the little old woman, and to me too it had begun to seem that in fact there was nothing she lacked. Her wrinkled skin even smiled at me: what does a Jewish woman need?

NUMBER 42

Notebook in hand, I proceed from house to house in the order of their numbers. From Number 41, though, the beadle leads me to 43.

"How about 42?" I ask.

"There!" he says, pointing to something ruinous in a narrow lane between 41 and 43.

"Did it fall down?"

"It was pulled down," answers the beadle.

"Why?"

"On account of a fire wall."

Walking had tired us, so we sat down on a nearby bench. The beadle resumed, his Yiddish teeming as ever with Hebraisms: "According to the Gentiles' law, you see, if a house hasn't been built far enough away from the one next to it, the two roofs have to be separated by fire walls. How great the distance must be, I don't know—as the psalm says, 'Of such ordinances they know nothing'[4]—but I think it has to be more than the Talmud's proverbial four cubits. For Gentiles a fire wall is a sovereign remedy for incendiary peril. But that hovel was built by Jeroham Ivankhovker, a mere children's teacher and a man eminent for poverty, and of course he couldn't put up a fire wall.

"To tell the truth, there was no basis in the first place for his decision to build. You'll hear how afterward the whole thing developed into a suit according to Jewish law. During the trial his wife, Malke, may she rest in peace, recounted everything that had happened—starting, as is the way of the world, with the Six Days of Creation. And this is what it was all about:

"For about fifteen years Malke hadn't talked to her husband. She was a woman with a stubborn, cunning nature, though I shouldn't say so; tall, skinny, dark, with a nose as pointy as a pickax. She hardly ever talked about anything but Making a Living—there was a market woman for you! Not that she needed to talk! Her look was enough to chill your heart and to make the other market women shiver with mortal fear—that was the kind of eye she had. It isn't hard to understand why her silence gave so much pleasure to Jeroham. And neither did he ever speak a word to her. Still, their not speaking to each other didn't keep them from being blessed with two male sons and three girls.

"But the lustful passion to become householders made both of them talkative. The conversation went like this:

" 'Malke!' She doesn't answer.

" 'Malke?' She remains silent. He 'Malkes,' and she doesn't budge.

"Then Jeroham stands up and lets out a yell: 'Malke! I want to build a house!'

"Malke couldn't stand it anymore. She raised an eye and opened her mouth. 'I thought,' she said afterward, 'that he had gone mad!'

"And indeed it was madness. From a great-grandfather he had inherited that narrow little plot of ground you saw, and in money not even a cent. Later, when his wife's so-called jewelry—junk, really—had to be sold, it didn't realize any more than three times eighteen gulden. Anyway, it used to be with the pawnbroker all year long, except that for Sabbaths and holy days Jeroham would retrieve it by signing a note making him liable to excommunication for failure to return the pawn.

"But as the psalm says, 'O Lord, who could stand' when lust enlists the aid of fantasy?[5] He was convinced that all he had to do was put up the house and he would have everything he needed. His credit would be good, so he would be able to borrow enough to buy a goat and have food in the house. He would rent out one room for a store or, God willing, his wife would be the storekeeper. Above all, the children would be provided for! The boys would in any event be sent to a yeshiva, he would give each of the girls half of a male's share in the estate, and that would be the end of it!

"And the wherewithal for building the house? He had that figured out:

" 'I,' says he to her, 'am a teacher and you are a peddler, so we have two incomes. We'll live on one income and build with the other.'

" 'What are you saying, you crazy man?' Malke says to him. 'Even with two incomes we don't have enough to live on.'

" 'God helps those who help themselves,' he tells her. 'Just look at our neighbor Noah the Teacher. His wife is sick, so she doesn't earn anything; and they have six little children, may they live and be well. Yet the whole family is able to live on the income from his tuition fees alone.'

" 'What are you talking about? He's a very good teacher, so his pupils are rich as rich can be.'

" 'And why do you suppose that is?' says he. 'Do you think he's a better scholar than I am? Of course not. But when God sees that Noah has only the one income, He gives him that in abundance. Do you want another proof? Look at Black Berakhah—a widow, with five children, like us, and she is only a peddler.'

" 'What are you talking about? Are you insane? If only my business were as good as hers! It must be worth thirty rubles.'

" 'That isn't what's important,' he explains to her. 'What's important is that Berakhah means "blessing" and for her the blessing can come only by way of her apples. The Sovereign of the Universe governs the world by the laws of nature!'

"He also persuades her that they will be able to save money. There are lots of things they can do without.

"And that's how it was decided. Jeroham went without his snuff and the whole family without such luxuries as sour milk in particular and the evening meal in general. They began to build!

"It took them years. Only by the time they came to the fire wall, Malke had no merchandise left, Jeroham was exhausted, the oldest son had gone off to beg, the youngest child had died, and there was a fortune still to pay out—forty rubles for a fire wall!

"What to do? What they did was to put something into the palm of the town clerk and move in without putting up the fire wall.

"Since he was a member of the Burial Society, the society sprang for a Dedication of the House. I'm not exaggerating when I tell you that they put away a whole barrel of beer, not to mention the liquor and raisin wine. I tell you, it was one joyous celebration!

"But the joy didn't last. A certain householder got into a fight with Jeroham's neighbor Noah the Teacher. Now this Noah had himself once been one of our more prosperous householders, a very rich man, in fact. Besides what he had inherited, he owned a nice few hundreds of his own, and he bought and sold honey. Then came that dissension in our community about the Lithuanian rabbi. Somebody turned informer against Noah's son—he's still in the army, with a bad lung—and Noah was put on trial for arson against the rabbi.

"It was murder! Talebearing we're used to, but spreading twigs around a house and then setting fire to them—that's truly murderous. Whether or not he did it, together his son and the costs of the trial made Noah as poor as poor can be, so he set up as a teacher. He was too new at the game to have learnt deference to his employers. One of them got insulted, took his scion away from Noah, and entrusted him to Jeroham.

"Noah resented it. He knew sneaky tricks, was at home in the seat of government, and was skilled with tongue and pen. So he made sure that the story about the wall got around, and down came a senior inspector.

"By the time this happened, though, Noah had come to regret what he had done. He bestirred himself, and the weight of a coin or two sank the legal proceedings into oblivion.

"Everything would have stayed fine if not for the controversy about the thread of blue that we are commanded to put in the fringe of the four corners of our garments.[6] I don't need to remind you that the rabbis of the Talmud were themselves no longer sure of the proper dye for that blue and ruled in favor of all the threads being white. Neither do you need me to tell you that the followers of the Rodzin rebbe believe that their master rediscovered the secret of the genuine blue, and make their fringes accordingly.

"Well, Jeroham was a Rodzin Hasid. Noah wasn't. He was a fervent Belz Hasid, and therefore abominated Jeroham's Rodzin blue. One word led to another, the fire wall surfaced again, and the proceedings were reinstituted. In a judgment by default Jeroham was given a month to build the wall, failing which the house would be torn down.

"They didn't have a cent. The quarrel had become so bitter that this time Noah didn't feel remorseful and wouldn't listen to anybody or anything. Jeroham summoned him before the rabbi, but Noah kicked out the beadle bearing the summons.

"When Malke saw that all was lost, she grabbed Noah right in the middle of the street and dragged her prey to the rabbi's. The marketplace was full of Belz Hasidim, but who would want to start up with such a woman? As the Talmud says, 'There is no justice for a man killed by women.'[7] Noah's wife went along with them, hurling deadly curses at Malke. She too was afraid to come near.

"In the rabbi's house Malke told the whole story from beginning to end and insisted that Noah should either have the wall built himself or have the court proceedings sink from sight again.

"Our fine little rabbi knew that no matter how he ruled, one or the other group of Hasidim would have it in for him. Like the learned Jew he was, he knew how to squirm out of his fix by matching 'on the one hand' with 'on the other hand'—proximate cause of damage versus remote cause, and so on, blah-blah-blah. Neither side would agree to compromise, so he commended them to their respective rebbes.

" 'The defendant's court has jurisdiction'—that is the legal principle. Noah stood firm, Jeroham had no choice, and off they went to Belz.

"Before leaving, Jeroham gave his power of attorney to his brother-in-law, together with the few rubles he had been able to borrow from compassionate lenders, and asked him to use the money to appeal the court's ruling.

"Everything afterward was a disaster. Maybe the brother-in-law used the money for himself or maybe, as he claimed, he lost it. Malke was first heartsick and then fatally sick. Noah's own rebbe in Belz found for his opponent, Jeroham, and awarded him the cost of constructing the fire wall plus the expense of litigation, but even that didn't help. On the way back from the Austrian kaiser's Belz to the Russian tsar's Tishevitz the two of them, Noah and Jeroham—both without passports, of course—were nabbed at the border and brought home in the prisoners' van. By the time Jeroham returned, Malke had passed on to the World of Truth and the house had been torn down."

THE MASKIL

You mustn't think that Tishevitz is at the end of the world. It too has a maskil—the genuine, old-fashioned article, a middle-aged man, unschooled, unread, bookless, without even a subscription to a newspaper: in short, a not very enlightened enlightener.

Not that he shaves; to be a maskil in Tishevitz it's enough that he trims his beard. So the townsfolk say that he's the sort to curl his locks even during the Ten Days of Repentance! Nor does he dress European-style. For that matter, the local barber-surgeon doesn't dress European-style either. He wears a long coat and honors the injunction in Leviticus against cutting the hair at the side of the head.

Our maskil discharged his obligation by polishing his boots and wearing some black ribbon around his neck. He retains a trace of his side hair, for which he compensates by wearing a cap. It's simple, people say. That's what Moses meant by "Jeshurun waxed fat, and he kicked."[8] He's got it made, they say—a thriving shop, a grand total of three children. What more does he need? So he's a maskil.

What exactly his being a maskil consisted of was unclear, but it sufficed that people knew that he was a maskil. Everybody said he was a maskil, and he himself admitted as much. And what served to clinch the whole thing was the authority he arrogated to himself of passing judgment—"against the Lord and against His Messiah," as the psalm says.[9]

I was to discover that the maskil, taking me for a fellow maskil, had expected that if I did not actually stay with him I would at any rate begin my work as a scrivener with him.

"For something like this," he said to his neighbors, "brains are needed. What could donkeys like you do for him?"

Unaware of Mohammed's existence, the mountain did not come to him, so Mohammed went to the mountain. The maskil tracked me down at the house of a certain widow and challenged me with his version of the Wicked Son's question in the Passover Haggadah. The Wicked son asks, "What is the point of this fuss that you're making?" The maskil asked, *"Moj panie"*—and continuing in Yiddish—"and what may you be doing here?"[10]

"What do you mean, 'here'?" I ask.

"You must think I'm some kind of ignorant yokel, without a clue as to what's going on in the world, just because I live in Tishevitz. Our patriarch Jacob said, 'I have sojourned with Laban'—only sojourned, not settled.[11] I may live here, but I have a nose for what's going on."

"All right, you have a nose and know what's happening in the world. What are you asking me about?"

The beadle pricked up his ears, and so did the handful of idlers who had been dogging my footsteps. A look of intense pleasure spread over their faces, and on their brows I could almost read the verse in which Abner says to Joab, "Let the young warriors duel for our entertainment"—in this case, "Let's watch two maskilim gore each other!"[12]

Now the maskil is really annoyed. "I don't need any more of this poking fun at me," he says. "You're not the only one who can use his tongue, you know. I can too. Do you think I like the companionship I can find here, with these Tishevitz jackasses? Just look at those nobodies!"

I am in a bit of a quandary. After all, I can hardly come to Tishevitz's defense when its own householders, at the windows and in the doorway, are smiling complacently at his insults. He continues: "Just tell me, what exactly is going on here, what notes are you taking?"

"Statistics."

"Statistics shmatistics! We've heard such stories before! What's the use of it?"

I explained it to him—or not so much to him as to the others. I wanted them to have some idea of statistics.

He laughed loud and long. "You may get these Tishevitz jackasses to believe you, but not me! Why do you record whether people are living in a house with or without a wooden floor? What difference does that make to you, ha?"

The object, I tell him, is to show that Jews are poor, and thereby . . .

"Thereby, nothing," he interrupts. "All right, let it go. But why do you have to know precisely how many boys and how many girls in a family? And how old each one is? And so on and so on, with all that other stuff in the notes you're taking?"

"They suspect us Jews of evading military service. You must know that the birth registers aren't accurate, so what we want to do is show . . ."

"All right, I suppose that's logical. I'll grant you that. But how about business licenses? What's your reason for recording who has one, and for what amount of business?"

"To prove that Jews . . ."

The maskil doesn't let me finish. "Don't tell me those fairy tales. What will happen is that the authorities will find out that this one or that one hasn't paid a big enough license fee for the amount of business he does, and they'll make things hot for him!"

Instantly, as soon as his words had left his lips, all my hangers-on at the windows disappeared. The beadle took his leave of me, and the maskil, who actually had meant no great harm, was left as though turned to stone.

Everyone who had heard this was frightened, and in the space of two hours all Tishevitz resounded with my name. I was suspected of being a tax agent. It made sense. Who could be a more useful agent for the tax office than a Jew? Who would be better placed to sniff out Jewish secrets?

This time I was alone as I made the circuit of the marketplace, the shtetl holding itself aloof. The lone maskil tagged along at my heels, wishing to talk with me. I, however, didn't wish to talk with him. I was heartily sick of him and couldn't bring myself even to look at him.

The faces of the people in the street have grown grave and ominous, and I begin to think of escape. I don't like the way they are looking at me out of the sides of their eyes and whispering.

I decide to take a last stab. I remember that the current rabbi of Tishevitz used to be a member of the rabbinical tribunal in my hometown. He will know me and at least testify that I am not what people think I am.

"Where does the rabbi live?" I ask the maskil.

Gratified, he answers, "Come. I'll take you."

THE RABBI OF TISHEVITZ

Only if you have seen the rabbi of Tishevitz's dressing gown will you know the reason why Mrs. Rabbi, his third wife and barely middle-aged, has to wear such large eyeglasses on her nose. The dressing gown is a wondrous thing of threads and shreds, and she has ruined her eyes patching and repatching it.

"If the town gave me two gulden more a week," he bemoans himself, "I could get by. As it is, things are bitter. But I'll win out! It's true that they can do without me for judging their disputes, because they have their wonder workers—or they can actually resort to the Gentiles' tribunals. Likewise, when it comes to deciding whether a pot or pan has become unkosher, any infants' teacher claims he's an authority. Feminine matters, now—it would be foolish to think that *they* could be postponed. But I'm going to win. All I have to do is wait for the communal elections. No rabbi, no valid elections! Can you imagine a city—'a mother city in Israel'—without, *Keyn eyn hore*, elected communal officers?[13] And if even that doesn't work, I won't certify the slaughterers' knives as fit for kosher slaughter. Oh, I've got them!"

It was hard to distract the rabbi from his own troubles, but the maskil succeeded by promising to do his best to influence the community council to grant a rise in salary. Thereupon, the rabbi invited us to be seated, and listened to our account.

"What foolishness!" he said. "I know you! Tell those idiots I know you."

"But they avoid me."

"Avoid you? What do you mean, 'they avoid you'? Who avoids you, and why? Well, since you say so—'avoid you!'—I'll go down with you myself."

"And what will you wear?" It was a woman's voice, from behind the stove.

"Give me my coat," answers the rabbi.

"How can I give it to you when I've taken it apart?"

"No great tragedy," says the rabbi. "We'll go tomorrow."

I let him know that it's only noon and that I wouldn't want to waste the rest of the day.

"Well, what else can I do?" asks the rabbi as he clasps his hands. "My wife had to pick just this time to work on my caftan."

"Tell them to come up here."

"Telling them is easy enough, but will it do any good? They won't listen to me. Maybe it would be better to go down in my dressing gown?"

"That wouldn't look right, Rabbi," interjects the maskil. "The policeman is making his rounds."

"If it were up to me," says the rabbi, "I would go; but since you say no, I won't."

The decision is that the three of us will call through the window to invite the people in the street to come in, but opening the window is more easily said than done. The last time it was opened was about fifteen years ago. The putty is dried out and the panes, cracked by the sun, rattle at every footfall. Woodworms have bored holes in the shutters, kept fastened to the wall only by rust. Whether the shutters still have hinges is doubtful.

We finally managed to do the deed without inflicting damage, tugging first at one side and then at the other. The rabbi stations himself between the maskil and me, and we call to the throng in the marketplace. In a few minutes the house is full.

"Gentlemen," the rabbi tells them, "I know this man. . . ."

"No notes. We don't want any report," a few voices cry out together.

The rabbi loses his courage. "If you say no," he says softly, "then it's no."

Meanwhile, the maskil has mounted the table. He calls out: "Jackasses! Notes have to be taken! *Pro bono publico!*"

Pro bono publico, he is prepared to lie. He tells them that he and I have analyzed my work in all its particulars, that what he said earlier about me was said in jest, and that I have even shown him missives from rabbis.

The question is shouted from every side: "What rabbis?"

He continues to trumpet his fabrications: "From the rabbi of Paris . . . the rabbi of London." Nothing less would be good enough for him.

"Jews, let's go home," someone breaks in. "Those aren't our kind of people."

The crowd scattered as quickly as it had assembled. Only we three were left—and the beadle, who sidled up to me and said, "Give me something for the day."

I gave him a few ten-gulden notes. He stuck them uncounted in his pocket and left without saying good-bye.

"Well, what do you think, Rabbi?" I ask.

"I hardly know what to think. I'm very, very much afraid that it's going to hurt me."

"Hurt *you?*"

"Who else? You? If you don't do your statistics, people will manage without them. As the psalm has it, 'Behold, the Guardian of Israel neither slumbers not sleeps.'[14] I'm thinking of those two gulden a week."

In the meantime, the rabbi's wife, she of the large eyeglasses, has emerged from behind the stove. "I keep telling you," says she, "not to meddle in communal affairs, but do you listen to me? Is the community a rabbi's business? How can that concern you?"

"All right, wife," he answers her quietly, "that's enough for now. You know what kind of man I am. I'm softhearted, I feel for others. But it's a pity about those two gulden a week!"

TWICE-TOLD TALES

"With head covered in mourning"—I say it of myself, though in Scripture it is said of the wicked Haman—I went down from the rabbi's house, together with the maskil, and into the street.[15] There we meet the beadle, who assures us that in his opinion note-taking can resume tomorrow. Two impoverished householders—now, poor souls, in dire need—created the hullabaloo: one a shady tavern keeper and the other a horse trader.

For his part, the maskil promises me that between afternoon and evening prayers he will discuss my enterprise with the people. "And my name isn't Shmerl"—for that can be a maskil's name in Tishevitz—"if I don't turn the shtetl around! They may stand on their heads, but notes will be taken! As the Talmud says, 'The mouth that forbade is the mouth that permitted.' "[16]

Say this for our maskil, at least he has had a basic Jewish education. That is more than can be said for some maskilim in the wider world.

I return to my lodgings, accompanied by the beadle. My host the widower is still in mourning, so men assemble there for prayer twice a day to allow him to say the Kaddish. Between afternoon and evening prayers they talked politics. After evening prayer their talk descended to the Jews.

Most are terribly optimistic. First of all, the anti-Jewish measures in the offing aren't directed at *them*. Second, our enemies won't be able to outfox the foxy scions of our patriarch Jacob. Third, things change: as with the turning of a wheel, what is down will be up. Fourth, God will help. Fifth, the "Good Jews"—the prayer virtuosi, the wonder workers—will prevent it.

The same old song!

A man with small, darting eyes under a low forehead knows what needs to be done. "Believe me," he exclaims, "believe me, what's needed is unity among all Good Jews. The reason for our weekday penitential supplications is that the Temple has been destroyed and we are in exile, unredeemed, still waiting for the Messiah to come. If all Good Jews stood together and agreed to stop saying the penitential supplications, Messiah would *have* to come."

"The rebbe of Kozinitz, may his memory be for a blessing, stopped saying them," someone objects.[17]

"One swallow," retorts the first man, "doesn't make a summer. It would be especially useful if they imposed the prohibition on all of

Jewry. There comes a time when you have to be resolute and fight back!"

"If they issued the prohibition," someone jokes, glancing at me, "the unbelievers would start praying just to say the supplications and make sure Messiah doesn't come."

"But what can you expect," someone else asks, "when the leading rebbes themselves are so disunited?"

Everyone groans.

I had no doubt that each of them was recalling the sufferings inflicted on him by the community's failure to stand together. The most convincing evidence that the dissension had caused Tishevitz grievous damage was that in all the discussion in the interval between afternoon and evening prayers, one question was not discussed: who was responsible for the hostility between the leading rebbes? People were afraid that even to ask the question would cause new dissension.

I suggested that poverty was mostly to blame. When people can't buy in order to sell, when they are unemployed and idle, they go looking for spiteful bickering to occupy themselves with. Contrast the big cities. Everyone is busy with his own affairs there, so calm prevails. I add: "If someone injected a couple of thousand rubles into Tishevitz, these things would be forgotten."

"Being rich isn't such a big deal," one of them calls out. "If I had only had a pinch of sense, I could have had all of Tishevitz in my pocket by now. It was touch and go, only my resolve wasn't firm enough."

"It's the truth, it's the truth!" they testified.

No doubt. As the maxim has it, what is known to all needs no proof.

The man who would have been rich if only he had had a pinch of sense or a somewhat firmer resolve was the very embodiment of poverty—skinny, sallow, hunched, mournful, and in a coat for which the only match was the rabbi's dressing gown.

In comes the maskil. Naturally, he laughs. "Reb Elye," he says, "you must have sold your winning ticket just before the draw."

"Look at him, the scoffer!" says Reb Elye. "As if he really didn't remember what happened!"

"I forgot long ago what you're talking about, and my head has been clear ever since," swears the maskil. "That is, assuming I ever heard your lies in the first place."

"Lies? Lies, is it?" Reb Elye has taken offense. "According to you, that isn't the only thing that's a lie."

I butt in to ask what he is referring to.

"You have surely heard of the holy Vorke rebbe, may his memory be for a blessing," Reb Elye begins.

"Surely."

"Of course! Everybody and his cousin knew about him. Then you know that not only God-fearing Gentiles used to flock to him, but even Germanized Jews—and even Lithuanian Jews, unbelievers that they are! May I have a piece of gold for every Lithuanian I saw there! There's a story I could tell you about the Tosaphot explication of the Talmud. Lithuanians have to show everybody how smart they are, so this one raised a question about the Tosaphot on a passage in the tractate *Nedarim*.[18] The rebbe, of blessed memory, gave him a wrong answer—on purpose, of course. The Lithuanian couldn't contain himself. 'How can you say that, rebbe,' he came back, 'when the Tosaphot dealing with the same subject matter in the tractate *Rosh Hashana* explicitly says the opposite of what you have just said?' Well, it was only a heaven-sent miracle that kept our fellow Hasidim from putting an end to him then and there. But that's by the way.

"The point I want to make is that the Vorke rebbe dealt with the Sovereign of the Universe—if it were permissible to say such a thing—as if he were dealing with a brother and friend. For instance:

"Once, after pacing around in his room, he stood still and said: 'Sovereign of the Universe, wouldn't You say that Your Jews have suffered long enough from this heat? How can they sit and study Torah?'

"He must have heard an answer from above, because then he said: 'All right, that's different. I'll go along with future payment for present hardship. But Sovereign of the Universe, how about a little payment in *this* life?'

"Again you could sense from his appearance that he had heard a response, because he answered: 'All right, if You say no it will have to be no. Your credit is good. We can wait.'

"But that too is by the way. The heart of the matter was his presiding over rites of circumcision, the entering into the covenant of our father Abraham. As to that, he was made of steel and would not bend. His signal awaited Above, and all he had to do was give a nod for the thing to be accomplished from Above. He said that when going to preside over a circumcision, when merely bethinking himself of the circumcisor's knife, he was transported to a state of awe. The result was, as the psalm puts it, that 'He fulfills the desire of them that fear Him.'[19]

"Grieving that people had become aware of these powers, he knew that he was not long for this life. Unless he was soon called to the

Academy on High, the world could not be sustained. That mystery was not meant to be revealed!

"But people did find out about it. So did I. As a matter of fact, I found out earlier than most. My first wife's brother-in-law Moses was a kind of secretary-cum-bodyguard of the rebbe's, and he blabbed the secret. When he was punished by being removed from his position for half a year, it hurt him so much that the rebbe had pity and reinstated him. But that too is by the way. Suffice it that I knew.

"Our father Jacob 'kept the matter in mind,' and so did I.[20] I wasn't going to bother the rebbe about trifles, so I waited. At the time I didn't live more than a mile from Vorke. My first wife was still alive and things weren't going too badly for her. Though it was hard to make a living, I earned a bit as a marriage broker, and she helped to support us with her stall in the marketplace. She was even able to lodge and feed my elder daughter and her husband, a first-rate scholar. What more did I need?

" 'And it came to pass upon a day' that my son-in-law is in Ger with his rebbe, the fair is in town, and my daughter is giving birth for the first time. Things are grim. Three days go by, she's in great pain, and Beyle-Bashe the Midwife doesn't know what more to do than she has already done. Cupping, bleeding—nothing helps. It is definitely not good.

"Now I get word that the rebbe is coming for a circumcision! Do I need to tell you that 'the Jews had light and gladness'?[21] We couldn't have been happier, our spirits revived in us. Our only prayer was for God to keep her alive another day and a half, because people weren't admitted to the circumcision until an hour before the ceremony. In the meantime, my daughter's condition was growing even worse. Her life was in danger.

"A couple of hours before the ceremony was to begin, her condition improved, or so it seemed to me. She came to, opened her eyes, insisted that her mother go to the fair, and called me to her bedside.

"Silly woman!—but then, every woman has it in for her husband when she's giving birth. She tells me that she dislikes her husband Shmulik, never did like him, didn't want him from the moment she first saw him, can't stand him, doesn't want anything more to do with him, would rather die. The reason why she sent her mother out is that she's afraid of her. And it's true that my wife, may she rest in peace, was harsh with our children. She was actually going to slap my daughter as the bridal veil was being put on her!

"Naturally, I give my daughter to understand that all women are

that way, that some women even vow not to live with their husbands
anymore, that to dissolve such vows the Sin Offering was brought
when the Temple stood, and that the Talmud's principle is still
valid: 'People are not held accountable for what they say in their
pain.'[22]

"She is unaffected by what I have told her. She needs neither vows
nor oaths, she says, because she is going. She tells me good-bye: 'I'm
fading like a candle.'

"To tell the truth, I don't take her very seriously. I can sense that
she's improving. She has recovered her wits, and there's only half
an hour to go before the circumcision. She's even looking quite
attractive.

"So I sit at her bedside and talk with her. The midwife has left to
buy a cradle at the fair. I look at the clock, and it's time to go. I look
at her and she seems fine, healthy. Still, I don't want her to be alone,
practically the only one in town without company.

"In our town," he explained, "the fair was held once a year for
three days, and those three days had to provide everyone's livelihood
for the entire year. Even at the rebbe's nobody was home. They
were all at the fair.

"So I wait a little.

"Half an hour later things suddenly get worse. She grips my hand,
falls back on the pillow, gestures, begins to wheeze. It isn't good.

"I cry out, but there is no answer from even one of the thousands
of people and peasants whose din I can hear in the marketplace.
They don't hear me, you could think it's a wilderness. I want to
leave and call somebody. I try to remove my hands from hers. She
won't let go.

"A minute passes, two minutes. I'm going to be late. Bad as her
condition is, I tear my hand away and run to the other side of town,
to Tsemakh's house. The circumcision is to take place there.

"Over carts and over piles of merchandise I fly and fly. It's taking too long. Though it's summer and I'm running, I shiver with
cold.

"Tsemakh's house is coming into view. As the Talmud says, 'A
man's heart knows his own dire need'—my heart is pounding within
me as if I were a bandit: at home a soul is departing.[23]

"I reach the first window of the house. I don't want to wait till I
get to the door, I'll break through the panes. I look and the rebbe
is there, pacing about. I'm going to go in like a robber. It's as if I
can hear my daughter's voice calling, 'Papa, Papa!' I summon my
last reserve of strength, and I leap."

He had difficulty breathing, so he rested for a moment. With the tears thick in his eyes he resumed, his voice low and broken.

"But it wasn't meant to be. In front of the window was a pile of manure mixed with stones, so I fell and almost broke my neck. I still bear the scar on my forehead. When I was allowed to see the rebbe, he made light of the matter.

"I returned home—and how I managed to do that, I'll never know—and found her lying on the ground. Either she had fallen as she died or I had pulled her off the bed when I tore my hand away."

We were all silent, each of us with a stone weighing on his heart. The maskil recovered soonest.

"Well," says he, "I can only say, 'Blessed be the True Judge.' But you still haven't told us how you almost became rich."

Reb Elye wiped his eyes with his sleeve, smiled a sad little smile, and went on with his story.

"I only wanted to show you what 'not meant to be' means," he said.

"Afterward my troubles heaped up. My wife passed away. I couldn't make a go of her little business—what does a man know about market stalls? I was left with the children to feed, and didn't have a crust. When I remarried, I purposely chose a woman who wasn't young. What I wanted was a woman who could make some money from the stall. What I got was what the Talmud might call deceptive marriage, because she gave birth year after year. The business done in our fairs fell off steadily, and the stall wasn't worth a whistle.

"Then I said to myself, 'This can't go on! I'll give up my marriage-brokering, get rich, and sit and study.' Only, how do you get rich?

"So I write to my first wife's brother-in-law, the rebbe's man, and beg him by all that's holy to let me know the next time the rebbe attends a circumcision. Before the month is up I get the word. I rush to Vorke—right to the rebbe's, no detours."

"Into a bigger pile of manure?" cracks the maskil.

Reb Elye looks daggers at him and says: "The rebbe of the Vorke Hasidim, may his merit shield us, was entirely dedicated to ritual purity. Of all the ways of serving God, devotion to ritual purity was the rebbe's special way. . . ."

"Just look how he's looking at me!" cries the maskil. "You ingrate! When you came to town, who was it that helped you? A fellow Vorke Hasid? Or maybe your own uncle, the rebbe? Or was it me? Well? If it hadn't been for me, you would have starved to death long ago!"

Then, turning to me: "And what do you think he does now? He's *my* children's teacher. If I were to fire him, good-bye livelihood! Good-bye his last crust of bread!"

The Jew in question looks down and says nothing.

The maskil was growing more repugnant to me by the minute, though earlier he had winked and then gestured to signal that thanks to his efforts I would be able to get back to work the following day.

I address the hapless Jew: "Go on, and tell us more."

"Just take a look," says he to the maskil, "take this recorder, here. Anybody can tell from his appearance that he's more of a maskil than you are, but *he* doesn't poke fun. It's possible to disagree without being disagreeable. We don't think the less of Maimonides, may his merit shield us, for disbelieving in witchcraft.[24] A Jew should . . . It isn't right. . . . Making fun of people doesn't prove anything, it just stabs you in the guts."

"All right," the maskil says, less harshly. "Spill the rest of it."

"I'll make it short," the pauper begins. "I come in to where the rebbe is. I haven't written out a request to show him, I'm unprepared, I don't even have the honorarium—not that that was the occasion for an honorarium. When it comes to presiding over a circumcision, it is as the Psalm teaches: there can be no question of a ransom, whether offered to God above or to man here below.[25]

"The rebbe's countenance is so terrifying that my hands and feet tremble. I stand mute while he, may his merit shield us, paces back and forth with giant strides. Suddenly, he notices me and lets out a roar like a lion's: 'What do you want?'

"I become even more frightened. I force out an answer: 'I want to be rich.'

"The rebbe seems to have trouble believing his ears. He thunders: 'You want to be rich?'

"I answer, and my voice is lower than ever: 'Anyway, to make a living.'

"He shouts again: 'What do you mean, 'make a living'?'

" 'At least not to starve to death.'

"He keeps pacing about. Then he stops and asks: 'And what else?'

"I thought I would die! It's as if somebody else—and that's how it still seems to me—took possession of my tongue to speak for me. I hear myself say: 'That my son Joseph should be a scholar.'

"And that was it. I barely escaped alive from the encounter and he, may his merit shield us, passed away the week after. So I didn't get rich, but I missed by no more than a hairbreadth. And it was strictly my fault that I missed. If I had only been more resolute and stuck it out . . ."

"Aside from that," I ask, "is your Joseph a distinguished scholar?"

"I'm sure he could have been," came the stammering answer. "But the desire is lacking and against that no rebbe can prevail. My son simply refuses to study, and nothing anybody can do will help."

Here the maskil breaks in: "Don't make things so complicated. Your story has a simple moral: first, nobody should pile manure under a window; second, take a rebbe's honorarium with you if you're going to ask him for anything; and above all, don't let any rebbe scare you!"

Instantly, Reb Elye's sallow face crimsoned, his eyes burnt, his form straightened, and the room echoed to the pair of slaps delivered to the maskil.

I fear that neither will Reb Elye's second request be granted, and that he will yet starve to death.

A LITTLE BOY?

I can't stop thinking about the innkeeper's sweet-faced little boy, the one with the unpleasing mannerisms and the curls full of feathers. In my mind's eye I see him holding a scallion and weeping for an extra one, or I remember him at the afternoon and evening prayers saying the Kaddish in childish tones so tearful and so earnest as to pierce my heart.

The frightening drama of the Hasid slapping the maskil had turned the boy's ruddy face greenish-gray. I took him by the hand and led him out. "Let's go for a walk," I said.

"A walk?" he stammered, as his color returned.

"Don't you ever go for a walk?"

"Not anymore. May she rest in peace, when Mother was alive she used to take me for a walk on Sabbaths and holy days; but may he live long, Father says I can spend the time better by looking into a sacred book."

Now we were in a long entryway that was dimly lit by the reflection, suggesting a Star of David, from a distant lantern. I couldn't see the child's face, but his thin little hand was quivering in mine. We went out into the street.

The sky hung over Tishevitz like a dark blue uniform with dull silver buttons. To my companion it must have seemed a silver-spangled curtain before the ark in a synagogue. Maybe he was dreaming of a comparable blue silk, spangled bag for his future phylacteries. In five or six years this child might be receiving one as a present from his bride.

At night the shtetl looks altogether different. The humpbacked, lurching hovels vanish into "the poetic, still bosom of the night," while the windows and shutters look like wide, fiery, purple-streaming eyes.

On the stoves potatoes or else dumplings and beans should already be cooking in their pots of boiling water. The statistical data show the average per capita income in Tishevitz to be thirty-seven and a half rubles a year, or about ten kopecks a day. You can do the arithmetic: tuition fees; two sets of kitchenware and tableware, one for milk and one for meat; Sabbaths and holy days; illness; something for those who pray efficaciously for you—add it all up and you will understand why the stoves are so seldom used for preparing a fine meal, why the dumplings are made without a single egg, and why the potatoes may be served dry.

And those are not the worst houses. Others are completely blind, indeed eyeless. Here the diet consists of a crust of stale bread, with or without a scrap of herring. It may even be that the tenants must say the bedtime prayer without having had any supper at all. In one such house, doubtless, lives the old widow whose needs are so few, tapping at her heart with scrawny hand as she recites the Long Confession. Maybe she is measuring her shroud again, or maybe she recalls the wedding dress she wore so long ago, with its borders of gold thread. Maybe her ancient eyes let fall a tear or two, and maybe she smiles in the darkness of the night: what does an old Jewish woman need?

Those are not my little orphan boy's thoughts. Hopping about, he lifts his face to a moon floating with lordly insouciance behind and between the wispy clouds. He sighs. Has he seen a falling star? No.

"Oh," says he, "how I wish Messiah would come!"

"And why is that?"

"I would like the moon to get bigger! It's a pity about her. She committed a sin, sure, but hasn't she been punished long enough? It's almost the sixth millennium now."[26]

Those are his only petitions: of his earthly father, an extra scallion; of his Heavenly Father, growth for the moon. I have to curb a fierce impulse to say to him: "Forget it. Your father here below will soon remarry, you will soon have a stepmother and be a stepchild, and then you'll be crying for a piece of bread. You're better off as is, even without the extra scallion and a bigger moon."

By now we have left Tishevitz behind. A breath of spring wafts toward us from the fields. He draws me to a tree and we sit. It occurs to me that this is where he must have sat with his mother. She must have taught him what was grown in the townspeople's narrow furrows, because he recognizes wheat, rye, and potatoes.

"And these are thorns growing here! Does anybody eat thorns?"

"They say donkeys eat thorns."

"Why," he wants to know, "did God make every different creature eat different things?"

He doesn't know that if all creatures ate the same, they would all resemble one another.

THE RABBI OF YARTSIEV

He will be the first to tell you that he is a man with all the advantages, everything worth having. His salary is four rubles a week, which is, like the Israelites' contributions for the sanctuary in the desert, enough and more than enough. Why shouldn't it be, for an old gent and his old lady? He used to be an associate rabbi in a bigger city, where he also made four rubles a week. But there that income meant that from one Sabbath to the next they had to live on herring, the staple of the poor, although for people of their standing the proper diet was: breakfast, let's see now, oatmeal with milk; dinner, half a pound of meat; at night, a glass of tea with a day-old bagel. The expense choked them. As the Aramaic proverb puts it, "Every river has its own current." Which is to say, every place has its own usages.[27] Big-city dinners are a major cause of poverty. Here the pressure is off.

It is no hardship for him to have some borscht in the morning and wait till supper for his next meal. That's the Yartsiev way, and it's the good way. The other way was not good. Really, when he was there, he didn't miss the meat they couldn't afford. As a matter of fact, he doesn't like meat. Meat makes for what the rabbis called a full meal—not to say overfull—and that isn't appropriate for weekdays. Weekdays he likes an onion with a bit of sour milk, sour milk being his favorite food of all. That's his nature.

"My wife can't hear us," he says, smiling in her direction, "so I can tell you that she used to resent it. A Jewish woman knows how to be envious. 'What right has the slaughterer's wife to serve sausage while I, the associate rabbi's wife, don't even have a meat bone in the house? It's an outrage!' Now I'm rid of all that. In Yartsiev, thank God, nobody has meat except on the Sabbath, and at that it isn't beef but mutton. As long as there's no one for her to envy, all's well."

"What do you mean, 'envy'?" The rabbi's wife is now heard from.

"I know, I know." The rabbi's chuckles cause his old eyes to moisten and his head to shake. It is small, wrinkled, and framed by a soft pointy beard. "I know that you didn't care about the sinful appetites of the flesh but only about the honor due the Torah. An associate rabbi outranks a slaughterer, and it wasn't fitting that the slaughterer should have meat and the rabbi not. But be that as it may, now I'm rid of all that. Here an entire week can go by without fresh meat being available."

What makes him especially happy is the fresh air. In the big city the burghers occupied the middle floors of their houses, renting basement below and attic above to the poor—including, naturally, communal servants.

In the summertime he used to stifle, so much so that his wife felt obliged to purloin his snuffbox in order to keep him away from snuff. But she had to return it. Deprived of snuff, he doesn't know what to do with himself, can't concentrate. Even when he isn't actually taking snuff he has to keep fingering the box when he reads or indeed, as now, when he talks. Otherwise, he becomes incoherent in thought and speech.

"Well, just imagine. When I first saw that Yartsiev's broad marketplace was also grassy, I could have wished for a band to play and express my joy." In fact, that is what happened later, on his arrival to be installed as rabbi. To the accompaniment of music in his honor, the whole community turned out to receive him.

Something else that gladdened his heart was that all the houses were so modest—tiny, no bigger almost than a stick of tobacco, and made of wood. The only exception, in the middle of the marketplace, was a large, walled structure belonging to the local nobleman.

As for stairs, here the rabbi no longer has to contend with them. With his bad feet and knees, he would have been laid low if he had had to remain in the big city another year.

And the blessed peace and quiet! No barking dogs and—not to mention them in the same breath—no wrangling children. There are about thirty children in all, with maybe six teachers in charge. Which means that these children are supervised, unlike big-city children. Of course, sometimes there's noise, on Purim, Hanukkah, name your holiday. Otherwise you can hear a pin drop.

But the greatest blessing of all that the good Lord has vouchsafed him is that this is a shtetl wholly lacking in contentiousness. It has two or three resident Blue-Thread Hasidim, to be sure. "But you may take my word for it that I pray for long life to them. *Keyn eyn hore*, when their time comes—may that be a hundred years from now—there will be a real to-do about burial. In the meantime, quiet reigns."

The livelihood of the entire male Jewish population of the shtetl depends on their fanning out to the neighboring villages—runners, the men are called. Even the artisans go forth in search of customers rather than wait at home for customers to come to them, and the barber-surgeon himself makes the rounds with his cupping glasses. Sunday mornings you can see them all pouring out of their chicken-coop houses. At the edge of town they remove their boots, hang them on a stick over a shoulder, and scatter to the four winds. Friday night they are back. The very slaughterer can absent himself for a full week. Who has the time to be contentious?

Sabbaths and holy days offer the best opportunity, and then something does occasionally happen—but only a poor imitation of the real thing. They are amateurs. Besides, everybody is tired.

So the rabbi can sit and study undisturbed.

"Every now and then it does comes about," he says with a smile, "that a little controversy will arise—and at that it's for the sake of Heaven, between the slaughterer and me. You will understand why questions of kosher or unkosher aren't asked very often. During the week people eat milk foods and on the Sabbath meat foods, so the two kinds of kitchenware are never on the same stove at the same time. Likewise, only once in a blue moon will a doubt be raised about the lung of a meat animal.[28] Such challenges are so rare that when we do get hold of one we aren't in a hurry to let go. We pursue the matter through the entire Talmud and all the codes, and a contro-versy is born. The slaughterer is the kind of man who denies his own faults and attributes them to others. He is very obstinate, and he calls *me* obstinate."

The rabbi concedes that even in Yartsiev he had difficulties at the beginning on account of yeast and on account of their house—and all, he said with a smile, the doing of Mrs. Rabbi.

Here is what happened about the yeast: After accepting the

community council's offer of a stipend of four rubles a week, the same as his predecessor's, he discovered that they had concealed from him their grant to his predecessor of the exclusive right to sell yeast. On the first Sabbath before Passover the traditional sermon he preached was about the prohibition of leaven.[29] The townspeople were beside themselves with enthusiasm.

"Everybody," says he, "even a certified ignoramus, can tell when something is good. That is because all Jewish souls stood together at Mount Sinai and received not only the written but also the unwritten Torah—including, as the Talmud says, 'whatever discovery or innovation may be made in the future by an as yet unborn scholar.'[30] Consequently, even when a Jewish soul has forgotten what it once learned, it still knows when it is in the presence of the supernal. And in fact, no sooner had the first two days of the festival gone by than the town voluntarily offered me the yeast monopoly. I swelled with pride, and He soon punished me for it.

"The yeast gave me no end of trouble. You understand that it was my wife and not I who actually did the buying and selling. Well, all week long there were disputes between the housewives and her. One said that the yeast made her bread too hard; another, too heavy; a third, too runny. They suspected her of watering the yeast. What did I know? I never saw anything, and she denied it.

"Well, it was embarrassing. The rabbi wasn't going to sit as the judge in a dispute involving his wife. So I compromised. If a woman came on Friday, I would give her my loaf in exchange for hers. On other weekdays I would give a complainant additional yeast for dumplings. In short, no end of troubles. Finally, God be praised, a tailor solved my problem for me. He brought me caked yeast."

And here is what happened about the house: He had noticed that his wife was putting money aside for herself. Well, if that was the way she wanted it, fine, why should he care? Their children were doing all right, so maybe the money was for a grandchild. Again, why not? Even if he objected, he was not going to do battle with a woman. And possibly, he thought, she had something else in mind.

"This is one of those things it's better not to talk about, but you and I know that a lot of women prepare for later, when they are widowed. My own philosophy is the psalm's 'Blessed be the Lord day by day.'[31] No need for us to worry, when we die our shrouds will be waiting." He wasn't going to get involved.

The affair of the yeast had subsided when something new came up.

"Once, in the study house, they tell me a story: the rebetsin, my wife, has bought some lumber. I come home, and it's true. She has even hired some workmen. She's building a house! Why? She doesn't like being a tenant."

He wasn't going to get involved this time either. Let her build. So she built and moved in, and he brought over his volumes of the Talmud.

"Now I was a homeowner too!" Unfortunately, it was very far from the study house.

"May you never experience it, but my feet aren't what they used to be. I don't have many rabbinical texts at home, and I can't borrow them from the study house. Nobody is allowed to, the rabbi or even the head of the community council. The result was that when a legal problem came before me I was handicapped. It was a nuisance.

"What did God do? A small fire breaks out and a few houses burn down, mine among them. God be praised, the other homeowners didn't sustain a heavy loss. They were insured. I wasn't. As you see, the community board has partitioned off a kind of miniature study house for me."

LASHCHEV

In the dark of a summer's night, between eleven and twelve o'clock, I arrived in Lashchev. Again a marketplace, surrounded by the customary structures. In the middle lie scattered white rocks. I approach and the rocks stir, acquire horns, and resolve themselves into a flock of spanking white goats.

The goats are shrewder than the inhabitants of Tishevitz; I don't scare them. One or two raise their heads, contemplate us sleepily, and resume scratching one another or grazing in the street.

Lucky goats! No one levels false accusations against you and you don't need to be afraid of statisticians. Granted, you're slaughtered. So what? Which of us doesn't die untimely? There can be no doubt that you suffer less.

I call to mind what they told me in Tishevitz: "It will go better and smoother for you in Lashchev. The inhabitants there are more placid, less excitable. Nobody will hound you."

The community and the goats would seem to be a good match, resembling each other. Yet my host, an old acquaintance, makes me a little uneasy. He says that things are not so rosy as people think.

"What do you plan to do," he asks, "go from house to house?"

"Why not?"

"I hope they don't give you a hard time."

"Why should they?"

"A Jew doesn't like outsiders counting the money in his till."

"Why, are people afraid that that will keep the blessing out?"

"No, they're afraid it will keep the curse in, by letting credit escape."

FIRST TRY

Next morning, even before the beadle comes, a few Jews come by to see the recorder. My fame has preceded me.

I make a trial attempt and address one of my visitors: "Good morning, sir."

He answers, "Good morning—*Sholem aleykhem*," and holds out a tentative hand.

"What's your name, sir?"

"Levi Isaac."

"And your last name?"

"Why do you need to know?"

"What's the matter, is it a secret?"

"Secret or no secret, tell me why you need to know. *That* can't be a secret."

"Don't you know why?"

"Not exactly."

"Just for fun make the effort and tell me your name."

"Berenpeltz." He seems embarrassed to be named Bear-Fur Coat.

"Married?"

"Well . . ."

"What does 'well' mean?"

"He wants a divorce," someone answers in his stead.

"How many children?"

To arrive at an answer he counts with his fingers. "With my first wife one, two, three of mine and one, two of hers. With my second wife . . ." He tires of counting. "Let's say six."

" 'Let's say' won't do. I have to know exactly."

"That's just it. 'Exactly' isn't so simple. 'Exactly!' Why do you have to know exactly? What are you, some kind of clerk? Do they pay you only when you're exact? Does someone follow you around and check on you. 'Ex-act-ly!' "

"Tell him, you fool, tell him!" the others urge him. "Finish what you started." They want the interview to continue so that they can hear the rest of my questions.

He resumed counting with his fingers and this time, thank God, discovered three more children. "Nine, may they be strong and well."

"How many sons and how many daughters?"

Again he had to count: "Four sons and five daughters."

"How many are married?"

"Do you have to know that too? Explain it to me."

"Tell him, tell him!" the impatient spectators call out.

"Three daughters and two sons married," someone else answers on his behalf.

"Is that so?" my respondent challenges. "And how about Israel-Srolik?"

"But he hasn't been married yet!"

"You're a jackass! This coming Sabbath in the synagogue he's going to be called up to the Torah as a bridegroom-to-be. What difference does a week and a half make?"

I record this and ask further, "Have you served in the armed forces?"

"I paid four hundred rubles instead. How I wish I had the money now!" he groans.

"And your sons?"

"My oldest has a tumor under his right eye. Also—may you never know what it is—he suffers from a hernia. He was in three different hospitals, and the medical expenses came to more than a wedding would have cost. He barely survived to get a medical discharge from the army. My second son is exempt, and my third is in the service."

"And where is his wife?"

"What kind of question is that? She's staying with me."

"She could be staying with her own father."

"He's too poor."

"Do you own a house?"

"Of course."

"How much is it worth?"

"If it were in Zamość it would be worth something. Here it's just about worthless, except that it's a place for me to live in."

"Would you take a hundred rubles for it?"

"God forbid! It's an inheritance. I wouldn't take three hundred. Five hundred, now—that would be a different story. I could rent a house for myself and have something to put into a business."

"What is your business?"

"Who has a business?"

"Then how do you live?"

"Oh, is that what you mean? I manage to live, that's all."

"From what?"

"From the good Lord's bounty. When He gives, people have enough to get by."

"God doesn't throw an income down from heaven."

"Yes He does! How should I know where my living comes from? Here, figure it out for yourself: I need a lot of money, four rubles a week at least. Besides giving me a place to live in, my house yields twelve rubles a year in rent; deduct nine for taxes and five for maintenance and repairs, and I'm out of pocket at least two rubles a year."

He becomes transported by a kind of perverse pride.

"God be praised, I have no money! Not me, not these other Jews here, not Jews in general—with the possible exception of the Germanized ones in the big cities. Jews like us have no money! But the good Lord wants me to live, so I've managed to live for more than fifty years now. And when the time comes to pay for a child's wedding, the wedding takes place, come what may!"

"To sum up, what are you, really?"

"A Jew!"

"What do you do with yourself all day long?"

"I study, I pray—what does a Jew do? After breakfast I go to the marketplace."

"What do you do there?"

"What do I do? I do whatever needs to be done. Take yesterday, for instance. While circulating I heard that Jonah Borik wanted to buy three rams for some landowner, so first thing this morning I was with another landowner, who once complained that he had too many rams. Jonah and I made a deal and, thank God, we were able to split a profit of a ruble and a half on the transaction."

"Which means that you're a middleman?"

"Is that what I am? Sometimes the chance will come my way, and then I'll buy a little grain for resale."

"Sometimes?"

"That's what I said. When I have a ruble or two."

"And when you haven't?"

"Then I try to get it."

"How?"

"What do you mean, 'how?'"

In an hour I slowly piece all of it together: Levi Isaac Berenpeltz is something of an associate rabbi and arbitrator, a bit of a middleman, in part a merchant, fractionally a marriage broker, and even, sometimes, when the occasion arises, a traveling agent or courier. From all such "occupations," both those he has mentioned and those he has not, he succeeds with great difficulty in eking out enough to feed wife and children, including the married daughter with the pauper of a father-in-law.

SECOND TRY

I am conducted to a store. Inventory: a few boxes of matches, a few packs of cigarettes, needles, pins, hairpins, buttons, a few bars of yellowish-greenish homemade aromatic soap, some groceries, and other trifles. Incongruously, by the side of the table lies an old plowshare. That must be a sideline.

"Who lives here?" I ask.

"You see who!" answers a woman. She is busy combing the hair of a girl who seems to be ten years old. The girl jerks her head up from under the comb to stare wide-eyed at the novelty of a Gentile who speaks Yiddish.

"Put your head down, you bad girl!" screeches her mother.

"What is your husband's name?" I ask.

"Moses."

"And the last name?"

She suddenly begins to scold. "His name is that he should have been home by now! It's four hours since he went to borrow a pot from a neighbor and he hasn't returned yet."

"Stop carrying on," says the beadle, "and answer the questions."

She is afraid of him. The beadle is also an official of the local government and collects taxes. Besides, he has influence with the authorities.

"Who's carrying on? What are you talking about? You mean I'm not supposed to say a single word about my husband?"

"What is his last name?" I ask again.

The beadle, remembering the name, tells it to me: "Yungfreyd."

"How many children do you have?"

"Please, sir, I beg of you, come back later, when my husband is here. This sort of thing is for him. I've got too many other responsibilities. I have to worry about the store and take care of the house, as well as six good-for-nothing children. Do me a favor. Don't you bother me too!"

After I have recorded that she has six children, I ask her how many of them are married.

"Married? I wish they were married! Then our hair wouldn't be all gray."

"You have only girls?"

"Three boys too."

"What do they do?"

"What should they do? They make trouble for me. They eat us out of house and home."

"Why don't you teach them some trade?"

She sniffs, glares, and stops answering.

I have an idea. I buy a pack of cigarettes from her, and she looks a little less cross. So I ask, "How much does your husband earn?"

"Him? How much does *he* earn? Can you even depend on him when you send him to get a pot from his neighbor? As sure as pork is forbidden, he's four hours late! If there *is* a meal for me to eat tonight, do you think I'll have him to thank for it?"

Since her rage kept blazing, I decided I might as well leave and intercept her husband outdoors. When I saw him, I recognized him by the pot he was carrying.

AT THE SLAUGHTERER'S

From the slaughterer's house a mixed chorus of noises greets us. Chanticleer crows his cock-a-doodle-doo as triumphantly as if there were no such thing in the world as a slaughterer's knife; seeming to suffer from hunger, a bound calf lows mournfully; in cheery contrast, hundreds of birds are chirping between the laths and under the high, leaky roof. Having wings to fly with, they can laugh at the slaughterer. It is summertime, the air is warm, and even the poorest and most miserly human leaves crumbs for them. Cheep-cheep-cheep, cheep-cheep-cheep! The nest is finished and furnished, the male flaunts his resplendent colors, the modest female is quiet, and the fledglings have eaten their fill. They are warm, and not listed in any governmental file.

In vain will you ask them to elucidate "a blemish in the sacred offerings." That problem occupies two young men, barefoot, skull-capped, and stripped down to the pious Jewish man's "little cloak"—

the four-fringed undergarment normally covered by a shirt. These young men are ignorant only about merely practical things, like business licenses. They know everything there is to know about such things as calves intended for the messianically restored sacrificial altar.[32]

While God was parceling out the world—the farmer acquiring the soil; the fisherman, the streams; the hunter, the forest; the gardener, fruit trees; the merchant, weights and measures; and so on—the poet dallied in the grove.[33] The nightingale trilled to him, the trees whispered their sylvan secrets, and his eyes, his poetical eyes, couldn't tear themselves away from the washerwoman, paddle in hand, kneeling beside a brook. By the time he thought to claim his share, nothing was left. For him, God had kept only clouds, rainbows, dew, and summer fowl. To cap it all, on his return to the grove the washerwoman was gone. She had hired out as a wet nurse.

"You have imagination. Create your own worlds," God told him.

And how they envied the poet his best of all worlds! Only with sweaty exertion does the farmer cultivate the soil. The fisherman is no idler either—breaking through the ice in winter is not an easy or pleasant task. The hunter wearies himself chasing his prey. The gardener has his work cut out too, since oak apples, though they can be gathered without strain, can find no buyers. To avoid starvation even the merchant must do something, as a last resort using false weights and measures. The poet alone can lie on his belly and make worlds for himself.

But it is a mistake to think that the poet's lot is enviable. It turns out that his soul is nothing more than a camera and that the great world, with its great muck and its swine wallowing in the muck, merely produces a photographic image of itself within him. As long as the swine knows its place, things are bearable. When a swine seats itself at the head of the table, the poet's world becomes as swinish as ours.

No, only our two young men, the slaughterer's son and son-in-law, are to be envied. There is no contact between the world of "a blemish in the sacred offerings" and our world with its swine, nothing in common between the worlds of Them and of Us, no bridge, no overlap.

Which is why, when I came to their world from ours, they closed their volumes of the Talmud. Fright and wonder appeared on the young men's faces, as if indeed they were beholding a visitor from another world.

The slaughterer has gone off to some village or other, and that is why the calf is still bleating in the house. The slaughterer's wife is in her little dry-goods store.

The daughter-in-law and a daughter are standing by the fireplace. They are blushing, for three reasons: first, pride and joy that their men are so learned; second, the crackling fire; and third, bashfulness in the presence of a strange male—and a Germanizer at that. One has captured a corner of her apron in her mouth, and the second has moved backward a few steps, as if completing the Kaddish.[34] With wide eyes both gaze at me from under the woven headbands girding the upper half of their foreheads.

The young men recover soon enough. They have heard of "the registrar," and they guess who I am.

The interview proceeds quickly.

The slaughterer's income is four rubles a week, besides what he makes in the villages. His situation would be even better if he didn't have some irregular competition. The little shop isn't very profitable, but it can be depended on for a bit of ready cash. God be thanked, they make a living! The children are provided for, and will never have to worry about a roof over their heads or food in their stomachs. There is no lack of meat at the slaughterer's! After a hundred and twenty years, in God's good time, the children will inherit. One will succeed to the slaughterership and the other will get the shop. They will have joint ownership of the house.

They look better off than all the others in the shtetl—merchants, householders, artisans—better off than the very tavern keepers and barber-surgeons. A time will yet come, I thought as I left, when even teaching will be one of the better ways to make a living.

Things aren't as bad as people think. Besides the religious pursuits—those of rabbi, slaughterer, beadle, and teacher—there is another good one.

A woman lodger in the slaughterer's house pays a rent of fifteen rubles a year. The door to her lodgings is shut, but through a window I can see an attractive room: two neatly made beds with white pillows piled high; wooden furniture painted red; near the chimney, copper utensils hanging on the wall; and a glossy brass chandelier. The room bespeaks comfort and ease.

"She's got silver too," somebody tells me. I see a large chest covered with a layer of brass. That must be where she keeps her Sabbath candelabrum, and perhaps jewelry as well.

"You may not know it," someone says, "but she's got so much money that the whole town is in her pocket! She's a widow, with three children. Weekdays her lodgings are shut, because she comes home only for the Sabbath—except before the fast of the Ninth of Av, when the pickings from Jewish almsgivers are particularly good. Mostly, she's out of town, begging with all three of her children."

THE RABBI OF SKUL'S WIDOW

Among the things that the Talmud says about Queen Esther is that she was beautiful not because of her complexion, which was sallow, but because of the thread of divine grace wound around her.[35] The complexion of Esther the rabbi of Skul's widow is likewise sallow, but her countenance is radiant with graciousness, as if not one thread alone but a whole spoolful were wound about her. She is an old woman, and spare. Her little head is covered with a shrunken, thin pink film of cloth. Like a citron on Sukkoth, it nods over the red kerchief on her breast. This citron has two exceedingly sharp eyes.

She was born here and lives alone. For good and sufficient reasons she does not want to live with any of her children, who are married and dispersed. No one can vouch for a daughter-in-law or son-in-law; a man will stick up for his wife and a woman for her husband. (The holy Torah knows whereof it speaks when it says, "Therefore shall a man leave his father and his mother, and shall cleave unto his wife, and they shall be one flesh." One flesh is what actually happens.)[36] "Thou shalt not put a stumbling block before the blind." She doesn't want to give her children a possible occasion to transgress the commandment of honoring Mother.[37]

"When the good Lord created human beings," she says, "He saw to it that they wouldn't recognize the flaws of those closest to them. Otherwise, there would be as many bills of divorcement as marriage contracts!"

In the second place, the rabbi of Skul told her more than once that a widow who had to live with her children was a wife deserted twice over. "And what the rabbi of Skul used to say should be set in gold and hung around the neck like a locket." With a quiet sigh she acknowledges that nowadays lockets are seen as old-fashioned, less desirable than modern imitation pearls.

She couldn't remain in Skul. Ever since her husband the rabbi of Skul died—may his memory be for a blessing—the city had become repellent and repulsive to her. "The rabbis were right," she says. "When a righteous man departs from a place, so also do its glory,

splendor, and beauty depart."[38] She travels to Skul once a year, on
the anniversary of her husband's death, but can't bear to stay for
any length of time. "Nothing is left there!"

They were together for forty years. Those who knew him say that
she had become his double.

He was, may he forgive me for saying so, a misnaged—no friend
to Hasidism. Hence her own lack of regard for rebbes. His service
of the Lord having been Torah pure and simple without mystical
admixture, she in turn is always poring over comparable edifying
reading for women. With every other word of hers the rabbi is
recalled—voice, gestures, usages, and all.

After all those benedictions of her husband's on the arrivals and
departures of the Sabbath, she will not stoop to anyone else's. She
chants them herself, over the raisin wine or her Sabbath loaves. Her
benedictions are from the same mold as his: quiet, decorous, and
sweet.

The food she eats is supererogatorily kosher.

For a woman she is unusually learned and doubtless could solve
the kinds of problems that are submitted to rabbis. For forty un-
interrupted years, while her husband sat at the table and studied
aloud, she stood by the chimney with her kindly face half-turned
toward him, taking in with her dovelike eyes his every movement;
and with her ears, half-hidden beneath the kerchief on her brow,
his every word. She was a true "helpmeet for him."[39] His every
thought was reproduced in her mind, and his goodness in her heart.

The imprint made by water in ancient times is preserved in the
hard rock of the dry riverbed. The rabbi of Skul's life and character
may have flowed by somewhat stiller than a raging torrent, and his
lady's heart was even less to be compared with flinty rock. Yet her
heart preserved his imprint.

She does not think well of the modern world. "Not because Jews
are less pious than they used to be and should be. About that, let
the Sovereign of the Universe worry. If His Jews are as they are, no
doubt that is how He wants them to be." It is the decline in standards
that most displeases her. The best fabrics now are as flimsy as
cobwebs, and even sewing is done the easy way rather than the right
way. Altogether, flash and glitter have elbowed aside substance. "And
believe me, the result is even uglier than before—at least in my
opinion."

But she harbors ill will to none. "My husband the rabbi of Skul,
of blessed memory, may have been a misnaged, but that doesn't
mean that he persecuted Hasidim. God forbid!"

Once, she remembers, the leading citizens complained angrily to him that the local Hasidim were as unpunctual as their fellows elsewhere about reciting the Shema.[40] From his saintly mouth she heard this responsum: "In one and the same army different soldiers bear different weapons and have different customs, but they all serve the same king. Even boots," he added with his little smile, "are not all made according to the same pattern."

She remembers all his aphorisms, and guides herself accordingly.

He used to become angry if an artisan rose deferentially before him. He strongly affirmed that verse in the psalm, "When thou eatest the labor of thy hands / Happy shalt thou be, and it shall be well with thee."[41] When she moved here with her few hundred rubles, therefore, she was determined to earn her keep. She would make and sell potash.

"A Jewish woman is exempt from prayer at fixed times,"[42] says she, "but not from self-support." When her new neighbors parted her from what little money she had, her potash became all she could depend on.

"It could be a so-so living," she tells me. "Thank God, before the festivals I can make as much as two or three rubles a week! Praised be His dear Name, my potash enjoys a good reputation in these parts. The trouble is that you have to extend credit, and sometimes my customers don't pay what they owe."

Looking around, I see neither supplies nor equipment.

"For making potash," she explains, "you don't need such things. You take ash from the fireplace, mix it with potatoes and other vegetables, stir it, boil it, let the liquid evaporate, and you get unrefined potash. Repeat the process, and you get the refined product."

Worried and embarrassed, she asks a question as I am about to leave: "I beg your pardon, sir, but when your writings reach the hands of the authorities, won't they make me take out a business license?"

INSURED

A calm summer night. On the horizon loom, very black, the famous woods on the tree trunks of which our ancestors are said to have carved a record of the tractates of the Talmud they had studied, and concluded with fitting celebration, on their journey here. When

they halted, not far away, the exilarch said, "*Po-lin*"—"Here stay" in
Hebrew. That is how Poland got its name; except that the nations
of the world don't know how to spell.[43]

The woods have still another distinction: they are but a short
way from Jerusalem. There was once a nanny goat that belonged to
one of the thirty-six unknown righteous men whose merit in every
generation sustains the world. The goat knew the way. Every morning
at dawn it would hasten to graze on the Temple Mount and then
would return with three gallons of milk in its udder for the righteous
man.

To the right of the woods, beside a brook, lies the shtetl. It is
divided into two parts. One part is a long, straight, paved street on
both sides of which are walled houses with metal roofs, fastened
irrevocably to the earth by their foundations. This part is materiality
itself. The inhabitants are certain that here they will live and here
they will die; and let every wind in the world blow, they will not be
moved.

Then comes the second part. It is as different as can be, immate-
riality itself: slight, infirm houses; pine and thatch everywhere; few
shingled roofs. A breeze will make all disappear. Do those who live
here hope to discover the immortal nanny goat's short way to the
Temple Mount? Or are they gambling on fire insurance?

How the houses resemble their inhabitants!—pigeon-breasted,
with somber window eyes, and hunched under tilted straw headgear.

From their coops the poultry cackle, quack, and hiss. From the
swamp, which laps with the proverbial seventy tongues at its neighbors' doorsills, the frogs' croaking makes a respectable din. Now and
then a Jewish calf joins in with a bleat, and is answered by a Gentile
dog barking from the long thoroughfare.

Tomorrow morning I will record information.

I know in advance what I'll come up with: if not an average of
thirty-six rubles a year, then thirty-three, or thirty-two; many occupations and few jubilations; kitchen-made potash; unoccupied
houses. The beadle will tell the old story: *he* is a messenger; *she* has
a stall in the marketplace; two daughters are in service, one in Lublin
and the other in Zamość; an unmarried son is a teacher's assistant;
another is in the army; the daughter-in-law has gone home to Father
and Mother with her three (or four, or five) children.

I will find waifs next to the geese and ducks in the water at the
edge of the swamp; infants in the cradle, crying their lungs out; the
helpless sick in bed; boys, hardly more than children, boarding with
strangers in order to study Talmud; young married women, modest

or immodest in their coarse wigs. No sooner do I close my eyelids than I visualize a horde of faces utterly feeble, sallow, ashen, and twisted, hardly a one with a smile, hardly a one with a dimple; the men unvirile, lumpish; the young women with runny eyes, bearing things—a bushel basket of fruit, or a sack of onions, or a baby plus the sack of onions.

I know in advance that I will find an unlicensed gin mill, a couple of horse thieves, and more than a couple of smugglers.

What will be the upshot of the statistics? Will statistics tell us how much suffering is needed—empty bellies and unused teeth; hunger so intense that the sight of a dry crust of bread will make the eyes bulge in their sockets, as if drawn out by pliers; indeed, actual death by starvation—to produce an unlicensed gin mill, a burglar, a horse thief?

While medical science has perfected an instrument for recording the heartbeat, statistical science toys with inane numbers. Does it know the frequency, strength, or intensity of the heartache suffered by the descendant of an exiled Jewish hidalgo or by the author of a work on the laws governing kosher slaughter, or for that matter by an ordinary householder, before any of them did what the law says should not be done?[44] Does it know how long their hearts continued to bleed afterward? Can it count the sleepless nights that preceded and followed the first illegal act, or the times when children writhed with hunger cramps and limbs tossed with fever before the first glass of unlicensed liquor was poured?

Through parched, discolored lips the ghastly faces floating in air rasp to me:

"Twenty-four days without fire in my fireplace."

"Ten days in a row we had nothing to eat but potato peel."

"Three died. They had no doctor or medicine. The fourth I myself had to keep alive."

The hoarse words scratch at my heart like a dull knife. I flee from the window at which I have been standing, but there is no escape from the ghosts. The room is full of them.

By the stove stands a ruddy, overfed Jew, laughing. "Stealing, receiving stolen goods?" he asks. "What kind of business is that? It can cost you at least a month in jail, and in that time I would lose a fortune. I'm an honest man, an honest man! All the landed gentry will testify to that."

His voice screeches like a saw, and irritates me even more. I throw myself onto the bed and close my eyes. The rabbi of Skul's kindly widow appears.

"After the reckoning is made," says she, "if it comes out tolerable, will you say: 'Thy people, all righteous / Shall inherit the land forever; / The branch of My planting, the work of My hands / Wherein I glory'?"[45]

I seem to feel her kindly, dovelike blue eyes, with their magically sweet radiance, soothing my brow. So I fall asleep, to dream of the Angel of the Inclination to Good and the Angel of the Inclination to Evil. I see them as they fly down from heaven at dawn, both of them enveloped in a fine, rosy mist.

The Angel of the Inclination to Evil holds in one hand a blue document with a large dark eye at the top left—evidently something legal, the title to a house, maybe, or an estate; and in the same hand untold quantities of garments and accessories of silk, velvet, satin, and fur, men's as well as women's, traditional as well as Germanized, together with gems and objects of gold. In his other hand he holds potato peels.

The Angel of the Inclination to Good is stark naked and empty-handed, as God created him.

I have the impression that the Angel of Good is trying to tell me something. He opens his mouth, but the sound that wakes me is not his voice. Rather, it is a loud "Fire!" I spring out of bed. The house just across is going up in smoke!

A tongue of flame stretches toward me. I think I hear it say: "Don't be scared. Insured!"

THE FIRE'S VICTIM

It was Reb Chaim Weitsenzang's house that stuck out that tongue of flame at me. As the tongue swelled, the house shrank until, to the frightened accompaniment of wailing and loud outcries, it collapsed. Luckily, no one was home when the fire started.

By the time a pretty pink sun rose behind the bathhouse, like a pious bride after her monthly immersion, it was already too late to glimpse the long black outlines of men raking through the embers. During the night the men had searched among the leavings of Weitsenzang's house for the leavings of Weitsenzang's riches.

Around the ruin little groups of sallow, pale-lipped women gather. With a hand that has just had water ritually poured over it for the morning meal, each holds her soiled scarf on her unwashed head. Moaning, they lament the fate of the house.

A breeze arrives. If it had come during the fire, it would have been a commanding presence, but now it can barely make the remaining old chimney sway gently, like a palm branch in the synagogue on Sukkot. The chimney groans sadly, a mourning widower. While the innkeeper tells me about this latter-day Destruction of the House, it seems to be nodding its head in agreement: "He is telling the truth, the truth."

Even less readily than you can gather up all of life's threads and specks of dust, which the Angel of Sleep uses in fabricating the phantasmagorical dreams he sends us, can you come to the end of all the doings a Jew must engage in before he is able to hear the sweet clink of a copper penny.

If I wished to record everything, the Jewish town would require a blank sheet of parchment—something like the fabled silver-spangled curtain that the Sovereign of the Universe has spread between the Divine Presence's lower extremities and our heads, lest mortal eyes behold His expression, if I may be allowed the anthropomorphism—when your average burdened paterfamilias rises, lifts his head, and begins to pray.[46] His brain is burnt out, the light of his eyes is extinguished, his throat quivers, and with cracked, bony hands he clutches an empty, shriveled belly. His tongue does not move, his prayer is voiceless, speechless. It is his blood that calls out: "Sovereign of the Universe! I have done all I can, now You must help. Sovereign of the Universe! Sustain me as if I were a raven." (He is recalling the Psalm which declares that God gives food to the young ravens when they cry.)[47] Our silent petitioner continues: "Am I of less account than a bird? Sovereign of the Universe! Where are *my* crumbs? When in the ritual calendar am *I* supposed to be fed?"

In truth, if we were to judge by skin alone, he is very like a bird. The only difference is that he lacks wings, as well as a nest and crumbs.

It must be granted that Jewish occupations can be so specialized as to bear comparison only with a futuristic, twenty-first-century vision: one medical specialist raising the patient's upper eyelid, a second pulling down the lower lid, and a third actually looking at the eye.

Endow a veal roast or a rag in the paper mill or an exported egg with the power of speech, and also with the memory of the legendary rabbi Reb Heschel.[48] Those gifts would not be enough for them to enumerate all the Jewish hands through which they had passed, coming and going, from peasant's stable to roasting pan, from dump to mill—from bondage to freedom, as the Haggadah says.

What is more, a Jewish livelihood is like the ladder our father Jacob saw in his dream after he had laid his head to rest on the stone that the midrash says was formed when all the stones in the vicinity, each vying for the honor of serving as that righteous man's pillow, coalesced into one. The ladder "was set up on the earth, and the top of it reached to heaven."[49] How deep it sank into the earth, only the worm beneath it knew; and only the star shining upon it knew how high it rose.

To look up high and ever higher dizzies the likes of us; to look down ever lower twists the bowels into knots and makes faces lose for good whatever color they once had. With ease and grace the angels go up and down the ladder. It is otherwise with mortals, who expend all their strength climbing and fall back exhausted. Even after a Jew has given thanks in the synagogue for escaping without a broken neck, he no longer has the strength to try climbing again.

Such was the ladder on which crawled the victim of the fire.

He had started as the humblest of humble village peddlers, treading barefoot the scorching soil. Not the voice of his brother's blood rang in this Cain's ear but the voice of wife and children calling to him, "Food!"

With God's help, for a couple of years he was able to buy cheap and sell dear. A couple of years later he had risen in the world somewhat. Now there was a full week's supply of food at home when he left on his rounds, his mind was less agitated, and he could take the time to reflect that a father of six should really stop abusing his swollen feet if he wanted them to bear him at least until a bar mitzva in the family.

God was good to him and helped him again. The village peddler, thank God, was transformed into a village merchant. This meant walking only when there was no chance of a ride—i.e., no peasant to ride with from one village to another. When there was such a peasant, the merchant could afford to pay a kopeck and rest his feet.

Once again God was good and helped. After a couple of years the merchant owned his own horse and two-wheeled cart.

Time did not stand still, he did not cease from his labors, and God continued to help. The one horse became two horses, the small cart became a wagon, and he hired someone to drive it. He was a grain merchant, no longer doing business with peasants but with gentry. Since God continued to favor him, men favored him too. In his business with the nearby noble lord, he worked his way higher and higher up the hierarchy of retainers, from barn foremen at the bottom to managers and stewards and then the majordomo. At last he dealt directly with his lordship.

Now he was a well and truly established citizen. He got rid of his horse and wagon and replaced the driver with a manservant. In his pockets were the nobleman's IOUs.

To the shtetl he seemed like a sun. Around him revolved lesser merchants, like planets, and brokers, like comets. As the sun radiates the beneficence of light, so he radiated to the shtetl the beneficence of credit. In a more hostile view of him, he was a spider at the center of the web he had spun, and among the flies trapped in the web was a nobleman.

In time our sun-spider or spider-sun enlarged his house, saw to marriages and dowries, bought his wife pearls and himself a fur coat, and employed better teachers for the boys—as well as a tutor for the girls so that they would at least learn how to write a letter in Yiddish.

Unexpectedly—for the shtetl, at any rate—the nobleman went bankrupt and our spider-sun or sun-spider lost everything all at once.

If I had arrived a month earlier I would have recorded the following: a house worth 1,500 rubles; a distillery license; lumber and grain; moneylender, with loans totaling 15,000 rubles at 10 percent to the nobleman—IOUs unsecured by a mortgage.

That is what I would have recorded a month ago. Now I write only: "Burnt out."

I could add: "Jew, 82 years old; swollen feet; household of 17."

THE EMIGRANT

I open a door. The room is bare, unfurnished, the floor littered with hay and straw. In the middle stands an overturned barrel, surrounded by four unkempt little children eating from a large yellow earthenware bowl containing sour milk. They dip into it with tarnished spoons in their right hands. In their left hands they hold small pieces of gritty bread.

In one corner a pale little woman sits on the earthen floor, tears spilling from her eyes onto a potato she has begun to peel. In the opposite corner lies the man of the house, stretched out on the ground.

"You're wasting your time and effort, sir," he says to me, not rising. "I don't belong here anymore."

When he sees that I have no intention of leaving, he slowly picks himself up.

"Well, where am I supposed to ask you to sit?" he asks, annoyed.

I assure him that I can write standing.

"I have nothing to tell you. I'm just waiting for the ship ticket. You can see I've sold everything in the house, down to my tools."

"You have a trade?" I ask.

"I'm a tailor."

"And why are you emigrating?"

"Hunger."

Hunger was plain to be seen on his face, on her face, and above all in the burning eyes of the children as they ate the sour milk.

"No work here?"

He shrugs. Translation: he can't remember the last time there was work here.

"Where are you going?"

"To London. I was there once, made good money, sent my wife ten rubles a week, was able to live like a human being myself. My bad lack dragged me home again."

His bad luck, I assumed, was his wife.

"Why didn't you take your family with you?"

He doesn't answer. "Something within me drew me back. London is as dark as midnight. Every time I began to doze off, I would dream about the shtetl—the brook, the woods. I felt I was choking, and I kept being pulled back home."

"It really is beautiful here," I say.

"Clean, fresh air—no charge. With God's help we've been swallowing the air for three years now. I'm leaving with my wife and children. We can't take any more."

"Won't you miss the woods again?"

"The woods?" He smiles bitterly. "When my wife went into the woods the day before yesterday to pick berries, the locals gave her their special welcome—accompanied by a few touches of the whip."

I wanted to distract him: "But there's the stream you have. . . ."

His pale face turned paler. "The stream? This summer it took a child from me."

I manage to escape.

THE LUNATIC

When I return to my lodgings, I am drained. For a long time I lie sleepless on the hard sofa. Finally, I fall asleep, only to be awakened by a rustling sound. Someone is trying to steal into my room through the window. I see two skinny, dirty hands on the sill. Above them hovers a disheveled head, eyes burning in a bloodless face.

"Don't you want to register me?" the head asks quietly.

I don't know what to say. He, acting on the principle that silence gives consent, comes through the window and stands in the middle of the room.

I am frightened, but my curiosity exceeds my fright. I keep a steady eye on him.

"Write!" he says impatiently. "You want pen and ink?" Not waiting for an answer, he brings to the sofa the little table with my writing needs. "Write, please. Write!"

The voice is so mild and quiet, it insinuates itself so gently into my heart, that I lose my fear. I sit up to write, and the questions and answers begin.

"Your name?"

"Jonah."

"And your surname?"

"Jonah the Goat is what they called me when I was a boy, and Jonah the Beanpole after I got married. But since my accident it's been Jonah the Lunatic."

"I mean your official last name."

"Oh, that? Let me think . . . Perlmann! Do you see my pearls?" He points to the torn red kerchief around his neck and says, "Not exactly real pearls, are they? But that's my name and I can't do anything about it."

"Your wife?"

"Her maybe you shouldn't register. She doesn't live with me, hasn't lived with me since my accident. A fine woman. I'd be glad to give her a divorce, but the rabbi won't allow it. He says I would have to be of sound mind. A fine woman!" His eyes have dampened. "She took the child. It's better for him with her. What would I do with him, carry him around with me? They throw stones at me, so on top of everything else the boy would be hurt."

"You have one child?"

"That's right."

"What kind of accident did you have?"

"May you know no more bad in your life than I know what happened. Everybody says it was a dybbuk. The medic says that a stone hit me on the head and then my soul—he calls it the vital element—sank into my belly. I don't remember any stone, but I do have a bruise on my head."

He removes his cap and skullcap at the same time and shows me a bald swelling amid his hair. "That may have been done by a stone, I don't know. What I do know for sure is that I'm crazy."

"In what way?"

"Two or three times a day my soul is in my belly and then that's where I talk from. I crow like a rooster. For the life of me, I can't help doing it—not for the life of me."

"What did you do before the accident?"

"I didn't do anything. It happened in the first year after I was married, and I was still being supported by my in-laws in their house. That's why I have only the one child, may he live and be well."

"Do you have any money?"

"I had a few rubles of dowry. A lot of money went for medicine and rebbes, and the rest I gave her."

"How do you live?"

"On my troubles! Boys throw stones at me, so I can't move around in the marketplace. If I could, maybe I could do odd jobs for the merchants. They used to take pity on me sometimes and they were friendly, but now times are hard and I have to beg. I go begging before dinner, when the boys are in school.

"I don't have much to show for it. This is a small town and I'm not the only lunatic. For instance, they say that only yesterday what's-her-name, the lanky one, threw a pot at her maid and hit her on the head. That will make the maid crazy for sure. It's too soon to tell whether she'll crow like me, or trumpet with her fist like Solly the rabbi's son, or make no sound at all like Hannah in the women's bathhouse."

PROFILES

I don't want to reveal the name of this town, but I will say this: if in my travels I come across another like it, I too will begin to crow like a rooster.

Here are some profiles for you.

"Was a first-class shoemaker; handsomely supported wife and children (seldom fewer than four or five); won a fortune in the lottery. Began to drink. Drank everything away; wife and children reduced to beggary. He disappeared, no doubt soon to be discovered dead in a ditch."

If that isn't Jewish enough for you, how about his partner in the lottery·ticket?

"Had his own Jewish school. Won the lottery. In partnership with the rabbi leased a mill. The mill went bankrupt. Now beadle in a Hasidic conventicle. Receives no pay, but bootlegs where he works. Wife sells butter and eggs from door to door. Lame, so she doesn't make much. One son out of the house; a second apprenticed to a carpenter; a third at home, suffering from scrofula."

"Beyle-Bashe, widow (husband disappeared in the Turkish War), surname unknown; lives with daughter-in-law, soldier's wife. Daughter-in-law plucks feathers, works in the women's bathhouse, sits at bedside of women giving birth or sick women in general. On the landowner's sufferance picks berries in his woods in summer. Sickly; ekes out earnings by a little begging."

"Zaynvil Graf, prepares hides after years as accomplished fisherman. Bought fishing rights in a pond; landowner would have preferred Christian buyer; Graf had to pay through the nose. Fished all summer and couldn't catch anything kosher. Now poorest of the poor."

"Shmerke Bentzies, transacted business as far away as Danzig; twenty years ago returned home ruined; sells raisin wine for Kiddush; wife a seamstress, eyes going bad. No children, but hard to make ends meet because of raisin-wine competition."

"Melech Perels, fine young man, until recently supported by in-laws in their house. Went into partnership with grain merchant and lost his money. Father-in-law died in poverty. What will he do for a living? Only three children, no more."

I'm also asked to record a Jew (they have forgotten his name), with wife and children (they don't remember how many, exactly, but they know there are a lot), who will get here anytime now. The landowner didn't renew his lease. What he'll do is uncertain, but "you may as well register him."

THE HIDDEN SAINT

A teacher of small children tells me this story: "A *lamedvovnik*, a hidden saint, actually lived in our town. That's the truth."

"He said so himself?" I ask.

"A fine hidden saint he would have been if he had said so himself! He denied it from beginning to end. Ask him, and he would be incensed. But somehow or other, people became aware of it and then the whole kit and caboodle of the town *knew*, without question. People talked, and it was as clear as day.

"In the beginning there were a few skeptics, but they came to a bad end.

"Take for instance Jacob Joseph Wineshenker, an elderly gentleman, honorable, respected. It isn't as if he said anything in so many words. God forbid! But he must have done something, maybe wrinkled his nose while somebody was talking, that could be understood to mean, 'Please! Spare me your superstitions.' Well, what do you suppose happened? No more than five or six years passed and Jacob Joseph was gone, dead and buried!

"Or poor Leah the milk woman. So as not to step in the mud herself, she didn't make way for *him*. What shall I tell you? For a month the milk she sold her customers didn't stop turning! And it was no use begging his pardon. He would pretend not to know what you were talking about, and into the bargain he would rail at you."

I make a show of erudition: "A scholar's waiver of the honor due him has no effect."[50]

"Scholar? Does a *lamedvovnik* have to be a scholar? He couldn't even pronounce Hebrew correctly. As the joke has it, he wrote the two-letter name Noah with seven misspellings.[51] So what? In these parts we aren't finicky about Hebrew. He wasn't even able to review the weekly reading of the Pentateuch, but that didn't affect the powerful impact his recitation of the Psalms had in the worlds above. Our rabbi in those days, of blessed memory, said Velvl—that was the *lamedvovnik*'s name—could pierce all seven heavens. And don't think it was only his Psalms. I'll tell you what kind of man he was.

"Hannah the Bathhouse Woman had a nanny goat that got sick, so she decided to take it to the Gentile witch at the edge of town. The goat can hardly walk. On the way—this was truly heaven-sent, no two ways about it—the goat meets the *lamedvovnik*, and because it can't walk straight it brushes against his coat. What do you think? It was cured on the spot. Hannah kept her own counsel until something else happened, an epidemic among the goats. As with the Ten Plagues in Egypt, 'there was not a house without its dead.'[52] Then she let the others in on the remedy. They lured Velvl into the marketplace and set the goats at him."

"And they all got better?"

"What a question! They gave twice as much milk as before. The bathhouse woman was paid a groschen per goat. She got rich!"

"How about him?"

"Him? He got nothing. He was always denying it and getting angry and railing. Anyway, a rebbe may take money but a *lamedvovnik* won't. He can't let himself be revealed.

"In the beginning he was a shoemaker and a cobbler. (A *lamedvovnik* must work, if only as a water carrier. He must eat the labor of his hands.) It was his shoes that the old rabbi—long life to him— used to wear when presiding over a circumcision. But in later life he couldn't continue in his trade. His hands trembled so much he couldn't thread his needle, let alone patch a sole. So he ran errands, carried water, kept vigil at the bedside of the dead, recited Psalms for their benefit, was called up to the Torah when the frightening litany of God's curses was read, and in the winter, mostly, kept the oven going in the house of study."

"Did he collect the wood?"

"What an idea, why should we let him collect the wood?! Do you think nobody else was around? He was in charge while the others brought in the wood and put it in the oven, and he lit the fire. You'd think an oven was a lifeless object, but—forgive the comparison— the oven in our house of study knew him the way a wife knows her husband. A gale could be blowing strong enough to put your life in danger, but if he lit the oven, it stayed lit! Everywhere else ovens might smoke, but not this one. In this one the fire burnt. Yet it was as old as Methuselah, and full of cracks. If anyone else tried his hand at it, nothing doing! Either it couldn't be lit at all or it would belch smoke from every crack; and if neither the one nor the other, then all the heat would go up the chimney and at night you could just about freeze. After he passed away, they had to put in a new oven, because no one else had his mastery over the old one.

"It's a pity a Jew like him had to die! Before, people could make a living. Now, may God help us, you have to break your neck for a groschen. And we didn't need doctors."

"All by virtue of his psalms?"

"What kind of question is that? Just as almsgiving is a guarantor against death, so it was with his psalms. That was as clear as could be."

"So while he was alive nobody passed away?"

"Just like that, nobody passed away? You really think the angel of death had no say in the matter anymore? When even "The Jew" himself, of blessed memory, wished perfect healing to someone, Satan was often enough of a different mind?[53] In that case, do you suppose anything could help? An angel is still something to reckon with. And if the Court on High rules in his favor occasionally, what then? Still, in those days we had no need of a doctor, and in fact none ever lasted here very long. But now we have two doctors!"

"Besides that peasant witchman?"

"He's gone also."

"Croaked?"

"Don't say 'croaked' about anyone with those powers. You don't want to start up with Satan's camp—magic and demons."

THE INFORMER

"To make up for Tomaszow's having had a *lamedvovnik*, it also used to have an informer," the teacher of small children tells me. "It wasn't so long ago that he—I'm not sure how to say it—passed on? Died? Was taken away?"

The teacher says: "Don't think we're dealing with one of your run-of-the mill, straightforward informers. If this one happened to come across a false weight or a measure that wasn't what it should be, did he simply go and report it? Oh no, God forbid! He squeezed out hush money with threats: he was going to go, he was going to run, he was going to ride, he was going to write, he was going to send a messenger, he was going to do other things just as nice. He sucked the marrow from people's bones.

"Actually," the teacher continues, "he was as much sinned against as sinning. I can still remember when Jeroham brought him here. A fine young man! The only thing is that Jeroham promised him a marriage settlement and support, though he didn't know where his own next meal was coming from. And Jeroham was likewise as much sinned against as sinning. His brother Getzl—a notable, a real magnate—was most to blame.

"It's the old story: two brothers, one intelligent and good, the other stupid and bad. The intelligent good one is poor and the stupid bad one is very rich. As you might expect, the rich one doesn't want to help the poor one.

"Well, as long as Jeroham needed the money only to feed his family, he didn't complain. But when his little daughter Grune had become a grown woman of nineteen or twenty and was still unmarried, he raised his voice. The community and rabbi intervened and Getzl undertook in writing to hand over, not before a year after Grune's marriage, such and such amount of money. Any sooner, he said, and the marriage might not last or Jeroham might latch on to the money himself and demand a dowry a second time. Getzl wanted a three-year delay and would settle for no less than one year.

"When the year was up, he refused to honor his promise. He said it would not be enforced in the Gentile courts, and as luck would have it any countervailing Jewish influence had been greatly weakened. The old rabbi had passed away and his successor didn't want to get involved, fearing that the official rabbi—the one appointed by the government—would take the case away from him and turn it over to the Gentile courts. The upshot was, nothing! Getzl paid not a penny and Jeroham disappeared, either to ask for a rebbe's prayers or to go begging. And Beynish remained with Grune.

"God's ways are truly mysterious! This youth and this maiden form a married couple, and all goes topsy-turvy. The maiden becomes a woman, a dynamo, a Cossack, and the youth becomes not a man but a nothing, a mere sack or pile of bones. In her way, though, she tried to make something of him.

"She never stopped inciting him against Getzl: he should delay the reading of the Torah in the synagogue until justice was done, he should see that Getzl was denied the honor of being called up to the Torah, and so on. None of that helped in the slightest. Getzl gave him some resounding slaps, and thereafter the young man was ashamed to show his face in the study house.

"Once, when things had become desperate, Grune made Beynish go to her uncle again. She actually prodded him there with her broom! But it was no use. Getzl threw him out again.

"The things that can happen in this world! Something terrible happened then. My second-wife-to-be was still a divorcée and lodging with Grune. She was there and was an eyewitness when Beynish returned from the uncle half-dead and shivering as with a fever. She knew about such things because she had been the housekeeper in the communal guesthouse before it burnt down, and she understood immediately that Beynish was in a bad way.

"Grune was due to come home from selling bagels in the market-place and would no doubt add to his miseries. My wife-to-be took pity on him and advised him to lie down and rest behind the oven. He, God help us, obeyed like a golem: tell him to do this and he did this, tell him to do that and he did that. When Grune came home, my wife-to-be watched and said nothing. Beynish slept or pretended to sleep behind the oven.

"He couldn't have been in full possession of his faculties, because as Getzl was kicking him out, he had shouted something that he would never have said in his right mind. He called out that he would tell where Getzl's son Jonah had been hidden to escape being drafted.

"In any event, what he said made a profound impression on Getzl's wife. May my enemies have as much joy of their lives as Beynish had knowledge of where Jonah was hidden, but she was a Jewish mother and he was her only son; you can imagine how it was with her. She owned a grocery store, so she had a porter take a sack of Passover flour and follow her to Grune's house.

"She comes in. (It's a pity my wife isn't here now. She was there when it all happened, and when she tells the story, you could split your sides laughing.) The porter is told to wait in the entryway.

"'Good morning, Grune.' Grune doesn't answer, which Getzl's wife takes as a bad sign. She continues: 'Where's Beynish?'

"'How the devil should I know?' says Grune, and turns her back to skim the soup she was preparing. To Getzl's wife this means that Beynish has gone off to inform, so she calls in the porter and has him set down the sack of flour. Grune either doesn't notice or affects not to notice; who can fathom the mind of a woman like that?

"Getzl's wife pleads with her: 'My little Grune, we're kinfolk after all! Shouldn't blood be thicker than water? Call him back. Don't let him destroy me and damn his own soul!'

"At last Grune turned around. She was nobody's fool and it didn't take long for her to understand what was going on. She tricked Getzl's wife into giving her a few rubles as well, and then set forth (she said) to look for Beynish.

"In no time at all word got around the shtetl that Beynish had turned informer. Grune enjoyed that. She kept Beynish behind the oven while she threatened and squeezed every householder who was at all vulnerable."

"So she was really the informer?"

"Only at first. Later it was Beynish himself. He was so depressed that he took to drink and would reel from one tavern to the next. That was when he began to do the dirty work himself. He drank the money all up and Grune didn't see a penny. He had such potential. It's a shame what happened to him!"

"What did happen?"

"His insides got all burnt out, but not before he went crazy. He would run around in the street, or for a week at a time lie in the gutter somewhere. But go home to Grune? Never! Even when he was on his last legs, ten men couldn't drag him back there, he hit and bit so. Finally, they had to put him in the study house—the guesthouse had gone up in smoke—and that's where he passed away. They tried to save him. They called in a specialist, and they also recited Psalms."

"The *lamedvovnik* too?"

"Of course."

"So?"

"When a man's insides are gone, that's it."

1891 (translated by Milton Himmelfarb)

THE POND

The road, sandy and difficult, emerges from the sparse, irregular woods. According to Matthew, the coachman I'm riding with, cutting down the evergreens doesn't pay, so the grove remains a blunt wedge among the peasants' meager oat fields. Matthew points his whip and makes the same gloomy observation he has made about the trees: "Look at those oats there, still standing. You think it pays to harvest them?"

He interrupts himself to turn his attention back to the horses, which have taken advantage of their respite to have a go at the oats. The horse on the left, about to start chewing, gets a touch of the whip and a curse.

A quiet, melancholy night. Stars, sown as thin as the oats in the field, follow their courses as if weary and resigned. Though now only faintly audible, the fluttering of wings in the woods still follows us. Silently, to the right on the farther side of the field, there appears a loose chain of lightly wooded hills that withdraw slowly, ever so slowly, like misshapen, ill-shorn sheep. One has just mounted another and has been frozen in the act. In front of us the sun has set long since. At the edge of the sky a last bright strip darkens slowly under the plump clouds swimming by. To the left, between the thin oats, scattered flickerings can be seen.

"A village?" I ask.

"Our village," Matthew answers. Then, seeing I have no intention of letting him sleep, he sighs and surrenders. He takes out a clay pipe, stuffs it full of coarse tobacco, and lights up. The flare of the match casts a reddish glow on his face, which is half-turned away from me and framed between hairy headgear and luxuriant mustache.

"Our village," he repeats. "That's what it is."

"Why so spread apart?"

"That's how things turned out. The landowner and the commission got together, and . . . Did we understand what they were doing?"

"Do any Jews live with you?"

"Not with us. They aren't allowed in our fields, but in the land-owners' . . ."

"The landowners allow it?"

"For a price. Those who feel like it, . . . those who don't pay attention to the priest. . . ."

"They harm you, the Jews?"

"Harm?" He casts an inquiring glance. "I don't know about harm, but what good are they to us? They don't work in the fields—'not for the hands of the likes of them.' Besides, who will give them land? There was a time when they ran the taverns."

"How about you? Do you drink?"

"I'm a normal, sinful human being. I drink."

"On credit?"

"Sometimes. Before New Year's definitely."

"And the Jew used to write down what you owed?"

"Of course he did. Would you expect him to make me a present of it? Doesn't he have a wife and children too? Everyone has to look out for himself."

"Did he chalk up twice as much as you really owed?"

"Who knows? My wife used to say so, but that didn't stop her. She kept drinking on credit."

"Your wife?"

"Her too. You have to, often you have to. Once when she was drunk, she wanted to burn down Moshke's place."

"Moshke?"

"Moshke was the one with the tavern. Now he trades with us. An honest man, Moshke. Does he cook his accounts? I don't know, but otherwise he's a good man. A jack-of-all-trades: first aid, medicine, law. He knows everything, and he does business everywhere."

"So she didn't burn him out?"

"Of course not. She was running with a lighted torch in her hand to burn the tavern down when she tripped and fell in the street. Her hand was burnt in the fire, and she still has the scars to show for it. How she screamed! Later she asked Moshke to forgive her, and you know what? He did forgive her. He's a good person, Moshke. And that's him, standing over there."

Again he points his whip, in front of him, and I make out a shadow at the roadside.

"The thing that's shaking," says Matthew, "is his cloak, and what he's carrying on his shoulders is a sack. He's probably going for something in the village."

"Why is he standing there?"

"He wants a ride over the water."

"What water?"

"There!" He points to the edge of the village.

I had taken for dew the broad stripe glistening under the sky. It wasn't dew.

"Doesn't the gentleman know that this year we haven't had either rain or dew? It's water."

"Are we going to use a ferryboat?"

"What do you mean, 'ferryboat'? The water is stagnant, and it isn't any higher than your ankles."

"Rainwater?"

"Must be."

We ride on, and from the shadow a real Moshke materializes. I see that the skirts of his cloak are in fact shaking. His white beard quivers. When we reach him, he holds on to the edge of the wagon.

"Good evening, Matthew."

"Good evening, Moshke."

"Give me a ride over the water?"

"For ten groschen."

"I'll give you a cigarette."

"And a kopeck."

"Two cigarettes."

As Moshke accompanies the wagon through the heavy sand, he keeps on bargaining.

Finally, Matthew says to him, "Ask this nobleman."

So Moshke, a thin, graying Jew, switches hands, turns, and begins to address me in Polish: "*Pan*, with your permission . . ." He doesn't finish the sentence. Having a better eye for these things than the peasant coachman and speedily discerning that the nobleman is not quite a nobleman, he heaves most of himself into the wagon. But he is undecided where to sit. Should he perhaps favor the coachman? I, after all, am not clothed in the Jewish fashion. I settle the issue for him by making room beside me.

"Sit here, Reb Moses."

He needs no further invitation. Sitting down, he begins to talk: "First off, I greet a Jew with *Sholem aleykhem*. Next, thank you very much! That tobacco of Matthew's can make you drunk. And third, how does a Jew know my name? Have we met?"

When I tell him how I know, he is reassured.

"I'm only going to the other side of the pond," he says, "and then I'm turning right. No doubt you'll be going left?"

He starts questioning me, but I interrupt: "See how the water glistens. It's like a mirror."

"Bah! Water like that—" says he, and breaks off. I feel a reticence.

"What kind of water is it?" I ask. "Rainwater?"

"Rainwater!" he repeats, annoyed. "When was the last time it rained?"

"Then it must be a nearby spring."

"What makes you think there's a spring? There is no spring for ten miles around."

"What then, my friend?"

"What then? Nothing." He is concealing something.

"Still, what is it?"

"Why are we prattling about trivial things?" He wants to change the subject. "I would rather you told me what business a Jew is in."

Now I am certain there is a story about the pond, and that it isn't simple.

Unable to tear his eyes away from the pond, which shines so peacefully in the silent night, he is looking at it rather oddly. In his voice I hear uneasiness. I've got to make him talk.

"There's a story in connection with that pond," I say.

"So?"

He doesn't trust me. I offer him a cigarette. He doesn't smoke.

"How about a drop?" I say, and take out my flask.

"Before the evening prayer? I had just wound my kerchief around my waist so I could start the evening prayer when I heard the wagon coming, so I ran out to wait by the roadside.⁵⁴ The pond is only ankle-deep and ordinarily I just walk across, but I've been feeling a bit off this week—I hope you feel better—and I was afraid of catching a cold. Please understand, I'll say the evening prayer there"—he points his finger to the right—"but don't let that keep you from taking a drink. Life and peace to you!"

"I don't drink by myself," I tell him as I put the flask away.

"Perhaps you would like to pray now?"

"I don't pray while I'm on the road."

To encourage the horses uphill, Matthew breaks in with a "Giddyap!"

"You see how it is," says Reb Moses. "Go pray when you're with a peasant!"

Another pause, and then I try again. "And how are things with you, Reb Moses?"

"There's a Creator, which means that I get by."

He says no more, giving me nothing to take hold of.

"You know what, Reb Moses?"

"What is it?"

"Tell me something, anything. The quiet is making me uncomfortable."

"What do you suggest? What shall I tell you?"

"Tell me a little about the pond. You do have a story to tell about the pond?"

"Suppose I have. You want to hear it so you'll have something to laugh about."

"God forbid!"

"Then again," he says, changing his mind, "maybe not. Such crazy times! Zionism . . ."

"What has Zionism got to do with anything?"

"How should I know? All of a sudden everything is topsy-turvy. Young men in the yeshiva become Zionists, and then they throw away the Talmud and do all kinds of wicked things. Contrariwise, when German Jews become Zionists they recover their Judaism. Shaven beards, and Judaism! You mustn't think I'm referring to you." He smiles apologetically.

"What has that to do with the pond?"

"What has it to do . . . Please don't take this amiss. Let's assume a German Jew becomes religious again and it's the anniversary of his mother's death. He goes to a Jewish restaurant and for the repose of her soul orders kugel. Kugel is his Judaism. Maybe your Judaism is stories. Is this the anniversary of a death for you?"

He told me the story anyway. Perhaps he wanted to tell it even more than I wanted to hear it.

"Where the pond is now, there used to be a shtetl—not very big, just ordinary. The important thing was that people were able to make a living."

"What happened to it?"

"What happened to everything? This used to be a forest, hereabout. Where is it now? Forest all around, a fortune! On the other side of the forest there was a *palace*!"

"What I saw was a ruin."

"It's falling to pieces. In those days a count lived in it. At night you could see the palace seven miles away, it was so lit up with wax candles. The forest was a rattling, rustling, crackling, barking, living thing. The gentry fired their rifles, and blew their kind of shofars—not to confuse the sacred with the profane—and hunted their prey, and shot their guns, and made merry, and with their wives sat on the lawn by candlelight to the sound of music and they ate and drank; and how their hounds bayed!

"But it had already begun.

"Germans had moved in on one side and cut timber. On the other side shingle makers passed through. Every one of them would build a wooden hut if he needed it and gather wood for fire so his wife could cook and he would have light to work by. It was all very jolly. One shingle maker would sing and a second would accompany him on a fife, and so it went, over and over, all through the forest.

"Years and years ago a Jewish countryman was the leaseholder where the pond is now. As time passed, he acquired two sons-in-law, who came to live with him, and he maintained his daughters-in-law as well. He imported a teacher and a slaughterer, and built some cottages.

"Pretty soon it was a shtetl—and you could make a living there, as I say.

"The landowner would shoot hare, and behind his back the gamekeeper would deliver eleven, twelve skins for next to nothing. Or the dairy products—the yield from ten stalls! Or the landowner's bit of grain still standing in the field—as good as a steady job! That was what the Jews bought. They sold food, spices, candles, mead, all kinds of wine. The manor was insatiable!

"The handful of Jewish men applied themselves to their studies and the womenfolk transacted business. The rabbi was a full brother of the luminary who composed *Hemdat yomim* ('Most Delightful of Days').[55] He used to send the rabbi of Warsaw the occasional honey and two hens to accompany a learned request for a responsum. You know the style: 'Cherished colleague, seeing that . . .' et cetera. In due course the shtetl was home to outstanding scholars, sons-in-law

recruited from the greatest yeshivas. It may have been small, but—
what is the expression?—it was weighty: a weighty shtetl. Nothing
was lacking. There was even a *lamedvovnik*."

"A water carrier?"

"A capmaker, actually. Everyone thought that he was without
question an upright man, but also an ignoramus of the first order.
He always had his eyes in the prayer book, even for the 145th Psalm,
though we shouldn't need a book for it because we say it three times
a day. And you couldn't hear a peep out of him while he was
praying—not on Rosh Hashana itself, when the congregation sings
out: 'All ye peoples, clap your hands; / Raise a joyous shout to
God . . . !'[56] They thought, 'The poor fellow probably stumbles when
he tries to read Hebrew aloud.' Maybe.

"But pious! On Yom Kippur eve, for instance, symbolic strokes
of the whip to atone for sins aren't enough for him. He arranges
with the beadle for a real whipping, 'so that it hurts!' Again, on
Sukkot he stands waiting for hours at the rabbi's door because he
insists on reciting the benediction over the rabbi's own *etrog*. For a
whole day he disappears, and when he returns, only the Creator
knows from where, he's loaded down with twigs more beautiful than
you can imagine, for striking against the ground on Hoshana Raba,
the seventh day.

"It's nothing special that he doesn't keep remnants of the cloth
provided by his customers.[57] In those days, who kept remnants? But
suddenly something happens. It was during the intermediate days
of Passover—that's when it was, Passover. Or was it Sukkot? Anyway,
it was during the intermediate days of one of them. It's nighttime
and a couple of men are coming back from somewhere—from a
celebration, maybe, or from visiting the sick. Study-house regulars,
young fellows. Maybe they've been delayed because they were arguing
about a text they were studying. As they're crossing the marketplace,
they see light through the capmaker's shutters. They become suspicious. Young people!

"A fair comes right after the holiday. He must be making goods
now—during the holiday—to sell then! It's only an intermediate
day, sure enough, but still, not a workday for a really observant Jew.
Isn't it written in the *Chapters of the Fathers*: 'The ignorant man cannot
be a pious man'?[58]

"They want to catch him red-handed, and it's easy. All they have
to do is knock away a bar holding the shutter closed. No sooner said
than done, but then what do you see? By a tallow candle the capmaker sits poring over a holy book, and crying! They can plainly

see him crying! Tears are pouring down, he's looking into his book and the tears are flowing. What's more, no tallow candle ever gave light like the light in that room. The capmaker is so engrossed that he hasn't heard the shutter being opened. They're scared, and quietly they close it. They agree to keep what they have seen secret: who knows what it can mean?

"That's the first thing that happened. The second thing happened a few years later. A persistent rumor is born: After the rabbi of some town in the region passed away, the community invited two rabbis to come and take his place. That is to say, the householders invited one rabbi and the Hasidim invited the other. Nowadays we're used to such things, but then it was a desecration of the Name, no more and no less.

"Dissension arises. One meeting is held, and then a second, and a third—everybody running back and forth, and nothing settled. Finally, the rabbi of Lublin is asked to adjudicate. What makes things so difficult is not only that both rabbis are scholarly, upright men but also that both were brought in on the same day. One arrives from the east and the other from the west, and they meet right in the middle of the marketplace! How are you going to decide who should be sent away?"

"So what did the Lublin rabbi say?"

"That's the point. He didn't say anything. He said he had no scales for weighing rabbis. Do you know what happened then? Here's where the story really gets interesting.

"People have never stopped believing that the rabbi of Lublin gave the townsfolk the name of this shtetl and advised them to send two representatives here to consult Leybl the Capmaker—that was his name, Leybl—and do what he said should be done. That's what people believe.

"Who started the rumor? Nobody knows. Did strangers come? Apparently. Two strangers were seen. They couldn't have come on business, because they didn't buy and they didn't sell. And then they disappeared. Somebody says he saw them near Leybl the Capmaker's house. When the rabbi of the shtetl is asked about it, he says he knows nothing and they should ask Leybl. So they go to ask, and what do they find? Leybl is packing.

" 'Where are you traveling to, Reb Leybl?' They now use the honorific 'Reb' when they talk to him.

"He's going to the Land of Israel.

"What a how-do-you-do! Hardly is he revealed than he goes off to the Land of Israel."

"Did he go?"

"He went."

Matthew has fallen asleep.

The wagon collides with a fallen bough. We get a scare, but no one is hurt. We ride on carefully and Reb Moses resumes his tale.

"Where did I leave off? Oh yes, Leybl the Capmaker was going away.

"There was another upright man in the shtetl, but impulsive, excitable, and generally eccentric. He was a children's teacher, Yosl Bertsies by name. And he's the one that Leybl chooses to send for before leaving! Leybl has to impart something to him.

"The coach is crammed full of passengers and ready to depart, but everybody has to wait for Leybl and Yosl to finish whispering in each other's ears. It turns out that they were talking about something important.

" 'Be informed,' Leybl says, 'that the Prince of Fire is angry at our community.' "

"Why?" I ask.

"That's what Yosl Bertsies asked too, but he got no answer. He was told only that it was a long and complicated story and there was no time to go into details, because everybody was waiting and Leybl didn't want the coachman to start cursing. It was enough to know that the Prince of Fire was angry and wanted to burn down the whole shtetl.

" 'Well,' says he, 'as long as I was here, I didn't allow it. Night after night, the whole night through, I would sit over the holy books. The Prince of Fire would drop a spark on a thatched roof, I would drop a tear on the book, and the tear on the book would put out the spark on the roof.' (Now do you understand what was going on that night in the intermediate days of the festival?) 'For years he the fire and I the water wrestled. Now,' says he, 'I'm going away. I want you, Yosl Bertsies, to take my place as protector of the community. You must be my replacement.'

" 'Sit up all night over a book and cry?' Yosl asks.

" 'No,' says he, 'you're not strong enough. You would fall asleep. What I'm going to do is entrust two names to you. The first name is for rain. Call that name to mind once, and mist will form. You won't see the clouds yet, but it will become misty. Call the name to mind a second time, and clouds will come and it will drizzle. A third time, and new clouds will come, as big as mountains, and cover the entire sky, and a rain will pour down heavy enough to put out any fire.

" 'When you see that there has been enough rain, that's the time for the other name I'm entrusting to you—the one for dryness. Almost before you're finished calling it to mind, an east wind will come and sweep away the clouds and scatter them to the four corners of the earth. A summer sun will come out, a sun to rejoice your heart. In the twinkling of an eye, all will be as warm and dry as if behind the stove.

" 'But you must be very careful not to call that name to mind more than once at a time. Otherwise, fiery heat will come and burn all the crops and all the greenery, and—God forbid—people and cattle and wild animals and birds will all go raving mad. A year of dearth and famine will follow, God help us!' "

Only after a long pause did he take up his story again:

"And so it was!

"Not a week has gone by since Leybl went away when there arrives from the devil knows where someone who claims to be a German Jew and starts making inquiries about doorsills and other lumber products. He doesn't do any buying; he just walks around with a pipe in his mouth and asks about prices and takes notes—smokes his pipe and takes notes. So one evening a little breeze springs up, snatches a spark out of his pipe, and speeds off with it to a thatched roof. Evening time, that's when it was.

"All the men are at afternoon and evening prayers when some market women burst in and shriek, 'Fire!' So-and-so's barn is burning. In no time at all the fire isn't a fire anymore, it's a conflagration.

"People are running around, yelling. They go to the well for water, but when they get there—no rope! They have to run to the manor for rope, and the fire won't wait.

"But there's Yosl Bertsies. They run to him; he runs to the ritual bath, immerses himself once, twice, three times, comes forth, calls the name to mind, and mist begins to form. Once more, and a drizzle! But it's too late for that. The fire has been growing stronger, and the raindrops only snap and crackle as they turn into steam. So he concentrates again on calling the name to mind. Well, what can I tell you? Black clouds gather from the four corners of the earth, and there's a downpour—or better, a flood."

"So the fire was put out?" I ask.

Reb Moses becomes mournful. "In hardly any time at all, the shtetl was annihilated."

"Too late?"

"That, first. And second, Yosl Bertsies had forgotten the other name! The flood drowned what survived the fire. The pond you see there is a vestige of all that water. To this very day it hasn't dried out."

"But the rain did stop. How was that?"

"That's foolish," he answers. "In the end it had to stop. We have been promised there will be no second Flood."[59]

The wagon enters the water.

"Wonder of wonders!" Reb Moses blurts out.

"What is?" I ask.

"Think about the pond. The horses are plodding through it, and Matthew is smoking his pipe, just as if this were only commonplace, ordinary water!"

1904 (translated by Milton Himmelfarb)

SHORT
STORIES

Peretz was best known as a writer of short stories, many of which were written for the miscellanies and periodicals that he edited and published himself. In the early 1890s he began contributing to the socialist Yiddish newspapers that had been founded in the United States, and when the Yiddish daily press exploded in Poland at the beginning of the twentieth century, he was one of its most sought-after contributors. He also wrote stories in Hebrew, and translated or supervised the translation of his work from one language to the other.

Peretz used the story form for the most diverse ends. He wrote mood pieces to express a gnawing dissatisfaction that afflicted him all his life. His sharp exposures of poverty and suffering introduced a new standard of realism into Yiddish literature. He wrote satires, skirting the censor through the use of fables or veiled allusions. By the turn of the century Peretz was less concerned about abuses within Jewish society, the main focus of his writing in the 1890s, than he was about defections from Jewish society on the part of young Jews espousing internationalist ideologies or simply drifting into assimilation. He wrote stories dramatizing the moral attainments of the Jewish way of life, the vigor of Jewish debate, the charm of Jewish folklore, the troubling grandeur of Jewish history.

In an attempt to explain the contradictory impulses in Peretz's writing, some critics have tried to periodize the stories, tracing a progression from the radical Peretz of the early period to the neoromantic of the later years. Although Peretz did constantly shift his attention to whatever problems seemed most immediate, all his work was characterized by a dialectical tension between the romantic and rational impulses of his character, between cosmopolitan, worldly yearnings and practical Jewish concerns, between personal erotic desire and public accountability. These struggles are not always resolved in the stories, even in those that appear to be most pointed and straightforward.

Like all Yiddish writers of his generation, Peretz struggled to find a natural narrative voice in what was still a raw literary language. In the story "Stories" he treats the psychological and creative dilemma of the estranged Jewish writer who cannot write authentically for either Jews or Gentiles. But even the narrators of such apparently folkish stories as "Three Gifts" or "If Not Higher" stand somewhat apart from the worlds they are describing, and comment on their subjects from various angles and degrees of distance. The final story of the collection, "Yom Kippur in Hell," may be read as a parable of the modern writer who happens to have a "divine" voice, an accidental asset that he turns into a moral cause.

The stories appear in the order of their original appearance in Yiddish, with dates given. In the case of two stories that originally appeared in somewhat different form in Hebrew, the translations are based on the Yiddish version, and both dates are supplied.

VENUS AND SHULAMITH

▼

In a little prayerhouse two young yeshiva students, Hayim and Zelig, were seated by the stove. Hayim was reading aloud from Zelig's notebook and Zelig was listening while mending his shoe with a needle and thread.

" '. . . And beautiful was Hannah like Venus. . . .' Tell me, Zelig, please, what does this word 'Venus' mean?" asked Hayim.

"Venus is a mythological goddess," answered Zelig, driving the needle into the shoe.

"Mythology? What's all that?"

"You know nothing about that either? Think back a little: remember the strange-looking man who appeared a week ago wearing an apron and a red cap, the one who sold licorice cookies and other such things for practically nothing?"

"Yes, so?"

"He was a Greek and there is a whole group of people called Greeks."

"And they all sell licorice cookies?"

"Don't be silly, they have their own land: Greece. They are an ancient people, mentioned in the Bible. Their land is called in Hebrew Iavan and they are called Ivanim."

"What? Iavan? And from this comes Ivan in the Russian?"

"God forbid! Greeks are Greeks, with their own kingdom. They once were a very strong and learned people. I'm sure you've heard of Aristotle and Socrates. Our talmudic sages and even Maimonides knew about them. Aristotle, for example, believed the world was created out of chaos. Such were the Greeks. And even though they were very learned and knew how to paint, sculpt, carve, and appreciate fine things, they were nothing but idol worshipers serving false gods."

"How sad!"

"So you see, the stories and tales of the gods, of the idols, are called mythology."

"Well then, what is Venus?"

"Understand that with the Greeks each trade and each craft had its own god. Just as we say that each people has its own genius, such as sculpture, poetry, beauty, health, prowess . . ."

"And they all have gods? Then what do you mean by 'goddess'? A little god?"

"No. A god is a he and a goddess is a she."

"What? They allowed unmarried women to roam about in heaven?"

"Oh, Hayim, why only men and not women?"

"It's true, Zelig, but I thought that gods should be neither male nor female."

"Hayim, you must understand that Greek gods are just like humans, with the difference that they are immortal. Therefore, they have children, wives, and mistresses just like us, only they never die! Even Jupiter, the greatest of their gods, who holds thunder in his hands and makes all the other gods tremble with fright, even he is only a henpecked husband. To his wife, Juno, he's like a little Hebrew teacher snubbed by the rabbi's wife. I told you once about the philosopher Socrates' wife, Xanthippe, the shrew. Why, she was small fry compared to Juno! If you could imagine how Jupiter suffered at her hands! At least ten times a day he wished he was dead. But it's impossible, he can never die."

"I get the point. And Venus?"

"Venus is the goddess of beauty. Now I'll read to you about her life."

Zelig put aside the half-mended shoe, drew out a soiled piece of paper from his breast pocket, and began to read from it.

" 'Venus, Aphrodite, Apogenena, Pontogenea, Andiametha . . .' "

"I don't understand a word you are saying," said Hayim, bewildered.

"Little fool. Those are the names by which Venus was known in the various parts of Greece and later in Rome."

"She has more names than Adam. What's the use of all these names? Get to the story."

Zelig continued reading: " 'Under her many appellations she was held sacred as the goddess of love in various towns and cities.' "

"No longer of beauty?"

"It's all the same! 'She was not born of a mother but sprang forth from the sea. She is the ideal image of womanhood and very alluring as well.' "

" 'Alluring'? What does that mean?"

"It means she knows how to entice everyone, excite them, and get them hot, etc."

"I see!"

" 'She was represented as either scantily dressed or entirely naked.' "

"That doesn't sound so good."

" 'Her husband was Vulcan.' "

"What manner of beast is that?"

"Another god, a god of fire similar to Tubal-Cain. He invented the forging of iron and founded the blacksmith's trade. Understand?"

"A little. . . ."

" 'But she had no children by him.' Gods do not divorce or marry according to the laws of holy matrimony. 'Therefore, she had children by other gods and even by mortals.' "

"Just like that? Do you know what they call such children? Bastards, that's what they're called!"

"Don't be a fool, Hayim! Gods are not bound by the laws of marriage, sanctity, or divorce. They have no shame about sexual things or having bastards."

"Of course, if you don't accept the laws, why pay them lip service?

If you don't wash your hands, why say the blessings? But you said she lay with mortals too?"

"Well, what about it? Didn't some of our own saintly men, mentioned in Scripture, go in for—"

"Read on, read on!"

" 'She had two children by Mars—' "

"Morris?"

"No, not Morris, *Mars*, the god Mars, the god of war! 'Two by Bacchus, the god who oversees the making of wine and other spirits.' "

"He must be like Lot, a real drunk."

" 'Two by Mercury—' "

"And who is he?"

"Mercury is the god of swindlers, traders, and messengers."

"Quite an unsavory pair."

" 'And one by Anchises, a mortal whom Venus, disguised as a shepherdess, happened to meet near a river. A child was born from that encounter. Once the following incident took place. A band of cutthroats chased Venus. She took refuge in a cave and called for Hercules.' "

"Who?"

"A powerful god, not quite a full god but only a demigod. All by himself, he cleaned out thirty-six stalls in a stable."

"Get to the point, Zelig; this is becoming irritating and a little confusing."

" 'Hercules came into the cave and let each cutthroat enter one by one. He settled accounts with each in turn.' "

"How disgusting!"

" 'Venus used to take revenge on people who spurned love. She metamorphosed townspeople into oxen.' "

"Enough," blurted Hayim, jumping out of his chair. "Enough! I'm absolutely sick. This you call a goddess! And she had a thousand men massacred, run through, and slaughtered! And she gives herself to adultery, whoring, and murder! It's sickening!"

Hayim spat and Zelig stood foaming with rage.

"Do you know what you are saying and spitting at?" Zelig shouted. "You are taking a nice garment, turning it inside out, and making it into a clown's outfit. I used Venus only as a comparison, an ideal figure in a particular setting, as, for instance, Shulamith in the Song of Songs."

"And that is an accurate comparison? Really! You should be ashamed of yourself, Zelig. As if they were alike! Her brothers called her into their vineyards, so she neglected her own vineyard. Her face is swarthy but not like a gypsy. Her neck is like fine marble. She smells sweeter than all the fields, woods, and gardens. She does not glance up from bashfulness and does not swell with pride like a turkey cock. She looks straight ahead and has nothing to be ashamed of. She has fine, warm, and sincere eyes like two pretty doves. And she has lips—two thin, red feathers! She never sneers with her little mouth or makes ugly faces. She speaks openly and honey flows from her mouth. You know very well that she does not make any evil thoughts come into your head; on the contrary, you forget about whatever you were thinking. She casts her eyes upon you and your own turn away like a thief. Your very heart begins to quiver and tremble like a freshly killed hen. She is simple, pure, and clean as the new-fallen snow. As the summer comes forth, so new life returns to the field and the garden. The turtledove begins to coo, the flowers begin to bud, the fig tree blossoms, the grapes sparkle. Everything comes back to life, everything awakens to a new life, and her heart knows a new sensation. A new feeling suddenly comes over her with intense power. Stronger than death is her love, deeper than hell is her jealousy; and her love is forever. Rivers cannot carry it off, the sea itself cannot extinguish it. She has but one love, a young, handsome shepherd. She does not know that the shepherd wears a crown on his head, and that he is the greatest king in the world. She is simple, open, and noble. She cannot assume a role, or act fickle. It hurts her that he is not her brother from the same father and mother so that she can kiss him openly and freely on all the streets. Such is Shulamith. She is the ideal of a true Jewish maiden. Not like your Venus, that hussy!"

"You are forgetting one thing," interrupted Zelig. "You forget that everything called mythology is just fables that contain hidden philosophic and religious thoughts."

"Oh no, it's you that have the argument backward. It's just the opposite. How can profound thoughts be clothed in shabby examples? How can one wrap diamonds in dirty rags? And do you think we Jews do not read the Song of Songs as a parable? Isn't Solomon the Almighty Himself? And isn't Shulamith the Jewish people, the innocent but persecuted Jewish people! But why all these hidden meanings? Shulamith is Shulamith and Venus is . . . Why, there are a hundred thousand million differences between them. It's not even worth talking about. Do you hear, Zelig! Blot her out! Erase her name from your book and write the name of . . . what's the name of the girl you are describing? Hannah, wasn't it?"

"Hannah."

"Yes, so write that she was as beautiful as . . . No, don't write anything! You hear? Don't you dare! It would be impudent of you. Let your Hannah be compared to whomever you like: to Miriam with her timbrel, to Abigail, to Rehavah, to Delilah, even to Queen Esther; but not to Shulamith! No one can be compared to her, absolutely no one, you hear?"

1889 (translated by Seth L. Wolitz)

WHAT IS THE SOUL?
The Story of a Young Man

▼

1

I remember, as in a dream, that a small, thin man with a pointed beard used to walk around in our house. He used to hug and kiss me all the time.

Afterward, I remember, this same little man was lying sick in bed. He groaned a lot, and my mother stood by, beating her head.

Once I got up at night and saw the room full of people. A wailing cry frightened me and I began to scream. One of the men came over to me, dressed me, and took me to a neighbor's house to sleep.

The next day I didn't recognize our house: straw lay strewn on the floor, the mirror was turned around to face the wall, the hanging lamp was covered with a tablecloth, and my mother was sitting in her stocking feet on a small stool on the floor. When she saw me, she let out a terrible cry, and began to wail: "The orphan, the orphan!"

A light was burning in the window. Near it stood a glass of water, and a piece of cloth was hanging there. I was told that my father had died, that his soul washed itself in the glass of water and dried itself on the cloth, that if I did a good job of saying the Kaddish, his soul would fly straight up to heaven.

And I imagined that the soul was a little bird.

2

Once the teacher's assistant was escorting me home. Several birds flew quite low and near us. "Souls are flying, souls are flying!" I sang to myself.

The assistant looked around. "You foolish boy," he said to me, "those are ordinary birds!"

Afterward I asked my mother: "How can you tell the difference between a soul and an ordinary bird?"

3

When I was fourteen years old, I was already studying the Talmud with commentaries at the home of Zorakh Pinch.

To this day I don't know whether that was really his name, or whether his students gave him this nickname because he pinched us without mercy. He didn't even wait until you deserved to be pinched—he paid in advance. "Remind me," he said. "I'll deduct it from the next time!"

Since he also performed circumcisions, he had a pointed fingernail which he used during the ceremony. This meant that you felt his pinches all the way down to your toes.

He used to say: "Don't cry over nothing! I only pinch your body! What harm can it do you if the worms in the grave will have less to eat?"

"The body," Zorakh Pinch said, "is only dust and ashes, and you will see the proof if you rub your hands together." We tried it and we saw for ourselves that the body really is dust and ashes.

"And what is the soul?" I asked.

"Something spiritual!" the teacher answered.

4

Zorakh Pinch hated his wife with a passion, but his only daughter, Shprintse, was the apple of his eye. We students hated Shprintse because she used to tell on us to her father. But we loved the teacher's wife because she sold us beans and peas on credit, and more than once she saved us from the teacher's hands.

I was her favorite. I used to get the biggest portion, and when the teacher started up with me, she would shout: "Murderer, what do you want from an orphan? His father's soul will take vengeance on you!" The teacher let me be, and his wife got what was meant for me.

Once, I remember, on a winter night, I came home from school so thoroughly pinched and frostbitten that my whole skin ached. I raised my eyes to heaven and prayed: "Dear Father! Take vengeance on Zorakh Pinch! . . . Lord in Heaven, what does he want from my soul?!"

I had forgotten that he pinched only my body.

As it says in the Talmud, "A man is not held responsible for what he says when in distress."[1]

5

But sometimes, when Zorakh Pinch declared a holiday, closed the Talmud, and began to tell stories, then he became a different person. He took off his fur hat, and you could only see a headful of feathers (his yarmulke was hidden in it). He unbuttoned his coat and smoothed his brow. There was a smile on his lips, and his voice took on a gentler tone.

He taught with the harsh, coarse, and angry voice that he used when speaking to his wife. But when he told stories, he spoke in the same soft, small voice that he used in talking to his "dear soul" Shprintse.

We were always begging him to tell us a story. We didn't realize that Zorakh Pinch only knew one chapter of Talmud—the fifth chapter of *Bava Metzia*—with which he began and ended the semester, and he had to fill in the time with stories, especially during the winter, when there weren't even any holiday breaks! Like fools, we used to pay for every story with beans and peas, and once put our money together to get a red velvet jacket for Shprintse.

For that velvet jacket Zorakh Pinch told us how the Almighty chooses a soul from His treasury and blows it into a body. And I imagined that in the Almighty's treasury the souls were laid out like the merchandise in my mother's shop, in all kinds of boxes—red, green, white, blue—and tied up with string.

6

"And when God," the teacher told us, "chooses a soul and decrees that it must enter the sinful world, it trembles and cries. Afterward an angel comes to it inside the mother's belly and teaches it the entire Torah. But when it comes time to be born, the angel gives it a fillip under the nose, and it forgets everything it has learned. For this reason," said the teacher, "all Jewish children have a dent above their upper lip. . . ."

That same evening we were skating behind the town, and I saw that the Gentile boys Yantek, Voytek, and Yashek all had dents above their upper lips, the same as we did.

"Yashek!" I risked my life and asked him in Polish, "You have a soul too?"

"And you, you dog's soul, what's that to you?" was his blunt retort.

7

Besides studying with my teacher, I also took writing lessons from a tutor.

This tutor was considered a great freethinker in the town, and the neighbors didn't trust him to keep the dietary laws. He was a widower, and people didn't believe that his daughter, Gitele, a girl my age, knew how to kosher meat.

But he was an accomplished man, and my mother wanted her only son to know how to write. "I beg of you, sir," she said, "not to study any freethinking things with him, no Bible, no Scripture—just teach him how to write a letter in Yiddish, a simple, ordinary letter!"

Yet I don't know if the tutor kept his word. When I raised with him the difficult question of the dent above the upper lip, he became terribly angry. He stood up quickly, kicked away the bench with his foot, and began pacing the room shouting: "Boors, murderers, bats!"

Gradually, he quieted down, sat down again, wiped his glasses, and drew me to him. "Don't believe such foolish things, my child," he said to me. "Did you take a good look at the Gentile boys who were skating? What are their names?"

I told him their names.

"Well," he asked me, "do any of them have a different kind of eyes? Do they have hands and feet or other limbs that are different from yours? Don't they laugh and cry the same way you do? Why shouldn't they have a soul the same as you do? All human beings are the same, children of the same God, inhabiting the same earth! True, today the nations hate each other; each nation considers itself the crown of all the others, the exclusive preoccupation of God. But we hope that a time of better understanding will come when all men will acknowledge one God, one law; when the words of our holy prophets will be fulfilled, and all wars will end, envy and hatred will disappear, all men will serve the one Creator, and it will come to pass, as the prophet says, 'For out of Zion shall go forth the law, and the word of the Lord from Jerusalem.' "[2]

I remembered that verse from saying it when we took out the Torah scroll at services.

The tutor talked quite a bit more, but I didn't understand very much of it; I couldn't believe that "a Gentile also has brains," that all human beings are the same! I knew that the tutor was a free-thinker; he didn't even believe in the transmigration of souls. Yet when Wild Fradl died I myself saw a black dog hanging around the roof of the house where she had lived.

Also, the tutor didn't cut his nails in the prescribed order. He just threw the cuttings out the window—the mark of a wicked man, according to the Talmud![3]

I would have run away from him a long time ago and told my mother that he spoke "against the Lord and against His anointed," except . . .

No doubt you've already guessed what and whom I mean.

8

But one thing the tutor said did stick in my mind—that a time would come when the other nations of the world would come to us to learn Torah, and that this could happen any day now.

In our town we really felt that the time of the Messiah was at hand. Someone had found a strong hint in the Book of Daniel that this was the year; there were allusions to it in the Midrash Neelam of the Zohar, and word got around that the Kozinitzer rabbi had stopped saying Takhanun, as though every day were a holiday or festive occasion. Another clear piece of information came from the Land of Israel: this year no fox was seen by the Western Wall, and the words of Lamentations were thus no longer fulfilled.[4]

Every day Messiah the Son of Joseph was really expected; the community piled up debts and held back on taxes. When Messiah came, who would remember such trifles?!

The women got the worst of it. The steps of the ritual bath had fallen in already a year before. Time and time again the Torah scroll wasn't taken out of the ark until money was collected for new lumber to replace the steps.[5] They finally collected the amount needed, thank God. And yet it seemed a shame to hire a workman, a waste of a couple of rubles!

And I was sure that soon the same Yashek who had tripped me the day before when I was skating figures and almost caused me to break my neck; and the same Voytek, who always turned up the corner of his jacket into a pig's ear; and the same Yantek, who taunted us with insults—the three of them would come to me bowing and prostrating themselves to ask about some ritual law, such as the items that may not be handled on the Sabbath!

And I, full of mercy, would not remember all the evil they had done me; I would tell them what they wished to know. I would treat them as friends and tell them the hidden meaning of the iron and paper bridges in the days of Messiah, the paper bridge that would support the righteous while the iron bridge would collapse under the wicked. I would tell them to be extremely careful not to approach the iron bridge; the best thing, I thought to myself, would be for them to stay away from both bridges so that they could save their souls.

9

On the eve of Rosh Hashana I finished the chapter of the Talmud I had been studying with Zorakh Pinch, and I felt as though I had been liberated from Egyptian slavery.

I was told that Reb Yoyzl, my new teacher, did not pinch. He didn't even hit you just for the sake of hitting. I had seen Reb Yoyzl a lot at services. He was a tall man with bushy eyebrows; you couldn't even see his eyes. He used to wear his coat open, and under the two points of his long white beard his *talis kotn* stuck out. He walked quietly and he talked quietly, as though everything were a secret. He nodded his head very slowly, raised his eyebrows, furrowed his brow, stuck out his lips and his mustache, and put both hands in his belt; it seemed that each word was weighty and important.

Reb Yoyzl had been the agent of one of the great Hasidic rabbis. To this day he still sold goods from such rabbis on commission: oil over which incantations had been said, special coins, amulets, and talismans. He was the most reliable person in town for charming away evil eyes, and when our rabbi was indisposed, Reb Yoyzl would deliver the sermons on the Sabbath before Passover and on Rosh Hashana, and the occasional eulogy. Our rabbi was an old, sickly man, and it was expected that when he completed his allotted hundred and twenty years, Reb Yoyzl would take his place.

In addition, Reb Yoyzl was well known for blowing the shofar on Rosh Hashana, and when he said the accompanying blessing, as the expression goes, "the fish trembled in the water."

I was proud that I was to become one of Reb Yoyzl's students.

Even before Yom Kippur I had a chance to talk to Reb Yoyzl about the soul. The soul had become a kind of *idée fixe* for me; it was never out of my thoughts for a minute. The first thing that Reb Yoyzl did was to knock out of my head friendship with the other nations, and to knock into my head our chosenness.

"It is not in vain," he said, "that we suffer exile, humiliation, and other plagues that are not even mentioned in Deuteronomy's list of curses! If our situation were the same as that of the other nations, we would share the same kind of life in this world as they have. The child that the father loves, he spanks, so that he will learn and inquire into all the gates of understanding. . . . But even among us Jews, not all souls are the same. There are coarse, ordinary souls like Zorakh Pinch. Your tutor, the freethinker, has a soul like the rebellious Korah. Then there are great souls, very great souls that come from beneath the Throne of Glory. There are very great and elevated souls like the most refined flour."

I didn't understand very well about the different gradations of souls, and especially not about the origin of some souls from beneath the Throne of Glory; but I did know what the most refined flour meant, and I imagined the distinction between the souls to be like that between rye flour, corn flour, wheat flour, and the flour used to make the Sabbath loaves. The greatest souls must be those with saffron and raisins!

10

"But the main thing," said Reb Yoyzl, "relates to suffering. No soul is ever lost; they must all return to their original level, where they were before they descended into this world—and souls are cleansed only through suffering. The Creator in His great mercy sends us suffering so that we remember that we are only flesh and blood, broken vessels, insignificant. At a mere glance of His, we disintegrate and become as the dust of the earth. But in the next world the souls are cleansed."

Then he told me what is done to all the poor souls in the seven departments of hell.

11

During the High Holiday period I had more time to pay attention to things at home. Before the Feast of Tabernacles we used to do a big wash.

One night I dreamt that I was in the next world. I saw how the angels stretched their hands from heaven and caught up souls that were returning from this world. The angels chose among them; only the pure ones, those white as snow, flew up from their hands like doves straight into paradise. The dirty souls were heaped up in a huge pile that was thrown into a frozen sea, where black angels with rolled-up sleeves stood and scrubbed them. After that they were boiled in huge black pots lit by the fires of hell. And as the dirt was squeezed out of them, and as they were pressed, you could hear the souls crying out from one end of the world to the other.

Among the dirty washing I saw my tutor's soul; it had his long nose, his sunken cheeks, his pointed beard, and it was wearing his big blue glasses. But the more his soul was washed, the blacker it became.

And an angel called out, "This is the soul of the tutor, the freethinker!" Afterward the same angel said angrily to me, "If you follow in his ways, your soul will become as dirty as his, and every night it will be washed until it is lost in the tortures of hell!"

"I won't follow in his ways!" I cried out in my sleep.

My mother woke me up and took my hands off my heart. "What

is it, darling?" she asked me, startled. "You're covered with sweat!"
She spat three times to ward off the evil eye.

"Mother, I was in the next world!"

In the morning my mother asked me very seriously if I had not
seen my father there. I said, "No."

"What a pity, what a pity!" she said, disappointed. "He surely
would have given you a message for me."

12

But what was the use of this dream, since my tutor even ridiculed
dreams! For his sake, and even more for Gitele's sake, I wanted to
save him. I told him my entire dream. But he said that dreams were
foolish; he paid no attention to such things. He wanted to bring
proofs from the Bible and the Talmud that dreams are nonsense; I
stopped up my ears with my fingers and wouldn't listen.

It was obvious to me that he was lost, and that his punishment
would be severe; that I must avoid him like the plague; that he
wanted to destroy my soul—my young soul!

But what was the use? I promised myself a hundred times that I
would tell my mother everything, but I never kept my promise.
Many times I had already opened my mouth to begin speaking—
but every time it seemed to me as though Gitele were pleading with
me from behind my mother's shoulders, her delicate hands stretched
toward me, begging me silently, "No! Don't say it!"

The plea in her eyes was stronger than my piety. I felt that for
her sake I was willing not just to go through fire and water but to
be thrown into hell itself.

And yet I had misgivings, for my mother and my teachers had
high hopes that I would turn into a great Jewish scholar.

13

I was now rid of Zorakh Pinch with his sharp fingernail, but I was
no better off.

By then I was sixteen years old. Matchmakers were already putting
pressure on my mother, while I still indulged the childish habit of

collecting wax at the end of Yom Kippur from the reader's desk in synagogue and kneading it under the table during class.

The synagogue attendant, who had his own designs on the wax, became my eternal enemy on account of this, and I got into trouble in class as well.

"What do you have in your hands?" asked Reb Yoyzl.

I was caught off guard, and I put my whole hand on the open volume of the Talmud: all five fingers, with the piece of wax.

Reb Yoyzl turned pale with anger. He opened the drawer, took out a thin piece of string, and tied my thumbs together so tightly that it hurt me to the quick.

But that wasn't all he did. He took the broom and very deliberately pulled out a flexible, thin stick. With this stick he whipped my bound hands—for how long? It seemed to me that it went on forever. But the amazing thing is that I accepted the suffering gladly; I felt that the Almighty was sending me this suffering so that I would repent and stop going to my tutor.

When my hands had swollen quite a bit and my skin had turned every color, Reb Yoyzl put away the stick and said, "Enough! You will not knead wax again!"

Nevertheless, I did knead wax again. My greatest pleasure was to make the wax into whatever I wanted. I felt that I had to be busy creating something.

I used to knead the head of a man. Then I made it into a cat or a mouse; next I drew wings out of its sides, and split the head in two to make the two-headed imperial eagle. After that I braided the two heads and the two wings into a Sabbath loaf.

But I myself was also a piece of wax, kneaded by Reb Yoyzl, my tutor, my mother, and anyone else who had the urge. Most of all by Gitele!

14

They kneaded me like wax, but it was painful!

I remember very well how it hurt me! But why should it have happened? Why was I so concerned about the soul? My friends mocked me, "the soul-boy," and as foolish as the name was, that's how much pain it caused me.

Sunk in thought, I wondered how I would wind up, and when I would finally have the strength to break away from Satan's grip. I reproached my soul and called it to account. Suddenly, someone would give me a fillip on the nose: "Soul-boy!"

I wanted to forget my troubles. I immersed myself in a difficult problem, linking together a difficult Tosaphot with a hard passage from Maimonides, mixed with some arguments from the Pney Yehoshua and from the Tumim.[6] I was in another world; the tutor, Gitele, the soul were all banished. It was all beginning to fit together in my brain, I just about had the answer, the right word was already on the tip of my tongue, when suddenly someone whistled in my ear: "Soul-boy!" It echoed in my head, bursting something in my brain—Maimonides, Tosaphot, Pney Yehoshua, Tumim were all banished. I was back on earth!

I stood praying the Shimenesre; my heart was full and my eyes were full of tears. "Heal us, O Lord, that we may be healed," I prayed with fervor—and I didn't mean, God forbid, my body; I meant my soul. "Master of the Universe, heal my young soul!" "That's the soul-boy," said someone in the middle of my prayer— and gone was my fervor!

Day and night I suffered.

15

Gitele was considered to be very clever. Her father always called her "my clever girl." Neighbors used to say that she was as bright as day—and were she as pious as she was smart, she would cause her mother to rejoice in paradise. My mother also praised her intelligence, and said she would make a perfect daughter-in-law if she were only more trustworthy at koshering meat.

Once, when I didn't find the tutor at home and Gitele was alone, it occurred to me that I should consult with her about the soul.

My legs were trembling, my hands shaking, my heart quivering, my eyes stuck in the ground like a knife being ritually purified,[7] but I managed to ask: "They say, Gitele, that you are smart. Please tell me, what sort of thing is a soul?"

She smiled and answered, "I certainly don't know."

But suddenly she became sad, and her eyes began to fill with tears. "I remember," she said to me, "that when my mother, may she rest in peace, was alive, my father always said that she was his soul. . . . They loved each other so much!"

I don't know what came over me, but at that moment I clasped her hand and said, trembling, "Gitele, would you be my soul?"

She answered very softly, "Yes!"

16

How lucky I was in everything!

Lucky that Gitele was an only daughter and I an only son, and both of us orphans—so that it was easier for us to get our way; lucky that the tutor had laid aside a few hundred rubles as dowry, and my mother needed it for her shop; lucky that I had suddenly—and undeservedly—gotten a bad reputation as a freethinker, and no one else would have me. And the greatest piece of luck was coming up with the idea of sending for Tsipe the Cottonmaker, a matchmaker with a mouth on wheels, whom I promised a bonus out of my own money!

For all that, my mother still cried over me: "If your father were to rise from the grave and see who I'm giving you to, he would return to the grave in shame."

That gave me an idea. In the middle of the night I began crying out as before. I was again in the world beyond, but this time I delivered my father's greetings to my mother, saying that my father approved of the match.

That is how I acquired a new soul.

1890 (translated by Michael Stern)

IN THE MAIL COACH
▼

1

He told me everything at once, in a single breath; within minutes I learned that his name is Chaim, that he is Yona Hrubeshover's son-in-law, Berl Konskivoler's son, and that the wealthy Merenstein from Lublin is related to him, an uncle on his mother's side. This uncle, he gave me to understand, has an almost goyish household; perhaps he doesn't go so far as to eat nonkosher food, but he himself saw him sit down to a meal without first washing his hands, as prescribed by ritual.

They are very strange people, he intimated: they have long cloths laid out on the steps; before entering the house one has to ring a bell; everywhere inside there are more embroidered cloths hanging on the walls . . . people sit as if they were in jail, walk about stealthily like thieves . . . it is as silent as, God preserve us, among the deaf.

His wife has the same kind of family in Warsaw, but he never visits them, the beggars. "What use are they to me? Eh?"

His uncle in Lublin may be lax in observing God's commandments, but at least he is rich. Nu, you rub against a fat person, some of the fat rubs off; chopping wood gives you splinters, at a feast you can lick a bone—but there, paupers!

He even expects that in time the Lublin uncle will give him a job. Business, he complains, is not good. These days he deals in eggs; he buys them in the villages and sends them on to Lublin. From there they are shipped to London. They say that in London they put them in a kiln until chicks hatch. "It must be a lie . . . the English must simply like eggs!" But in any case, business is bad.

Still, it's better than dealing in grain. Grain is completely dead. Right after his wedding he became a grain dealer. Since he was a yeshiva student, they found a partner for him, an old merchant who talked him to death and simply lorded over him.

2

It was dark in the mail coach; I could not see Chaim's face, and to this day I don't understand how he knew that I was a Jew. When he entered, I was sitting in the corner, dozing—I might have given a Jewish sigh. Perhaps he felt that my sigh had an affinity with his.

He told me that his wife comes from Warsaw, that even now she dislikes Konskivola.

"She was born, you understand, in Hrubeshov, but she was raised in Warsaw, by her 'unkosher' family—she was an orphan. In Warsaw she tasted other things. She knows Polish, she can read German addresses, she even claims to play an instrument, not a fiddle, but some other kind of instrument.

"And who are you?" he asks, suddenly clutching my hand.

I gave up trying to sleep and, I must admit, he began to interest me. A story about a young man from a small town, his bride, brought up in Warsaw, who detests the small town. . . . "Something might come of this," I think to myself. I must get more details, add something of my own to the plot, and I will have a novel. I will put in a convicted robber, mix in a few bankruptcies, throw in a dragon for good measure; it might even be interesting.

I bend over toward my neighbor and tell him who I am.

"Oho!" he says. "So it's you, of all people. Be kind enough to tell me, won't you, where a man gets the time and the patience to think up stories?"

"You see for yourself."

"How should I know? You might have inherited a bundle and are living on the interest."

"God forbid! My parents are both alive, may they live to a hundred and twenty."

"Then you must have won the lottery."

"Not that either."

"Then what?"

I honestly did not know what to answer him.

"And you make a living from this?"

I give the typical Jewish answer: "Beh!"

"And your entire income comes from writing?"

"For the time being."

"Ah! Tell me. What do you get out of it?"

"Not much."

"So yours is another dead profession?"

"Dead . . . or put to death."[1]

"Times are bad," my neighbor sighs.

For a few minutes there was silence; but my traveling companion could not remain quiet for long.

"Tell me, I beg you, what good are these stories? I don't mean yours, of course," he quickly corrects himself. "God forbid! A Jew must earn a living. Even if he has to squeeze it out of the bare walls—there's no question—what doesn't a Jew do for a living? Take my case, for example. I had no other choice but to go by mail coach, and only God knows if I am not, at this very moment, sitting on a ritually forbidden mixture of cloth.[2] But I mean the readers. What do they get out of these stories? Is there anything of value in them? What do you write in your books?"

He doesn't wait for a reply, but answers his own questions.

"It must be some new fashion for women, like the crinoline."

"And you," I ask him, "have you never read these kinds of books?"

"To you I will admit the truth. I do happen to know something about them—this much. . . ."

He probably indicated the tip of his finger, the nail and a bit of the flesh above it—it was dark.

"Did it capture your interest?"

"Mine? God forbid! I read them for my wife's sake. This is what happened: It was five or six years ago, six years, a year after the wedding—we were still being supported by my family while I studied in the *beysmedresh*—and something happened to my wife; she was not herself. Not that she was actually sick, God forbid. She was up and about, but she was not in the best of health. Once, when I asked her what was wrong . . . But"—and he suddenly drew back—"why am I bothering you with these things?"

"Not at all," I say to him. "Tell me, my friend."

My traveling companion laughs. "And bring straw to Egypt? You don't need my stories—surely you can think up better ones on your own."

"Go on, friend, tell me."

"You write lies for others, I see, and want the truth for yourself."

It doesn't even occur to him that one might write the truth! Nevertheless, he complies with my request.

3

"Nu," my neighbor begins his story, "it's nothing to be ashamed of. We had a room of our own in my father's house. I was a young man, readier to talk about these things, so I asked her what was troubling her. She began to sob—I was filled with pity for her. Not only is she my wife—may the Evil Eye have no power over her and may she live, please God, for a hundred and twenty years—but she is also an orphan, far from home and lonely."

"What do you mean, 'lonely'?" I wonder out loud.

"You must understand that my mother, may God grant her peace, died a year before I married, and my father, may God grant him peace, never took another wife. My mother, may her merits preserve us, was a pious woman, and my father could not forget her. So my young wife was alone in the house—my father had no time to spare. He spent almost the entire week in the villages; he dealt in produce, anything you might think of—eggs, butter, old clothes, pigs' bristles, canvas."

"And you?"

"I was always in the *beysmedresh*, studying Torah. I figured my wife was frightened to be alone all the time. But that still did not account for her crying. No, she's not frightened, she says. She is bored. . . . Bored? I don't even know what that means—I saw that she wandered about like a sleepwalker. Sometimes when I talked to her, she didn't hear me, sometimes she looked at the wall, lost in thought, just staring and staring, sometimes she moved her lips but not a sound came out. What is it to be bored? Something for women only, no doubt. These women are an unknown tribe. A man is not bored, a man has no time to be bored. A man is either hungry or full, he is involved in business affairs, or he is in the study house, or he sleeps. If he has an extra minute, he smokes a pipe—but bored?"

"Don't forget," I tell him, "a woman doesn't study Talmud, she takes no part in public affairs, she isn't even responsible for carrying out the six hundred and thirteen precepts."

"That's the point exactly! I soon understood that being bored meant having nothing to do, a kind of idleness that can drive a person mad. Our rabbis long ago understood this—are you well versed in the commentaries? 'Idleness leads to boredom!' According to Jewish law, a woman is not permitted to be idle. So I said to her, 'Do something!' She wants to 'read,' she told me. 'Reading' was also a strange concept to me, even though there were already Jews among us, especially those who had learned to write in the profane tongue, who 'read' books and newspapers instead of studying sacred texts. At that time I did not yet know how educated she was—she spoke to me even less than I spoke to her! She is quite a tall woman, but she used to hang her head and keep her lips closed as if she couldn't count to two—a quiet person, a sheep. And her face always looked strained and worried, as if her shipload of sour cream had just sunk. She wants, she says, to read. Read what? Polish, German, even the Yiddish translation of the Bible, so long as it is something to read. And here, in Konskivola, there is not even the shadow of a book! I felt so sorry for her that I couldn't deny her this, so I promised her that when I went to my uncle in Lublin I would pick up some books for her.

" 'Don't you have any?' she asks.

" 'I? God forbid!'

" 'Then what do you do all day in the study house?'

" 'I study!'

" 'I want to study too,' she declares.

"I make it clear to her that Talmud is not a storybook, that it is not meant for women, that the Gemara even teaches that women are not permitted to study Talmud, which is holy. But nothing helped! If the people of Konskivola had known, they would have stoned me. And they would have been right! I won't go into all the details—I'll be brief. She begged me, she cried, she swooned, she carried on for so long that I finally gave in. I used to translate a page of Gemara for her each evening, but I knew from the beginning how it would end."

"And how did it end?"

"Don't ask! I translated a page from 'The Four Categories of Damages'—the ox, the pit, the grazing animal, and the incendiary—together with the commentaries of Rashi, the Tosaphot, and the Maharsha.[3] I recited the lesson in the traditional singsong, and she fell asleep as I read to her, night after night—it is not for women! But that winter I had a stroke of luck when a peddler strayed into Konskivola during the great blizzard and sold me a whole crate of storybooks. Now the situation became reversed. She read to me and I fell asleep. To this very day," he continued, "I can't understand what there is in these stories. Men surely won't find anything in them! Tell me, do you write only for women?"

4

Meanwhile, daylight broke. My neighbor's sallow, long, thin face became visible in the dimly lit carriage—and so did his black, tired, bloodshot eyes.

Apparently, he wanted to go to the front of the wagon to say the morning prayers; he was wiping the mist from the mail-coach window when I interrupted him.

"Please don't take offense, my friend, but tell me, is your wife content now?"

"What do you mean, 'content'?"

"Is she no longer bored?"

"These days she has a stall with salt and herring, one child at the breast, two to comb and wash—just wiping noses keeps her busy all day."

He continues to clean the windowpane, and I disturb him again. "Tell me, my friend, what does your wife look like?"

My neighbor stands up, glances at me sideways, scrutinizes me from head to toe, and asks me harshly:

"Say, do you know my wife, from Warsaw perhaps, eh?"

"Of course not," I answer him. "I ask only so that if by chance I get to Konskivola I might recognize her."

"You want to be able to recognize her?" He smiles, reassured. "All right! Here is a sign: she has a mole on the left side of her nose."

5

The man climbed down from the mail coach, and not until he reached the bottom step did he say a cold good-bye. Apparently, he suspected me of being acquainted with his wife and perhaps even of belonging to her "unkosher" family in Warsaw!

I was left alone in the coach, but sleep was out of the question now. The early-morning air enveloped me; the coat that my literary life permitted me was padded with wind and the cool morning crept into my every limb. I moved to the back and huddled in a corner. Outside, the sun began to shine. It is possible that I was riding through a breathtakingly scenic area; the first rays of the sun may have been kissing the peaks of the tree-lined hills and dancing across a blue, crystal-clear river, but I did not have the courage to open the little window—a Jewish writer has respect for the cold. I sat and began to "dream up" a story, as my Jewish companion would say— but other thoughts intervened.

Two separate worlds, a man's world and a woman's world—a world of the talmudic "Four Categories of Damages," and a world of storybooks, bought by the carton.

When he reads, she falls asleep; when she reads, he falls asleep. It's not enough that we have different sects, not enough that we classify people according to French noses, English canes, German hunters, Lithuanian pigs, Polish beggars, Eretz Yisrael wanderers, not enough that every part of the body lies in a separate stall and has a different-sounding name, not enough that every one of these parts is further separated into different sections—Hasidim, misnagdim, "Germans"—but we are also divided into males and females, so that in each and every narrow, damp, squalid Jewish home there are two distinct worlds.

When he reads, she falls asleep; when she reads, he falls asleep. At the least, I think, we ought to unite the two worlds. It is the debt of every Yiddish writer—but Yiddish writers have too many debts of their own. If only we had some supplement to our income!

The driver interrupted my ruminations on income by several sharp tugs on the reins. I did not leave the coach. It was getting a bit warmer and the sun began to show its generosity.

Another passenger joined me in the coach; and in the morning light, not only could I see him clearly, but I even recognized him. He was an old acquaintance. As children we used to slide on the ice together and often played at making mud pies; we were like buddies. Later, I went to the dark and grimy Jewish boys' kheyder, and he went to the bright and emancipated gymnasium.

When I didn't know the lesson, I was whipped; when I revealed a particularly good grasp of the basic questions with which the commentators dealt, I received a pinch on the cheek. One was as painful as the other. Sometimes he received the highest grades; at other times he was locked up for punishment. I broke my head over talmudic legal problems, and he broke his teeth on Greek and Latin. All this time we remained inseparable. We were neighbors. Secretly, he taught me to read languages other than Hebrew, and he lent me books. As adolescents, lying on the grass by the river, we made plans to change the world. I intended to invent a powder that could be shot over a great distance, as far as a hundred miles; he, a balloon that could fly to the stars, so that we could introduce order there too. We felt a great pity for the wretched world, which had somehow gotten stuck in the mire—how do we drag it out? A wagon with ungreased wheels, with lazy horses, and the driver asleep!

Afterward, when I got married and he left for the university, we didn't correspond. I heard that something went wrong; his plan to become a doctor never materialized and he became a druggist instead, in a small town somewhere.

When he entered the coach, I almost shouted for joy; my heart warmed with pleasure, my hands reached out to him, my whole body bent toward him, yet I controlled myself; with all my strength I held back.

It's unbelievable, I think. It really is Janek Polniewski, the town administrator's son; it really is my old friend who wanted to embrace the whole world and kiss each part, except for the disgusting warts that needed to be excised! But who can tell these days? Perhaps he has become an anti-Semite; perhaps we Jews are today's warts that have to be excised from Europe's beautiful nose. Perhaps he will survey me with a pair of cold eyes, even hug and kiss me, but say that I am different from the other Jews.

But I was mistaken. Polniewski recognized me and fell on my neck, and before I even had time to raise the question, he asked me what I thought of the vile anti-Semitism.

"It is"—he speaks in Polish, of course—"a kind of cholera, an epidemic."

"Some say that it is political."

"Don't believe it," Polniewski declares. "Politics doesn't create new realities. It can only take advantage of those that exist, suppressing some parts and intensifying others. It can blow up a tiny spark into an inferno; but it can't kindle a new spark. Human nature, not politics, spins the threads of history. Politics only picks up the threads, twists and tangles them and ties them in knots. Anti-Semitism is a disease, and politics stands by the sickbed like a stupid, vicious doctor who wants to prolong the illness. Politics makes use of anti-Semitism: A stone flies into the air, so Bismarck's assistant directs it at the window of the synagogue; if not, other windows would shatter. A protesting fist is raised, so they shove an emaciated, stooped, Jewish back under it; if not, other bones would crack. But the stone, the fist, the hatred, have an existence of their own. Who generally succumbs to illness? Weak children, old and feeble men and women, sick people. Who succumbs to a moral epidemic? The child of the masses, the effete aristocrat, and a few madmen who jump out of the crowd and lead the ailing in a wild dance! Only healthy minds endure!"

"How many healthy minds are there among us?" I ask.

"How many? Very few, unfortunately," answers Polniewski.

We were both sadly silent. I do not know what my traveling companion was thinking. I was thinking that even healthy and strong minds become infected also. There are at least two possibilities in history: sometimes the most gifted and capable person leads the masses; and sometimes the crowd drags the best and most intelligent people down with it. The leader of the masses is a Columbus who seeks a new destiny for mankind, a new America. As soon as bread and water become scarce, the ship's crew mutinies and takes the helm! As a first step, someone must be slaughtered; his sacrifice stills both the hunger for food and for violence.

"And don't think"—Polniewski interrupts my sad thoughts—"that I flatter myself into thinking that I am the powerful spirit that can resist the epidemic, the tall cedar that no storm can move. No, brother," he continues, "I am no hero. I might have been just the same as the others; the wind might have plucked me too and blown me about like a decayed leaf from the tree of knowledge. I might have believed, along with all the decayed leaves, that we were at a ball, dancing enthusiastically to the accompaniment of the wind, our hired musician, who accompanies us on his pipe. . . . I was saved by a coincidence. I happened to become acquainted with a Jewish woman. Listen to this!"

I bent toward my traveling companion; his face had become even more earnest and grim; he leaned his elbows on his knees and pressed his head into his hands.

"And don't think," he tells me, "that this woman I met was the heroine of a novel, some steely character who breaks fences and walls and then goes proudly on her way; don't think of the exceptional woman either, the intellectual with new ideas, or of any ideal type. Not at all. I met a simple Jewish woman, one of the better class, but one of the unfortunates of that class. I grew to love her; this is the truth. And when I hear or read something bad about Jews, she floats out of my memory and with her limpid, melancholy eyes implores, "Don't believe it, I am not like that!"

He becomes lost in thought, then rouses himself and continues.

"The story is very simple. You and I did not correspond during this period and you don't know what happened to me. I'll make it short because I'm going only as far as Lukova. After the gymnasium I entered the university to study medicine, but I never finished. Although to some extent I hold friends and teachers responsible, mostly I have only myself to blame. I had to leave, became a druggist, married, and with my dowry I established myself in the shop of a small town selling pills and castor oil. But I did have some luck: I had an honest father-in-law who gave me the dowry money right after the wedding, my wife was good and beautiful, and the small Jewish town was tolerable.

"My wife's name was Maria. Even now I can see her standing before me. She turns to me helplessly from the mirror—the golden tresses will not surrender to her tyrannical comb. The curls scatter merrily in all directions—they refuse to remain suppressed under the garland then in style. She was slender, with such kind, lively, laughing, sky-blue eyes.

"The practice didn't tax us much. The small town was too poor for that, and a pharmacy without a doctor is not very useful. I earned little, but it was really like paradise. In the summer we would stand on the veranda holding hands, looking into each other's eyes, our lips touching.

"And what else should have interested us? We had an income. Go places? Where to? From our veranda we could see almost the entire town, the low, crooked houses, with tall, wide, black, wooden attics that bent, as if in pity, over the bagel and fruit sellers who tended their poor stalls below, as if wanting to protect the shrunken, old faces of the women from the sun.

"The small town had once been prosperous. The attics used to be filled with produce and fruits, the marketplace with carts, with peasants, with merchants; among the white aprons and the gray smocks one could sometimes see a great landowner too—at least that's what they told me. But the highway and the train made the town superfluous in the world of trade; the streets are empty now, the attics filled with decaying onions and moldy pieces of cheese, the only legacy remaining from the good old days.

"Poor! It's hard to imagine how poor! Ten grain dealers throw themselves on every measure of rye that a peasant brings. This raises the price. Then they come to an agreement on the price, or they buy in partnership, but when it comes to paying, all ten scrape their pockets. They have no money to buy the grain and end up borrowing at interest. And one hundred tailors for one pair of overalls, fifty shoemakers for one small repair. Such poverty! I've never seen anything like it!

"We isolated ourselves as much as possible from the life of the town—the fortunate are self-centered. . . .

"But across from us, vis-à-vis our house, we noticed a young woman, probably no more than eighteen, twenty at the most. And neither of us could take our eyes off her, nor she from us. An unusual phenomenon—imagine a beauty, a picture in a shabby frame, as charming as a Jewish window can be in a small town, under a dilapidated, crumbling roof. Imagine a pair of sorrowful, dreamy, tear-filled eyes in an alabaster-white face, under a kerchief. God, she made a poignant impression on us!

"For hours on end she would lean over the windowsill, her arms bent, looking mournfully at us, or at the stars above, swallowing her tears! We saw that she was always alone, forlorn—your men never have time—always despondent, homesick, unhappiness written all over her pale face. She probably came from far off, from a better, less confined home. She always gazed far into the distance. Her heart craved a freer life—she wanted to live, to love and be loved.

"Say what you will, there is an injustice among you. You sell your daughters. It is true that with time they become accustomed to their fate, with time they forget—they are pious, they are good, they are long-suffering. But who can count the bitter tears that fall on their woeful faces before their eyes dry up? Who can measure the suffering in their breasts before they become reconciled to a living death? Is this their reward for being good and pious women?

"You should see the woman's husband: hunchbacked, sallow. I saw him twice a day—when he left in the morning and when he returned at night. A crime."

I confess that I had no answer for Polniewski.

We both sat in silence for a while and then he continued his story.

"Once the woman failed to appear. For one entire day she did not come to the window. 'She must be ill,' we thought. In the evening her husband, the sallow one, came to our shop and asked for medicine.

" 'What kind of medicine?'

" 'How should I know?' he says. 'Medicine!'

" 'For whom?'

" 'That too you need to know? For my wife!'

" 'What's wrong with her?'

" 'I have no idea—she says that her heart aches.'

"This," says Polniewski, "was our first meeting. I'll make a long story short. I'm something of a doctor, after all, so I went to see her."

Polniewski started to speak indistinctly; he groped for cigarettes, then matches, and finally he opened his traveling bag and busied himself with the contents for several minutes.

In the meantime I had some disturbing thoughts.

I began to see Polniewski in a different light; his story began to weigh on my spirits.

Can one ever know another person? Can one know what he is made of? The thought crossed my mind that sitting across from me may be a Christian skunk who sneaks into the chicken coop. He polemicizes a bit too much about the Jewish woman's lot, he searches too long for his matches; somehow, he is embarrassed in my presence. Why doesn't he want to give me more details? Why won't he tell me everything the way it was? Who knows what part he had in this business? Perhaps he played the old role of the snake in the Garden of Eden? What do you think? That his conscience would hold him back? From a young Jewish wife! Why not? Once, to gain glory, it was necessary to bring Jews to baptism; today it is enough to corrupt a Jewish woman by drawing her away from her God, from her parents, from her husband—from her whole life.

It is called liberalism to visit a prison, bringing a fresh breath of air and some sunshine, to awaken the prisoner, to give him a piece of cake, and then to disappear—not to see how the prisoner gnashes his teeth when the rusty key turns the lock once again, how anguished the face becomes, how spasmodically he breathes in the constricted air, how he tears his hair and rips his flesh, or how, if he can still cry, he waters his moldy, mouse-bitten crust of bread with bitter tears. To arouse an unhappy, repressed Jewish woman's heart to the peals of sweet, romantic music, to a new, wild, unknown or long-forgotten emotion, to kiss, and then adieu! Close the door, and leave her to a life of gall and wormwood. . . .

We are so glutted with poison, with bitterness and hatred, that when we are offered bread and salt we are sure that it is contaminated. Even when the hand trembles with compassion, the eyes fill with tears of pity, and the lips speak words of comfort, we find it hard to believe! We too have been infected, the epidemic is upon us too.

Meanwhile, Polniewski found his matches and I took a cigarette from him, unwillingly. We smoked; the carriage became filled with blue smoke rings, and looking at them I thought, "Good and evil cannot coexist any longer than they!"

"We became friends," my Christian traveling companion continues, "but nothing more than that."

"Why?" I ask, taken aback.

"From a distance we continued to think of each other as the best of friends, but she dared not visit us, nor we her. Just imagine what would have happened if she had come! The town is extremely religious and conservative. Aside from the barber-surgeon and a young ladies' tailor, everyone wore the traditional dark garb of the Orthodox. I don't know myself what held us back, but that's not what I was getting at.

"During this time I was struck by the greatest misfortune that can befall a man. The pharmacy brought in very little and my wife became ill. With each passing day I was more certain that she was dying, yet I didn't have the means to save her. She needed Italy, and I didn't have money for food.

"As you know, a dying patient is often full of hope, believing that the crisis is past! I had to suppress my terrible pain and sorrow, and bury it deep inside my heart. While my heart bled, I had to smile; no hint of worry dared wrinkle my brow. While I felt myself dying with her, I made plans with her for the coming year: to enlarge the house, to buy a piano. . . ."

His voice became hushed.

"I can't tell you everything, to relive my troubles, but my misfortune brought me closer to the young housewife's misfortune, and we recognized ourselves in one another."

Lukova appeared in the distance.

"In the few moments that remain I must tell you that in all my life I have never seen anyone as unhappy as that woman, yet with so much feeling and sympathy for others, and so unaffected, so natural, nothing excessive. She didn't move from Maria's bed. She prevailed upon her husband to arrange a loan at low interest for me. She watched over us; she was our housekeeper, our cook, our most devoted friend. And when Maria died she was, perhaps, even more inconsolable than I. It was then that I realized that the hatred between nations is unnatural. As soon as things are bad and the hotheaded or the downtrodden want to protest, then the hypocritical writer or the politician denounces the Jews. My experience has taught me that Jews are not our enemies, that we can live together in peace!"

We were drawing closer and closer to Lukova, and I, still apprehensive about the conclusion, interrupted him to ask: "And what happened to the woman?"

"I don't know. I buried my wife, sold the pharmacy, wept when I parted from my dear neighbor and . . . nothing! Now I live in Lukova and things are no better for me."

"And tell me, what's the name of the small town where you used to live?"

"Konskivola."

"And your neighbor—is she tall and pale?"

"Yes!"

"And slender?"

"Yes. Do you know her?" he asks, surprised.

"Does she have a beauty mark on the left side of her nose?"

"What kind of beauty mark?" Janek laughs. "What are you thinking of?"

I begin to believe that I was mistaken and ask: "Perhaps it's on the right side of her nose."

"What kind of beauty mark? What are you talking about?"

"Perhaps you didn't notice. But her husband, is his name Chaim?"

"I think not, but it could be; the devil only knows."

"But her name is Chana!"

"No, of course not! Sarah! I remember: Sarah, for sure. I used to call her Saruchna. I could never forget her name."

What a fool I was! Was there only one Jewish housewife who fit this description?

1891 (translated by Golda Werman)

BRYNA'S MENDL

▼

Bryna's Mendl—there were no family names in those days—was a "tent dweller," as it was said of Jacob:[1] he was a man who liked to devote his time to study. This meant that Mendl belonged to the spiritual elite of his town—more or less. He was not a great scholar, but he did recite psalms before praying, peruse the *Eyn Yakov* after praying, and in the evening read a chapter from the Mishna. Quite often he brought home a guest, and every morning he put money into the charity box of Rabbi Meir the Miracle Worker.[2] He was also called upon to read the portion from the prophet Jonah on Yom Kippur, and to join the consortium of those who opened the holy ark. In addition, he was a man much preoccupied with doing good. When a preacher came to town, or someone had to collect alms for the poor so that they would have matzas, or firewood, or potatoes; when the Sabbath limits needed to be marked, or a monument erected over a tomb, or any such matter, then Bryna's Mendl would assume an air of expansive sagacity, take in hand his thick walking stick with the brass knob, and venture forth with the rabbi, or the inspector, or some other distinguished member of the community.

He considered it a good deed to carry the collection box himself, even though the sexton walked just behind him.

During the winter he did not have a moment to himself. He recited psalms, prayed, read the *Eyn Yakov*, breakfasted, gave alms, attended the afternoon service, then the evening service, studied a chapter of the Mishna, ate supper, recited the evening prayer, slept, awoke for the midnight service, and slept some more. There was never any time left to spare from his day. But to make up for this, during the summer he would have a long stretch of unscheduled time after the evening meal. This time too he spent in the study house, but then he would discuss worldly matters, the latest inventions, politics.

Bryna's Mendl was not clever. In kheyder he had been called Stupid Mendl. When he got married, the general opinion softened and he became known as Foolish Mendl. It was only after he had stopped boarding at his father-in-law's and become master in his own house, when his wife, Bryna, had opened a grocery shop and was earning her weight in gold, that he was crowned with the title "Bryna's Mendl." And since Bryna's Mendl stood in no one's way, never said a mean word to anybody, and profited the study house and the community with his contributions, no one recalled what once had been, and no one laughed aloud when he punctuated every fifth word with "I'm no fool now, am I? Don't you agree that I am clever?"

"It is true that I'm no fool," Reb Mendl once said. "Nevertheless, I don't understand how they can produce such thin, hollow strands of straw to fill the straw mattresses. I purposely pulled out about forty straws, one after the other. All are hollow as whistles. I wanted to ask my Bryna, but she had already left for the shop."

Before anybody had time to laugh, he answered his own question. "The peasants probably import the straw from England." Bryna's Mendl had heard a lot about England. He thought the world of that country—and then some.

This occurred after the battle of Sevastopol. The entire study house was abuzz with news of the latest English military strategies. The stories were circulated by war veterans who had witnessed the marvels with their own eyes.

Truly, there had been wonders, recounted a prominent member of the study house. For instance, a cannon. What, my friends, is the use of a cannon? A cannon fires a cannonball. So what? First, you have to convince the enemy to stand in the line of fire. Since the enemy is by no means a fool, he won't be talked into any such thing.

Sometimes he even resorts to tricks. He stands, you shoot, and he sneaks away. Matters had so degenerated on the battlefield, you would have thought that the end of the world was at hand. But those clever bastards, the English, had heard the story of the plague of frogs in Egypt, so they too looked for something that multiplies. They invented an enormous cannon that fired not cannonballs, but entire cannons. And each of these cannons, when it fell, crashed into the ground, exploded, and disgorged ten new cannons, and those cannons fired the cannonballs. Well, try and hide from that! Now you can appreciate what kind of slaughter this caused. You think it was magic? Heaven forbid! It worked by means of a simple lever.

If someone asked why, after the war, the Russian Empire did not reproduce just such cannons, the answer was that immediately after the end of hostilities all the kingdoms had come together to make a pact among themselves, each one swearing, on oath, that in order not to destroy the world, they would never fire on anyone again, not with sheets of boiling millet and not with such cannons.

From that time on, Bryna's Mendl thought the world of England, and then some. Whenever he saw something that his mind could not comprehend, then it was clear that the thing must come from England. That watches originated in England—about that there could be no doubt. But the first lever must also have been made by an English smith. Bryna's Mendl spoke with great enthusiasm about England, her wise men and her blacksmiths. "They must all have great minds over there!"

Bryna's Mendl would have liked to live in England, but he wanted to die—after a hundred and twenty years—in the land of Israel. First, for reasons of faith. Second, it was simply his nature to enjoy a peaceful existence, and whenever he recalled that at the time of the Resurrection the dead were required to roll underground until they reached the Holy Land, he lost his appetite for three days.[3] But since he nevertheless continued eating despite his loss of appetite, he suffered from stomachache for six days after that. So he was overjoyed to learn from a reliable source that the Land of Israel was even further than England. "Good," he thought. And from that time on, he seriously began making plans for a trip to Israel, because the way to the Holy Land must lead through England.

He would long since have sold the grocery store with all the household effects and set out on the road, if not for Bryna.

Bryna was very devoted to her Mendl. She wished nothing better for herself than to be his footstool in paradise. She pampered him and stuffed him with food. She worked like a donkey to support him, to shoe and clothe him and their five children—three girls and two boys. The greatest pleasure she took in this world was to look out from the shop and see her Mendl pass by carrying the charity box in his left hand and holding the walking stick with the brass knob in his right. For a pittance she sold her seat in the women's gallery, because the window there looked out on the synagogue. She then paid an extravagant sum for a seat near the study-house window, so that she could see how Mendl was called up to read the Torah and how sweetly he pronounced the blessing. Her heart melted when Mendl prompted the cantor to announce that "for the sake of the woman Bryna, daughter of the honorable . . . ," he pledged a contribution of eighteen times eighteen.

She was never happier than on Sabbaths and holidays, when she accompanied him to the synagogue to pray. When they parted in front of the two staircases, she would remain standing on the bottom step of the women's staircase and look back to see how her Mendl walked up the men's stairs. After the service she waited for him in the entranceway to the synagogue, and when she saw him and heard him call out, "Good Shabbes," she would blush, as if she were a bride who had just emerged from under the wedding canopy. Nevertheless, she was aware that Mendl was not clever in the foolish ways of the world, that his intelligence was limited to the domain of the printed word. He was brilliant in the study house, but otherwise, in more mundane matters—not quite. That was her province.

"No, Mendl, my dear," she objected placidly, "we can't just get up and leave. We can't just sell off all our merchandise. Maybe later, when the children are all married and the sons-in-law have boarded with us, and we have lived to see at least one grandchild born and maybe even a great-grandchild—then, you see, I wouldn't mind. Then we could transfer the business to the children."

Mendl knew that Bryna was an absolute wizard when it came to worldly affairs, so he waited, because after Jerusalem and England, Bryna was the closest thing to his heart.

Not all of his children had yet been married off, however, when he came home one day very downhearted. "You see, Bryna," he said, "I have received a summons to the heavenly court." He showed her a gray hair in his beard.

Bryna consoled him. "Don't talk nonsense, Mendl. You are not knowledgeable in these matters. My father, may he rest in peace, went gray at the age of fifty. And, may you live a long life . . ."

"May we both live long lives," Mendl corrected her.

"May we both live long lives—my father lived for another thirty years."

"But our generation is weaker. We don't have the strength of our forefathers," Mendl said, lowering his eyes.

Bryna talked him out of his distress, and began to pamper him even more. From the butcher she bought an additional half pound of meat for supper.

"Eh, Bryntcha," said the butcher. "You must be having the in-laws over for dinner. May it bring you good luck."

"No," Bryna answered. "It's just that our generation is so weak." And at mealtimes, she always added to Mendl's plate another piece of this and another bite of that. "Eat this. This is a delight," she would say. And as she looked at Mendl, she prayed, "May he eat in good health. People today are not what they used to be."

She claimed that, having washed her hands at a neighbor's, she had eaten a roll at the shop. Once she said that a relative had cooked a new type of potato soup and brought her a few spoonfuls to taste. Another time, she maintained that she had eaten at a circumcision, although she could not remember the name of the child's mother. In any case, she was not hungry at mealtimes, and only pleaded: "Eat, Mendl, eat. Why do you compare yourself to me? Studying Torah takes strength."

"You mean it gives strength, Bryna."

"Let it be 'gives strength.' Or, as it is written in *Chapters of the Fathers*, 'Im eyn torah, eyn kemakh'—If you study Torah, you must eat."[4]

Mendl smiled at this new mistake. Bryna had reversed the order of the Hebrew saying.

"As for me," continued Bryna, "what do I do? Either I sit around all day with nothing to do, or I warm myself at the firepot. If a customer comes in, I measure out a quart of beans, or cereal, or flour. If no one comes, then I don't. That's why I don't need to eat so much."

Mendl believed in the roll, in the potato soup, in the circumcision, even though he had just recited the prayer of supplication, and should have known that no circumcision had taken place.[5] Perhaps he really did need to eat more. It was no small matter to read two portions from the Psalms, a chapter of the Mishna, a few pages of the *Eyn Yakov*, and on top of it all, to recite the daily prayers, carry the charity box, and drag along his walking stick.

He was very pleased that his virtuous Bryna led such a quiet life, sitting idly next to the firepot, her hands folded, awaiting a customer. If a customer appeared, then he appeared, and if not, not. That was as it should be. Let her, at least, not work as hard as he did. Let her, at least, rest her bones. So Mendl stuffed himself with even more food, that he might have the strength to prolong his days and live to see England and then die in Jerusalem.

Apart from the pleasure he took in Bryna, Mendl also rejoiced in his children. His eldest son had been married to a girl from another town. The son was now boarding at his father-in-law's. God be praised, ever since his wedding he had not written a single letter home. This was a sign that all was well, that he was in good health. Whoever arrived from the town where his son lived brought regards.

Next in line was Mendl's second son, a kheyder boy, who would soon also be of marriageable age. Bryna hired tutors, paid their fees, made sure that the boy studied on the level of his peers. For his part, Mendl tested him on his lesson every Sabbath. But he hated doing this before the meal. After dinner was better, more comfortable. Which was also the reason why Mendl always dozed off during the recitation and did not awake again until he heard the tutor toast, "*L'chaym.*" Then he pinched his son's cheek, and that was that.

In addition, Mendl had three daughters, young children who still played at marbles, fine girls all. Respectful children. Quiet children. Always clean and washed, a pleasure to look at. He did not actually notice when they were washed or combed, or when Bryna patched or mended their clothes. He could hardly comprehend how they came to be so clever and well bred.

"These really are my children," he thought with pride. "They take after me." He thanked and praised the Holy Name that Bryna led such a peaceful life, not like other mothers whose children drove them crazy. And the children were so obedient! For instance, if he asked for a glass of water. Bryna had a habit of repeating everything he said, so no sooner had she repeated, "Bring your father a glass of water," than a child would run and bring it. It was a pleasure to have such children. When he walked into the house, Bryna had only to say, "Your father is home," and the house fell silent.

Praised be God, a match was proposed for the second son, and an excellent match it was too. Bryna thought they should go and view the bride. She told Mendl that she wanted to make the trip during the Christian holidays. But when Mendl found out that the road to his future in-laws did not pass through England, he decided to relinquish the honor of the voyage to his wife. Let her have the pleasure of the journey. Why not? All in all, she made only four trips a year and those were to buy merchandise. From these trips she returned tired and worn-out from running around, appraising, and bargaining. At least once let her take pleasure in her travels, and let the world see what a wonderful wife he had. He himself would reserve his appearance for the engagement ceremony, perhaps even for the wedding itself. It was Bryna who had gone alone to interview the prospective bride of the eldest son, and the result proved that she was fortunate in such matters. As for him, he would in any case be doing his share of traveling. . . .

A few more years passed. When God bestows blessings, He does so with a free hand. He even bestows peace of mind. The second son also married, and married well, and now he too was boarding with his in-laws. Mendl, however, knew very little of the what and the how. It had all floated past him like a dream. The wedding did not even cause him to miss a single day's recitation of the psalms. He suffered no headaches, except on the morning after the big night, when he did not get enough sleep.

And Mendl rejoiced. It only remained for the three girls to be married off—Bryna managed these things quickly—and then, finished! They would transfer the business to the children, rent a wagon wide enough to lie down in, bed it down with English straw, and off they would go! In truth, Mendl felt that somehow his legs were no longer what they used to be, and recently he had begun to have trouble breathing. But Bryna would not let him despair. She consoled him and doted on him even more. She assured him that he would live to realize all his dreams.

One day, as he was sitting over the *Eyn Yakov* in the study house, Mendl heard a scream. It sounded like his daughter, but that could not be. What business would his daughter have in the courtyard of the study house? And a girl of marriageable age did not cry. Someone was running up the stairs shouting, "Father! Father!" Surely that was her voice. But after all, it was not possible.

He wanted to consider the matter and took out a pinch of snuff. But even before he could insert the snuff into his nostrils, his daughter stood before him pulling at his lapels. "Help, Father! Mother has collapsed."

And before Mendl could fully grasp what she was saying and run home, Bryna was dead.

In the space of one day Mendl's hair did indeed turn gray. Now he really did have trouble breathing and his feet were truly swollen. It had never occurred to him that Bryna would not outlive him. Not with such a husband, such children, such comfort.

Bryna, who had attracted no notice in life, was barely visible on her deathbed. She was so thin!

1892 (translated by Goldie Morgentaler)

A MUSICIAN'S DEATH

▼

A skeleton lies in bed, a skeleton in taut, dry, yellow skin. Mikhl the Musician is dying. On a crate beside him sits his wife, Mirl, with swollen eyes. Their eight sons, musicians like their father, crowd the narrow room. No one speaks. There is nothing to say. The doctor and the barber-surgeon have long since given up on the patient, and even Reuven of the almshouse, who is considered an expert on these matters, says he should be readied for the world to come.

There will be no inheritance. The shrouds and grave site will be provided by the Burial Society and brandy by the Society of Pall-bearers. Everything is settled and in the open. There is nothing to discuss.

Only Mirl is unwilling to give up. Long after everyone else had accepted the verdict, she stormed the synagogue demanding psalms for her husband's recovery; she has just returned from measuring graves at the cemetery.[1] She keeps insisting that Mikhl is dying for his children's sins. God, blessed be He, is taking their father because they don't keep the faith, because they act so wild. . . .

"The musician's band is losing its glory. There will never be a proper wedding again. No Jew will be able to enjoy a true celebration."

God's mercy is great, she insists. If they would only cry out, plead with God, try to rouse Him! But these pitiless sons won't wear their ritual fringes. If not for them, her uncle the slaughterer, well placed as he probably is in heaven, might be interceding up there on her behalf. He liked to caress her when he was alive, and no doubt he still thinks well of her, and he would certainly do his best for her, if not for their sins! Their sins!

"You play at the balls of Gentiles, you eat their bread and butter and God knows what else! My uncle can't do the impossible. He is probably trying his best, but your sins stand in his way!"

The sons don't answer. They stand, each in his corner, staring at the ground.

"There's still time!" she sobs. "Children! Have mercy! Repent!"

"Mirl, Mirl," the sick man calls out. "Leave it alone. It's all over. I'm played out, Mirl, and I want to die."

Mirl explodes in rage.

"A plague on you. . . . Die! He wants to die! And what about me! I won't let you die; you have to live. I'll scream so loud that your soul will not be able to leave your body!" It seems that in Mirl's heart an old, unhealed wound has torn open.

"Leave it alone, Mirl," pleads the sick man. "We've already had our full share of cursing. Enough. It isn't right to go on like this at the threshold of death. . . . I've sinned . . . you've sinned . . . but enough! I feel as if icy death is creeping from the tips of my toes to my heart. I'm dying, an inch at a time. Don't scream, Mirl, it's better this way."

"Because you want to get rid of me," Mirl interrupts in bitter tears. "That's what you've always wanted. You had your heart set on dark Peshe . . . you were always saying you wanted to die. Oh, what misery! Even now, you won't repent."

The sick man gives a twisted smile. "It wasn't only dark Peshe, there were many dark Peshes, and blondes and redheads too. But I never wanted to get rid of you, Mirl. A woman is a woman, and musicians are drawn to them the way your hand is drawn to a wound. . . . But a wife is a wife. They are two different things. You remember the time black Peshe said something mean about you— and right there in the middle of the street I let her have it.

"Hush now, Mirl. A wife will always be a wife. Except when there's a divorce . . . and even then there's a lot of regret. Believe me, Mirl, I will long for you . . . and for you too, my sons. You caused me a lot of trouble too, but never mind . . . that's all in the fiddle, as we say. I know that you loved me, even if you didn't always treat me with respect. If I ever took an extra nip, I heard you muttering, 'The drunk.' . . . It wasn't right to talk that way about a father, but never mind. . . . I had a father too and I didn't treat him any better. Enough of this—you're forgiven!"

Talking had exhausted him. But within seconds he revived. "You're forgiven." Raising himself a little on the bed, he took the measure of his audience.

"Just look at you—you dumb bulls," he suddenly cried, "with your eyes glued to the ground as if you couldn't count to two! So you're sorry to lose a father, eh—even if he is a drunk!?"

The youngest son raised his eyes. His lashes trembled and he began to sob. The others joined in. A minute later the cramped house filled with their cries.

The sick man enjoyed the scene.

"Well," he erupted with a fresh burst of energy, "enough of this. I'm afraid you're going to make me sorry to die. That's enough now. Listen to your father."

"Murderer!" shouted Mirl. "Let them cry, you murderer! Maybe their tears will soften the heart of Heaven—"

The invalid cut her off. "Be quiet, Mirl. I've told you already that I'm played out. I've had enough! Chaim! Berl! Jonah! All of you! Listen, now—take up your instruments!"

The boys stared.

"I command it. And I beg of you. Do me this favor. Take your instruments and come close to the bed."

The boys surrounded their father: three fiddles, clarinet, bass, horn. . . .

"Let's hear how the band will sound without me," he said. At the same time, he asked Mirl to call in their neighbor, the head of the pallbearers.

At first, Mirl did not want to do his bidding, but there was such a plea in his eyes that she had to surrender. Later she would say that he called her "Mirlshe" and looked at her that last time before he died (forgive the comparison) just the way he did after the wedding. "You remember," she would say, prodding the children, "his sweet voice and his eyes!"

When their neighbor, the head of the pallbearers, came into the room, he took one look at the invalid and told Mirl to assemble a minyan.

"There's no need," the sick man protested. "Why do I need a minyan? I have my own minyan—my band!"

He turned to his children.

"Play without me, children, as you played when I was with you. . . . Play well . . . don't clown around at a poor wedding. Take proper care of your mother. . . . And now—play my confession. Our neighbor will recite the words."

The tiny house filled with music.

1892 (translated by Ruth R. Wisse)

THE PIOUS CAT

▼

Three canaries, who had all once lived in the same house, were killed by the cat one after the other.

This was no ordinary cat; she was a truly pious soul who did not wear her glossy Jewish white coat in vain. Heaven shone in her eyes!

And devout! She lived for ablutions, washing herself ten times a day. And she always took her meals alone, silently, off to the side or in a corner. During the day she ate nothing but dairy products; only after dark did she taste meat, kosher mouse meat.

She didn't rush through her meal or pounce on her food and gulp it down like a glutton. She was always dainty, delicate. Let the mouse live another minute or two. Let it frisk around a little longer, tremble a bit, say the confession. A pious cat does not pounce.

When we brought the first canary into the house, it touched the cat's heart and she was filled with pity. "Such a beautiful, delightful little bird," she sighed, "yet it will have no place in the world to come." The canary will never enter paradise, of that the cat is certain. First of all, instead of washing its hands in the traditional way, it thrusts its whole body into the water bath; second, even though it is a sweet and tender young songbird, the experience of being locked in a cage must make the creature wild; unquestionably, it trusts more in dynamite than in the Code of Jewish Law!

You can tell that by its singing alone, by its licentious warble and song as it looks fearlessly up to heaven. And by its periodic attempts to escape from the cage into the world of sin, into the free air, out the open window.

Was ever a cat locked up in a cage? Did a pious cat ever sing like the wicked Zimri of the Bible?[1]

"What a shame," weeps the tenderhearted cat; "it is a living creature for all that, a precious soul, a spark from above."

Tears well up in the cat's eyes. "The problem is that the sinful body is so beautiful and this world is so attractive and the evil inclination is so strong. How can such a sweet little bird resist such a powerful evil inclination? The longer it lives, the more it sins, and the greater will be its punishment."

"Ah!"

And with that the cat, inflamed with holy ardor—the ardor of the biblical Pinkhas, son of Eliezer son of Aaron the High Priest—jumps up onto the table where the canary's cage stands. . . . [2]

Feathers fly around the room.

The cat got a sound beating. She accepted the blows as a sign of love and groaned as she recited her painful confession. She will never sin again! The clever cat understands why she was beaten, and resolves never to do anything that will earn her a beating. She believes that she was punished for sending feathers flying through the house and for getting bloodstains on the white tablecloth.

She will heed the judgment carefully and devoutly. No feather will fly again, no single drop of blood will be spilled. When we brought home a second songbird, the cat choked it fastidiously and swallowed it whole, feathers and all.

The cat was given a whipping.

Now she begins to understand that the issue is not the feathers or the bloodstains. The point is that one must not kill! One must love and be merciful. Death sentences that were once meted out to evildoers by the courts will not reform the sinful world. One has to preach penitence, to teach morals, to speak to the heart! A repentant canary may reach a level of righteousness that even the most pious cat cannot attain.

The cat feels her heart swelling with joy. No more hard and evil times! No more spilling of blood. Only mercy, mercy, and more mercy!

She approached the third canary tenderly.

"Don't be frightened," she purred with the gentlest sounds that ever poured from the throat of a cat. "You have sinned, but I will do you no harm because I pity you. I will not open the cage, I will not even touch you.

"You're silent? Very good! Better silent than singing impudent songs. You tremble—better yet! Tremble, tremble, my child, but not on my account. Tremble before the Creator of the World, before his Holy Name!

"If only you would remain as you are, silent, pure, and tremulous.

I will help maintain your awe. From my pious soul I will breathe sweet silence and virtue upon you. My breath will pervade your body with faith, your little bones with the fear of God, your tiny heart with repentance and regret for past sins!"

The cat begins to feel how good it is to forgive, and how gratifying to inspire piety and honesty in others. The devout heart of this most pious cat swells with rapture.

But in this atmosphere the canary cannot breathe. It dies of suffocation.

1893 (translated by Golda Werman)

THE GOLEM

▼

Great men were once able to perform great miracles.

When the ghetto of Prague was under attack and marauders wanted to rape the women, roast the children, and murder everyone, when it seemed that all hope was lost, the Maharal Rabbi Judah Loew put aside his Gemara, went out into the street, and, from the first suitable mound of clay that he found in front of the schoolteacher's doorstep, molded the shape of a body. He blew into the golem's nostrils—and it began to stir. Then he whispered a name into its ear, and our golem strode out of the ghetto. The Maharal returned to his books in the house of study and the golem attacked our enemies who had surrounded the ghetto, thrashing them as with flails. They fell like flies.

Prague filled with corpses. They say that it went on like this right through Wednesday and Thursday. On Friday, with the clock striking noon, the golem was still intent on its labors.

"Rabbi," pleaded the congregation, "the golem is slaughtering all of Prague! Soon there won't be any Gentiles left to heat the Sabbath ovens or to take down the Sabbath lamps."

Once more the Maharal interrupted his study. He went to the pulpit and began to recite the psalm in honor of the Sabbath.

The golem stopped its work. It returned to the ghetto, entered the house of study, and approached the Maharal. Again the rabbi whispered something into its ear. The eyes of the golem closed, the soul departed from its body, and it returned to a mere image of clay.

To this very day the golem lies concealed in the uppermost part of the synagogue of Prague, covered with cobwebs that have been spun from wall to wall to encase the whole arcade so that it should be hidden from all human eyes, especially from pregnant wives in the women's section. No one is permitted to touch the cobwebs, for anyone who does so dies. Even the oldest congregants no longer remember the golem. However, Zvi the Sage, the grandson of the Maharal, still deliberates whether it is proper to include such a golem in a minyan or in a company for the saying of grace.

The golem, you see, has not been forgotten. It is here! But the name that could bring the golem to life in times of need, that name has vanished into thin air. And no one is allowed to touch the cobwebs that thicken.

Do something—if you can!

1893 (translated by Ruth R. Wisse)

THE SHABBES GOY

▼

The rabbi of Chelm, in ragged fur cap and tattered satin robe, a tiny Jew with a prominent Adam's apple and laughing gray eyes in a shriveled face.[1] . . . Between one talmudic problem and the next, the cheerful, gray-headed rabbi gets up, surveys with confidence the open Gemara through glasses on the tip of his nose, his shawl popping out of his chest, and, as his rightful share of worldly pleasures, takes up the wooden snuffbox.

A softhearted person, a being contented with his lot, he smiles at the snuffbox and taps on the cover, drumming lightly with his small fingers as though asking: Is there a little something there?

And when the snuffbox replies softly, "There is a bit left, there is!" he opens it leisurely, takes a crumb of a morsel between his fingertips and brings it to his nostrils, presses gently to the right, gently to the left—and then again. His eyes brighten, his heart gladdens, he strolls about the House of Judgment almost dancing, and gives praise to the world's Creator in singsong: "Ay, ay, Gottenyu, dear God, what a sweet world you have created!"

"What splendid creatures walk about in your dear world! Jews, and—to be exact—others. Ay, people made of gold, of velvet, of satin. . . ."

Suddenly, someone drops in: "Rebbe, help!"

He is alarmed.

"What happened to you, Yankele? Yankele!"

He recognizes him. The rabbi knows everyone in Chelm, for he has been godfather to almost all. And when he sees Yankele's bloodied mouth: "Oy, Yankele, who wronged you so, Yankele?"

Yankele is already seated on the bench in front of the table of justice holding on to his cheeks with bloodstained hands and rocking away without stopping, from left to right, this way and that.

"Oy, Yankele, who wronged you so, Yankele?"

"Oy, oy, the Shabbes goy, Rebbe."

The rabbi of Chelm stares in amazement. "In the middle of the week, how do you come to the Shabbes goy, Yankele?"

"A destined thing, Rebbe Leyb. I'm walking as usual in the marketplace. Just walking. And do you think, Rebbe Leyb, that I have the Shabbes goy in mind? I have nothing else to think about but the Shabbes goy? A Jew thinks about making a living, that's what he thinks about. Soon I'll be going home with empty hands—and I don't stop worrying. What will my wife have to say? That shrew of mine . . . but you know her well, Rebbe Leyb! So he comes toward me, the Shabbes goy, and I look and see he's eating pumpkin seeds . . . and with such skill! He throws a handful right into his mouth— a single crack and already he's spitting out the shells, to the right and to the left. So I stop and observe this great dexterity.

"He becomes friendly, like an equal, and says, 'Yankele, come on, open your mouth, Yankele!'

"Well, seeing that a goy pleads, I open my mouth supposing, Rebbenyu, dear Rebbe, that he wants to throw some nuts into it. I open wide . . . so he takes his fist, and—bang!—right into my mouth!"

"At this, Yankele starts crying afresh: "Oy, the murderer, the murderer. . . ."

But this does not please the rabbi of Chelm at all. He draws nearer and reproaches him: "That I don't like, Yankele. How can you say such a thing, just so, about one of God's creatures—*murderer*?"

"But take a look, he knocked out three of my teeth," sobs Yankele, and shows him the teeth.

The rabbi looks closely, shakes his head and says incredulously, "Tell me the truth, Yankele, are these *your* teeth?"

"Whose then, Rebbe? Here, Rebbe, look!"

The rabbi looks and marvels.

And Yankele opens his mouth wide to show him the holes.

"Wonder of wonders," says the rabbi after a pause, "that a Jew should have such teeth. . . ."

"What kind of teeth, then, should a Jew have?" asks Yankele, by this time alarmed.

"Here, look!" answers the rabbi and shows him the old "furniture" in his aged mouth. "Some have no teeth at all—in any case, not *such* teeth! After all, I wasn't born yesterday. Never have I seen such teeth in a Jew's mouth!"

And the rabbi proceeds to ponder two questions at once: How does a Jew come to have such large, strong teeth? As to the Shabbes goy, what impels him to knock out strange teeth?

He ponders and ponders, and then jumps up. "Aha! That is to say, solved!

"It's all very clear, Yankele! The one depends upon the other. Just like that, you say 'murderer.' About one of God's creatures, *murderer*? There's no such thing. If there were murderers in the world, would God permit the world to exist? So what then? But since you are relating an incident that happened, after all, and I believe you, and I see with my own eyes the knocked-out teeth, I must conclude, you understand, thus . . ."

He pauses to catch his breath and expounds: "The guilt, Yankele, in reality belongs to your teeth!"

Yankele leaps up to his full height. "How is it possible, Rebbe— my *teeth*? And the goy?"

"Wholly innocent he is not, Yankele, that's not what I'm saying! The basic fault, however, lies in the teeth; that is to say, not *your* teeth. . . ."

"What do you mean?"

"Listen with attention, Yankele! By nature the goy is an amiable creature. He was eating pumpkin seeds, he saw you, he really wanted to be hospitable and give you some, so, 'Open your mouth!' he says, and wants to throw nuts into it—after all, they're fond of doing favors and little tricks. But when you, Yankele, obeyed and he saw such fine teeth, that is to say, *his teeth in your mouth* . . . you understand, a goy, and his teeth in your mouth, so naturally he becomes excited. And since he's a goy, what else can he do when he gets excited? So he hits out with his fist.

"Do as I tell you, Yankele," the rabbi concludes. "Don't make a fuss about it. Go home to your wife and tell her I told you, that I explicitly told you, she should make you a mouthwash out of figs. . . ."

As Yankele submissively departs, the rabbi calls after him: "And the next time a goy tells you to open your mouth, open just a little bit, not more than a bit—a crack! He doesn't have to see anything, that a Jew has teeth. . . ."

The rabbi of Chelm returns to his books, studies with gusto, and derives much joy from the holy Torah—and from time to time helps himself to a pinch of worldly paradise from the wooden snuffbox. His heart expands with joy!

"Oy, a dear world, a sweet world. . . ." And he glances again through the ancient, moldy pane of the House of Judgment's narrow window into the marketplace.

"Such precious people, Gottenyu, silky, satiny . . ." But he does not finish his praises, for here comes Yankele again. A full month has not yet elapsed.

The rabbi stares in wonder. "What I dreamed last night, just the other night . . . What happened this time, Yankele?"

"The Shabbes goy, Rebbe! The Shabbes goy again!" yells Yankele, and collapses on the bench.

Benignly the rabbi scolds him, "What a pest you are, Yankele! Still bothering with the Shabbes goy? A murderer, God forbid, he's not, but what do you need him for?"

"He stole up on me from behind," explains Yankele, "*from behind*, Rebbe Leyb! I'm walking through the alley, I'm on my way home. I'm carrying a loaf of bread for my family, I bought a loaf of bread for my wife and little ones, his Dear Name destined a loaf for me! Under my arm I'm carrying it when suddenly, from behind, a blow on my head. I fall down, I faint, I've scarcely come to, and I see the Shabbes goy walking away with a full mouth, chewing—and the loaf of bread lies at my feet, bitten off. Here, look, Rebbenyu. Oy, my head, my head!"

He shows the rabbi the loaf and grabs his head.

The rabbi examines the bread and says, "The head is a triviality; from a blow, God forbid, one doesn't perish! But consider, Yankele, who was in the right? Here, take a look—*teeth!* A goy, as you see, has teeth! Do you see? One bite, and half a loaf gone at once! *I* couldn't do it!"

"Yes, Rebbe," admits Yankele, "but what's to be done with the murderer? All Chelm is in danger!"

"And don't think, Yankele"—the rabbi turns to him—"that I'm not suffering on account of this. I know what half a loaf of bread means to a person like you, with so many mouths in your house to feed, I know what it means. Alas, there won't be enough to go around. If it depended on me, and I tell you this in confidence, I would positively request that the community compensate you for half a loaf. Why not? True, the community is poor, but still, a Jew has suffered a loss from *everybody's* Shabbes goy. And half a loaf is not merely blows—the community wouldn't be impoverished—but you know yourself, Yankele, that I have no say."

Yankele starts screaming, "So that's how it is? It means only one thing—there is no judge and there is no justice in this world—the murderer goes about scot-free!"

" 'Murderer,' " replies the rabbi serenely, "is not necessarily the proper word. I explained that to you once before; if it were so, the world would not be permitted to exist. There are no murderers!"

"So what then?"

"The guilt, I tell you, Yankele, lies in the bread. In the holy books it is written, 'A man sins because of bread.' You know the small print yourself. 'A man sins on account of a crumb of bread.' And all the books say that there are times when a Jew transgresses the commandment 'Thou shalt not covet'—sometimes even 'Thou shalt not steal.' A goy, to make a distinction, may transgress 'Thou shalt not steal'—sometimes even 'Thou shalt not kill.' But this too, however, not by nature. It's all the fault of the bread. You have no idea, Yankele, of the evil impulse that lies hidden in bread. Basically—now tell me your opinion frankly, Yankele—why should it exasperate the Shabbes goy when he sees that Yankele walks about on the street, feeds his little ones, and praises God? Hah? But when he sees *bread*, that Yankele is carrying a loaf of bread! Yes, Yankele—I see you comprehend me now. Chew it well!"

And the rabbi goes over to him, puts his arm about Yankele's shoulder, and says with great compassion, "You know what, Yankele? After all, you know that I am a humble person, by nature a humble person, and I don't like to do such things. However, I will do it for you, for your sake. I will pray to God especially for half a loaf on your account."

"Thanks, Rebbenyu!" Yankele jumps up overjoyed and starts to leave the hut.

But the rabbi detains him. "Listen carefully, Yankele. Don't ever carry bread exposed and uncovered that his Dear Name has destined for you! It is forbidden to tempt the evil impulse. You have a coat—cover it!"

A pacified Yankele takes leave of the rabbi and, after a short while, returns for the third time with a cry for help; again the Shabbes goy.

"It is now beyond comprehension," says the rabbi, "that in the course of a single season a Jew should meet with the Shabbes goy three times—and three times get beaten up! It doesn't stand to reason.

"There's something more to this than meets the eye!" he says, wrinkling his forehead, and proceeding to cross-examine. "Did you show him the teeth?"

"God forbid, Rebbe! Since you told me not to!"

"Did you keep the bread uncovered?"

"What bread, when bread, Rebbe?"

Ah, if he'd only had bread, he would not have come to this pass. He was on his way home without bread . . . his wife had met him with the poker . . . so he ran away, she ran after him . . . he ran beyond the town to the bathhouse . . . a Jewish wife doesn't run outside the town . . . finally he reaches safety on the slope behind the bath, where the Shabbes goy is reclining on the grass. He jumps up and wants to kill Yankele. With his bare fists he'll kill him dead, he says, and punches away. He could barely tear himself away. . . .

"Do you know what, Yankele?" the rabbi says softly after a contemplative pause. "You will forgive me, but I don't believe you."

Yankele pulls off his coat. "Rebbe, I wish you pieces of gold as big as the blue marks I have."

And he wants to disrobe completely, but this the rabbi does not permit.

"Little fool, that's not what I mean," says the rabbi. "It's not the least bit necessary to undress. I'm only acting in harmony with my conviction. I can't possibly believe that the Shabbes goy, one of God's creatures after all, should, just like that, without a reason, be a murderer. The concept lacks reality. Tell me, Yankele, does it make sense—a murderer? Could you be a murderer?"

"No!"

"Nor I," says the rabbi.

He falls into a trance, and after a while comes to. "A-*ha!* That is to say, solved!" and he breaks into a smile. "You know what, Yankele? Listen carefully to what I have to say!"

And he stands up, the better to savor each of his words.

"I tell you, Yankele, in the rear of the bath must be the place where Cain, as it says in the holy Torah, killed his brother Abel. The place itself, more or less, is capable of murder, but particularly is it a dangerous spot for 'an offspring of Noah' who cannot by nature control himself."

Yankele opens mouth and ears. "Ah!"

"What do you say?" smiles the rabbi. "It makes sense? Apparently, that's how it is! And I maintain that the goy doesn't even know he is guilty.

"So listen to me, Yankele, and forget about the whole thing! If you wish, call an apothecary; if not, apply cold compresses yourself.

"And on the Sabbath—it's true I don't mix in community matters, but still in times of danger—on the Sabbath, God willing, I will announce in the synagogue and in the study house that everyone should avoid going to the rear of the bath.

"And perhaps the council will decide to move the entire bath into town, into the marketplace. Why not? Wouldn't it be better? But that's already outside my sphere. A good day to you, Yankele."

Hardly a month had gone by when Yankele showed up again.

He had no teeth to exhibit, he hadn't been to the rear of the bath, but he did have broken bones. The Shabbes goy had come upon him behind the synagogue.

This time the rabbi had to admit: "What a bandit! Indeed, quite a bandit!" And "A peril for all of Chelm. . . . For me personally, no. I hardly ever step outside the door of my house. . . . Why should I? But, the rest of Chelm!

"Why," he queries, "how are you in greater danger than any other Chelmer? *Your* name is Yankele, another is called Groinem. It has nothing to do with the name. And I don't even know if the Shabbes goy is acquainted with people's names—how that one is called, whose candlesticks he is taking down. . . .

"We must," he sighs, "call a meeting right away, yes. . . . And do you know for what purpose? Can you guess my fear, Yankele?"

"What, Rebbe?"

"On Yom Kippur, when the goy comes into the synagogue to light the candles before the final prayer, he can destroy all of Chelm. He can at that moment, God forbid. wipe out the entire community at once!"

And with the rabbi of Chelm it's this way: when he comes to a decision, he acts without delay.

On the Sabbath, in all the houses of prayer, large signs with glaring letters are already hanging: "A MEETING WILL BE HELD! THE WHOLE TOWN IS IN DANGER!"

Danger? The notables gather, the ordinary citizens come running, they sit packed together, cheek by jowl.

"Now tell us everything; what's it about, Rebbe Leyb?"

"Let Yankele say," says he.

So Yankele tells his story. Then the rabbi tells how the supposition was revealed to him, but that, nevertheless, Yankele is in the right throughout.

"A murderer," yells Yankele, "a murderer!"

"So what's to be done, Rebbenyu?"

The rabbi does not keep them in suspense and speaks as follows. "Were I," he says, "to have a say in the community, if I were to be asked in all sincerity, this is what I would say: In the first place, and before anything else—to satisfy the Divine Name—in fact, right away, tomorrow before dawn, Yankele should go away, someplace else, because on him the Shabbes goy has a claim already—more than a claim—a *fixation*.

"Now, in order to appease his resentment, and with the object of redeeming the entire community from dire peril, let us give the Shabbes goy a raise: a larger portion of the Sabbath loaf and *two* drinks of brandy instead of one. And what else? Perhaps he'll have compassion!"

You're laughing?

Still, there's a little of the rabbi of Chelm in each of us.

1894(?) (translated by Etta Blum)

THE POOR BOY

A Story Told by a "Committee Man"[1]

▼

"Give me eight groschen for a hostel."[2]

"No!" I answer sternly and walk away.

He runs after me with a doglike entreaty in his burning eyes; he kisses my sleeve—it doesn't help! "My income doesn't permit such daily handouts!"

"Poor people," I think, leaving the soup kitchen where I had treated the beggar boy so harshly. "Poor people quickly become a nuisance."

The first time I saw the dirty, skinny little face, with its sunken, blazing, sad, but clever eyes, it went straight to my heart. Before I even heard him speak, my heart began to ache, and a ten-groschen coin flew out of my pocket into his skinny hands.

I remember distinctly that my hand did this *by itself*. It didn't ask my heart whether it felt compassion, nor the auditor, my mind, if a man on a monthly salary of forty-one rubles and sixty-six kopecks could afford five kopecks for charity. His entreaty was an electric spark that shocked every last corner of my body. Only later did my mind factor in the new expense, after the boy, jumping for joy, had already left the soup kitchen.

Caught up in my own and others' business, I quickly forgot about him. But not entirely, it seems. Somewhere inside me there must have been a planning conference. Because the very next evening, when the same boy stopped me once again, and in his shivery ragamuffin voice asked me for a hostel bed, from somewhere within me ready-made thoughts emerged: a seven-or-eight-year-old boy shouldn't be begging, shouldn't be hanging about the kitchen; eating in the kitchen before the dishes are collected only turns him into an idler; he'll never become a proper person that way.

My hand again slipped into my pocket, but this time I discovered it there and restrained it. Had I been pious, I might have thought: Is the good deed worth the eight groschen? Or couldn't I get by just as well with afternoon prayers? Or with an ardent groan while praying? *Not* being pious, I kept the boy's welfare in mind. With my eight groschen I would do him *harm*! Turn him into a lifelong beggar!

And yet I did give him something then. When my hand finally tore out of my pocket, I did not restrain it. Something ached around my heart; my eyes turned moist. Again he left the kitchen rejoicing, and I felt my heart grow easy and a smile spread across my face.

The third time it all took longer, quite a bit longer. I had already calculated that my salary didn't allow me to hand out eight groschen a day. It was certainly a pleasure to see the shy, tearful youngster dance for joy, see his eyes shine, know that because of my eight groschen he wouldn't sleep in the street, but in the hostel, where he'd be warm and in the morning even get a glass of tea and a roll. All this was a pleasure, but I, with my income, dared not allow myself such "joys"—not for anyone!

Naturally, I didn't say all this to the boy. Instead, I determined to teach him a lesson, what else!

I gave him to understand that he spoiled himself with begging, that every man—and he too must grow up to be a man—has the responsibility to work—work is a holy thing! And, when you *look* for work, you find it! And I preached other such nice things I'd seen in books, none of which could replace the hostel for him, nor even serve him for a night as a borrowed umbrella against the rain or snow.

He just stood there kissing my sleeve, raising his eyes to mine looking for a spark of compassion, trying to see if his words were having the least effect. His hopes were not in vain. Under the dogged plea of his eyes, I felt my cold thoughts warming up. I with my battery of ledgers and morals would shortly surrender. And this is what I decided: I would give him something, but tell him once and for all that he should never beg again. Hard and sharp, so he'd remember! I had nothing smaller than a five-kopeck piece, so I changed it and gave him eight groschen.

"Here! But never, you hear me, never beg from me again!"

Where had that "from me" come from? Apparently, I wasn't so selfless after all. I hadn't wanted to say those two words, and I would gladly, for any number of kopecks, have swallowed them. I felt a chill in my soul, as if I had suddenly torn away its ragged covering and now the spot was naked. But this lasted only a flash. My stern face and sharp voice, my right arm extended and left foot planted forward, had done their work. I had a powerful effect upon the boy. Standing as if on burning coals, straining to rush from the kitchen to arrive early at the hostel, he nevertheless paled at my words, and a tear trembled on his lash.

"But no more begging," I concluded my moralizing. "Do you hear? The last time!" The boy caught his breath and fled.

Today—I gave him nothing! I will not break my word. I'm not one of your Jewish hypocrites who use "No vow, no commitment" to get away with anything.[3] A word is a precious thing. Unless people stand firm, there will be no order in anything!

So calculating once again what I'd done and said, I felt very pleased with myself. I can't afford to hand out eight groschen charity every day, and yet that was not the main thing. The main thing was that I was concerned about his welfare, and about public welfare too. For what is charity worth without order, and what kind of order can there be without firm authority? To the boy I spoke plain Yiddish; to myself somewhat more pedantically: "Beggary is the worst germ in society's body. Whoever does not work, has no right to live," and so on.

As the door of the soup kitchen closed behind me, my feet sank in the mud, my face hit the wind, and I stepped body and soul into the dark night.

A terrible wind was blowing. The streetlights shivered as if cold, and their flicker cast thousands of reflections in the wet mudholes, making me dizzy. An awful voice piped along, as though a thousand souls were begging for redemption, or a thousand boys—for a hostel bed.

Damn! That boy again.

It would be a sin to drive a dog out in this weather! And yet the boy would spend the night in the street. But what should I do? Three handouts weren't enough? Let someone else take care of him now! For my part, wasn't it sufficient that despite a sore throat and a cough I had checked in at the soup kitchen? No one on the Charity Committee would have required me to do this, especially in such weather, and without a fur. If I were pious, this would all be self-serving: I'd run quickly home, throw myself into bed, and fall asleep, while my soul flew up to heaven to add another little good deed to my account. The good deed would be my "credit" toward a fat morsel of Leviathan on Judgment Day.[4] But in going to the soup kitchen, I hadn't given a thought to such rewards. My good heart led me there.

Praising myself somehow warmed me up a bit. Had someone else praised me, I would have had to wave him off in embarrassment, but to myself I could listen without shame. And I might have continued to discover other good qualities in myself, but unfortunately, my half soles—and God knows that I wore out the other halves on my way to the soup kitchen!—my half soles stepped right into a mudhole. The Talmud says, "Emissaries of good deeds come to no harm," but this seems to apply only when you're going, and not on your way back; afterward, as the newly created angel rushes up to heaven, you're liable to break every bone in your body.[5]

My feet were wet and my entire body chilled; I felt sure I was going to catch cold, if I hadn't already. I felt the onset of a coughing fit, of stabbing pains in my chest, and was overcome with fear at the thought that I'd just spent four weeks in bed! "One dare not do this!" something inside me rebelled. "No! You may sacrifice yourself, but what gives you the right to risk the welfare of your wife and child?"

Had I been reading this sentence in someone else's manuscript while holding a pencil in my hand, I would have known what to do with it. But the sentence was my own.

Suddenly, I felt that I really had caught cold. There I was, still far from home, and my boots filled with water, cold and heavy. Across the street I noticed the brightly lit windows of a tearoom, the worst in all of Warsaw, disgraceful tea, but since there was no choice, I hastened across the street and into its warm fog.

After ordering a glass of tea, I picked up an illustrated paper. The first cartoon to catch my eye was a reflection of things outside. Under the caption "Who has too much of what?" two figures approach each other on a rainy, windswept street. One, a heavy, middle-aged woman, bursting at the seams, in a silk dress, velvet coat, and white, feathered hat, had apparently gone for a stroll or a visit while the sun was shining, and was caught unprepared by the sudden change of weather. Her face is anxious: she's afraid of the rain and the cold—but perhaps only for her coat. As she hurries along, unsteadily, drops of sweat appear on her white forehead. Both her hands are filled. One, passed through her muff, clasps a silk handbag already edged with mud, and the other, a small silk umbrella that barely shields the feathered hat on her head. Although the lady has too much of everything else, she still needs some more umbrella!

Approaching the lady is a young girl—skin and bones! Her hair may be long and beautiful, but as she obviously has little time for it, it flies around, disheveled by the wind and smacking across her skinny shoulders. Her flimsy dress has many patches, and the wind clings to it, seeking a hole through which to reach her body. Her steps, in a pair of mud-spattered boots, are also unsteady against the wind, and both her hands are also filled, one with a big pair of men's boots—obviously her father's that she's bringing in to repair. (The split soles don't allow the suspicion that she's taking them to a tavern to pawn for a bottle of whiskey.) The father obviously came home tired from work, the mother is cooking dinner, and she, the eldest daughter, was sent out to have the boots repaired. She hurries, knowing that if the cobbler can't finish the boots by morning, there will be no fire in the hearth all day. She pants, the big boots are too heavy for the child, but even clumsier is the burden in her other hand, for she wields overhead an enormous umbrella! She carries it with pride; it was entrusted to her by her father.

The child may lack many things: warmth in winter, clothes and nourishment all year long. Yet she has too much umbrella, which I am certain the wealthy lady envies her at that moment.

The skinny little girl with the roguish eyes, though nearly bowled over by the wind, smiles up at me from the page: "So you see? We too sometimes have our pleasures! I'm laughing at the expense of that lady!"

But when paying for the unfinished tea, I'm reminded again of my begging boy. For him there's no umbrella, nor is there a home, not a dry potato either, nor even the least bit of space at the foot of a father's or a mother's bed. Even the unfortunate lady would find nothing in him to envy!

What made me think of him like that? Oh yes—it occurred to me that the ten groschen I paid for the nearly untasted tea might have provided the poor boy with half a bowl of soup or a piece of bread, and—a place to spend the night. Why had I ordered tea? At home, waiting for me, was a steaming samovar, food on the table, and sitting by it someone with a ready smile. I, however, had been embarrassed to sit in the tearoom without ordering tea. "Well," I console myself, "dealing with my shame has its price too!"

The wind outside was even fiercer than before.

It tore furiously at the roofs, like an anti-Semite pursuing Jews. But the roofs are iron and they're in their element. With murder in its heart the wind swooped down on the streetlamps, but they remain unbent and continue to shine like scholar-heroes in the days of the Inquisition. Descending even lower, it tore at the pavement, but the stones are deeply buried, and the earth doesn't give its neighbors up so easily. Angrily, the storm rose up again, ever higher, but the heavens are distant, and the stars look down with indifference or derision.

Passersby, bowed and bent, shrink into themselves to take up less space, twist against the wind to catch their breath as they continue on their way. "But the poor, weak boy"—I'm filled with fear—"what will become of him?!" All my philosophy abandoned me, and compassion awakened in its stead.

What if it were *my* child, my own flesh and blood, and he had to spend the night in the street in such a wind? Or, even if he had managed to beg eight groschen, and had to walk in such a storm to Praga, across the Vistula, over the bridge! Is he worth less just because he isn't mine, or because his parents lie somewhere in a grave under a headstone, does he shiver any less from the cold?

The desire to go home left me. I felt I had lost the right to a warm house, to a steaming samovar, to a warm bed, especially to the smiles of those awaiting me. I felt that with a word like "murderer" or "Cain" surely stamped on my forehead, I couldn't show myself before anyone.

"If only—the devil take it—I were pious!" It wouldn't hurt to know that He who lives higher than all the stars, above all the heavens, never abandons our world for an instant, and would never forget the boy. Why should he lie on my heart? I would rather cast him freely on the whole world's heart. Not for an instant would he stand before my eyes if I were certain that he was under the great Cosmic Eye, which, should it close for but one instant, God forbid, entire worlds would be snatched by the devil, but within Whose sight the tiniest worm may not be lost without a reckoning, without a judgment, without justice. . . .

Instead, with my sore throat and wet feet, and in such weather, I had now to return to the soup kitchen to look for someone else's orphan. It was a shame and a disgrace!

Exactly why and for whom I was ashamed, I do not know to this day. And yet, because of the "shame" and "disgrace" I didn't go to the soup kitchen directly, but rather circled several streets before finally arriving.

The front room, the dining hall, was empty. The day's hell had begun to cool off, and the ascending mist from the wet floor found a new heaven, a new firmament, between the lower waters from the feet of the poor and the drops of mist condensing on the ceiling. Here and there drops rained down, and through the little window into the kitchen I could see the sleepy cook, her wig awry, leaning one hand on the great kettle, and lazily raising the big ladle to her lips with the other. Meanwhile, the "assistant cook" chopped noodles for the next day and the "supervisor" counted out the lunch tickets against the committee's account. There was no one else there. I glanced under the tables—no trace of the boy! I had arrived too late! At least no one had seen me, I thought as I left the kitchen.

Suddenly, I realized that I'd been wandering the streets for several hours. "What the devil's got into me?" Suddenly angered, I began to stride home.

I was glad that everyone was already asleep. Taking off my boots in the foyer, I stole into the apartment and into bed—but I had a bad night. Exhausted and soaked through and chilled, it took me some time to finish coughing and warm up. A constant shiver ran through my bones. When very late I fell asleep, it was only to be tormented by nightmares, and I awoke bathed in a cold sweat. I leaped out of bed straight to the window. The heavens were filled with stars, like diamonds mounted in an iron sky, serene and very far away! The wind still raged, and the whole house trembled.

I tried returning to bed, but now I only dozed a bit, and kept having half dreams, always with the boy in their midst. Each time I see him in another place. Here he drags along the street somewhere, there he sits doubled over on the steps beneath a shop roof, and sometimes I even see demons playing catch with him, tossing him through the air from one hand to another. Later I find him frozen stiff in a trash barrel.

I barely survived until morning, and ran straight to the soup kitchen.

There he was!

Had I not been embarrassed, I would have washed the mud from his face with grateful tears. Had I not been afraid of my wife, I would have brought him home as my own child. He was here; I was *not* his murderer!

"Here!" I handed him a ten-groschen piece.

He accepted it wonderingly, with no idea of the favor he had done me.

May he live and be well!

The next day, when he begged me again for a hostel bed, I didn't give him anything, but now I didn't moralize. What's more, I felt embarrassed and displeased with myself.

I really cannot give him anything, but my heart aches: why can't I?

Not for nothing did my grandfather, may he rest in peace, used to say: "The unpious live with heartache and die unconsoled."

1894 (translated by Michael C. Steinlauf)

BONTSHE SHVAYG

▼

Here on earth the death of Bontshe Shvayg made no impression. Try asking who Bontshe was, how he lived, what he died of (Did his heart give out? Did he drop from exhaustion? Did he break his back beneath too heavy a load?), and no one can give you an answer. For all you know, he might have starved to death.

The death of a tram horse would have caused more excitement. It would have been written up in the papers; hundreds of people would have flocked to see the carcass, or even the place where it lay. But that's only because horses are scarcer than people. Billions of people!

Bontshe lived and died in silence. Like a shadow he passed through this world.

No wine was drunk at Bontshe's circumcision, no glasses clinked in a toast; no speech to show off his knowledge was given at his bar mitzva. He lived like a grain of gray sand at the edge of the sea, beside millions of other grains. No one noticed when the wind whirled him off and carried him to the far shore.

While Bontshe lived, his feet left no tracks in the mud; when he died, the wind blew away the wooden sign marking his grave. The gravedigger's wife found it some distance away and used it to boil potatoes. Do you think that three days after Bontshe was dead anyone knew where he lay? There was not even a gravestone for a future antiquarian to unearth and mouth the name of Bontshe Shvayg one last time.

A shadow! No mind, no heart, preserved his image. Nothing remained of him at all. Not a trace. Alone he lived and alone he died.

Were not humanity so noisy, someone might have heard Bontshe's bones as they cracked beneath their burden. Were the world in less of a hurry, someone might have noticed that Bontshe, a fellow member of the human race, had in his lifetime two lifeless eyes, a pair of sinkholes for cheeks, and, even when no weight bent his back, a head bowed to the ground as if searching for his own grave.

Were men as rare as horses, someone would surely have wondered where he disappeared to.

When Bontshe was brought to the hospital, the corner of the cellar he had called his home did not remain vacant, because ten men bid for it at once; when he was taken from the hospital ward to the morgue, twenty sick paupers were candidates for his bed; when he was carried out of the morgue, forty men killed in the fall of a building were carried in. Think of how many others are waiting to share his plot of earth with him and well may you wonder how long he will rest there in peace.

He was born in silence. He lived in silence. He died in silence. And he was buried in a silence greater yet.

But that's not how it was in the other world. There Bontshe's death was an occasion.

A blast of the Messiah's horn sounded in all seven heavens: "Bontshe Shvayg has passed away! Bontshe has been summoned to his Maker!" the most exalted angels with the brightest wings informed each other in midflight. A joyous din broke out in paradise: "Bontshe Shvayg—it doesn't happen every day!"

Young, silver-booted cherubs with diamond-bright eyes and gold-filigreed wings ran gaily to greet Bontshe when he came. The flapping of their wings, the patter of their boots, and the merry ripple of laughter from their fresh, rosy mouths echoed through the heavens as far as the mercy seat, where God Himself soon knew that Bontshe Shvayg was on his way.

At the gates of heaven stood Father Abraham, his right hand outstretched in cordial welcome and the most radiant of smiles on his old face.

But what was that sound?

It was two angels wheeling a golden chair into paradise for Bontshe to sit on.

And what was that flash?

It was a gold crown set with gleaming jewels. All for Bontshe!

"What, before the Heavenly Tribunal has even handed down its verdict?" marveled the saints, not without envy.

"Ah!" answered the angels. "Everyone knows that's only a formality. The prosecution doesn't have a leg to stand on. The whole business will be over in five minutes. You're not dealing with just anyone, you know!"

When the cherubs raised Bontshe on high and sounded a heavenly fanfare, when Father Abraham reached out to shake his hand like an old friend, when Bontshe heard that a gold crown and chair awaited him in paradise and that the heavenly prosecutor had no case to present, he behaved exactly as he would have in this world—that is, he was too frightened to speak. His heart skipped a beat. He was sure it must be either a dream or a mistake.

He was accustomed to both. More than once in this world of ours he had dreamed of finding gold in the street, whole treasure chests of it, only to awake as great a beggar as before. More than once some passerby had smiled or said hello only to turn aside in disgust upon realizing his error.

That's how my luck is, Bontshe thought.

He was afraid that if he opened his eyes the dream would vanish and he would find himself in a dark cave full of vermin. He was afraid that if he uttered a sound or moved a limb he would be recognized at once and whisked away by the devil.

He was trembling so hard that he did not hear the cherubs sing his praises or see them dance around him. He did not return Father Abraham's hearty greeting or bid the Heavenly Tribunal good day when he was ushered before it.

He was scared out of his wits.

His fright, moreover, grew even greater when his eyes fell involuntarily on the floor of the courtroom. It was solid alabaster inlaid with diamonds! Just look where I'm standing, he thought, too paralyzed to move. Who knows what rich Jew or rabbi they've mixed me up with? In a minute he'll arrive, and that will be the end of me!

He was too frightened to hear the presiding judge call out, "The case of Bontshe Shvayg!" adding as he handed Bontshe's file to the defense counsel, "You have the floor, but be quick!"

The whole courtroom seemed to revolve around him. There was a buzzing in his ears. Gradually, he began to make out the counsel's voice, as sweet as a violin:

"The name of Bontshe Shvayg, Bontshe the Silent," the counsel was saying, "fit him like a tailored suit."

What is he talking about? wondered Bontshe just as the judge remarked impatiently:

"No poetry, please!"

"Not once in his whole life," the counsel for the defense went on, "did he complain to God or to man. Not once did he feel a drop of anger or cast an accusing glance at heaven."

Bontshe still understood nothing. Again the brusque voice interrupted:

"You can skip the rhetoric too!"

"Even Job broke down in the end, whereas this man, who suffered even more—"

"Stick to the facts!" warned the bench.

"At the age of eight days his circumcision was botched by a bungler—"

"That doesn't mean the gory details!"

"—who couldn't even staunch the blood."

"Proceed!"

"He bore it all in silence," continued the counsel for the defense. "Even when, at the age of thirteen, his mother died and her place was taken by a stepmother with the heart of a snake—"

That does sound like me, marveled Bontshe.

"No hearsay evidence!" snapped the judge.

"She scrimped on his food. She fed him moldy bread and gristle while she herself drank coffee with cream in it—"

"Get to the point!"

"She didn't spare him her fingernails, though. His black-and-blue marks showed through the holes in the old rags she dressed him in. She made him chop wood for her on the coldest days of winter, standing barefoot in the yard. He was too young and weak to wield the ax, which was too dull to cut the wood, which was too thick to be cut. He wrenched his arms and froze his feet more times than you can count. But still he kept silent, even before his own father—"

"His father? A drunk!" laughed the prosecutor, sending a chill down Bontshe's spine.

"—he never complained," continued the defense counsel. "He hadn't a soul to turn to. No friends, no schoolmates, no school . . . not one whole item of clothing . . . not a free second of time—"

"The facts!" repeated the bench.

"He even kept silent when his father, in a drunken fit, took him by the neck one snowy winter night and threw him out of the house. He picked himself out of the snow without a peep and followed his feet where they took him. At no time did he ever say a word. Even when half-dead from hunger, he never begged except with his eyes.

"At last, one dizzy, wet spring evening, he arrived in a great city. He vanished in it like a drop of water in the sea, though not before spending his first night in jail for vagrancy. And still he kept silent, never asking why or how long. He worked at the meanest jobs and said nothing. And don't think it was easy to find them.

"Drenched in his own sweat, doubled over beneath more than a man can carry, his stomach gnawed by hunger, he kept silent!

"Spattered with the mud of city streets, spat on by unknown strangers, driven from the sidewalk to stagger in the gutter with his load beside carriages, wagons, and tram cars, looking death in the eye every minute, he kept silent!

"He never reckoned how many tons he had to carry for each ruble; he kept no track of how often he stumbled and fell; he didn't count the times he had to sweat blood to be paid. Never once did he stop to ask himself why fate was kinder to others. He kept silent!

"He never even raised his voice to demand his meager wage. Like a beggar he stood in doorways, glancing up as humbly as a dog at its master. "Come back later!" he would be told—and like a shadow he was gone, coming back later to beg again for what was his.

"He said nothing when cheated, nothing when paid with bad money.

"He kept silent!"

Why, perhaps they mean me after all, thought Bontshe, taking heart.

"Once," continued the counsel for the defense after a sip of water, "things seemed about to look up. A droshky raced by Bontshe pulled by runaway horses, its coachman thrown senseless on the cobblestones, his skull split wide open. The frightened horses foamed at the mouth, sparks shot from under their hooves, their eyes glittered like torches on a dark night—and in his seat cringed a passenger, more dead than alive.

"And it was Bontshe who stopped the horses!

"The rescued passenger was a generous Jew who rewarded Bontshe for his deed. He handed him the dead driver's whip and made him a coachman, found him a wife and made him a wedding too, and was even thoughtful enough to provide him with a baby boy. . . .

"And Bontshe kept silent!"

It certainly sounds like me, thought Bontshe, almost convinced, though he still did not dare look up at the tribunal. He listened as the counsel went on:

"He kept silent when his benefactor went bankrupt without giving him a day's pay. He kept silent when his wife ran off and left him with the little infant. And fifteen years later, when the boy was strong enough to throw his father into the street, Bontshe kept silent then too!"

It's me, all right! decided Bontshe happily.

"He even kept silent in the hospital, the one place where a man can scream.

"He kept silent when the doctor would not examine him without half a ruble in advance and when the orderly wanted five kopecks to change his dirty sheets. He kept silent as he lay dying. He kept silent when he died. Not one word against God. Not one word against man.

"The defense rests!"

Once again Bontshe trembled all over. He knew that the defense was followed by the prosecution. Who could tell what the prosecutor might say? Bontshe himself hardly remembered his own life. Back on earth each minute had obliterated the one before. The counsel for the defense had reminded him of many forgotten things; what might he learn from the prosecution?

"Gentlemen!" The voice of the prosecutor was sharp and piercing. At once, however, it broke off.

"Gentlemen . . ." it resumed, although more softly, only to break off again.

When it spoke a third time, it was almost tender. "Gentlemen," it said. "*He* kept silent. I will do the same."

There was a hush. Then, from the bench, another voice spoke tenderly, tremulously, too. "Bontshe, Bontshe, my child," it said in harplike tones. "My own dearest Bontshe!"

Bontshe felt a lump in his throat. He wanted to open his eyes at last, but his tears had sealed them shut. Never had he known that tears could be so sweet. "My child"; "my Bontshe"—not once since the death of his mother had he been spoken to like that.

"My child," continued the judge, "you have suffered all in silence. There is not an unbroken bone in your body, not a corner of your soul that has not bled. And you have kept silent.

"There, in the world below, no one appreciated you. You yourself never knew that had you cried out but once, you could have brought down the walls of Jericho. You never knew what powers lay within you.

"There, in the World of Deceit, your silence went unrewarded. Here, in the World of Truth, it will be given its full due.

"The Heavenly Tribunal can pass no judgment on you. It is not for us to determine your portion of paradise. Take what you want! It is yours, all yours!"

Bontshe looked up for the first time. His eyes were blinded by the rays of light that streamed at him from all over. Everything glittered, glistened, blazed with light: the walls, the benches, the angels, the judges. So many angels!

He cast his dazed eyes down again. "Truly?" he asked, happy but abashed.

"Why, of course!" the judge said. "Of course! I tell you, it's all yours. All heaven belongs to you. Ask for anything you wish; you can choose what you like."

"Truly?" asked Bontshe again, a bit surer of himself.

"Truly! Truly! Truly!" clamored the heavenly host.

"Well, then," smiled Bontshe, "what I'd like most of all is a warm roll with fresh butter every morning."

The judges and angels hung their heads in shame. The prosecutor laughed.

1894 (translated by Hillel Halkin)

KABBALISTS

▼

When times are bad even Torah—that best of merchandise—finds no takers.

The Lashchev yeshiva was reduced to Reb Yekel, its master, and a single student.

Reb Yekel is a thin old man with a long, disheveled beard and eyes dulled with age. His beloved remaining pupil, Lemech, is a tall, thin young man with a pale face, black, curly sidelocks, black, feverish eyes, parched lips, and a tremulous, pointed Adam's apple. Both are dressed in rags, and their chests are exposed for lack of shirts. Only with difficulty does Reb Yekel drag the heavy peasant boots he wears; his pupil's shoes slip off his bare feet.

That is all that remained of the once-famed yeshiva.

The impoverished town gradually sent less food to the students, provided them with fewer "eating days," and the poor boys went off, each his own way. But Reb Yekel decided that here he would die, and his remaining pupil would place the potsherds on his eyes.

They frequently suffered hunger. Hunger leads to sleeplessness, and night-long insomnia arouses a desire to delve into the mysteries of Kabbalah.

For it can be considered in this wise: as long as one has to be up all night and suffer hunger all day, let these at least be put to some use; let the hunger be transformed into fasts and self-flagellation; let the gates of the world reveal their mysteries, spirits, and angels.

Teacher and pupil had engaged in Kabbalah for some time. Now they sat alone at the long table. For other people it was already past lunchtime; for them it was still before breakfast. They were accustomed to this. The master of the yeshiva stared into space and spoke; his pupil leaned his head on both hands and listened.

"In this too there are numerous degrees," the master said. "One man knows a part, another knows a half, a third knows the entire melody. The rabbi, of blessed memory, knew the melody in its wholeness, with musical accompaniment, but I," he added mournfully, "I barely merit a little bit, no larger than this"—and he measured the small degree of his knowledge on his bony finger. "There is melody that requires words: this is of low degree. Then there is a higher degree—a melody that sings of itself, without words, a pure melody! But even this melody requires voicing, lips that should shape it, and lips, as you realize, are matter. Even the sound itself is a refined form of matter.

"Let us say that sound is on the borderline between matter and spirit. But in any case, the melody that is heard by means of a voice that depends on lips is still not pure, not entirely pure, not genuine spirit. The true melody sings without voice; it sings within, in the heart and bowels.

"This is the secret meaning of King David's words: 'All my bones shall recite. . . .' The very marrow of the bones should sing. That's where the melody should reside, the highest adoration of God, blessed be He. This is not the melody of man! This is not a composed melody! This is part of the melody with which God created the world; it is part of the soul that He instilled in it.

"This is how the hosts of heaven sing. This is how the rabbi, of blessed memory, sang."

The discourse was interrupted by an unkempt young man girded with a rope about his loins—obviously a porter. He entered the house of study, placed a bowl of grits and a slice of bread beside the master, and said in a coarse voice, "Reb Tevel sends food for the master of the yeshiva." As he turned to leave he added, "I will come for the bowl later."

Shaken out of his reverie by the porter's voice, Reb Yekel rose heavily and, dragging his feet in his big boots, went to wash his hands at the basin. He continued his remarks, which now lacked enthusiasm, and Lemech from his seat followed his voice with great eagerness.

"But I," Reb Yekel's mournful voice trailed, "have not even merited to understand to what degree that melody belongs, through what gate it emerges. See," he added with a smile, "but I do know the fasts and 'combinations' required for this purpose, and I may even reveal them to you today."

The pupil's eyes bulged. His mouth opened in his eagerness not to miss even a word. But the master broke off abruptly. He washed his hands, wiped them, pronounced the benediction, and, returning to the table, recited with trembling lips the blessing over the bread.

With shaking hands he raised the bowl. The warm steam covered his bony face. Then he replaced it on the table and took up the spoon in his right hand, warming his left hand against the bowl. His tongue pressed the first bite of salted bread against his toothless gums.

Having warmed his face with his hands, he wrinkled his forehead, pursed his thin bluish lips, and blew upon the bowl.

All this time the pupil regarded him intently, and as the master's trembling lips stretched to meet the first spoonful of grits, Lemech's heart seemed to contract. He covered his face with both hands and seemed to shrink all over.

Some minutes later another young man came, carrying a second bowl of grits and bread. "Reb Yosef sends dinner for the pupil," he announced. But Lemech did not remove his hands from his face.

The master put down his spoon and approached his pupil. For a moment he looked at him with loving pride; then he wrapped his hand in the wing of his coat and touched his shoulder.

"They brought you dinner," he reminded Lemech gently.

The pupil slowly removed his hands from his face, which was now even paler, and from his eyes, which burned with a still wilder fire.

"I know, Rebbe, but I will not eat today."

"The fourth fast in a row?" the master wondered. "And you will fast alone? Without me?" he added with a touch of resentment.

"This is a different kind of fast," the pupil answered. "It is a penitence fast."

"What are you saying? You, a penitence fast?"

"Yes, Rebbe, a penitence fast. A moment ago, when you began to eat, a sinful thought flitted through my mind, a covetous thought."

Late that night the pupil woke his master. They slept on facing benches in the house of study.

"Rebbe, Rebbe!" he called in a weak voice.

"What is it?" The master awoke in fright.

"Just now I attained a high degree. . . ."

"How?" the master asked, still not entirely awake.

"Something sang within me."

"How? How?"

"I hardly know myself," the pupil replied in a still weaker voice. "I couldn't sleep and I pondered your words. I wanted to know the melody. I grieved so at not knowing it that I began to weep— everything within me wept; all my limbs wept before the Almighty.

"And even as I wept I made the combinations you had revealed to me. It was strange; I did not recite them by mouth, but somehow deep within me, as if it happened by itself. Suddenly, there was a great light. My eyes were closed, but I saw light, much great light."

"And then?" The master bent down to him.

"Then I felt so good because of the light; it seemed to me that I had lost all weight, that I could fly."

"And then, then what?"

"Then I felt very gay and cheerful so that I could laugh. My face didn't move, nor my lips, yet I laughed. It was such joyous, good, hearty laughter."

"Yes, yes, from joy."

"Then something within me hummed, like the beginning of a melody."

"Well? And then?"

"Then I heard the melody sing within me."

"What did you feel? What? Tell."

"I felt as if all my senses were deadened and shut off, and that something within me sang, the way it is necessary to sing, but without words, simply melody."

"How? How?"

"No, I can't describe it. I knew it before. Then the song became— became—"

"What became of it? What?"

"A kind of music . . . as if I had a violin within me, or as if Yonah the musician was within me and he was playing as he does at the rabbi's table, except that he played still better, more delicately, with more spirit. And all this time there was no sound, no sound at all, pure spirit."

"You are fortunate! You are fortunate! You are fortunate!"

"Now it's all gone," said the pupil sadly. "My senses are awake again, and I am so tired, so tired . . . so that . . . Rebbe!" he shouted suddenly and grasped at his chest. "Rebbe! Recite the confession with me! They came after me! A singer is missing in the heavenly host! A white-winged angel! Rebbe! Rebbe! *Shma Yisroel!* Hear, O Israel! *Shmaaa . . . Yis . . .*"

The entire town was unanimous in wishing for themselves a death such as this. Only the master of the yeshiva was not satisfied.

"Only a few fasts more," he said, sighing, "and he would have died with the Divine Kiss!"

1894; in Hebrew, 1891 (translated by Shlomo Katz)

A CONTRIBUTION FOR A WEDDING

▼

Reb Oyzer Hofenshtand was, may God protect him, a very rich man, perhaps even a millionaire. He had a say in the affairs of this world—and in the affairs of the next world, even more so.

Here he is sitting at table having his dinner.

And what a table it is! Would that all who wished me well had such a table. The feast begins with herring, pilchards, and sardines. The silverware—as plentiful as if it were wood—glitters on the table and gleams in the open credenza. On the walls all around the room hang about ten silver trays for which there is no room in the credenza. Above the cabinet glitters a large menora with candle holders carved in the shape of flower stems, and on either side of the menora, as if on guard, stand two enormous Sabbath candlesticks.

Reb Oyzer himself is a small, thin Jew who appears entirely lost in the depths of a large armchair upholstered in red velvet. On his head gleams a high, broad green velvet hat whose stiffly raised top barely reaches above the back of his chair. The style of the hat is his own invention: it will make his name in the oral history of the

Hasidim, his renown passing from mouth to mouth for eternity. When he is already in paradise reading the Mishna (having begun with rudimentary vocalization), our great-grandchildren (he hopes) will still be wearing their hats in the style of an Oyzer head-covering.

He eats in silence, his forehead and eyebrows drawn together in a serious expression, without a glance at those on either side.

All the seats at the long table are occupied. On his right side, a row of women—his wife, two daughters, a daughter-in-law, and three granddaughters. On his left sit the men—a son, two sons-in-law, and their three sons, all kheyder boys.

Reb Oyzer's wife wears an embroidered headband with broad, fluttering flame-red ribbons under a deep bonnet. His daughters wear wigs; but his daughter-in-law has reached the stage of wearing her hair in bottle curls covered by a scarf. The young girls do not need to hide their hair. Their bangs dangle freely over their narrow foreheads. Who knows what will happen when the time comes to shave their heads for marriage?

Just a few years earlier, the seat of honor had been occupied by Reb Oyzer's mother, a formidable matron who wore a head scarf, dangling earrings, and a hooded shawl around her shoulders. But Reb Oyzer's mother now lies in the cemetery.

The men too are dressed in various styles. Reb Oyzer himself wears his version of the Hasidic "top hat." His son wears a pointy yarmulke, while his sons-in-law wear yarmulkes that are flat and square. The kheyder boys wear visored caps, at which Reb Oyzer frequently casts angry glances. The hatmaker had made the caps too narrow and too short.

The week before there had also been present at the table a tutor dressed in a caftan with lace. But the tutor has since been engaged as a rabbi in some shtetl, so now Reb Oyzer must travel to the rebbe and seek his recommendation for a new tutor. He has no intention of letting just anybody into his house. "Not in such times as these," he sighs.

He looks around and notes how with every passing minute Time tears away another stone from the walls that he has so craftily constructed to seal himself off from the great profane world, a world to which he properly belongs by reason of his wealth. This modern age seeps like water into his old ark, where he had hoped to ride out the flood of "enlightenment," so that not a single member of his family would ever get so much as a toe wet. But the effort has been in vain.

One granddaughter had barely learned a little writing before she was caught reading a novel. Oyzer's daughter-in-law had reported the matter. Doubtless no good could come of reading novels.

Another grandchild—this one a boy—was suddenly possessed by an evil spirit. The child stubbornly demanded to be sent to a worldly school. Nothing helped, not arguing or pleading or fainting. Not even a beating made any impression on him. He was barely bought off with a gold watch.

The crease between Reb Oyzer's brows deepens. He can see clearly with the same weepy old eyes that had helped him to recite so many psalms, to count so much money, and to take in so much of the world, that the times have no pity, that they erase and efface the old, the moldy, and the sacred.

The door opens. The Jew who enters is stooped, with a white, unkempt beard tangled in the threads of his frayed old gabardine. His face is pale under his greasy cap.

Poverty itself has entered.

"Welcome, Mendl," the millionaire calls out.

"Greetings to you," answers Mendl Poverty approaching the table.

The master of the house wraps his hand in a serviette and shakes Mendl's hand. The sons-in-law do the same, as do the grandsons, all but one, who makes a face. Had they bought the boy a pendant to go with the watch, he might not have grimaced.

But Mendl smiles and does not notice. "You seem to have too many women at your table, Oyzer."

"They are all family," Oyzer answers with a sigh. But in his heart he doubts that a daughter-in-law can be considered family.

"You know what, Oyzer?" Mendl continues. "I will have a glass of brandy."

"Go ahead."

"Well, rascals, let me sit down." Poverty squeezes himself in between two of the grandsons, so that he sits on the edges of both of their chairs at once, and helps himself to the brandy. "And something to eat with it?" he asks, raising his moist eyes to the mistress of the house.

Oyzer, his temper rising, casts an angry eye on the long row of women. What is the matter with them? Don't they see that the man needs food to go with his drink?

His wife understands his look, but apparently is not in the mood to get up. "Help yourself to a drumstick," she says.

"That won't do," Mendl replies. "For that I'm required to wash my hands. In the meantime—sponge cake. I deserve some sponge cake. Tell me, Sarah," he continues to the lady of the house, "didn't somebody here get married during my absence, eh?"

One of the granddaughters frowns and brings over a piece of sponge cake from the credenza.

Mendl Poverty makes a toast and eats his sponge cake. "Now I am going to wash." He looks around for the water basin and goes over to wash his hands.

A maid enters carrying a tureen of boiling soup. Oyzer directs another furious look at his wife. "Take it back for now," his wife commands. "A guest has come."

The maid throws a sour glance at Poverty and retreats.

After the meal and the collective blessing, the acrid smell of the smoke rising from Mendl Poverty's pipe chases the women from the room. Mendl smiles with satisfaction, looks around, and finds what he is looking for—the sofa. His head feels heavy. It has been a long time since he has had so much to eat. He raises himself with effort from the chair, wobbles over to the sofa, and stretches out.

Oyzer asks: "Would you like to sleep a little?"

"Yes. I will speak to you later." Mendl yawns before adding, "God willing, I will be staying with you for a few days."

"Well then, sleep," says Oyzer as he leaves the room. The other members of the household follow him out.

A few hours later Oyzer returns to find Mendl lying with his eyes open. "So how are you doing, Mendl?" he asks, seating himself on a chair near the head of the sofa.

"So-so," Mendl replies. "Don't you have any tea?"

Oyzer rings, and when his wife appears in the doorway, he orders her to bring the samovar. Mendl yawns. "What exactly are you doing here?" asks the rich man.

Mendl Poverty repeats the question: "What exactly am I doing here, you want to know? I'm arranging a marriage."

"For your son Shmerl?"

"No, I still have an older daughter."

"Really?"

"What did you think?"

"So?"

"So, so. As you may imagine, I need money for a dowry."

"You can count on me for twenty-five rubles."

Mendl sits up. "That's very generous of your father's son!"

"So how much do you want?"

"How much do I want? I need five hundred rubles."

"Five hundred rubles?" The millionaire is surprised.

"I gave my word on it."

"So what if you gave your word?"

"Idiot! I never intended to keep it, but something has gone wrong. Listen to what can happen. My daughter has fallen ill. Nothing worth mentioning, the whole story's not worth a pinch of snuff. How should I know what's the matter with her? But you know that wretch Motie the Bum, don't you? Well, he and I had a falling-out. We had to go for arbitration. Then—may his name be erased—he goes and writes to the groom's father."

"You don't say." Reb Oyzer looks disgusted.

"As you hear."

"A real scum. A traitor in Israel."

"So now I'm on my way to see the rebbe. Motie will get what he deserves. But the damage is done. Do you know what that villain—may his name be rubbed out—wrote in his letter? That she has epilepsy. Believe me, she only had one fit. Maybe two. But on my oath of honor, not more than that." Mendl pauses to rest his mouth and puffs a little on his cold pipe.

"Have a cigar," offers the rich man.

Mendl takes the cigar, lights it, and continues: "And now, you understand, the groom's father says that he wants the entire sum."

"The arrogance of the man!" rages Oyzer.

"Of course, obviously, the dog wants to get out of the match. So he wants to get rid of me without paying the dowry penalty."

"He's no fool," jokes Oyzer.

"I couldn't care less about him. But I have to stop that vile mouth of his. That's why I need the entire five hundred rubles."

"But why do you want it all from me?"

"Aside from this," Mendl Poverty continues his own train of thought, "there are wedding expenses, as usual. Mind you, the trousseau has already been taken care of."

"And you want the entire sum from me?" Reb Oyzer asks again, not very pleased. "Why don't you ask Berl, or Chaim?"

Mr. Poverty grows angry. "I beg your pardon, but what do you want from my life? You think I have the energy to walk up and down your cobbled streets, or to climb all the stairs in your town? At my age, I should be ringing doorbells?" He gets up from the sofa. "People in this town," he spits out angrily, "live on streets that are as long as the diaspora. They live in houses that have more steps than rooms. And here I am, suffering from asthma, and I should go knock on their doors? You go! Either that, or give me the money and don't go. What do I care? When I had money, I gave."

Oyzer is silent, and Mendl sits down again. "Where is the tea?" Mendl asks impatiently.

Oyzer rings again, and from the other room comes his wife's reply that the tea will soon be ready. Mendl yawns some more.

"Honestly," continues Oyzer, "do you expect me to pay for everything? You ought to have a drop of Jewish charity in your heart."

"Heaven forbid! It needn't all come from you," Mendl answers. "Get the money from wherever you like. But I can't do it. I just can't."

"Is that my fault?"

"Listen, Oyzer. I need five hundred rubles for a dowry and another fifty rubles for wedding expenses. As I said, some of the trousseau has already been taken care of. As for the rest, I intend to pull a little cheat on that old miser. In total it comes to five hundred fifty rubles, and not a penny less."

Oyzer shakes his head. He is about to make another objection.

But Mendl cuts him off: "And to help matters along, I have this." He draws from his bosom pocket a greasy linen money bag and throws it onto Oyzer's lap. "Count it," he says.

Oyzer opens the bag, digs out a wad of balled-up banknotes, and counts out 164 rubles.

"I sold my house," Mendl explains, "so I have this money."

Oyzer stuffs the money back into the bag and is about to hand it back to Mendl.

"No." Mendl draws away. "My legs are swollen. I don't intend to do any walking. You keep the money. But you owe me five hundred fifty rubles. You can take your time about it. I'll be staying here for a few days, so you will have plenty of time. By the way, I will be resting up at your place and eating as much as I please. You understand? So there is no rush. Before I leave, you will give me a down payment on the five hundred rubles, fifty rubles in cash for wedding expenses and a five-ruble note to travel to the rebbe in Ger. You can take the money from whomever you like. That's not my business."

"Well," murmurs Oyzer.

"I will remain in Ger," continues Mendl. "But if the spirit moves me, I may drop by your place again for a few weeks."

"Well," mutters Oyzer again.

"If I do come," says Mendl, "I will sleep on this sofa. It's such a fine sofa."

1894 (translated by Goldie Morgentaler)

THE DEAD TOWN

▼

Once, while traveling through the provinces in connection with a Jewish census, I came across a Jew trudging along a sandy road. He was dragging one foot after another as though each step were his last, and I felt so sorry for him that I offered him a ride. At once, sitting himself down beside me with a "How do you do?" he began to inquire about the latest news from civilization.

"Where are you from, my friend?" I asked him.

"From a dead town," he replied.

I assumed he was joking.

"Exactly where is this town?" I asked. "In never-never land?"

He smiled. "As a matter of fact, it's here in Poland."

"You mean there's such a place in this country?"

"There certainly is. It's just that the Poles don't know about it and haven't given it a name. It's a hundred percent Jewish."

"You don't say!"

"But I do! I suppose you've studied geography and think it's all-inclusive. Well, you're wrong. There are Jews who don't live in geography at all. You won't find the place I'm speaking of listed anywhere, but people come to it from all over and travel from it all over too. Why bother with geography when any coachman can take you there? . . . You think I'm making it up? Ask me anything you want to know about it."

I remained silent.

"It's an honest-to-goodness place. Our rabbi corresponds with the greatest talmudic scholars in the world. He doesn't make a major decision without consulting them. It's never too late with him. Not long ago, for example, he declared an abandoned woman eligible for remarriage even though she was no longer alive. Well, why not? The point wasn't the woman, it was the reasoning behind it."

After a pause he continued:

"Every child knows about our town. We have lots of visitors. No one comes away disappointed."

"And here I've never even heard of such a place!"

"Amazing, isn't it? I suppose you're not from these parts. But it's a real Jewish town, and a good-sized one at that. It has everything a town should have, even a couple of certified madmen. And it's a place for doing business, believe me!"

"You mean stuff comes and goes?"

"What's that?" he asked uncertainly. "Oh, you mean merchandise!"

I nodded.

"Of course. We export tfiln and import earth from the Holy Land. But all that's just on the side; the main thing is what goes on locally. We have taverns, inns, an old-clothes trade—it's your typical Jewish economy."

"I suppose you have poverty too, then."

"What's poor and what's rich, I ask you? We get by. Whoever's hard pressed can always count on some help from town or nearby. Usually, it's from someone in town. Stick out your hand and it won't stay empty for long. And there are all kinds of odd jobs around too. If you don't mind working on commission, you can pick them up right in the street. God sees to it that no one's left out in the cold. Every orphan is assigned a house to eat in and has his studies paid for; if it's a girl, she can always find work as a cook or a housemaid, or, in the worst case, try her luck out of town. Widows, divorcées, abandoned women (there seem to be a lot of those lately!)—they may dream of a world where fresh rolls grow on trees, but they do it while snoozing in a kitchen full of steaming pots. We all live quite respectably, I assure you!"

"But from what?"

"From what? From the same things everyone else does! Our poor folk live on hope, our merchants live on air, and our gravediggers make a living from the soil. . . ."

Was he putting one over on me, this skinny bag of bones with a strange gleam in his sunken eyes? And yet there wasn't a hint of a smile on his gaunt face, which resembled a piece of yellow parchment. Nevertheless, there was something decidedly odd about his voice.

"But just what sort of town is it?" I asked.

"What do you mean, 'what sort of town'? It's a town like any other! There's a synagogue that once, or so they say, had paintings of fabulous beasts on the walls and of King David's harps and lyres on the ceiling. That was before my time, of course, but I've heard the old folk mention it."

"And now?"

"Now? It's full of dust and spiderwebs. All that's left is a chain carved from a single piece of wood that hangs down from the ceiling to the ark, whose curtain was embroidered by some old women. No one knows who made it, but he must have been a master. It's something worth seeing!

"As for the congregation," continued the Jew, "it's mostly made up of simple workingmen. Except for the tailors, who pray by themselves, and the butchers and coachmen, who rented a place of their own this year. Hardly anyone who attends services there knows the meaning of the words in the prayer book. The better-off and better-educated Jews pray in the study house. It's quite a big building—why, you should see all the books in it! And the Hasidim, of course, have their own little places to pray."

"I suppose you fight a lot among yourselves."

"I'll say we do! It won't stop until we're all in our graves, because the cemetery is the one place that belongs to everyone. Plus, of course, the bathhouse and the ritual bath."

"Is there any other communal property?"

"What else do we need? Once we had a hostel, but it isn't kept up anymore. Travelers can sleep in the study house if they like. There's no one there at night. And we also have a sick ward."

"You mean a hospital?"

"I wouldn't call it a hospital. It's just a room. It used to belong to the bathhouse keeper until it was decided that two rooms were too much for him and that one should be set aside for chronic cases—I believe there are three women in it now. One is a bedridden paralytic; one can't use her hands; and one is a madwoman whose husband ran off and left her. Each has a corner with a bed in it, and in the fourth corner there's a heating stove. Sometimes, when we find an unidentified dead body, the room serves as a morgue too."

"You're pulling my leg, my friend," I interrupted him. "The town you're describing is Tsiachnovka.[1] In fact, it's Tsiachnovka to a T, with all its goings-on and good deeds! Why call it a ghost town?"

"Because it is! It's a place that hung from a thread from the day it was founded—and now that the thread has been torn, it's hanging in air. There's nothing supporting it at all. It's a ghost town, all right—if you'd like, I'll tell you the whole story."

"I wish you would," I said.

. . .

Meanwhile, it was getting on toward evening. In the west, where the sun had set, the sky turned red as blood; in the milky east, like a bride beneath her veil, a full moon swam into sight, its pale, shimmering beams blending with the flickering phantoms of the silent, melancholy night. . . .

It was an eerie sight.

We entered a small forest. The moon shone down through the trembling leaves. Little circles of light danced like silver coins among the fallen leaves and branches on the ground. There was magic in the air, in the quiet rustle of the woods. . . .

I stole a glance at my companion. His face seemed different now, so sad and earnest, simple, yet utterly dependable.

Could he be some kind of demon or troll?

He was speaking again:

"The place hung by a thread from the start, because it was built on an illegal site. As soon as there were ten Jews living there, enough for a prayer group, they got together on the fiction that that they were a suburb of another town nearby and proceeded to build a ritual bath, a synagogue, and a bathhouse, and even to buy some ground for a cemetery. It was only then that they remembered to hire an operator to try to register them in the right places."

"To which he came hat in hand!"

"Don't we always come that way? When haven't we?"

"You've got me there!"

"Anyway, that's what happened. It wasn't quite as difficult as you might think. You see, there was a rich Jew there who, like a lot of rich Jews, happened to have a few connections, or maybe it was a lot of them—anyhow, he was someone important. Everything was registered in his name: the synagogue, the bathhouse, the ritual bath, even the cemetery. The police kept their mouths shut—I already told you he was a big shot. The idea was that once the papers came through he would make everything over to the community, which could then stop paying out bribes."

"At which point, I'll bet your rich Jew decided to remain sole owner and proprietor!"

"No, my good man, he did not. Rich Jews like that weren't the fashion then. They never even thought of such tricks. But listen to what can happen in this world of ours nonetheless!

"It wasn't the rich Jew who caused all the trouble, it was the operator. On his way to the right places, you see, he suddenly had the bright idea of running off with all the money and the papers.

He ditched the town and left it in the lurch like a man who leaves a wife with little children."

"Wasn't a second operator sent in his place?"

"Not so fast! By the time the town found out he'd absconded, the rich Jew had died and left behind, among other things, a small son. The boy couldn't put his signature alongside his brothers' until he turned twenty-one."

"Wasn't there some way of speeding that up?"

"The best that could be done was to have a new operator, maybe even two, ready to start out the day the boy reached his majority."

"I hope the town at least kept good records."

"That's just it! The records were fine—it's just that they couldn't be found. Rumor had it they'd been burned. They were kept by the president of the congregation, who, it was said, spilled some brandy on them one Saturday night and set them on fire with a Havdala candle.

"Meanwhile, the place grew; we Jews, praise God, have a knack for multiplying. And Jews came from other towns too: one brought his son-in-law, another his daughter-in-law—in a word, the town kept getting bigger. As luck would have it, though, the rich Jew's heirs began to disappear. The widow remarried and moved away, the sons took off one by one for God only knows where—no one was left behind but the little boy, who was now a young man. The townsmen appointed a legal guardian for him, married him off to a girl from a good home, and even found him an experienced partner to go into business with."

"And to lead him around by the nose."

"But good! The young man didn't get along with him, and he got along with his wife even less. To make matters worse, he signed a bad note, didn't have a cent to pay it back with, and cleared out of town in a hurry. Was there ever a stink! The case went to court, and the court appointed a bailiff. Well, the estate had no cash and the widow had taken all her husband's personal possessions—what could the bailiff do but attach the synagogue and the cemetery?

"The town was thunderstruck. And it all came out of the blue, you see, because no one had known anything about the whole business, which had been kept a dark secret until the last minute. Suddenly, without warning, the town found out that it was hanging, as I've told you, by a thread.

"What could be done? Lawyers were called in, but the only advice they could give was for the bailiff to auction off the attached property so that the town could buy it back. Needless to say, that was an expensive proposition! And to complicate matters further, the town couldn't even prove it was a town, since all the records had been lost. The best solution was to find another rich Jew and again put everything in his name. This time, though, the town wouldn't wait to register until he either dropped dead or disappeared.

"At first glance, it didn't seem a bad idea. The town was used to shelling out. The only problem was that by now there wasn't just one rich Jew living in it, there were several, to say nothing of all the operators! In whose name should the property be bought and who should get the town registered? Everyone wanted the honor and would be insulted if he didn't get it. A public meeting was held at which the matter was discussed, and discussed, and discussed for so long that it turned into a feud. And with us, you should know, a feud is more easily started than ended. Every time it finally begins to die down, along comes some peacemaker, pours fresh oil on the fire, and the whole thing blows up again!"

The Jew wiped his pale brow and went on.

"But meanwhile, something else happened that could make your hair stand on end. It's really too much to expect you to believe, except"—he smiled at me—"that this is a night for the animal we call 'Faith.'" He pointed up at the moon. "It's so quiet out that a person could believe anything."

"It is indeed," I admitted reluctantly.

"It's a real ghost story. One day the bailiff went to have a look at the cemetery before selling it. The dead heard he was there and panicked. Gravestones began rocking back and forth—before long corpses were crawling out from under them. Can you believe that?"

"I'm no freethinker, God forbid," I replied. "I believe in an afterlife. But—"

"But what, my friend, but what?"

"What I mean is, I believe in the immortality of the soul, which goes to another world, not in that of the body, which rots—and however you look at it, without the soul the body can't move an inch, let alone rise from its grave."

"Bravo!" my fellow traveler praised me. "I couldn't have put it better myself. I'm glad to see that you're an educated Jew. But you've forgotten something, my friend—and what you've forgotten is the World of Illusion. You say the soul goes to another world—agreed. But what world does it go to? If it's been good it goes to heaven and if it's been bad it goes to hell, am I right? Each soul gets what it deserves: the righteous soul feasts in paradise on the flesh of the Leviathan and the wine of Creation, and the sinful soul gets a barrel of hot pitch! Of course, all that's just in a manner of speaking, but reward and punishment do exist. And why do they? Because as long as a man is alive, he is free to choose. If he chooses, he can do good, and if he chooses, he can do evil—and once he's made his bed, he has to lie in it, don't you think?

"But what would you say about the case of a man who has slept away his life, so that he was never really a man, his life was not a life, and nothing he did was ever done, either for good or for bad, because it all happened as though in a dream? What happens to a soul like that? Should it be sent to hell? But why? It never harmed a fly! Should it be sent to heaven? What for? It never even got its feet wet."

"What really does happen to it?" I wondered.

"Nothing, that's what! It goes right on living in the World of Illusion. It never leaves its body at all. The only difference is that before it dreamt it was living on the earth and now it dreams it's living in the earth!

"No one in our town ever really died, because no one in our town ever lived, or did good or evil. We had no saints or sinners, only daydreamers in the World of Illusion. And when such a daydreamer ends up in the grave, he goes right on dreaming. All he's done is moved from one home to another.

"That's why dying was such a joke with us. Why, in our town you could put a feather beneath a living man's nose and it wouldn't stir! No one even bothered to chase away the flies. Of course, you can't expect a man to put his heart into everything, but what kind of a man is it whose heart doesn't beat? After a while none of us even worried about making ends meet anymore. And it wasn't just in our town either.

"The same waking dream, the same World of Illusion—it began spreading to other towns too. We weren't the only place where corpses crawled out of their graves and completely forgot that they had already made their last confessions and died. The minute the shards fell from their eyes, they went straight to the synagogue, or to the bathhouse, or home to have supper, as if nothing had happened at all."

I don't know if it was just the moon or if I wasn't my usual self, but I believed every word and even asked: "Did all the dead rise in the cemetery?"

"Who knows? Nobody took attendance. Maybe there were a few freethinkers who thought it must be Judgment Day and decided to stay put on principle. But there certainly were a lot of people. They picked themselves up and took off for the woods to escape the clutches of the bailiff."

"Why for the woods?"

"They couldn't go into town in midday because they were all wearing shrouds and would have given the pregnant women such a fright that they would have given birth to corpses themselves."

"Of course. And the bailiff?"

"What can you expect of a goy? He didn't notice a thing. Maybe he was drunk. He made a few notes, and that was that."

"And the cemetery was sold?"

"Don't be in such a rush. There weren't any buyers for it yet."

"What about the dead, though?"

"The dead? Ah, yes!"

He paused to rest for a moment and continued his story.

"As soon as night fell, the dead came into town. They all headed for home, slipped in through a door, a window, or even a chimney, went straight to the closet, put on their pajamas, yawned, lay down in bed, and fell asleep. The next morning they were all over the town."

"And the living didn't say anything?"

"They were too busy feuding to notice—that's all they had room in their heads for. Besides, how do you tell the difference between a living man and a dead one wearing clothes? It's not so easy. If a son saw his dead father, for example, he spat three times against the Evil Eye and said, '*Tfu, tfu, tfu*—and here I'd dreamt that I'd already buried you and inherited all your money! May all my enemies have such dreams.' Or if a wife saw her dead husband, she gave him a box on the ear for playing such a practical joke on her. Why, she had even been foolish enough to spend good money on brand-new shrouds!"

"But what if she had remarried in the meantime?"

"How could she remarry? By then the feuding had gotten so bad that the synagogue and study house had been burned down, along with the wedding canopies that were kept in them. It was a regular free-for-all. There was hardly a soul in town who hadn't been booked at least once by the police."

"Well, what happened then?"

"Nothing at all. The dead went back to their old lives and the living kept on dying—from the squalor, from the bad air, and most of all, from hunger."

"You mean there was nothing to eat?"

"No less than anywhere else. But now there were extra mouths to feed, because the dead took their place at the table and expected to eat too. And suddenly spoons were missing: when you tried helping yourself from the serving bowl, there weren't enough spoons to go around. Since every housewife knew she had exactly one spoon for every member of her family, someone was obviously stealing them—unless (as some of our more pious folk thought) they were being spirited away by black magic. But one way or another, once everyone realized that it was happening all over, and that no one had enough food anymore, it was decided there must be a famine in the land, in which case there was no choice but to go hungry. And that's what we've been doing ever since.

"Before long the dead took over. Today they're the bulk of the community and its leaders. Naturally, they don't bring children into the world; but whenever anyone dies, they steal the corpse from its deathbed or its grave and there's one more dead person in town.

"After all, what more could they want? They don't have a worry in the world—and best of all, they're not afraid of dying; they eat in order to say the Lord's blessing, but it's not as if they suffer from hunger, or for that matter, from thirst or congestion; a hundred of them can live together in one room, since they don't even need any air to breathe.

"Nothing bothers them at all. The more knowledge, the more sorrow, it says in Ecclesiastes[2]—and they know nothing and are happy knowing it as long as they can stay asleep in the World of Illusion. The problems of life don't concern them. They ask no questions, have no doubts, feel no anguish, never eat their hearts out over anything.

"You think our rabbi is any different? He may once have been an active, living man, but today he's just a ghost. He walks around in the World of Illusion regarding life as though in a dream. And the judges of our rabbinical court are all corpses too—which doesn't keep them from handing down decisions for the living as well as for the dead, let alone presiding at circumcisions, officiating at weddings, and reciting blessings on public occasions.

"Who leads the prayers in our synagogue? A corpse! He's perfectly well versed, though he looks dead and sounds dead and drops everything and runs if a rooster crows.

"Our most prominent citizens, our public benefactors, our communal leaders, the whole who's who of us—they're dead men, every one of them, who were buried long ago.

"That's why, wherever you go, there's such a stench in the air—

in the synagogue, in the bathhouse, in the street—there are corpses all around you."

"And you, my friend?" I asked. "What exactly are you?"

"I'm only half-dead," answered the Jew—and jumping out of the wagon, he disappeared among the trees. . . .

1895 (translated by Hillel Halkin)

UNCLE SHAKHNE AND AUNT YAKHNE

▼

My uncle's name was Shakhne and my aunt's name was Yakhne. Whether this was purposely arranged by a special providence to spare me the trouble of thinking up rhymes for their names if I should decide to write a poem about them, or whether it was purely accidental, I don't know! The truth is that if a special providence *had* dedicated itself to providing me continuously with rhymes, I would never write prose at all—only bad rhymes. And then there would be nothing for a literary annual. Readers want only prose, and ordinary prose at that, nothing complicated—"like a man speaking to his friend." True, they like to read, it's an inherited trait, but they see no point in learning anything. Still, one wants the honor.

But let's get back to Uncle Shakhne and Aunt Yakhne. Not only were their names a perfect match, but they were the same height and weight, and they had identical noses and eyes!

I'm not really obliged to tell you how I know this. An author has the right to know everything, including what a person has under his fingernails, and especially in his mind and heart. According to convention, he can discuss even those things that no one ever talks about. But there are so many foolish and unworthy privileges in the world, so many idiotic and asinine conventions, that it would be a disgrace for a decent person to defend his own use of a privilege or to justify himself on the basis of an accepted convention.

Therefore, I must tell you that they were both at my wedding! And, since I was married at thirteen and I knew the cantor and the rabbi and my parents, and since the bride's face was covered with a veil and no young people came to my wedding because of the big parade outside the town, I watched Uncle Shakhne and Aunt Yakhne, who were standing directly opposite me, and I noticed that they had exactly the same small eyes, which were in constant motion as if they were searching for a place to hide in shame and fright. It looked so comical to me that I burst out laughing right under the bridal canopy, and my father, may he rest in peace, put his finger to his nose, always a sign that he was about to twist my ear, or even worse. I was saved by the rabbi, who just then began the marriage invocation.

At the wedding feast, while we were eating the special "golden soup" prepared for us, it occurred to me that I had the beginning of a poem:

> My Uncle Shakhne,
> My Aunt Yakhne,

and that I could send it off secretly to the Warsaw newspaper I knew about. I would rather have written it in the holy tongue:

> *Dodi* Shakhne,
> *Dodati* Yakhne,

but at that time the buds of modern Hebrew literature had not yet begun to sprout.

That they were both exactly the same height I found out for certain only the next day. This is the story. My father's house was very crowded. I had, God be praised, a grandfather, parents, and seven brothers and sisters, and my wife and I were still at home too, being supported by my family! My father owned the house. With 10 rubles of his own and 290 on loan with interest, he had purchased a house and a pigsty from someone in the city. The house remained a house, and the pigsty was turned into a storage shed for wood. When I was married off without being sent off, they had a brief deliberation and decided that the wood could just as well be left in the yard, especially since they didn't always have wood to store—most of the time there was some, but some of the time there was none. In any case it wouldn't freeze, and it could easily be dried in the oven, and if we did remove the wood, there would be room for two beds in the shed and enough space to get in and out too. And, as everyone knows, two beds are all a young couple need.

The marriage broker had suggested this plan when my father held out for "them" to provide us with the first three years of support while he paid off his 290-ruble debt on the house; after that he would be in a position to add a little apartment to his house.

"And really," he argued, "how can one put children where they used to keep pigs?"

This bothered my mother less: "Bah!" she said. "Why make a fuss over three years? They will be over before you know it!"

And that's how it was.

The day after the wedding my wife Chavele absolutely refused to crawl out of the pigsty into the bright daylight. When I left for the synagogue, I looked over toward her bed and saw the cover and the pillow but nothing at all of her face.

And I was very anxious to see what my wife Chavele looked like, even though last night at the wedding feast I hadn't thought to glance her way; the big parade was on my mind then. Now I didn't know what to say to her: "Chave" is too familiar. "Wife" sounds vulgar. Does everybody have to know that she's my wife?

The truth is that to this day I don't like the "liberal" custom of husbands and wives walking everywhere together, and arm in arm, so that no one will, God forbid, mistake it, everyone must know what happened—who and with whom! There's no sense in it! And these same liberal Germans make fun of the washbasin in the study house because we rinse our hands in public.

But I'm getting off the track; I wanted very much to call her but didn't know how. I tried "Listen here," but it stuck in my throat; that's the way you talk to a servant, not to a wife. So I just stood glued to the spot, thinking about it, until my father shouted in to me: "Are you coming?"

Trembling, I went out without making a decision.

I could tell from the shape of the quilt that my wife Chavele was lying curled up like a ball; she was completely covered and had buried her face in the pillow.

On the way to the synagogue it dawned on me that she must be homesick; my father-in-law and my mother-in-law, her parents, went home right after the wedding supper. He was a sexton in a nearby village where a rich family's wedding was scheduled for the following day; she had a stall with ribbons and buttons and "the moment she turns her head her daughters-in-law reduce her to poverty."

At their departure my wife Chavele wept bitterly. Her impatient father shouted at her: "Be quiet, snotnose!" Her mother promised to send her a present, some patterned calico, I think.

And we could barely win her over.

Now, I suppose, she was probably yearning for home, and I felt so sorry for her. All during the prayers I couldn't stop thinking about her. I wanted to fly home, to see if my wife Chavele had stopped crying, but I had to wait for my father.

At the door my mother greeted us in a rage:

"That's quite a lady *you* landed with your bargaining. Just see how you like this! She refuses to get up and I had to bring her coffee to her in bed!"

My mother was fond of the "truth"—she simply lived for it. "I want the whole truth," she would demand when I came home with a scratched face or a torn hat, and she was always coming up with false accusations against my father. The fact is that the match with Reb Yankele, son of Yente Bryna (this was my father-in-law's name), was mostly her doing. My father was still deliberating about it when she decided to close the deal—"Let's get it over with," she insisted. She had an ingrained weakness for saying "coffee" when it was really chicory.

Naturally, I didn't go into the shed, nor did my father, even though my wife Chavele wouldn't drink her coffee. Later on my Uncle Shakhne and my Aunt Yakhne came to visit, and when they were told that "the daughter-in-law refuses to get up" they marched straight in. And, since they both banged their noses against the upper lintel (the doorway was low, as is only natural in a pigsty), I saw with my own eyes that they were bruised in the very same places—on the tips of their noses.

Here you have the best evidence that my Uncle Shakhne and my Aunt Yakhne were the same height.

Furthermore, they looked as much alike as brother and sister.

They tell this story: My Aunt Yakhne was born in Hotzeplotz and came here only to marry my uncle. I don't know precisely when this took place, but I know that the story is true. At that time we had a mayor, a Jew-hater, who was determined that no one would get married without first registering with the civil authorities. Now if we followed government regulations, we would have to wait until the legal age of seventeen or eighteen—and if Jews, with their large families, were to wait for the oldest child to reach eighteen before marrying him off, they would never live long enough to celebrate the youngest one's wedding. After a circumcision party you can't simply decide to take a break before the next one, but after marrying off a child one needs a good couple of years to recoup enough money to make another wedding.

To make a long story short, the tyrant didn't know this and he used to call all the out-of-towners who were about to be married to his office, ostensibly to ask about their identity cards, but really to find out whether a secret religious marriage ceremony hadn't taken place. Do you get the point?

Generally, he didn't find out about them.

The married youngsters would shrug their narrow shoulders, signaling, "I don't know anything." Besides, who understood Polish? When the police officer, who knew Yiddish, would ask again, they would answer: "Who? When? What? Huh? Do I know?"

And nothing!

Now to send the groom is one thing, but it's not our way to permit a young bride to go to the mayor! So we used to take young boys, hide their sidelocks behind their ears, put dresses on them, and send them in place of the brides! We weren't afraid of disobeying the injunction that states, "A man may not wear women's clothes," because we didn't do it, God forbid, for sinful purposes.[1]

One time we almost split our sides laughing: the mayor took such a liking to one of the young brides that he spread his mustache and kissed her on the forehead, and then, to top it off, he gave her a caramel!

When it was my aunt's turn, they decided that the groom himself would take the place of the bride. They were sure that the mayor would not recognize him because my uncle never went out into the street with the other boys; he was sickly, may you be spared the same, and he always sat and studied the holy books. So how would he know him?

The mayor didn't keep him long, praised be God's beloved Name. In the middle of the conversation he had him thrown out: "Away with this abomination!"

"It was a miracle," our grandmother used to say; "our ancestors' merits saved him." Uncle Shakhne is not overly bright, and who knows what secrets he would have babbled away there?

As he was walking home, everyone in the street shouted that he was "the spitting image of the bride!" And he really was. In the house, before he had a chance to change back to his own clothes, his father-in-law, an absentminded type, gave him a box on the ear: "Yakhne! Why don't you wipe your nose?"

There was another incident too. My Uncle Shakhne was the first victim of the evil decree against beards that came into force at that time; he was at the magistrate's office paying his taxes when they grabbed him and cut off his beard and sidelocks. When people saw him that way in the street they began to shout that Yakhne had gone crazy and was trying to impersonate Shakhne!

He was so horrified and embarrassed that he ran out of town. But the young boys and the women ran after him: he ran to the fields, and they followed him; he ran into the forest, and they came after him, until finally he lost them among the trees.

When they got back to town and they saw the real Aunt Yakhne, what do you think happened? They tore off her bonnet in the middle of the street. If the police hadn't come to her rescue, not a shred would have been left of her.

They both became ill from the fright and the shame of it all; and when men and women came to visit the sick pair, they didn't know which bed to approach. It was impossible to tell who was under the covers—Shakhne or Yakhne.

But that's all in the past. Today it's easy to tell them apart: Uncle Shakhne has a beard that reaches to his belt, and even though Aunt Yakhne tried to keep up with him, the few hairs sprouting on her chin don't compare with his mop, with which you could sweep up the entire study house.

In short, there was a very strong resemblance between them. The mayor, with his goyish taste, who had called him an abomination, would have said the same of her. In my opinion, though, they were both good looking; but that's not part of the story. I want to continue on about their common features. I must tell you that even their voices sounded alike! When they were in the hut with my bride, I heard two deep voices that sounded identical and one whimpering voice that responded only later.

"Chavele," I heard, "what kind of behavior is this?"

"Chavele! You're causing your parents-in-law great grief."

"Everyone will laugh at you."

"What is the meaning of this? Why?"

"Who acts this way?"

"Guests will soon be arriving."

"My precious one, my darling, listen to your old uncle and aunt; they want only what is best for you!"

"You're not a child anymore! . . . You're a grown-up person!"

They showered her with questions like this, and advice, and pleas, and not once could I tell whether it was Uncle Shakhne or Aunt Yakhne speaking!

Only after this did a thin, weeping voice, smothered from under the quilt, respond: "I'm ashamed!"

But this doesn't belong to the story either.

Their married life was idyllic. If Aunt Yakhne said *bom*, Uncle Shakhne would strengthen it with *bim-bom!* If Uncle Shakhne shook his head yes Aunt Yakhne would say, "Yes, indeed, it is certainly so—how else would it be?"

At circumcision parties and at weddings they would look at each other, he from the men's table and she from the women's; each one always had the other in mind: "Shakhne, take that middle part." . . . "Yakhne, do you want some horseradish?"

At my oldest son's circumcision, my Aunt Yakhne didn't come because she wasn't well and my Uncle Shakhne couldn't really enjoy the meal. He took about thirty macaroons home for Aunt Yakhne.

At the second son's circumcision it was just the reverse: Uncle Shakhne was sick, and she took the head of a pike home to him.

And each one was always the last word for the other.

During a dispute, when the other side had the upper hand and my Uncle Shakhne had used up all his arguments, he would invariably hold fast with the comment "But my Yakhne says so!" That was his final statement, and both reason and logic were powerless against it.

Similarly, my Aunt Yakhne would begin every sentence with "My Shakhne says" or "My Shakhne thinks," and you could build brick houses on whatever her Shakhne said or thought.

In a word, it was an ideal life. I used to send my wife Chavele to my Aunt Yakhne for instruction in how to tend to one's husband; she, on her part, would send me to Uncle Shakhne to observe the proper way for a man to treat his wife.

When they were still in good health, my Uncle Shakhne and my Aunt Yakhne would often come to our house and make peace between my wife Chavele and me. Later, when they became weak and sick, we would go to them for advice, and their counsel helped us preserve our marriage!

The proof of it was that a few years after they died, both in the same week, our domestic peace finally collapsed once and for all— my wife Chavele and I were divorced. She took two children, and I took two. She remarried, and I remarried—we live in different towns and neither of us is very happy. But that is not part of the story.

The point is that Uncle Shakhne and Aunt Yakhne lie peacefully in their graves. And have you ever heard anything like this? The two tombstones have tilted sideways and lean toward each other; and between the graves a tree has sprung up whose branches envelop the tombstones, as if to draw them closer together.

With the passing years the inscriptions on the tombstones have worn away and now it's impossible to make out the names. The records of the burial society were destroyed in the third fire, and no one can remember whether it was Uncle Shakhne who was buried on the right and Aunt Yakhne on the left, or whether it was the other way around.

My former wife Chavele and I will not be lying in the same cemetery—but again that's not part of the story.

1895 (translated by Golda Werman)

IF NOT HIGHER

▼

Early every Friday morning, at the time of the Penitential Prayers, the rabbi of Nemirov would vanish.

He was nowhere to be seen—neither in the synagogue nor in the two study houses nor at a minyan. And he was certainly not at home. His door stood open: whoever wished could go in and out; no one would steal from the rabbi. But not a living creature was within.

Where could the rabbi be? Where should he be? In heaven, no doubt. A rabbi has plenty of business to take care of just before the Days of Awe. Jews, God bless them, need livelihood, peace, health, and good matches. They want to be pious and good, but our sins are so great, and Satan of the thousand eyes watches the whole earth from one end to the other. What he sees, he reports; he denounces, informs. Who can help us if not the rabbi!

That's what the people thought.

But once a Litvak came, and he laughed. You know the Litvaks. They think little of the holy books but stuff themselves with Talmud and law. So this Litvak points to a passage in the Gemara—it sticks in your eyes—where it is written that even Moses our Teacher did not ascend to heaven during his lifetime but remained suspended two and a half feet below. Go argue with a Litvak!

So where can the rabbi be?

"That's not my business," said the Litvak, shrugging. Yet all the while—what a Litvak can do!—he is scheming to find out.

That same night, right after the evening prayers, the Litvak steals into the rabbi's room, slides under the rabbi's bed, and waits. He'll watch all night and discover where the rabbi vanishes and what he does during the Penitential Prayers.

Someone else might have gotten drowsy and fallen asleep, but a Litvak is never at a loss; he recites a whole tractate of the Talmud by heart.

At dawn he hears the call to prayers.

The rabbi has already been awake for a long time. The Litvak has heard him groaning for a whole hour.

Whoever has heard the rabbi of Nemirov groan knows how much sorrow for all Israel, how much suffering, lies in each groan. A man's heart might break, hearing it. But a Litvak is made of iron; he listens and remains where he is. The rabbi—long life to him!—lies on the bed, and the Litvak under the bed.

Then the Litvak hears the beds in the house begin to creak; he hears people jumping out of their beds, mumbling a few Jewish words, pouring water on their fingernails, banging doors. Everyone has left. It is again quiet and dark; a bit of light from the moon shines through the shutters.

(Afterward, the Litvak admitted that when he found himself alone with the rabbi a great fear took hold of him. Goose pimples spread across his skin, and the roots of his sidelocks pricked him like needles. A trifle: to be alone with the rabbi at the time of the Penitential Prayers! But a Litvak is stubborn. So he quivered like a fish in water and remained where he was.)

Finally the rabbi—long life to him!—arises. First, he does what befits a Jew. Then he goes to the clothes closet and takes out a bundle of peasant clothes: linen trousers, high boots, a coat, a big felt hat, and a long, wide leather belt studded with brass nails. The rabbi gets dressed. From his coat pocket dangles the end of a heavy peasant rope.

The rabbi goes out, and the Litvak follows him.

On the way the rabbi stops in the kitchen, bends down, takes an ax from under the bed, puts it into his belt, and leaves the house. The Litvak trembles but continues to follow.

The hushed dread of the Days of Awe hangs over the dark streets. Every once in a while a cry rises from some minyan reciting the Penitential Prayers, or from a sickbed. The rabbi hugs the sides of the streets, keeping to the shade of the houses. He glides from house to house, and the Litvak after him. The Litvak hears the sound of his heartbeats mingling with the sound of the rabbi's heavy steps. But he keeps on going and follows the rabbi to the outskirts of the town.

A small wood stands just outside the town.

The rabbi—long life to him!—enters the wood. He takes thirty or forty steps and stops by a small tree. The Litvak, overcome with amazement, watches the rabbi take the ax out of his belt and strike the tree. He hears the tree creak and fall. The rabbi chops the tree into logs and the logs into sticks. Then he makes a bundle of the wood and ties it with the rope in his pocket. He puts the bundle of wood on his back, shoves the ax back into his belt, and returns to the town.

He stops at a back street beside a small, broken-down shack and knocks at the window.

"Who is there?" asks a frightened voice. The Litvak recognizes it as the voice of a sick Jewish woman.

"I," answers the rabbi in the accent of a peasant.

"Who is I?"

Again the rabbi answers in Russian. "Vassil."

"Who is Vassil, and what do you want?"

"I have wood to sell, very cheap." And not waiting for the woman's reply, he goes into the house.

The Litvak steals in after him. In the gray light of early morning he sees a poor room with broken, miserable furnishings. A sick woman, wrapped in rags, lies on the bed. She complains bitterly, "Buy? How can I buy? Where will a poor widow get money?"

"I'll lend it to you," answers the supposed Vassil. "It's only six cents."

"And how will I ever pay you back?" asks the poor woman, groaning.

"Foolish one," says the rabbi reproachfully. "See, you are a poor, sick Jew, and I am ready to trust you with a little wood. I am sure you'll pay. While you, you have such a great and mighty God and you don't trust him for six cents."

"And who will kindle the fire?" asks the widow. "Have I the strength to get up? My son is at work."

"I'll kindle the fire," answers the rabbi.

As the rabbi put the wood into the oven he recited, in a groan, the first portion of the Penitential Prayers.

As he kindled the fire and the wood burned brightly, he recited, a bit more joyously, the second portion of the Penitential Prayers. When the fire was set, he recited the third portion, and then he shut the stove.

The Litvak who saw all this became a disciple of the rabbi.

And ever after, when another disciple tells how the rabbi of

Nemirov ascends to heaven at the time of the Penitential Prayers, the Litvak does not laugh. He only adds quietly, "If not higher."

1900 (translated by Marie Syrkin)

A CONVERSATION

▼

The day was warm, as befitting a holiday, and two men set out for a walk outside the town—Shakhne, tall and lean, among the last of the old followers of the rebbe of Kotsk, and Zerakh, also lean, but short, a relic of the old Hasidim of Belz.[1] As young men they had been sworn enemies. Shakhne had led the Kotsk Hasidim in their fight against the Belzers; Zerakh, the Belz Hasidim against the followers of Kotsk. Now that the dynasty of Kotsk was no longer in its glory and Belz too had lost its fire, the two old men had quit their factions, leaving their study houses to younger men, stronger in body but punier in spirit.

They had made peace beside the study-house stove, in winter. Now, on the first of the intermediate days of Passover, they were taking a stroll together.

The sun shone in the distant blue sky. Flocks of birds flew about looking for their last year's nests. Grass sprouted from the ground, the attendant angel almost visible in his presence, encouraging each new blade to shoot up and grow!

Shakhne opened the conversation: "The Hasidim of Kotsk—I mean the Hasidim of old, there's no point talking about today's— authentic Kotsk Hasidim don't put much stock in the Haggadah."

"They don't care much for the Haggadah, only for the *kneydlakh*, the matza balls in the soup," Zerakh smiled.

"Don't joke about the *kneydlakh*," said Shakhne earnestly. "Do you know the relevance of the text "You shall not return a runaway slave to his master"?[2]

"For me," said the Belzer with proud humility, "it's enough to know the intention of the prayers."

Shakhne pretended not to hear. "The plain meaning of the text is clear: When a slave, a servant, a serf, runs away, the Torah forbids us to catch him, tie him up, and return him to the nobleman, to his master. If someone escapes, we assume that he couldn't stand it any longer, that it was a matter of life or death. The implied meaning of the text is equally obvious: The body is slave to the soul. If the body should lust for the slice of pork, for the married woman, and other idolatries, the soul has only to command—thou shalt not!— and the body must obey. Or the reverse; suppose the soul wants to perform a good deed. Though the body may be bone-tired, the hands have to function, the feet have to run, the mouth has to speak. Why? Because the soul, the master, commands it.

"Nevertheless, you shall not return a slave! It is forbidden to turn the body over completely to the soul, because the ardent soul would consume it, leaving only ashes. Had God wanted spirits without bodies, he would never have created the world. Consequently, the body is also entitled to something. It is said, for example, 'The man who fasts overmuch is counted as a sinner.'³ The body is expected to eat! If you want to travel, you have to feed the horse.

"Whenever a holiday, a day of rejoicing, rolls around, you too should celebrate. Down a glass! The soul will enjoy the blessing while the body warms to the brandy. It's Passover, the festival of liberation—so come along, slave, and celebrate your freedom. Come, body, and grab a *kneydel*. That way it fulfills the commandment of rejoicing. That is its way to ecstasy, to exaltation! My friend, don't mock the *kneydlakh*."

Zerakh conceded that this was an important matter, worthy of discussion. But matza balls were not for him, since he abjured all food that was soaked.

"Then you must take your pleasure in the matza itself."

"Who can ever enjoy his fill of matza?" Zerakh smiled. "Besides, who has the teeth for matza?"

"In that case, how *do* you fulfill the injunction to 'rejoice on the festival' with respect to the body?"⁴

"Who knows? If my body enjoys the taste of raisin wine, well and good. I myself happen to take fierce pleasure in the Haggadah. I sit and recite the Haggadah—I count the plagues, count them and double them and then multiply them again."

"Barbarian!"

"Barbarian? After so much suffering and persecution? When we've endured so long an exile? In my opinion we ought to introduce a custom of repeating the plagues seven times, and seven times the prayer 'Pour out Thy wrath on the nations that do not know Thee.'⁵ The plagues are all-important! They're my greatest delight. We should open the door then too, when we count off the plagues—let the Gentiles hear! What is there to be afraid of? Do they understand our holy tongue?"

Shakhne was silent for a while, then launched into the following anecdote:

"I'll tell you what happened once in our town. About ten doors down from the rebbe, of blessed memory, there lived a butcher. He's no longer alive, and I don't want to speak ill of the dead, but he was a man of the fleshpots, a butcher's butcher. He had the neck of a bull, eyebrows thick as brushes, hands like logs. When he spoke, he let you hear the rumble of thunder, of artillery. If I'm not mistaken, he was a Belz Hasid."

"Is that so?" muttered Zerakh.

"So help me," said Shakhne impassively. "He used to gesticulate wildly when he prayed, raising his voice to a shout and dropping it to a whisper."

"Spare me the details."

"Well, just imagine the racket this fellow made when he recited the Haggadah! You could hear his every word in the rebbe's house ten doors away. As you might expect, a butcher butchers what he reads. All of us at the table laughed aloud, and though the rebbe, of sacred memory, barely moved his lips, he was smiling too. Until our gentleman began to count out the plagues. When they came shooting from his mouth like bullets, and his fist hammered the table so you could hear the glasses clanging, the rebbe, of blessed memory, grew sad, and fell into a state of depression."

"Depression? On a holiday? On Passover? How is that possible?"

"That's exactly the question we put to him."

"And what did he say?"

"He said that even God Himself fell into melancholy during the exodus from Egypt."

"Where did he get that idea?"

"From a midrash. When the Israelites crossed the Red Sea and the waters closed behind them, and Pharaoh and his army were drowned, the angels began to sing the praises of God. Seraphs flew through the seven heavens with the wonderful news. The stars and planets sang and danced for joy. You can imagine the rejoicing of the heavenly spheres: evil had been destroyed! But God put an end to the celebration. 'My children drown in the sea, and you find that occasion for song?'[6] Pharaoh and his minions—the power of evil itself—are also God's creation. And His mercy extends to all that He has wrought."

"Is that so?" Zerakh sighed, then revived again after a short pause:

"But if it was only a midrash that he was repeating, what is his great accomplishment?"

Shakhne halted and turned earnestly to his companion:

"First of all, you Belz fool, no one is obliged to be original. 'There is no anterior and posterior in the Torah.' The old is new and the new is old. Second, he revealed why it is that we recite the Haggadah, even the catalogue of plagues, in a mournful, melancholy chant. And third, he explained the verse 'Israel does not rejoice in the manner of the nations.'[7] Don't engage in vulgar celebration like a barbarian. You are not a peasant! Vengeance is not Jewish!"

1900 (translated by Ruth R. Wisse)

BETWEEN TWO MOUNTAINS
▼

You have certainly heard of the Brisker rov and the Bialer rebbe.[1] But not everyone knows that the saintly rebbe of Biala, Reb Noahke, had originally been a distinguished pupil of the Brisker rov, and only after studying with the rov for many years had he disappeared, remaining in self-imposed exile for several years before surfacing again in Biala.[2]

Reb Noahke had left for the following reason: At the yeshiva of Brisk, they had studied Torah, but the rebbe felt that the Torah they studied was sterile. For instance, they learned the laws governing the conduct of women, or the regulations for meat and dairy, or those pertaining to commerce. Very good. Comes X or Y for a ruling, or a servant to ask a question, or a woman with a problem— in that moment Scripture comes alive. It bursts into life and has authority in the world. But without these questioners, the Torah— that is, the revealed part of the Law—is arid. This was not, the Bialer rebbe felt, the living Torah. And Torah must live!

In Brisk it was forbidden to study any kabbalistic texts. The Brisker rov was a misnaged, and by nature as vengeful as a snake. If anyone was found with a Zohar or a Pardes, the rov would curse, and threaten the miscreant with excommunication. Once, when a student was caught with a book of kabbalah, the rov allowed Gentiles to shave off his beard. What do you think happened? The man lost his mind and fell into the blackest despondency. And what was more amazing, no miracle worker could help him! There was no monkeying with the Brisker rov! On the other hand, how could anyone leave the Brisker rov's yeshiva?

In fact, for a long time Reb Noahke could not make up his mind to go, until one night he had a dream. He dreamed that the Brisker rov came to him and said, "Come, Noahke, I will lead you to the earthly paradise." He took him by the hand and led the way. They came to an enormous palace. In the palace there were no doors and no windows, except for the door by which they entered. In spite of this, the palace was full of light, because the walls were made of crystal—or so it seemed to Reb Noahke—and gave off a luminous gleam.

The two men walked on and on, endlessly.

"Hold on to my caftan," said the Brisker rov. "In this place there are so many chambers that should you break away from me you will be lost forever."

The rebbe did as he was told and they walked farther and farther, but nowhere along the way did the rebbe see a single piece of furniture, not even a bench.

"This is not a place for sitting," explained the Brisker rov. "Here you must keep walking forward." Each chamber they passed was larger and brighter than the one before; and the walls gleamed here with one color, there with another; some rooms were multicolored, others were all the colors of the rainbow. But they encountered no living person on their way.

The rebbe grew weary of walking. He broke out in a cold sweat and felt a chill in every limb. His eyes began to ache from the constant glare. He was overcome by a powerful longing, a yearning for his fellow Jews, for friends, for the people of Israel. This unpeopled world was no laughing matter!

"Do not wish for anyone," said the Brisker rov. "This palace is only for me and you. One day you too will be the Brisker rov."

The rebbe grew even more frightened and grasped at the wall in order not to fall. But the wall scalded him—not like fire, but like ice.

"Rabbi!" he cried. "The walls are not crystal, but ice, plain ice."

The Brisker rov did not answer.

Again the rebbe cried: "Master, lead me out of here! I don't want to be alone with you. I want to be with the people of Israel."

No sooner had he uttered these words than the Brisker rov disappeared, and Reb Noahke was left all alone in the palace.

He had no idea in which direction to go. A cold fear came at him from the walls. And the yearning to see another Jew, even if he were a cobbler or a tailor, grew ever more intense, until he burst into tears.

"Master of the Universe," he pleaded. "Take me away from here. I would rather be in hell with the rest of Israel than remain here all by myself."

At that very moment there appeared before him an ordinary little Jew with a coachman's red belt tied around his hips and a long whip in his hand. Silently, the little Jew took hold of the rebbe's sleeve and led him out of the palace. Then he disappeared.

This was the dream that had appeared to Reb Noahke.

When he awoke before dawn, just as the sky was turning gray, he understood that this had been no ordinary dream. He dressed quickly, intending to run to the study house to have his dream explained by the scholars who lodged there. As he passed through the marketplace, he noticed a covered wagon standing in the square. It was a large, old-fashioned, horse-drawn covered wagon, and next to it stood the driver, wearing a red belt around his hips and with a long whip in his hand—just like the little Jew in his dream.

The rebbe realized that something lay behind this. So he approached the driver and asked, "In which direction are you headed?"

"Not in yours," the driver answered quite brusquely.

"Even so," entreated the rebbe, "perhaps I could come along?"

The driver hesitated a moment before answering. "Why couldn't a young fellow like you go on foot?" he asked. "Do your own traveling."

"And where would I go?"

"Wherever your eyes lead," the driver answered, turning away. "It's no concern of mine."

The rebbe understood, and set out on his self-imposed banishment.

As I have said, he surfaced again several years later in Biala. (The story of how this happened has been passed down by word of mouth, so I won't retell it here, although it would set your ears on fire.) About a year, more or less, after the rebbe's reappearance, Reb Yekhiel, a prominent citizen of Biala, hired me as a tutor for his children.

At first, I did not want to take up the position. Reb Yekhiel, you must understand, was one of those old-fashioned, wealthy Jews. He endowed each of his daughters with a dowry of a thousand gold pieces, and he married them into the most distinguished rabbinical families. In fact, his last daughter-in-law was the Brisker rov's daughter.

From this you may conclude that if the Brisker rov and the other in-laws were enemies of Hasidism, so Reb Yekhiel must of necessity be an enemy too; whereas I was a Hasid, a disciple of the Bialer rebbe. How, then, could I have dealings with such a house?

Nevertheless, I was drawn to Biala. To be able to live in the same town as the rebbe was not a small consideration. I turned the matter over in my mind—and I went.

Reb Yekhiel turned out to be a truly unassuming and decent man. I would even vouch for the fact that his own heart was powerfully drawn to the rebbe. Because, to tell the truth, he was not much of a scholar. He looked at the Brisker rov, as they say, with the blank eye of a rooster contemplating a human being. So he did not forbid me to follow the Bialer rebbe, but he himself kept his distance. Whenever I brought up the subject of my rebbe, he pretended to yawn, although it was obvious to me that he was listening with both ears. But his son, the Brisker rov's son-in-law, frowned and gave me a look of anger and derision. He did not argue with me, however, being by nature a man of few words.

The day came when Reb Yekhiel's daughter-in-law, the Brisker rov's daughter, was about to give birth. Certainly, there is nothing out of the ordinary about a woman giving birth; but that was not the whole story. It was known that because the Brisker rov had once ordered a Hasid to be shaved—that is, to have his beard and sidelocks shorn by Gentiles—the rov's good name had been tarnished in the eyes of the saintly men of his generation. Both his sons died within five to six years after the event—may God protect you from such a fate! And none of his three daughters had male offspring. In addition, all three of his daughters, poor souls, were prone to painful labor, during which they were each time closer to the next world than to this one. But since it was the will of heaven that there should be disputes between misnagdim and Hasidim, everyone knew that this was a punishment imposed by the holy men of his generation on the Brisker rov. But the Brisker rov himself, despite his luminous eyes, did not see it! And perhaps he did not want to see it. He continued to carry on his campaign of opposition to the Hasidim with an iron fist, with excommunications and denunciations, just as in former times.

I felt very sorry for Gitele (that was the name of the Brisker rov's daughter)—first, because she had a Jewish soul, and second, because her Jewish soul was virtuous. Not a single poverty-stricken bride got married without her assistance—that was how generous she was.

To think that such a saintly being should have to pay for her father's severity! That was why, as soon I noticed that the midwife had begun to hurry about the house in preparation for the delivery, I set about moving heaven and earth to persuade the family to send for the Bialer rebbe. Let them send a note without a fee—as if he wanted or needed the money! The Bialer rebbe did not believe in fees.

I tried first to talk to the Brisker rov's son-in-law. I knew that his soul was bound up with Gitele's, since no matter how they tried to conceal it, the harmony between husband and wife radiated from every corner of the house and from all their gestures and expressions. Nevertheless, he was the Brisker rov's son-in-law! He spat and walked away, leaving me standing with my mouth open.

So I approached Reb Yekhiel himself. He answered: "She is the Brisker rov's daughter! I would not do such a thing to the Brisker rov, not even if her life depended on it, Heaven forbid."

I tried Reb Yekhiel's wife—a good woman, but common. She answered me as follows: "If my husband told me to, I would instantly send the rebbe my best holiday headscarf and my earrings, both of them treasures that cost a mint. But without his say-so, I wouldn't send even half a penny; not even a crumb."

"But just a note. What harm can it do?"

"Without my husband's knowledge, I do nothing!" she responded, exactly as a decent Jewish wife ought to answer. She turned her back on me, but I noticed that it was only to hide her tears. A mother's heart knows, and her heart had already sensed the danger.

So it was that as soon as I heard the first scream, I myself ran for the rebbe.

"Shmyeh," he said to me. "What can I do? I will pray for her."

"Give me something, Rebbe," I pleaded, "anything to help the woman in her labor. A charm, a coin, a talisman . . . something with your blessing."

"God forbid! It will only make things worse," he replied. "Without faith such things can do harm. And she has no faith in these things."

What could I do? These were the first days of the Sukkot holiday. Gitele was having a difficult childbirth, but I could be of no help. I might as well stay in the rebbe's house. I was quite at home there; so I thought that if I spent every moment of my time gazing imploringly at the rebbe, perhaps he would take pity and relent.

Word came that things were bad. Gitele's pains had already lasted three days. Everything that could be done had been done: there were prayers in the synagogue; they had measured the graves in the cemetery; they had burned a hundred pounds of candles in the synagogue and in the study house, not to mention collecting a fortune in charity![3] What more is there to say? All the clothes closets stood open, a mountain of coins of all kinds lay on the table. The poor came in and helped themselves to as much as they wanted.

I took the whole thing very much to heart.

"Rebbe," I said. "After all, it is written, 'Charity saves from death.' "

He answered as if he had not understood: "Perhaps the Brisker rov will come."

At that very instant Reb Yekhiel entered the room. He ignored the rebbe, as if he did not see him, but turned instead to me. "Shmyeh," he said, catching hold of my lapel. "There is a wagon waiting out back. Get in and drive to the Brisker rov. Tell him to come." Obviously, he already sensed what was at stake, because he added: "Let him see for himself what is going on. Let him decide what to do!"

His face bore such a look—how else to describe it? Corpses have been known to look better.

So I set off, thinking to myself that since the rebbe knew that the Brisker rov was returning with me, something was bound to come of it, perhaps a reconciliation. That is to say, a reconciliation not between the Brisker rov and the Bialer rebbe, since the two of them had never fought each other, but between their two factions. Because, after all, when the Brisker rov came to Biala, he would see for himself how things were. He had eyes, after all.

But, obviously, Heaven does not encourage easy solutions. We had no sooner driven out of Biala than a large cloud suddenly surged across the sky, a cloud as heavy and black as pitch! Suddenly, there arose such a gust of wind as if demons were flying in every direction at once. A peasant like my driver understands such things, so he crossed himself and, pointing his whip at the sky, announced that we were going to have a difficult journey, Heaven help us. Even as he spoke, the wind increased, piercing the cloud as if it were tearing apart a sheet of paper. The wind began to chase one piece of cloud into and over another, as if herding ice floes on a river. Clouds, two and three stories high, were already hovering over my head.

At first, I was not even afraid. Getting drenched was nothing new

to me and I am not afraid of thunder. First, because it never thunders
at Sukkot time, and second, what evil could befall me so soon after
Rosh Hashana? We Hasidim of Biala knew that for an entire year
after the rebbe had blown the ram's horn for the New Year, thunder
could do us no harm. But suddenly I felt a smack across my face, as if I
had been struck with a whip. Once, twice, three times, and the color
drained from my face. It was clear to me that the heavens were slapping my face, that they were driving me back.

And the driver added his plea: "Let's turn back."

I knew, however, that I had been sent on a matter of life and
death. Sitting on the wagon in the thundering storm, I could hear
the groans of the woman in labor and the cracking knuckles of the
Brisker rov's son-in-law as he wrung his hands; and I saw before me
Reb Yekhiel's dark face with its sunken, burning eyes. "Drive on,"
he pleaded. "Drive!" So on we drove.

Still it continued to pour. The water streamed down from above
and splashed from beneath the wagon wheels and the horses' hoofs.
The road flooded, until it was entirely submerged, and a foam
hovered over the water. It seemed as if the wagon were beginning
to float. And as if this were not enough, we had also lost our way.
But I made it through!

I returned with the Brisker rov on Hoshana Raba, the seventh
day of Sukkot.

If truth be told, as soon as the Brisker rov climbed on the wagon,
the storm subsided. The clouds split apart and the sun shone through
the crack, so that we drove into Biala hale and dry. Even the driver
noticed the change in the weather and remarked in his language,
"A mighty rabbi." Or perhaps he said, "A great rabbi." I don't
remember which.

But the main thing was our arrival at Reb Yekhiel's house.

The women fell on the Brisker rov like a swarm of locusts. They
virtually prostrated themselves before him and wept. There was no
sound from the next room, where the woman in labor lay, either
because she could not be heard above the lamentations of the others,
or—I suspected the worst—because, Heaven forbid, she no longer
had the strength to groan. Reb Yekhiel did not even notice us. He
stood with his forehead pressed against a windowpane, apparently
to cool his burning head. Nor did the Brisker rov's son-in-law turn
around to greet us. He had his face to the wall, and I could clearly
make out his body and his head trembling against it.

I thought I would collapse with tears and sorrow. All my limbs,
my very soul, seemed to shiver with cold.

But we are dealing here with the Brisker rov! Here was a pillar of steel, I tell you! He was very tall, with stature "from the shoulder and up," as they once said of King Saul.[4] He could inspire the awe of a king. His beard was long and white. I remember as if it were yesterday how one tip of his beard was tucked under his belt, while the other quivered above it. His eyebrows—white, thick, and long— hid half his face. When he raised his brows—God in heaven!—the women fell back as if they were retreating from thunder. Such eyes he had! Knives, naked butcher knives, glinted in his eyes. He roared like a lion: "Women, out of the way!" Then more softly: "And where is my daughter?"

He was shown to her room, and I was left utterly overcome. Such eyes! Such a look! Such a voice! He was altogether different from anything I was used to. The Bialer rebbe's eyes shone with such kindness and such mildness that they brought joy into your heart. When the rebbe looked at you, it was as if you were being showered with gold. And his sweet voice—God in heaven!—it caught at your heart and caressed it so tenderly, so soothingly. No one was afraid of him—Heaven forbid. Instead, he melted your soul with the sweetness of love, so that it yearned to leave your body and unite with the rebbe's soul, like a butterfly drawn to bright flame. But the Brisker rov was fear and trepidation. The majesty of ancient times. That such a man should enter the room of a woman in labor!

I was terrified. "He will reduce her to a pile of bones," I thought. So I ran to the rebbe.

The rebbe greeted me at the door with a smile. "Did you see?" he asked. "Did you see the glory of the Torah?"

I calmed down. If the rebbe is smiling, I thought, then all must be well.

And, in fact, all was well. Gitele delivered her child on the eighth day of Sukkot. And the day after that, Simkhat Torah, found the Brisker rov expounding the Torah at the table. I would actually have preferred to have been elsewhere, at someone else's table, but I was afraid to leave, especially since I was needed for the quorum. They were about to recite the blessing Nivrakh Aleynu.[5]

How can I describe for you the Brisker rov's commentary on the Torah? If the Torah is a sea, then the Brisker rov was the leviathan in that sea. With one plunge he swam through ten tractates; with one sweep he encompassed the Talmud and the Commentaries. His words resounded and surged, sizzled and boiled, just as the real sea is said to do. He made my head swim. But it is written, "The heart knows the bitterness of the soul."[6] My heart did not rejoice in the holiday. That was when I remembered the rebbe's dream, and I froze. The sun shone through the window and there was no lack of wine on the table; I saw that the entire company was perspiring. And I? I was as cold as ice. I knew that over there, at the rebbe's table, they were expounding another kind of Torah. There it was bright and warm. Every word was interwoven with love and steeped in ecstasy. One could sense the angels fluttering around the room; one could almost hear the rustle of their large white wings. O God of the Universe! But it was not possible to leave.

Suddenly, the Brisker rov interrupted himself and asked: "What kind of Hasidic rebbe do you have here?"

"A certain Noah," someone answered.

It cut me to the quick to hear this "a certain Noah." Ah, the fawning flattery of such a response!

"A miracle worker?" the rov asked again.

"Very few miracles. We don't hear of them. The women say he performs wonders, but who listens to them?"

"He just takes money and performs no miracles?"

So they told him the truth, that the rebbe seldom took money and gave a lot of it away.

The Brisker rov grew thoughtful. "Is he a scholar?"

"They say a great one."

"Where is he from, this Noah?"

No one knew, so I was obliged to answer. This led to a conversation between me and the Brisker rov.

"Was this Noah, by any chance, ever in Brisk?" he asked.

"Was the rebbe ever in Brisk?" I stammered. "I think he was."

"Aha!" the rov exclaimed. "One of his followers." And I had the impression that he looked at me as if I were a spider.

He turned back to the company. "I once had a student," he said, "whose name was Noah. He even had a good mind. But he was drawn to the other side. If I told him once, I told him twice. . . . And I would have told him a third time. I would have warned him, but he disappeared. Could this be the same man?"

"Who knows?"

So the rov began to describe his student: a thin man, small, with a black beard, curly black sidelocks, a dreamy type with a soft voice, and so on.

The company answered that it was possible that this was he; it was very likely.

I thanked God that at that moment they began the blessing. But after the blessing something happened that I would never have dreamed possible.

The Brisker rov rose from his chair, took me aside, and whispered: "Take me to my former student, your rebbe. But take care! No one must know."

Obviously, I obeyed. But on the way I asked with trepidation, "Brisker Rov, with what intention do you pay this visit?"

He answered me plainly: "It occurred to me during the blessing that up to now I have judged him behind his back. I want to see— I want to see with my own eyes. And maybe," he added after a while, "God will help me and I will be able to rescue my pupil.

"You know," he continued jestingly, "if your rebbe is the same Noah who once studied with me, he could become one of the great men of Israel. He might even one day become the rov of Brisk."

Then I knew for certain that my rebbe was the same man, and my heart began to pound.

So the two mountains converged. And the fact that I was not crushed between them I consider to be a miracle from heaven.

It was the habit of the Bialer rebbe—may his memory be blessed— to send his Hasidim out for a walk around the city on Simkhat Torah, while he himself sat on his balcony and looked on with pleasure.

Biala was not then as it is today. It was, at that time, still a little town. All the houses were small and built low to the ground, with the exception of the synagogue and the rebbe's study house. The rebbe's balcony was on the second floor, and from there he could see everything as clearly as if it were on the palm of his hand—the hills to the east, and to the west the river.

The rebbe would sit on the balcony, surveying the scene. When he noticed that a few of the Hasidim were strolling about silently, he threw them the beginning of a melody. They caught it up and walked away singing. One group after another would then pass before the balcony on their way out of the town, singing with true joy, with genuine delight in the Torah. And the rebbe never moved away from the balcony.

This time, however, the rebbe apparently heard a different kind of step; so he arose and went out to meet the Brisker rov.

"Greetings, Rabbi," he saluted him humbly in his sweet voice.

"Greetings to you, Noah," the Brisker rov responded.

"Please sit down, Rabbi."

The Brisker rov sat and the Bialer rebbe stood before him.

"Tell me, Noah," the Brisker rov said, raising his eyebrows, "why did you run away from my yeshiva? What did you lack there?"

"What I lacked, Rabbi," Noahke answered with composure, "was air. I could never catch my breath."

"What do you mean? What are you talking about, Noah?"

"It was not I," explained the rebbe in a soft voice, "but my soul that lacked air."

"Why, Noah?"

"Your Torah, Rabbi, is nothing but law. It is without pity. Your Torah contains not a spark of compassion. And that is why it is without joy, without air to breathe. It is nothing but steel and iron— iron commandments, copper laws. It is a very refined Torah, suitable for scholars, for the select few."

The Brisker rov was silent, so the rebbe continued: "Tell me, Rabbi, what have you got for ordinary people? For the woodchopper, the butcher, the tradesman, the simple man? And, most especially, for the sinful man? What do you have to offer those who are *not* scholars?"

The Brisker rov maintained his silence, as if he had not understood what was being said. Still the Bialer rebbe stood before him and continued speaking in his mild voice.

"Forgive me, Rabbi, but I must speak the truth. Your teaching was rigid and dry, because it dealt only with the body, not with the soul of the Torah."

"The soul?" asked the Brisker rov, rubbing his high forehead.

"Certainly. Your Torah, as I have said, is only for the privileged few, for the learned, not for the ordinary man. But the Torah must be for all. God's emanation must rest on everyone, because the Torah is the soul of all the people of Israel."

"And your Torah, Noah?"

"Would you like to see it, Rabbi?"

"See the Torah?" The Brisker rov was astonished.

"Come, I will show you. I will show you the glory and the joy that radiate from it and touch all of Israel."

The Brisker rov remained motionless.

"Rabbi, I beseech you. Come. It is not far." He led him out on the balcony. I followed silently.

Nevertheless, the rebbe sensed my presence. "You may come along, Shmyeh," he said. "Today, you too shall see. And the Brisker rov will see. You will both witness Simkhat Torah, a true rejoicing in the Torah."

And I saw the same thing that I saw every Simkhat Torah, but this time I saw it differently, as if a curtain had fallen from my eyes.

The sky stretched above us, enormous, infinite, and of such a brilliant blue that it was a delight for the eye to behold. Across the sky floated white silvery clouds. When you looked closely at them, the clouds actually seemed to be trembling, as if they were dancing in joy at Simkhat Torah. Below, a broad green belt girded the town. Its color was a dark green, but so vibrant that the breath of life itself seemed to waft from the blades of grass. Now and again, little flames appeared to dance among the tufts of grass, each time in a different spot, as if embracing and caressing them.

Across the meadow with its many little flames strolled group after group of Hasidim. Their satin caftans, even those caftans made of cheaper cotton, glittered like mirrors, the tattered ones as well as the whole. The flames between the blades of grass flickered up around the shining holiday coats, so that they seemed to be dancing around each Hasid with love and ecstasy. And all the groups of Hasidim looked up at the rebbe with an extraordinary passion. I saw clearly how their thirsty eyes sucked in the light that shone from the rebbe's face as he stood on the balcony. The more light they absorbed, the louder they sang, ever louder and louder, ever more joyful, more holy.

Each group sang its own melody. But in the air, all the melodies and all the voices merged, so that only one tune reached the rebbe's balcony, as if they were all singing one song. Everything sang—the sky, the constellations above, and the earth below. The soul of the world sang. Everything sang!

God in heaven! I seemed to be dissolving in sweetness.

But it was not to be.

"We must say the afternoon prayer," the Brisker rov suddenly announced in his harsh voice—and everything vanished.

Silence fell. The curtain closed again before my eyes. Above me, an ordinary sky, and below, ordinary pasture; ordinary Hasidim in torn caftans murmuring old tattered fragments of song. The flames were extinguished. I looked at the rebbe. His face too was somber.

They did not reach an understanding. The Brisker rov remained a misnaged, just as before. And that was how he left Biala.

Yet their meeting did have some effect. The rov never again persecuted Hasidim.

1900 (translated by Goldie Morgentaler)

THE MISSING MELODY

▼

Es iz yahdua lakol—the whole world knows of the joy with which the rebbe of Nemirov, of blessed memory, would worship: like sunbeams flooding the earth, making us Jews forget our exile and our sorrow, making us forget ourselves, making all souls pour into the flame of his being. What burning joy! Some zaddikim know this joy on the Sabbath and holidays—the Vonvolitzer rebbe, of blessed memory, knew it at the close of Yom Kippur—and others at a holiday meal, after the conclusion of the study of a tractate, at a circumcision; but our rebbe, of blessed memory, was filled with joy all his life, till the moment of death, each note of his singing, every movement of his dancing, touched with the Holy Spirit. "I declare," he once cried out, eyes burning in ecstasy, "I declare that this world is nothing but a song and a dance before the Holy One, blessed be He; all mankind, all Jews, are singers; each letter of the Holy Torah, every soul in every body, is a musical note; every soul in every body is a letter in the Holy Torah; all souls together make up the Holy Torah; soul and Torah are one song before the King, King of Kings, blessed be He!

"What is more," he said, "as numerous as the voices which carry the song are the instruments, each with a melody to cleave to it, which it alone can play; for the instrument is the body, the melody its soul. Every man too is an instrument and life is his melody, happy or sad, at the end of which the soul flies from its body and the melody is reunited with the great melody before God's Throne of Glory. Woe to the man who lacks melody—it is like having no soul. That is no life but a long-drawn groan. Each group has its distinct melody, the zaddik its kapellmeister, and every man knows the part he must play so as not to spoil the song. But the kapellmeister needs to know the whole melody so as to conduct it well and to drive out the false notes, God shield us, like a dybbuk. Happy are you to have joyful melody!

"Talmudic scholars," he continued, "with all their shallow knowledge, are like visitors to the king's palace who have the pleasure of seeing it from the outside but cannot enter. They do not even dare to knock at the door for fear that it will remain shut; they gaze at the walls, the windows, the chimneys, and the flags high above the palace. At times they may see smoke rising from the chimneys and catch sounds of servants' voices passing through the corridors. But those truly immersed in the Torah, whose souls cleave to the Torah, enter the palace; they see the full glory of the king, they hear the songs of praise to the king, they become one with the whole before the king.

"The scholars are no more than workmen who make musical instruments and repair them but know nothing about playing. This is why they cannot enter the palace. They may make the instruments with great skill but are tone deaf, or their hearts are stopped up and cannot feel. A great craftsman among them may sometimes put an instrument to his lips, but the sound is cold and soulless. Real playing even the greatest of them does not know how to do.

"But I, thank the Lord," he concluded, "though I am no scholar— no workman, that is—and I neither make instruments nor mend them, I know how to play them all. . . . They are the vessels, we are the melody, they the clothes and we the humanity! They the bodies and we—souls!"

Happy is the man privileged to hear such words! Happy is the man who witnessed the ecstasy in the rebbe's court, though all that was a drop in the bucket compared to the joy at his daughter's wedding! Whoever did not go to Feigele's wedding does not know the meaning of a *simkha*.

On that occasion the Shekhina herself descended, enveloping the guests with the Holy Spirit. One felt how the great and the small, even the cooks and waiters, and even the wagoners who had brought the guests, were uplifted and crowned with the radiance. And even the peasants, as the rebbe remarked, were promoted to the status of righteous Gentiles.

The oldest guest there, Reb Tzatz, told me—and Reb Tzatz was not one to exaggerate—that this was the first proper *simkha* since the Creation. . . .

And imagine the celestial tumult when the rebbe danced before the bride! I only wish that the mockers and disbelievers, the critics and kvetchers, could have seen that ecstasy! They think this world is what they want; they should know how this world can be transformed into the World to Come, as a room lit with joy bright as sunshine. They would have kissed the rebbe's feet.

The rebbe's dance, even his weekday dance, was a sixtieth of paradise, but on that day it was certainly a third, possibly even a half.

The musicians set a happy mood. The guests, as customarily at weddings, spread to all corners. Some danced or clustered in small groups, others sang, drank, and made a proper babble.

Suddenly the rebbe, of blessed memory, got up and went to the middle of the room. He paused; then he lifted a finger as a sign for the musicians to stop playing. And so he stood in the middle of the room, face flaming with the Holy Spirit, eyes lit like stars, satin caftan flashing and shimmering, fur hat glittering with hundreds of silver arrows—a breathtaking sight.

There was a breathless hush; all eyes were fixed upon the rebbe. The pendulum of the clock could be heard in the distance as in the sweet stillness the rebbe began his quiet melody.

Midway he broke off to let out a series of distinct ragged sounds—everyone knew immediately what these meant! They were greetings sent throughout the world saying that Feigele's marriage—long life and *mazel* to her!—was taking place. And I felt as if I could see snow-white doves flying from the rebbe's mouth; indeed, he later admitted that the sounds were *shamosim*, messengers sent all over the earth to the animals, trees and grasses, deserts and forests, seas and rivers, to heaven and hell and the Garden of Eden, to the patriarchs and the heavenly hosts, inviting all to the wedding.

Suddenly, the room became twice as hot, and when the rebbe, of blessed memory, saw that these guests had arrived, he returned to his sweet melody, singing with words, holy words. And he began to dance, and all eyes dropped and were joined with his holy feet. Happy the eyes that saw it!

Everyone knows that right after the rebbe's death trouble befell his son-in-law and Feigele too, of blessed memory, and we were left like a flock without a shepherd; I set out on a quest throughout the Jewish diaspora, and what I sought, what my heart craved, I never found. I looked high and low, but true joy I found nowhere. Sadness, depression, broken hearts, that was all—joy was corked in its bottle. The wholeness of melody had vanished with the rebbe's death.

There was no singing, but wooden voices; no dancing, as the feet were stuck to the floor: clumsy hands, sluggish bodies—cold, frozen. The one time when there were singing and dancing, on Simkhat Torah, the feet did not move in harmony. Words, melody, and feet were like three strangers, each going his own separate way.

With the rebbe's death, joy vanished. He alone knew the soul of the dance, the melody and the words, which motions belonged to which tunes, which sounds suited which words.

But let us return to the story. The rebbe was singing and dancing in the middle of the room and we stood listening, encircling him, and we all began to sing and dance. Even the musicians cast aside their instruments and joined in, and I had the privilege of dancing face-to-face with the rebbe. Just then I noticed the groom. The groom alone was silent; he neither sang nor danced.

"Rebbe," I cried in a voice not my own, "even the musicians are singing and dancing and he is not."

The rebbe replied as he danced with me, "Don't be afraid; have faith in Feigele's good fate."

And later, before the festive meal, he whispered to me, "You'll see, his words of Torah will fit the spirit of my dancing."

And so it was. What the groom said in his wedding address I forget: you know I am no expert in that sort of thing, particularly as he spoke in a deep Lithuanian style and so quickly that his fiery words whirled before our eyes. Yes, his explication of Torah was very deep. The crowd, including several tens of great talmudic scholars, gaped at him. Even the brilliant Dayan of Kovel, of blessed memory, who was not in the habit of hearing anyone out—finger jabbing, he would shout at the first opportunity, "Ignoramus!"—even he sat quietly, a sweet smile on his fine features, listening intently, his head rocking back and forth.

Everyone heard, but I alone knew the secret, that he spoke what the rebbe had danced. They heard the outer meaning, but only I knew the essence of the words; my eyes were open to the rebbe's dance!

As with the rebbe, so with the groom. There was such silence that the pendulum of the rebbe's clock could be heard at a distance. The groom was in the center of the room encircled by guests with flaming faces, eyes burning, breathless with wonder.

The glory of the Torah rested sunlike upon the groom, casting its burning light upon all the flaming souls who stood around him. And his lips danced the pattern of the rebbe's feet. All eyes hung upon his lips as on the rebbe's feet. All were filled with pleasure and devotion.

At that moment he too became a rebbe . . . the soul of the congregation. . . . They were fixed to him like iron dust to a magnet. . . . As if by witchcraft he carried them far, far away, through street and town, over mountain and valley, sea and desert. . . . His eyes shone like the rebbe's, his hand moved like the rebbe's holy feet. . . .

I sat as in a dream, when suddenly someone touched my shoulder—the rebbe: "Look! That's how I danced, but the melody did not penetrate. It was blocked at the door. He is a student of the Vilna Gaon after all. . . . Ach!"

That groan went through my heart like a knife.

Suddenly, he said: "Go, Chaim, give the Gentile wagon drivers some whiskey." What he meant by that, I still have not begun to understand.

1902; in Hebrew, 1894 (translated by David Aberbach)

STORIES
▼

He strolled along the bank of the Vistula, thinking, "Today she will come."

And so thinking, he saw it all in the most vivid colors: He is sitting on the bed in his room, in the darkness, waiting. Every sound on the stairs makes his heart beat faster, and he asks himself, "Why? I'm not in love with her, am I?"

And then it is really she; he recognizes the light, swimming step. He gets up and kindles the lamp on the table. She, meanwhile, pauses on the other side of the door. She is catching her breath; the flight of stairs is a long one. She is putting her hair in order; she stops and peeps in through the keyhole. Then she taps with one finger on the door, almost inaudibly.

"*Prosze.* Come in."

She opens the door, and asks from the doorway, "Got any stories for me?"

"Yes, I have."

If he hasn't, she turns back. She doesn't like him, she says. In fact she's frightened of Jews. But she loves his stories.

Their acquaintance began in Warsaw's Saxony Park, in a downpour of rain. She stood under a tree. She wore a thin white blouse, and she had no galoshes on. The tree afforded little protection, and she kept glancing up through the sparse branches, her face expressing mingled fright and hope. As he was carrying an umbrella, he went up to her and offered his assistance. She hesitated. He pleaded earnestly with her, and finally she yielded. She excused her hesitation: there are so many bad people about. . . . But his voice, she said, gave her confidence. Encouraged, he offered her his arm; still hesitant, she took it and gave him her address.

As they walked along the streets—he had not the money for a droshky—she told him she was a seamstress. (True, he had noticed that her fingertips were pitted with tiny holes.) And she learned from him that he was a writer. Does he write songs? No, stories. Stories! She loves stories! To which he answered that he could tell her no end of stories. Would she let him come to see her? No. She had no father, and her mother was mean. When she said this, her voice trembled a little. The idea! A man coming to visit her, and a— a Jew at that. She did not use the word "Jew" easily; she blushed and threw a comical sideways glance at him. He asked, "How do you know I'm a Jew?" The eyes, the hair, the way he spoke, and— well—the nose. She giggled. Her voice was pure and childlike; and yet the forehead was already wrinkled.

During the summer they used to meet in Saxony Park. During the winter she would steal up to his room, at rare intervals, for a story. When she planned to do that, she would leave a message for him in the morning with the janitor. This very day he had received such a note from her. Her Polish was illiterate—a dozen mistakes on every line—but so childishly warm.

"Jew, have a story ready for me. But a happy one, with a princess. Life is so sad. And you musn't dare to touch me. I'm not interested in you. You are so ugly. If you touch me, I shall scream and run away. Do you hear?"

And yet he had ways of softening her: the story he is telling takes on a mournful tone—the king's son and the queen's daughter are in danger. The lovers have been driven apart by a terrible slander, the work of false people. And if he feels like it, he can throw the queen's daughter into a dungeon, while somewhere else, in an alien land, the king's son is being led to the gallows. They're the victims of a horrible frame-up. And then the listener throws herself on her knees before him and catches his hand; or she strokes his face in sheer pity for the unfortunate lovers. Then, for one kiss on the lips, he conjures away the dangers and brings prince and princess together to the strains of the wedding march.

Why does he do that? What does he want her kiss for?

He is sorry for it every time it happens—and yet there is something

that draws them to each other. Both are filled with longing for
happiness; both have missed it; both are willing to be deluded for a
few minutes. Two lost, desolate souls.

Once he asked her, "Does your mother ever hit you?"

She turned pale and her eyes flooded. "I won't tell you. I'd rather
hear your stories." And he stroked her brown hair and went on.

Now, as he strolled along the riverbank, he felt that he had no
story for her. His mind was confused and restless, like the water
dashing up against the bank. His thoughts wandered vaguely, like
the formless clouds overhead.

What obscure thing was it that was eating at his heart?

He remembered suddenly that he had not yet eaten that day.

There had been a sort of restlessness, a running about and a
rummaging in his lodgings. The sun had unexpectedly broken
through the clouds that morning, and, getting out of bed, he had
left the house without even drinking a glass of tea. The streets too
were oddly agitated. What the devil was it all about? Now and again
passersby jostled him. He had barely managed to make his way
down to the riverbank, where it was his habit to stroll mornings. By
now he was quite faint. He felt in his vest pocket. Yes, he still had
some change. He turned and made for the restaurant where he
usually took his lunch; there he sat down by a window that looked
out on the Vistula.

The restaurant was empty. Blondie sat behind the food-laden
counter, dozing. She woke as he came in, and greeted him sleepily.
Still half-asleep, she served him, then went back to her perch to
doze again. He ate meditatively: There *had* to be a story of a king's
son and a queen's daughter. She, the queen's daughter, would have
to be asleep somewhere on a mountain peak. A magician or a witch
would have to be guarding her. Today he would add something—
there would be a serpent at her feet. He'd given her so many queens'
daughters—the serpent would make a special impression. And the
mountain peak would be a lofty one. He had never seen a high
mountain but he would say: "High, very high, very high up . . ."
and she would lift up her eyes and follow his forefinger. Below the
point where the queen's daughter slept, he would draw about the
mountain a circlet of clouds, and to make it prettier the clouds
would be edged with crimson. Down in the valley no one knows
about the queen's daughter; the clouds conceal her. All through the
year the circlet hangs there. That too is a piece of magic. But high
up, way above the sleeping princess, there is an eternally blue sky;
she lies between cloud and heaven, the serpent at her feet.

He finished his meal. A king's son would have to be found on the way home. Meanwhile, he had to pay the check. Blondie still dozed.

He tried to waken her in his old, approved fashion: He would make bread pills and flick them at her long nose. One in twenty would hit the target, and Blondie would start out of her sleep, frightened. "I beg your pardon, sir. Is that your idea of a joke? What did you have, sir?" He would smile good-humoredly, tell her, and pay.

This time it didn't work. He aimed countless bread pills, but never hit the waitress. Meanwhile, he kept thinking of his prince.

He clawed out a soft lump of bread, rolled a few pills, forgot to aim them. The prince! He saw him suddenly. There he was, marching across field and forest. A raven, which he had once rescued from certain death, had told him the secret of the sleeping princess. . . . The raven flies before him, showing him the way. But of course, it won't be as simple as all that. One can't let the prince reach the happy end of the story in a single chapter. For when the story is ended, the listener goes home, and he is left alone with his agitated nerves and his incomplete thoughts. Well, then, he will bring in a wolf, and after that a river. So the prince will uproot a tree and float himself across the river on it. After that an impassable mountain will confront the prince, whereupon the raven will take him on its wings and fly him over. No, not the raven, but an eagle, the raven's uncle. And then—and then—well, after that the prince will simply start feeling hungry. The banal and the commonplace always have to come in. Even a king's son can become hungry in the midst of his adventures. The raven sets out to get food for him, but it's a long way to the nearest village, and the raven does not return. The sun blazes overhead; the barren fields stretch in every direction. If only wheat grew hereabouts, he would forget his dignity as a king's son and tear a few ears from the stalks. But nothing grows here except bitter herbs, and before flying away the raven warned him: "Don't touch them. They are poison." That's the work of the magician who guards the sleeping princess; for now we are not far from the mountain, and more than one adventurer has eaten of these bitter herbs and been poisoned.

How hard, how frightfully hard, it is to wait for the raven. The prince's heart faints in him. His eyes burn. Meanwhile, a peasant girl passes, carrying a loaf of bread, fresh, odorous bread; the smell of it fills his nose tormentingly.

"Peasant girl," he calls out in a weak voice, "a piece of bread."

"Pay," she answers curtly.

"I have no money."

"Those who have no money don't eat."

"I am a king's son. When I return to my home, I will send you a king's treasure."

"Tell it to the wind. . . . Debts written in water . . ."

"I am dying of hunger."

"What's new about that? It's happened to your betters."

She walks on a little space, then turns back.

"I'll tell you what. I like you. Marry me and I'll give you bread."

"I can't. I'm in love with the queen's daughter."

"And you want to eat?"

"I'm hungry."

"Marry me and you'll not be hungry."

The peasant girl was obstinate; hunger gnawed at him, and he had to yield. He pledged her eternal faithfulness. A hare ran across the field, and they called it to witness the marriage. The king's son snatched a piece of bread, and followed the peasant girl to the village.

Blondie opened an eye and closed it again. The story wove itself on.

For a long time the prince lay sick in the village; the fresh bread had been too much for him. Then he became better and married the peasant girl. And since he could neither plow nor sow nor reap, but could read and write, he became the village teacher. Their married life was peaceful. The peasant girl used to call him, lovingly, "my little loony," and he would smile foolishly. But he kept the queen's daughter in a secret place in his heart. Who knew? The peasant girl used to work with the nobleman's automatic reaper; someday something might happen, then he would renew the quest. Of course, he never clothed the thought in words—quite possibly he was not even aware of the thought. The hope found a hiding place in an obscure corner of his heart, and he kept the secret to himself.

But nothing happened to his peasant wife. Indeed, she became sturdier and stronger from day to day. Not so with him. It may have been the coarse peasant fare, and it may have been the vain longing in his heart; in any case he aged early. And when he observed that his beard had turned gray, that his eyes were dimming, that his forehead was wrinkled, he called his pupils to him and, weeping, revealed to them the secret of the queen's daughter. They broke into laughter: Teacher had taken leave of his senses! And yet . . .

He became aware that the light had changed. Darkness had fallen.

He looked out through the window; the weather too had changed. A wet snow was falling. He felt a contraction of the heart. Hastily, he picked up a bread pill and threw it. This time he hit the target, and Blondie woke up.

"Come here, Blondie. I'll tell you a story."

"*Mnie poco?* What would I want stories for?"

"It's a pretty story, all about peasant boys in search of a princess."

"That's silly."

"No, it's not silly. The princess is asleep on a flowerbed on the summit of a mountain. The village teacher told them to look for her."

"Not a bad idea."

"Sure it's not a bad idea. The princess is good and beautiful and clever."

"Quit making fun of me. You'd better pay and go."

"Sure, sure. But the youngsters of the village armed themselves with wooden swords and wooden spears."

Blondie yawned.

"Are you tired?"

"God, what weather!" And she added irritably: "Whenever there's a Jewish holy day, there has to be bad weather."

"What sort of holy day do you mean?"

"It's their Easter."

So that was the meaning of the running about in his lodgings, the restlessness in the streets! Passover!

He paid and ran out.

In the street he burst into laughter.

Somewhere in him a reincarnated soul was stirring: a grandfather's, or a great-grandfather's. What a pang of homesickness! Every man is a carrier of reincarnated souls.

The first year he was away from home he nearly went out of his mind with homesickness when the night of the seder came around. The family where he lodged had been invited out for the seder, and he had the run of the house to himself. He went to bed early, having nowhere to go. But he had forgotten to pull down the shades, and the moonlight woke him. He came to with a painful beating of his heart. He lay there a long time, wondering what it was. Then he remembered. Suddenly, he sprang up, tore the sheet off the bed, wound it about him like the white ceremonial garment his father wore at the seder, and ran from room to room bellowing the seder prayers at the top of his voice, by heart. The second year, terrified by the recollection of his homesickness, he sold his overcoat and made a trip home for Passover. On the way home he kept repeating to himself that he was going to give in, give in completely. And indeed, he went with his father to synagogue, came home, let his mother prepare the seat for him at the seder table, with the ceremonial cushion; and at the right moment he asked the ritual Four Questions of the seder. But when it came to that part of the ceremony which recounts the Ten Plagues visited on the Egyptians, he could not stand it anymore. He simply refused to follow the hallowed custom of flipping a drop of wine out of his glass at the mention of each plague. And further on in the service, where the sages of old discuss the manifold character of the plagues—the plagues within the plagues, as it were—he almost ran from the room. It was all his mother could do to keep him there. But on the third day of Passover he left, without saying good-bye to his father. His mother waited for him outside the city.

He mounted the stone stairway from the riverbank.

He was sorry for that incident now. What sense had there been in hurting them so? In those days he used to justify himself by saying, "For the sake of the truth." Was there such a thing as truth?

His thoughts ran on. "We, the younger ones, must suffer. Our pains are creative; they drive us to new work, the production of new forms. But the pains of the old people are fruitless; they only end in futile tears, and the heart remains petrified."

He traversed Krasinski Park. The dairy stand was deserted. Belated people hurried along the walks. He drew near the hillock that looked out over Nalewki Street. He was tired, but it was still too early to go home. He sat down on a bench facing the hillock.

On its lower slope the hillock was bare, as if a barber had shorn it; higher up there were tufts and patches of grass and thorns, here and there a bush or even a clump of trees. Birds could nest and sing there. *She* was very fond of birds. Once she used to work in the country, and whenever she heard birds singing, the tears came to her eyes and she couldn't hold them back; it was as if her soul wept, she said, it was so sweet.

And there were times when she talked in such a strange, wonderful way. She would play with the tips of her long white fingers, with their needle scars; or she would touch the tips of her even whiter teeth. She would use expressions like "soul-star." Where had she picked it up? Perhaps she too was a concealed princess; her mother, with her washing bales, was no mother, but a witch, watching over her to see that no stranger prince approached and woke her up.

Well, if that was so, he wasn't the prince. The prince had to be free from sin.

A nurse with four little charges hurried by. The boys turned aside and began running toward the hill. Boys armed with swords and spears—"they ascend the mountain." The nurse became angry: it was time to go home; their parents would be worrying—it was a festival day. The boys paid no attention: "To the princess!"

He closed his eyes and saw the village schoolmaster's pupils mounting the hill to the princess, their wooden weapons in their hands. A cloud is spread between the "rescuers" and the princess. They do not see her; they only believe in her. Shall he let them reach her?

And here the old witch comes swooping down through a cloud, riding on her broomstick.

She takes one of the boys by the hand.

"Where are you going, little one?"

"To the princess."

"What have you to do with her?"

"I want to waken her."

"What for?"

"I want to marry her."

"What do you want to marry her for?"

"She's so good! Our teacher told us. And she's clever and sweet. Teacher knows."

"Sure he does! And you, of course, like good, sweet things."

"You bet I do. Mama calls me 'Sweet Tooth.' "

"Well, you silly little boy, what's the sense of crawling all the way up the mountain and getting tired out? I can see you're a noble and delicate child—"

"What's that got to do with you?"

"You silly fellow, don't you see I'm your auntie? Don't you know me? I'll give you all kinds of sweet things."

She waves her broomstick in the air. Hocus-pocus! And right at the boy's feet falls a basket full of the loveliest things; almonds in their yellow chemises, pressed figs, bunches of raisins, flaming oranges, chocolates, and other tempting things that the boy doesn't even know by name. He utters a cry of glee and falls on his knees before the lovely basket.

Meanwhile, the other three go on. Against them comes the magician, old, white-bearded, with heavy white eyebrows, and big blue spectacles on his nose.

He heard the creaking of the park gate and opened his eyes. The nurse and her charges had disappeared. He got up from the bench and hurried out into the almost deserted Nalewki Street. Meanwhile, the story went on weaving itself in his brain.

The old magician stops one of the three.

"Where are you off to, young man?"

"To waken the princess. I want to marry her."

"What for?"

"Teacher told us wonderful things about her. She's so clever."

"You want to learn from her how to be clever?"

"Sure I do. A man ought to be clever. If you're clever you get money and medals."

"Well, well, I can see that you're quite clever already. And if you want, you can become as clever as can be, without the princess."

"How?"

"Very simple. Here!"

The old man takes out of his inside pocket a little book bound in white leather and edged with gold, and hands it to the boy who is quite clever already.

"Sit down and read. When you'll have read one page through, you'll be cleverer than Daddy and Mama; after the second page you'll be cleverer than everyone in the village; and by the time you're in the middle of the book you'll be as clever as three professors."

The youngster snatches the book and sits down to read.

The last two have meanwhile gone on. Suddenly, a snake blocks their path. One of them runs away; the other remains, paralyzed with fear.

But the snake doesn't bite him. It draws its tail across its fangs and asks in a snakish-friendly voice:

"Whither away, young man?"

Well, he's going to the princess, to wake her up and marry her, because Teacher said she was beautiful.

"Do you like beautiful things?"

"Of course."

"Then come with me. Do you see that crystal palace over there? It's full of little dolls; they wear sateen dresses and slippers of white silk. They have cherry-red lips and eyes that flash like precious stones. You'll choose the doll that you love best, and look, you won't have far to walk; it's close by, no climbing."

But what about the fourth one, the one who ran away and returned? What's to be done with him? Let him reach the princess? That would be a pity. He would be the unhappiest of boys. He would be left without anything—he would not even have a vain longing to look back on or self-reproaches to cling to.

And yet for her sake he must do it. He must let the boy reach the princess.

After which, a wedding ceremony, music, dancing, a honeymoon trip, a stroll in the hanging gardens.

And *she*—she will close her eyes blissfully, and she will be so moved that she will let him put his arms round her and draw her on to his lap, and he will wonder what he is doing it for. She will put her hot cheek to his, he will feel her sweet breath, he will kiss her, and inwardly he will say to himself, "Swine!" She will jump from his lap, terrified, and she will start crying brokenly, and he will throw himself at her feet and implore her pardon, and in his heart he will say to himself, "Clown!" And she will forgive him at last, but for a long time she will not come to see him again.

Somebody elbowed him aside; he slipped and almost fell down on the wet pavement.

The staircase lay in shadow—only one oil lamp for two flights. He had no matches. His neighbor on the same floor had a flashlight, but he didn't envy him that; the man's wife was so ugly. Whenever he passed their door, he trembled lest she show herself. Ugliness is the greatest of all sins. And if the woman was ugly, the servant girl was uglier. He shuddered, partly out of revulsion, partly with the cold. He had forgotten that his spats were torn and he had stepped into puddles. In the night he would cough and perhaps run a temperature. The doctor would come and threaten him again with tuberculosis. Who cared? Let it be tuberculosis, as long as something happened.

He stood stock-still in terror.

There in the dark corner of the stairway a picture had suddenly risen before him. A seder table, a snow-white, gleaming tablecloth, three engraved red wine beakers, gleaming plates, silverware, candles in three tall, wrought-silver candlesticks: Mother stands there, saying the benediction over the candlelight. . . . She has her back to him. . . . Her shoulders tremble. . . . She is weeping into her hands . . . weeping for him. . . . Where is he? Where is he now?

"Ha, it's beginning!" In a rage he dashed up the remaining steps three at a time. And then suddenly he regretted the rage and the hurry. His mother might have turned around to him. What did she look like now? She wrote that she lay awake through the nights.

She'd sent him four pairs of socks a little while back. "Do be careful and keep your feet warm."

"Bah!" He shook himself. "A man must be a man."

He entered his room with firm footsteps; with firm hand he lit the lamp. He didn't like the dark. He looked around. "What poverty!" Cobwebs in the corners; but, as against that (he smiled bitterly), at least no scrap of the forbidden leavened bread. Well, tomorrow someone would invite him out; he would hang around the German synagogue at service time; he knew a certain teacher. . . .

He sat down on the bed. The lamp smoked a little; he got up to fix it, and forgot himself. What was it he had got up for? He sat down again, drew his feet onto the bed. His eyes fell on the mirror hanging by the bed. He took it down and examined himself.

He smiled. "I'm not as ugly as she makes me out." He hung the mirror up again. "Yes, rather dark, like a Tatar, but what eyes!"

He is proud of his eyes. Few women can look at them and not be moved. When he becomes intimate with a woman, she always kisses him on the eyes. His lips—well, they were a little too full—too ready to kiss, dangerous. Even in the old days, when he lived at home . . .

The thread breaks. What's happening at home just now? Has Father come back from the synagogue service?

He hears his father's greeting: "Happy Festival!" He hears his mother's answer. No happiness in the voices. How can there be, God help them? An only son, and he far away.

He tries to shift his thoughts to other matters, but without success. The seder refuses to be conjured away. This is the fifth year.

He gets up from the bed and walks over to the window. The wet stones in the courtyard below throw back in flickering ribbons the festive lights in the apartments opposite. He will not lift his eyes to the windows above. But he must. He lifts them slowly, but halfway to the first floor he stops again, as if paralyzed. Another picture:

A seder table, utensils of gold and crystal. Is it a family? No, it must be a gathering of several families. The women are in strange habit, fashions that have passed away many generations ago. Men in white, embroidered ruffs under their white covering garments— golden circlets, gold-embroidered skullcaps. What part of the seder service is this? A murmurous recitativo—

Then suddenly a knock at the outside door.

From outside a voice: "Open in the name of the law!"

Ha. The blood libel![1]

"Quickly! Look under the table!" At the patriarch's order they bend down and discover—a dead child. They freeze in horror.

The patriarch of the family stands up and issues commands in a tense but firm voice.

"Put it on the table and cut it up."

"Everyone take a piece on his plate."

It is done. The intruders are now banging at the inner door.

"Eat!"

The pieces are eaten up. Police and soldiers burst in then. They look everywhere in vain. They go out raging. And when they are gone, the furious cry of the prayer goes up from the assembly of celebrants:

"*Pour forth Thy wrath upon the heathen that know Thee not. . . .*"

"Not for me," he thinks. "That needs a stronger pen than mine."

Better, then, to lie down on the sofa, with closed eyes.

His strength is gone, eaten away by moodiness.

There are easier pictures to paint.

For instance: the famous seder where the Master of the Name, the Baal Shem, the founder of Hasidism, presided. No—that isn't it either. The seder he is thinking of was celebrated in the house of a rich Jew who was actually a misnaged, an opponent of Hasidism. The Baal Shem humbled himself and sought an invitation to the man's seder. Couldn't get it so easily either.

That was at the synagogue service before the seder. The Baal Shem *asked* for the invitation, saying humbly to the rich Jew: "Let me come. You'll find me useful."

The rich man consulted the rabbi. Was it permissible to have a Hasid at one's seder? The rabbi answered yes; it was a sin to shame a man by a refusal.

And the Baal Shem sits quietly at the seder. The first part passes— the Four Questions—and the passage beginning, "Slaves we were unto Pharaoh." And suddenly the Baal Shem speaks up and asks that an additional prayer book be brought, and an additional prayer robe. Laughter breaks out at the table. The tone of the Baal Shem changes. "I command it!" What's this? An hour ago he was begging for an invitation, and now he's issuing commands at table! The master of the house stares at him; the eyes of the Baal Shem are blazing. Fear takes hold of the host. He orders the prayer book and the robe brought and placed before the Baal Shem. Then the Baal Shem kicks at something under the table and says: "Yantek! Stand up!" And from under the table there crawls forth and rises to his feet a young peasant lad, his face bloodless, a corpse with closed eyes, and across his throat a cut. The guests start back.

"Yantek! Open your eyes!"

Yantek obeys.

"Yantek, put on the robe, tie up the girdle, put on the skullcap."

Yantek obeys.

"Give him a chair. Yantek, sit down!"

Yantek sits down in robe and skullcap.

"Open the Haggadah and say the prayers with us."

The celebrants tremble and mumble the prayers, and Yantek murmurs with them. Suddenly, the door is broken open. It is the old story. They have come to look for the corpse they planted under the table—there is no sign of it. The intruders withdraw, baffled and ashamed.

The Baal Shem turns to the resurrected corpse:

"Yantek! Close your eyes again, and go to the cemetery and bury yourself. And because it has been your privilege to wear a Jewish prayer robe, and say a Jewish prayer, your resting place will be the Jewish cemetery. And when you meet Father Abraham, you will say to him—"

A light tap on the door.

"Come in."

"Got any stories?"

"All kinds."

1903 (translated by Maurice Samuel)

REVELATION; OR, THE STORY
OF THE BILLY GOAT

▼

Reb Nakhmanke[1] told the story on a Sabbath evening, a few weeks after he had been "revealed"—that is, made manifest to the world in his capacity as zaddik.

The revealing of the zaddik is—or was—usually accidental, and certainly unsought. It goes something like this: A man or a woman in trouble will come to the zaddik and seek his advice; it may be concerning a match for his daughter, a remedy for the prevention of childlessness or illness, or merely a matter of a livelihood. The zaddik, whose spirit has been sojourning in the upper spheres, cannot refuse to receive the suppliant, and listening to the pitiful story, he is moved to say something. The words prove to be prophetic. They are fulfilled. This happens once, twice; then the truth swims out like oil on water. People begin to come from all over.

So it happened with Reb Nakhmanke, for he was never a man to refuse anyone. A light went up in Israel, and all the windows shone.

The town rejoiced, of course. What a break! On the one hand, there was misery aplenty; a zaddik would be extremely useful. On the other hand, it meant business. Jews would come from the four corners of the earth. And so little miracles multiplied, like mushrooms after a rain. The word went out among all the nearby villages: Here's a saint who refuses no one, and whatever he utters is law. Before the first week is ended, before the Sabbath has come, two walls in the zaddik's house are broken through; a table is laid along the length of three rooms. There will be guests from the big city, guests from the villages, and from the surrounding towns. Wines and fruits will be needed—and the harvest, as it happens, has been a good one.

On that Sabbath evening, two or three weeks after the revealing, the town was caught up in a wave of jubilation. The singing of Sabbath-evening songs and dancing about the laden table was such as to engage the stars in heaven to dance their accompaniment. Only Reb Nakhmanke sat apart. And when the time came for him to say the valedictory prayer to the departing Sabbath, a great sadness overcame him, and the wine cup in his hand trembled so that they feared he would let it fall. After the valedictory prayer he sat down again in a corner, murmured a last prayer to himself, then suddenly rose and left the room.

The congregation made as if to follow him, but he turned round and shook his head. They remained in the room, but crowded to the window to follow him with their eyes. They saw him cross the marketplace with faltering steps, stooped like a man in grief, and disappear into the fields beyond.

And now a real heaviness of heart settled on the assembled. Some returned to the table, a few went home; those who remained tried to strike up a melody—it did not take. They sent for brandy—no one felt like drinking.

What was it? What did the rabbi lack? What *could* a man in his position lack?

"Well, as far as his livelihood is concerned . . ." began someone coarsely, and went no further, for the looks that were turned on him froze the roots of his soul. And yet the question remained: a man who had attained that degree of sanctity should radiate only happiness.

Reb Joshua the Teacher, a sweet-tempered man who had once lived in the kingly presence (that is, he had known the Baal Shem in person), was moved to anger:

"Here is a man who can help thousands of Jews, and yet he is s-s-sad," he stammered. "He can even cause a harsh decree issued from above to be abrogated. Isn't that true?"

"Indeed it is," they chorused. For Reb Nakhmanke had already done much in these few weeks. And they began to recount his miracles. I will not set them down here; they are a drop in the ocean compared with his later wonders. But one little story I will tell out of those early days, for it shows his humility and his kindness.

There was an old woman in the town, a simple old soul, the widow of some tailor. All she had in the world was a nanny goat, and this is what she lived off. The nanny goat was not worth a bit of snuff, but it was enough for her. As the years passed, the old woman found it harder and harder to milk the goat. Her hands became very shaky, and so she would lose a few drops at every milking—and there was not, God knows, too much milk in the nanny goat at best. Finally, she dragged the animal to Reb Nakhmanke and lodged a complaint against it as lacking in respect for an old woman and refusing to stand still while being milked. Reb Nakhmanke listened patiently and smiled; then he said: "Go home, woman. Help will come to you." And help did come to her. Not that her hands became any steadier—the poor creature was every bit of eighty, or maybe nearer ninety; but a wonderful change came over the nanny goat. It became, as it were, another animal; it began to turn up at milking time; it would stand quietly with uplifted leg till the last drop of milk had been squeezed out of it.

The assembly was so absorbed in the various stories of Reb Nakhmanke's wonders that they did not notice his return. Suddenly, they heard his voice at the window: "Once again, Jews, a happy week to you all!"

There he was, his elbows on the sill, his head on his arms. His eyes shone with a queer kindly light—kindly, yet somehow not happy.

"I am going to tell you a story," he said. "Listen and do not think it strange."

They wanted to bring a chair out for him. No, he preferred to stand. So some of them came out, and some remained in the room, and standing thus in their midst, with the moon over him like a crown, he told them the story of the billy goat and of the meaning of "revealing."

"Once," he began, and his voice was steeped in sorrow, "there was a billy goat. A billy goat like all other billy goats. Or perhaps it was different, bigger. I don't know. No one ever measured it. For the billy goat loved loneliness and never ventured among other living things. Perhaps this billy goat was an eldest son—and perhaps not.

"Outside the village there was a ruin, which had been standing there as long as men remembered. It was said, and no doubt with truth, that it was the ruin of a holy place, a synagogue or a study house. Men had prayed here once, had studied the sacred books. When the building was destroyed, someone may have been martyred here, died for the Sanctification of the Name. Old stories, these were. Now grass grew in the ruin, a strange kind of grass that no one sowed and no one cut. In this ruin the billy goat lived, and this was the grass he ate.

"The grass that grows in these ruins is, as I have said, no ordinary grass. It is a wonderful specific for horns. The horns of an animal cropping here grow to an unbelievable length. Such horns are likewise remarkable in another respect—they are alive. They can curl themselves up at will, and they can unfold and become revealed. And as long as they remain curled up, no one seeing them would suspect anything. But when they unfold, they can reach to the uppermost heavens.

"This billy goat of ours was a Nazarite, a dedicated soul, attentive to his vows. No grass but such grass as grew in the ruin ever touched his lips. Nor would he eat at random even in the ruin. He had a great understanding of grass, and he chose only the richest and best, both for taste and for smell. Here was a patch that grew where the Torah had been devoutly studied; there was a patch that grew in memory of particularly soulful prayer; elsewhere—most precious to him of all—grass sprouted from soil that was soaked in the blood of a Jewish martyr. The billy goat ate carefully, and the horns grew faster and faster.

"Being a Nazarite and a hidden wonder, the billy goat kept his horns curled up. But in the night, when the town sleeps, save for those Jews who say their midnight prayers in the study house, in the night, when the heartache of the psalm 'By the waters of Babylon' is poured out between heaven and earth, an agony of longing would come over the billy goat.[2] Then he would stand up on his hind legs and straighten out his horns heavenward; and if there happened to

be a new moon there, recently sanctified by Jewish prayer, he would
hook the tips over the lower edge and say: " 'What news, holy moon?
Is not the hour of the Messiah come yet?'

"The moon would pass the questions on to the stars, and they, in
deep perturbation, would arrest their motion, and the moon's with
it. Then the night would stand still, and the song of the night would
break off. The attendants about the Throne of Glory, marking the
sudden silence, would send down a messenger to find out the cause;
and he would bring back word that moon and stars were motionless
until they were told whether or not the hour of the Messiah had
yet come. But the only answer from the Throne of Glory was a
melancholy sigh.

"Nevertheless, such questionings can have their effect—"

Here Reb Nakhmanke broke off. He covered his face with his
hands, and the listeners saw clearly how head and hands trembled;
and the moon, which hung over him like a crown, seemed to be
trembling too. Then after a time Reb Nakhmanke lifted up his head.
His cheeks were pale, and his voice shook as he continued:

"Mark well that it was no small act of grace on the part of the
billy goat that he remained among us, here below, on earth. Another
than he, possessed of horns that he could hook over the moon,
would have swung himself up and entered paradise while yet living—
what would he have cared about us? But this billy goat had a
compassionate soul; he thought of the congregation and could not
bring himself to abandon it.

"For life is hard here below. Years of hunger come, and the congregation begins to break up. The women sell their jewels, the men
the gold and silver ornaments on their prayer shawls. The times
grow harder; the little ones are taken out of school, there's no money
to pay the teacher. And still the misery grows, pestilence follows
starvation—and now he *must* do something.

"Up in the heaven there is the Milky Way, as human beings call
it. It is not a way at all, for no foot treads it and no wheels roll on
it. It is a stretch of great fields sown with precious stones, with
countless diamonds and pearls. These are diamonds and pearls for
the crowns of the saints in paradise. No one knows or cares to know
their number—they are like the sands on the seashore. They multiply
from year to year, while the number of crowns needed for newcomers
to paradise diminishes from year to year.

"Then at last the suffering on earth below becomes unbearable, and the secret owner of the hidden horns takes action. When it is midnight in the town, and voices in the study house are heard lamenting over the exile of Israel and the exile of the Divine Glory, the billy goat rears up on his hind legs, straightens out his horns, and directs them toward the Milky Way. There he pulls out a precious stone and flings it all the way down into the marketplace. The stone shatters into a thousand fragments, and Jews going home after their midnight lamentations see them sparkling on the ground—and so there is something to live on for a while.

"That is why the billy goat cannot abandon the community—"

Again Reb Nakhmanke broke off, to resume sadly after a while:

"And his kindness of heart was the undoing of him. Because of his compassion and sweetness he was 'revealed.' I mean—his horns. And the beginning of it was so trifling—the snuff habit."

And now there was something utterly fantastic in Reb Nakhmanke's tone; the listeners did not know whether it wept or laughed.

"The snuff habit," he repeated. "Jews took to snuff; it became a custom everywhere. They said it did them good: a sound sneeze cleared the eyes. And of course if people take snuff, they have to have snuffboxes. And snuffboxes are best made of goat's horn. So whenever a Jew finds a piece of goat's horn, he makes himself a snuffbox. Sometimes he stops a goat, asks for a piece of horn, and gets butted for his pains. But one day a Jew happened to be passing the ruin and chanced on our billy goat. He said:

" 'Billy goat, firstborn or not firstborn, give me a piece of horn for a snuffbox.'

"In the kindness of his heart the billy goat could not say no. He pushed out the horn, and the Jew cut off a piece and made himself a snuffbox. In the study house he offers the other Jews a pinch of snuff, and they say, 'Where did you get such lovely horn?' He tells them—and in a few days every snuff taker in the town has already sought out the billy goat among the ruins. He never says no to anyone. He bends down his head and lets them cut off a piece of horn. Before long the fame of his kindness has spread through the land. Jews come from every corner—and are provided with snuffboxes.

"And there is only one drawback to this kindness. Before long the billy goat will not be able to reach the moon with his horns, to inquire after the Messiah. Neither will he be able to pry a jewel out of the Milky Way and cast it down to earth."

With that Reb Nakhmanke stopped, turned from his listeners, and walked away. At the same moment a cloud covered the moon, and a mingling of sadness and fright fell on the assembly.

Yet, as we know, the matter ended well after all.

1904 (translated by Maurice Samuel)

THE MAGICIAN

▼

A magician once came to a town in Volhynia.

Although he arrived in the hectic days before Passover, when a Jew has more worries than hairs on his head, the newcomer made a great impression. Indeed, he was a walking mystery: he was dressed in rags but wore a creased yet still serviceable top hat, and while God had given him a clearly Jewish nose, his face was as clean-shaven as a Christian's. He had no travel papers either, and was never observed to touch food, whether kosher or treyf. It was anyone's guess who he was. If you asked him where he was coming from, his answer was "Paris," and if you inquired where he was going, it was "London." What was he doing in Volhynia? "I lost my way." And from the looks of it, he had come on foot! Nor did he ever go to synagogue, not even on the Sabbath before the holiday. If a crowd gathered around him, he would suddenly vanish as if swallowed by the earth and reappear on the far side of the marketplace.

Meanwhile, he rented a hall and began to put on magic shows.

And what magic! Before everyone's eyes he swallowed burning coals as though they were egg noodles and pulled colorful ribbons from his mouth: red ones, green ones, any color you wanted—and as long as the exile of the Jews! Once he even pulled sixteen pairs of turkeys from his boots. Turkeys? Each was as big as a bear! They were still running around the stage when he lifted his shoe and started scraping gold rubles from the sole, and the audience was still shouting "Bravo!" when he let out a whistle and fresh khallahs and rolls flew through the air as if on wings, danced in a circle on the floor, and stamped angrily on the ceiling. Another whistle, and it all

disappeared into thin air. Rolls, khallahs, turkeys, everything—gone!
Of course, it was no secret that the devil and his helpers could do
such tricks too. Didn't the Bible say that Pharaoh's sorcerers worked
even greater wonders in Egypt? The real riddle was: why was such
a talent such a pauper? The man scraped rubles off his shoes and
couldn't afford to pay for his hotel room! He whistled up more rolls
and khallahs than a baker could bake, pulled turkeys out of his
boots, and had a face so pinched that a corpse's was better-looking!
Hunger burned in his eyes like two bonfires. Instead of the Four
Questions, the townspeople said, this year at the seder there would
be five.

But before we get to the Four Questions, let's leave the magician
and have a look at Chaim-Yona and his wife, Rivke-Beyle. Chaim-
Yona was once a lumber merchant—that is, until he bought "at a
good price" the rights to a forest in which the government quickly
barred all lumbering, leaving him completely ruined. For a while he
worked as a forestry clerk, but eventually he lost this job too, and in
the months before the magician's arrival he had been unemployed.
The worst enemies of the Jews shouldn't have to live through such
a winter! And to make matters worse, after the winter came Passover.
Every item in the house had already been pawned, from the
chandelier on the ceiling to the last cushions on the couch. "You
had better go to the Poor Fund," Rivke-Beyle told her husband,
"and ask for some money for the holiday." But Chaim-Yona wouldn't
hear of it: he had faith in God and was not about to stoop so low.

Rivke-Beyle searched the house again, ransacking every corner,
and managed to find an old silver spoon that had disappeared years
ago. It was nothing short of a miracle. She gave the spoon to Chaim-
Yona, who went, found a buyer for it, and donated the pittance he
received to the Poor Fund. The poor, he explained to his wife,
needed money for Passover.

Meanwhile, time was not standing still. The holiday was just
around the corner. Chaim-Yona had faith: God, he said, would
provide. What could Rivke-Beyle do but bite her lips? A woman lets
her husband have his way. But the days went by one after another,
and at night, unable to sleep, she buried her face in the straw
mattress to keep Chaim-Yona from hearing her sobs. There wasn't
a sign of Passover in the house yet! And the days were worse than
the nights, because at night she could cry and feel better, while by
day she had to pinch her cheeks to put some color in them for the
neighbors. Not that the neighbors were fooled: each time they

stepped into her house, their pitying looks pierced her like nails. "When will you bake your matzas?" their stares said. "Where are the beets for your borscht?" Her closest friends told her:

"Look, what's with you, Rivke-Beyle? If you need anything, just ask. It's no problem."

But Chaim-Yona refused to accept "charity" and Rivke-Beyle couldn't disobey him. She had no choice but to invent all kinds of unlikely excuses, her face burning as she did. Seeing how things stood with her, the neighbors went to the rabbi. He had to do something! The rabbi, whose position was not to be envied, listened, sighed, thought a while, and said that Chaim-Yona was certainly a learned and pious Jew and that faith in God was faith in God.

In a word, it was already Passover eve and Rivke-Beyle didn't even have candles to light for the holiday!

That evening Chaim-Yona came home from the holiday prayer in the synagogue. In every house the windows were festively lit except in his own, which was like a mourner at a wedding, or like a blind man among those who can see. Still, his spirits did not flag. "If God wants us to have a Passover seder," he thought, "then a Passover seder we'll have!"

"Happy Passover!" he called out to his wife when he came home. "A happy holiday to you, Rivke-Beyle," he repeated.

"A happy holiday to you too," Rivke-Beyle's tearful voice answered from a dark corner.

Her eyes burned in the darkness like two coals. Chaim-Yona went over to her. "Rivke-Beyle," he said, "tonight is the celebration of the exodus from Egypt, don't you know that? We're not allowed to grieve! And what is there to grieve about? If the good Lord doesn't want us to have a seder here, we'll do His will and have it elsewhere. We'll go to somebody's house. No one will turn us away. All doors are open tonight—doesn't it say in the Passover Haggadah, 'Koyl dikhfin yeysey veyeykhul'?" In plain language that means 'Let whoever is hungry come and eat.' Put on your shawl and we'll go knock on the first friendly door we come to."

Never one to argue with her husband, Rivke-Beyle swallowed the lump in her throat, put on her tattered shawl, and made ready to go. Just then, though, the door swung open and in stepped someone who said:

"Happy Passover!"

"A happy Passover to you!" the two answered, unable to make the visitor out in the dark.

"I'd like to be your seder guest," said the man.

"We're not having a seder," replied Chaim-Yona.

"Yes you are," said the visitor, "because I've brought it with me!"

"In the dark?" asked Rivke-Beyle, her voice breaking in spite of herself.

"What a thought!" replied their guest. "Let's have some light. Abracadabra!" At once two silver candlesticks with burning candles appeared in midair and lit the room. Now Chaim-Yona and Rivke-Beyle could see the magician, whom they stared at too wide-eyed with amazement and fright to utter a word. Open-mouthed, each hung onto the other's hand and stood there. Meanwhile, the magician turned to the table that was standing abashed in a corner. "Hey, old man, cover yourself and come here!" he ordered it. No sooner had he spoken than a snow-white tablecloth fell on it from the ceiling and the table began moving toward the middle of the room until it stood beneath the candlesticks, which lowered themselves onto it. "Now," said the magician, "let's have something to sit on!" Three chairs left the other three corners of the room and assembled around three sides of the table. "Make yourselves wider!" said the magician, and they turned themselves into armchairs. "Softer!" he said, and in no time they were upholstered in red velvet with white cushions. Now everyone could sit in comfort!

The magician spoke again and right away a platter of matzas and everything needed for the seder appeared on the table beside three cups and a bottle of red wine, followed by a host of dishes fit for a king, and Passover Haggadahs trimmed in gold.

"How about some water to wash our hands with?" the magician asked. "I may as well conjure that up too!"

It was only then that the couple roused themselves. "Do you think we're allowed to touch all this?" whispered Rivke-Beyle into Chaim-Yona's ear. And when Chaim-Yona didn't know what to answer, she said, "Go, husband, ask the rabbi!"

"It's you who should ask the rabbi," said Chaim-Yona, "because I can't leave you here alone with the magician."

"No, it's you," said Rivke-Beyle. "If the rabbi hears such a story from a foolish old woman like me, he'll think I've gone out of my mind." In the end they both went, leaving the magician in the house with the seder.

The rabbi heard them out and said: "If it's black magic, nothing on the table is real, because magic is only illusion. Go home and see. If the matza can be broken, the wine can be poured, and the cushions are solid, you can consider it all a gift from Heaven that you're allowed to enjoy."

Their hearts in their throats, they went back home. The magician was gone. The table, though, was just as they had left it. They fingered the cushions, poured the wine, and broke the matza—and only then, realizing that their guest had been the Prophet Elijah, did they sit down to have a merry seder.

1904 (translated by Hillel Halkin)

THREE GIFTS

▼

THE SCALES OF HEAVEN

Once, long ago, a Jew died somewhere in this world.

Well, when a Jew dies, he dies. No ones lives forever. He was given a proper funeral and buried with all the honors.

The gravestone was laid in place, a son said the Mourner's Prayer, and the dead man's soul flew up to heaven to be tried by a tribunal of angels.

It arrived to find the balance used for weighing good and bad deeds already waiting for it.

The counsel for the defense, who was none other than the dead man's former conscience, stepped up with a snow-white bag in his hand and stood by the right-hand scale.

The counsel for the prosecution, who was none other than the dead man's evil urges, stepped up with a bag smeared with dirt and stood by the left-hand scale.

The white bag contained the man's good deeds, the dirty bag his bad ones. When the defense counsel poured the good deeds onto the right-hand scale, they smelled like the finest fragrance and shone like the stars in the sky. When the prosecutor poured the bad deeds onto the left-hand scale, they were, God help us, as black as coal and smelled like a barrel of pitch.

The poor soul stood gaping. It never had dreamed that there could be such a difference between "good" and "bad." Down below, in the world it had come from, it often couldn't tell them apart and confused one with the other.

The scales floated slowly up and down. One moment one was higher, the next the other. The needle of the balance shifted back and forth, now a hairsbreadth to the left, now a hairsbreadth to the right.

Never more than a hairsbreadth; the scales swayed imperceptibly. The man was an ordinary Jew—not much of a sinner and certainly no saint. His good deeds were as small as his bad ones: little crumbs, little bits of things, so tiny you hardly could see them.

Still, each time the needle moved a hair to the right, there was rejoicing in the heavens; each time it moved back to the left, there was such a sigh of sorrow that it reached all the way to the mercy seat.

Slowly, single-mindedly, the two angels emptied their bags, bit by bit and crumb by crumb, like Jews on Simkhat Torah bidding penny by penny for the right to carry the first Torah.[1]

But sooner or later every well must run dry. The two bags were finally empty.

"Finished?" asked the bailiff of the court, an angel himself.

The counsel for the defense and the counsel for the prosecution both turned their bags inside out: nothing was left. The bailiff stepped up to look at the balance.

He looked and he looked, and the longer he looked, the clearer it became that he was looking at something that had never happened before since the day the world was created.

"What's taking you so long?" asked the chief judge.

"It's a tie! The needle is right in the middle."

The good and bad deeds weighed exactly the same amount.

"Are you sure?" asked the chief judge of the Heavenly Court.

"Absolutely!"

The court recessed to consult and returned with the following verdict:

"Since its bad deeds do not outweigh its good ones, this soul cannot be condemned to hell.

"On the other hand, since its good deeds do not outweigh its bad ones, it cannot be admitted to heaven either.

"We therefore sentence it to be homeless.

"Let it wander back and forth between the heavens and the earth until God remembers it and calls it to Him in His mercy."

The soul was led out of court by the bailiff, bitterly bewailing its fate.

"What are you crying for?" asked the bailiff. "You may never know the joys of paradise, but you won't have to suffer the torments of Gehenna either. Fair is fair!"

But the soul was not comforted. "Better the greatest tortures," it replied, "than nothing at all. There's nothing more awful than nothing!"

The bailiff felt sorry for the soul and gave it a piece of advice.

"Go, my little soul," he said, "and return to the world of living men. Don't bother to look back, because what can you see from down there? Nothing but the stars—and the stars are bright but cold creatures that have no pity. You mustn't expect them to intercede with God for anyone.

"Only the saints in paradise will put in a word for a poor, lost soul like you. And they—do you hear me, my little soul?—like to be brought gifts. That's what the saints are like these days," confided the bailiff ruefully. And he went on:

"Fly down to the world of living men, my little soul, and take a good look around you. If you see any deed that is perfectly good, take it and bring it back to heaven; it will make a fine gift for the saints. Just knock on the gate and tell the angel on duty that I asked for it.

"Once you've brought them three gifts, the saints will see to it that the gates of paradise are opened to you. They won't hold your past against you. They don't like aristocrats. There's nothing they like more than a common soul that's managed to work its way up."

THE FIRST GIFT

And so the poor little soul flew back down to the world of living men to seek gifts for the saints in paradise. It flew hither and thither, over cities, towns, and hamlets; through brilliant sunshine, torrid heat, and foul weather with needle-sharp rain; in and out of cloudless summers that ended in showers of gossamers and winters with their endless snows—looking and looking until it felt that its eyes would pop out.

Most of all, it looked for Jews. And as soon as it saw one, it flew down to look even more closely. Could it perhaps be about to witness some act of great devotion to God?

Sometimes, at night, it even peered through the slats of shutters

in the hope of finding one of God's fragrant flowers—that rare
bloom, a perfect good deed—in the quiet room of some town.

In vain! Often it sprang away from the window with a shudder
or in a state of shock.

Thus, the seasons and the years went by and the soul grew
melancholy. It had seen whole cities turned into graveyards; graveyards plowed into fields; forests cut down by the ax; stones ground
by water into sand; riverbeds moved from their place; stars fall by
the thousands from the sky; souls fly by the millions up to heaven—
and yet never once did God remember it, nor did it find a good
deed that was perfect.

"This world," thought the soul, "is such a poor place; human
beings are so mediocre; their souls are so gray and their deeds are
so petty: where is one to find anything special? I might as well have
been condemned to wander about homeless forever."

It was in the middle of this thought when something flared red
in the night. The soul looked down and saw that the light came
from the window of a house.

Inside the house masked robbers were holding up a wealthy Jew.
One of them held a burning torch while another pressed a gleaming
knife to the man's breast and exclaimed: "Don't make a move, Jew,
or this blade will come out your back." The rest of the gang was
busy ransacking chests and closets and taking everything of value.

The Jew stood regarding the knife with perfect calm. Not an
eyebrow flickered, not a hair stirred in the white beard that came
nearly down to his waist. It was as though the whole matter failed
to concern him. The Lord giveth and the Lord taketh, he thought;
praised be the Lord's Holy Name! And his pale lips seemed to
murmur, "I wasn't born with any of this and I can't take it with me
when I die."

He remained untroubled even when the last drawer of the last
chest was yanked open and out came bags of silver, gold, precious
stones, and other valuables. Indifferent to parting with it all, he
simply looked on in silence.

Yet all of a sudden, as the robbers were taking one last little bag
from its hiding place, he gave a start. Eyes ablaze, he raised his right
arm protectively and opened his mouth to cry out.

"Don't move!"

A hot jet of red blood spurted out in place of a cry, spraying the
little bag. The knife had done its work.

The robbers fell on the bag and ripped it open, certain that it
held the most precious, the most valuable possession of all.

They were wrong. The Jew's blood had been shed for nothing. The bag contained no gold, no silver, no jewels—nothing, indeed, that had the slightest worth in this world. Its only contents were a bit of earth from the Holy Land that the rich Jew had wished to be buried with when he died. It was this he had laid down his life for.

The soul seized a handful of the bloody earth and flew straight to the gates of heaven with it.

The first gift had been brought.

THE SECOND GIFT

"Remember," the angel called after the soul as the gates of heaven swung shut again, "you still have to bring two more gifts."

"With God's help I'll find them," thought the soul cheerfully as it flew back down to earth.

Its good cheer did not last forever, though. Once more the years went by without its sighting a perfect good deed, and once more the soul thought sadly:

"Like a live spring of water, the world sprang forth from God and ran off into Time. Yet the further it runs, the muddier and dirtier it grows. Gifts fit for heaven are far and few between. Men have become diminished, their good deeds plainer, their bad ones drabber; you can look all over and not find a single one that is special.

"If God were to weigh in one weighing all the good and bad deeds of this world," thought the soul, "the needle of the balance would hardly move at all.

"The world is too weak to rise any higher or plunge any lower. Like me it is trapped between the starry heavens and the black depths, while the prosecutors and defense counsels go on endlessly feuding, just as light feuds with darkness, heat with cold, life with death.

"The world teeters this way and that, unable to go up or down. Human beings are born and die, marry and divorce, rejoice and sorrow, love and hate, hate and love, on and on and on. . . ."

A blare of horns and trumpets roused the soul from its thoughts. Looking down, it saw a city in Germany. (All this happened long ago, of course.) Oddly sloped roofs surrounded a town square, which was filled with a colorfully dressed crowd. Other townsmen pressed their faces to the windows or straddled the railings of the packed balconies that projected beneath the roofs.

In front of the town hall stood a table covered by a green cloth trimmed with fringes and tassles of gold. The town magistrates sat around it in sable robes with gold clasps and white-feathered hats with gleaming badges. Beneath a seal of a taloned eagle, the burgomaster presided over them.

To one side stood a Jewish girl in shackles. Not far from her, ten vassals restrained a wild horse. The burgomaster rose to his feet, faced the square, and read the verdict from a sheet of paper:

"This Jewish damsel has committed a grave sin—a sin so heinous, indeed, that God Himself in all His mercy could not possibly forgive her for it.

"Stealing out of the ghetto on our holy day, she polluted our pure streets. Her shameless eyes stained our sacred procession and the holy icons that we carried through our town with music and hymns. Her accursed ears heard our drums and the songs of our innocent children dressed in white. Who knows if the filthy devil himself, in the guise of this accursed rabbi's daughter, did not touch and defile our holy relics?

"Why did he, the devil, wish to inhabit such a beautiful creature? For I cannot deny that she is beautiful, beautiful as only the devil could make her! Just look at those brazenly bright eyes beneath their silken lashes; look at that alabaster complexion, which only grew paler and purer during her long imprisonment; look at those fingers, so fine and thin it is as though light passes right through them.

"Why did Satan inhabit her? Because he wished to tear your souls away from the rapture of our procession—and he did! 'Just look at that beauty!' he caused a young knight from one of our most distinguished families to cry out.

"Worse yet, it happened during the mass. Yet when the parade officials saw her and caught her, the devil put up no resistance. And why not? Because you, God's flock, were without sin, having just been shriven by confession, so that he had no power over you.

"We therefore sentence the devil, in the guise of this Jewess, to the following:

"Let her hair be bound by its long, devilish braid to the tail of a wild horse, which shall drag her until she is dead through the streets that her feet trod on in violation of our laws!

"Let her unstaunched blood wash the cobblestones that those feet polluted!"

A wild cry of joy resounded from every mouth. When it had subsided, the condemned was asked if she had a last wish.

"Yes," she replied calmly. "I would like to be given a few needles."

"She's gone out of her mind with fear," the magistrates remarked to one another.

"Not at all," said the girl in a cold, tranquil voice. "It is my last wish and I ask to have it granted."

She was given her request.

"And now," ordered the burgomaster, "tie her to the horse!"

With trembling hands the vassals tied the rabbi's daughter's long black braid to the tail of the rearing wild horse.

"Stand back!" the burgomaster ordered the crowd in the square.

The crowd parted noisily and pressed itself against the walls of the houses. Each hand gripped something—a whip, a rod, even a plain kerchief—to spur on the horse. All breaths were held, all eyes glittered, all faces were aflame; no one noticed in the excitement how the condemned girl bent over and thrust the needles through the hem of her dress and deep into her flesh to keep her body from being exposed as it was dragged through the streets.

No one but the wandering soul.

"Free the horse!" ordered the burgomaster. The vassals jumped back and the animal broke loose. A cry from the crowd broke loose too, and all the whips, rods, and kerchiefs slashed the air. In a wild frenzy the horse galloped out of the marketplace and through all the streets of the town.

The soul did not wait to see the end of it. Seizing a bloody needle from the leg of the rabbi's daughter, it flew straight up to heaven.

"That's your second gift!" cheered the angel at the gate.

THE THIRD GIFT

Back down to earth flew the soul in search of one last gift.

Once more long years went by, and once more the melancholy soul thought what a petty world it was, pettier than ever, full of little people and little deeds, the bad ones no less than the good.

Once it thought:

"If God, may His name be praised, ever visits His Last Judgment on the world, and if the counsel for the defense stands on one side shaking out the bits and crumbs from the white bag, and the counsel for the prosecution stands on the other side shaking out the grit and grime from the black bag, it would take forever to empty both—that's how tiny everything is in them!

"But when the bags are finally empty—what will happen then?

"The needle will stop in the middle once more!

"When all things are so small, nothing can outweigh anything. What difference can one more feather, one more wisp of straw, one more flake of chaff, one more particle of dust, possibly make?

"And what will God do then? What will His verdict be?

"To turn the world back into chaos? No, the sins will not outweigh the good deeds.

"To bring the Redemption? But the good deeds will not outweigh the sins either.

"What then?

" 'Carry on!' he will tell the world. 'Fly on between heaven and hell, between love and hate, between tears of compassion and rivers of blood—fly on forever and ever!' "

The sound of a drum awoke the soul from this oppressive thought.

Where was it coming from?

The soul had lost all sense of time and place.

Down below it saw a prison. Sunshine glanced off the bars of its small windows and glittered on the bayonets of the rifles stacked against one of its walls. The soldiers who had put them there now held knouts in their hands.

They were arranged in two rows, with a narrow passageway between them. Someone was about to run the gauntlet.

But who?

It was a Jew, his meager body dressed in a torn cloak, a skullcap on his half-shaven head. The soul watched as he was led out from the prison.

What had he done to deserve such punishment? God knows. It was long ago. Perhaps he was a thief, perhaps a burglar or a murderer. Perhaps he had even been framed. After all, it was all so long ago.

The soldiers smiled and wondered why there were so many of them. Their victim wouldn't make it halfway down the line!

Yet as the Jew started down the gauntlet, he walked steadily without stumbling or missing a step, taking blow after blow in his stride.

The soldiers were enraged. Who did he think he was, staying on his feet like that!

The knouts whistled through the air and lashed the thin body like snakes. The blood spurted out, more and more of it.

Halfway down the line a soldier aimed too high and knocked the Jew's skullcap off his head. A few steps farther on, the victim noticed it. He halted as though deliberating, and then, unwilling to continue bareheaded, turned around to retrieve the fallen cap. Bending over, he picked it up, turned around again, and started back down the line, soaked in blood but serene, his skullcap on his head. He kept walking until he collapsed.

As soon as he fell, the soul seized the skullcap and flew with it straight to heaven.

The third gift was accepted too. The saints interceded for the wandering soul and it was admitted to paradise.

And when the three gifts were displayed there, a connoisseur's voice was heard to say:

"Ah, what beautiful gifts! Of course, they're totally useless—but to look at, why, they're perfection itself!"

1904 (translated by Hillel Halkin)

DOWNCAST EYES

▼

1

A very long time ago in a village a few miles from Prague, there lived a Jew, a certain Yekhiel-Mikhl, who kept the local tavern.

The landlord of the village was not an ordinary nobleman, but rather a count of great repute, so that Yekhiel-Mikhl made a plentiful living, as they say, "with something to spare." He became a great personage, a man who dispensed both charity and hospitality. On the High Holy Days, Yekhiel-Mikhl would journey to Prague and there spend money with a free hand. Nor was Yekhiel-Mikhl an ignorant man. While in Prague he became something of a regular at the house of the rabbi, who was also the head of the yeshiva. From him Yekhiel-Mikhl would buy such necessities as the etrog for Sukkot and the ground matza for Passover. He asked as well for the rabbi's intercession with Heaven that he might be granted male offspring.

But through the assistance of the Holy Spirit the head of the yeshiva divined that Yekhiel-Mikhl was not destined to derive pleasure from his children; and sons who give their parents no pleasure might just as well not set foot on this earth. So he bluntly refused to intercede for him. This plunged Yekhiel-Mikhl into great sorrow. The rabbi consoled him by saying: "When the time comes, if with God's help you have collected a handsome dowry, and you come to me with the request, I will find you such a son-in-law that you will not have any regrets."

Yekhiel-Mikhl returned home somewhat comforted. Since he had two daughters, he began to set aside a sum of money toward a dowry, first for the elder daughter and then for the younger. After all, a learned son-in-law was nothing to sneeze at.

So he saved money and God helped him. When he had amassed the first five hundred thaler, he said to his wife, Dvoshe, "The time has come to marry off our elder daughter, Nekhama."

Dvoshe answered that this was an excellent idea. If they calculated three hundred talers for the dowry, two hundred for the trousseau, presents for the bride and groom, assorted wedding expenses, fees for the rabbi, cantor, and sexton, etc., as well as a feast for the paupers, they would have a wedding that Prague would long remember.

But things are more readily said than done; unforeseen obstacles arise. The count of the village sent Yekhiel-Mikhl here and there on business. Snow fell, making the roads impassable; in the summer it rained. When there was a Christian holiday, the tavern could not be left unattended. In a word, things did not proceed so rapidly. And in the meantime, as often happens, man proposes, but God disposes. . . .

2

Nekhama, the tavern keeper's elder daughter, certainly merited a bridegroom from the yeshiva in Prague. She was a quiet, golden-hearted girl, a kind soul. The goodness shone from her eyes, and she was docile. Whatever her father bid, or her mother asked, whatever all the pious people who stopped at the tavern requested, that she did. With great fervor she performed the ceremony of removing the piece of dough from the khallah, throwing it into the fire, and reciting the benediction.[1] She blessed the Sabbath candles and read the sacred texts fluently in Yiddish. In short, she deserved to be led to the wedding canopy.

The more so, because with her younger sister, Malke, matters had gone somewhat awry. Not that the girl had an evil nature, God forbid, but it was like this: She had somehow developed into a singular creature, forever dreamy and absentminded, who constantly let things slip from her hands. Sometimes she lowered her eyelids and walked around with a face as pale as chalk, absorbed in a world of fantasy. When someone called her, she jumped and nearly lost her balance, as if she had been summoned from the Other World. There were times when she turned such forceful, piercing eyes on a person that it made the flesh crawl.

And then Malke betrayed the beginnings of licentious tendencies. She could not be torn from the tavern, especially at night, when the music played and there was dancing. She would sit there night after night feasting her eyes on the young male peasants as they flirted with the peasant girls and danced in a dizzying circle, singing to make the tavern resound and tremble.

And if she was dragged away by force to the bedroom alcove that she shared with her sister, and put to bed next to Nekhama, she would lie there with her eyes shut, pretending to doze. No sooner did Nekhama fall asleep than Malke would jump out of bed, always barefoot whether in summer or winter, and peek through the keyhole, or through a crack in the door or the Prussian divider. Should her mother find her there and drag her away, her body would begin to burn feverishly and her eyes would seem to shoot sparks, so that Dvoshe grew frightened and ran back to Yekhiel-Mikhl to tell him what had happened.

"If only we could marry off the younger one first," sighed Yekhiel-Mikhl.

"We must consult someone," replied Dvoshe.

In the meantime, fresh difficulties arose, until there occurred the following incident.

3

The landlord of the village—the count, that is—had an only child, a son, whom he had brought up in Paris, as was then the custom among the greater nobility. Once a year the young man returned home for a short vacation, but even then no one saw him. He was a young nobleman and so spent his days and nights hunting in the forest. In the manor kitchen Yekhiel-Mikhl could purchase at a very low price the skins of the hares and other animals that the young nobleman shot.

One day, when it was so hot that the very air breathed fire, the young nobleman was riding along the road that passed the tavern. On an impulse he jumped off his milk-white horse, tethered it to the fence, and burst into the tavern to order a glass of mead.

Yekhiel-Mikhl served him the mead with trembling hands. The young nobleman raised it to his mouth, took a sip, and frowned. His father's cellar apparently contained a better quality of God only knows what vintage. He might have given vent to his displeasure by striking Yekhiel-Mikhl on the head with his glass, had he not at that moment caught sight of Malke sitting in a corner, her eyes staring into space and her face pale. So he carefully replaced his glass on the counter, threw down a taler, and asked:

"Moyshe"—the members of the greater nobility called all Jews "Moyshe"—"is this your daughter?"

Poor Yekhiel-Mikhl! His heart sank, and he replied with a stammer: "Yes, yes, my daughter."

The young nobleman stared and could not tear his eyes from the girl. The next day he returned to the tavern to drink mead, and on the third day he came again, and again on the fourth. The parents took the girl and hid her away. This angered the young nobleman, although he did not admit his rage, but sat there, eyes flashing, twisting his black mustache. Suddenly, he declared that Yekhiel-Mikhl was paying too little rent for the tavern, that there were Jews in Prague who were prepared to pay more. (And this was true, but the old count would never allow any other prospective tenants even to cross his threshold. It made no difference to him. If a Jew was already settled in the tavern, then let him earn a living.) Yekhiel-Mikhl grew increasingly ill at ease, especially since Malke had recently become even more absorbed in the world of her fantasies. In fact, he had been intending to seek counsel in Prague. But new difficulties constantly arose to prevent him from going, while the young nobleman continued his daily visits to the tavern, until one day, out of the blue, he said:

"Moyshe, sell me your daughter."

Yekhiel-Mikhl's white beard quivered and everything turned black before his eyes.

The young master laughed. "Is her name Esther?" he asked.

"No, her name is Malke."

"Then imagine that her name is Esther, and yours is Mordekhai, and mine Ahasuerus. What do you say? Don't expect me to place a crown on her head, but you will get the tavern rent-free and forever, for your children and your children's children."[2]

And he gave him some time to think it over.

<h1 style="text-align:center">4</h1>

Yekhiel-Mikhl realized that things were bad. At dawn he harnessed his horse to the wagon and drove to Prague, where he made straight for the house of the rabbi who headed the yeshiva. He found him studying the Gemara, greeted him with a hasty "*Sholem aleykhem*," and blurted out his question.

"Rabbi, may one marry off a younger daughter before an older one?"

The head of the yeshiva leaned his elbows on the Gemara and replied: "No, Yekhiel-Mikhl. We do not do such things here. It is not the Jewish way." And he reminded him of the story of Jacob and Laban.

"I know," said Yekhiel-Mikhl, "but if it's necessary?"

"For what reason?"

So Yekhiel-Mikhl proceeded to pour out all the bitterness of his heart before the saintly man, recounting everything that had taken place.

The holy rabbi of Prague considered the matter and said: "So be it. Everything is permitted in an hour of need."

Yekhiel-Mikhl gave the holy man an account of the excellent state of his financial affairs, told him of the five hundred talers set aside for a dowry, and reminded him of his promise to choose a bridegroom from among the students in the yeshiva.

The rabbi of Prague sank into thought, leaning his head against his elbows on the Gemara. Then he raised his head again and said, "No, Yekhiel-Mikhl. This I cannot do!"

"Why, Rabbi?" asked Yekhiel-Mikhl with a quiver. "Is the soul of my Malkele stained with a sin, heaven forbid? She's a young child, a sapling. Whichever way you bend it . . ."

"God forbid," answered the rabbi. "I do not say that she has sinned, Heaven forbid. That was not my intention. But it's not appropriate. Listen, Yekhiel-Mikhl, your daughter did not sin, but she is somewhat touched by sin nevertheless. Mainly, however," he continued, "it is your good that concerns me here, because your daughter requires attention, the care of a man, and not just any man, but a man of character, a merchant. In addition to this she needs the supervision of her father-in-law and mother-in-law and of the household staff. One way or another, these thoughts must be drummed out of her head. For this reason she must be brought into a household with many ears and eyes. When the evil spirit gets hold of a person, it requires a fierce battle to dislodge it. It is the same as with bitter horseradish. You plant it only once, but it grows forever. You pull it out, and it grows back. Don't you agree?"

Poor Yekhiel-Mikhl had no choice but to nod assent.

"And now," continued the saintly man, "come closer, Yekhiel-Mikhl, and consider this. Let's say I want to be good and keep my word. After all, I did promise you, and I want to keep my word and do as you wish. So I go and choose for you a son-in-law from the yeshiva. This means a poor young man, a forsaken boy. Will it do any good? Who is this boy? A scholar, who will sit and study. He knows nothing else, and wants to know nothing else. He is allowed to know nothing else. And where will the couple live? You certainly won't give them room and board in your house in the country."

"Certainly not. Not as long as the young nobleman is in the neighborhood."

"And who knows how long he will remain there? Who can tell what goes on in a nobleman's mind? People like that, if they take a fancy to something . . . ! Does he have any other worries? Does he need to earn a living? So to give them room and board at your house is out of the question. On the other hand, should you settle them in Prague, rent rooms for them, and send them money, what would the couple do then? The young man would sit day and night in the study house poring over the sacred texts. And what would the young wife do? What thoughts would she think? In what imaginary world would her mind wander?"

"You are right, Rabbi," Yekhiel-Mikhl conceded in a hoarse voice. "What then do we do?"

"Whatever we can," answered the head of the yeshiva. "And I will help you. I will send for the matchmaker myself and direct him where to look. It should be a household full of people in a town where one can enjoy the ordinary pleasures of life that are permitted and not forbidden. You will see, with the help of the Almighty, everything will work out.

"As a recompense, Yekhiel-Mikhl," the rabbi consoled him, "when you come to me about your other daughter, and God will have helped you to lay aside a sum toward her dowry, I assure you that you will be given a jewel of a son-in-law who will be worth his weight in gold. In the meantime, marry off your younger daughter."

5

So it was.

On the responsibility of the head of the yeshiva, and in the utmost secrecy, a respectable match was arranged for Malke. Until the very last moment, the girl did not know why the seamstresses appeared to fit her for clothes, or why she was being woken at dawn to be driven to Prague.

And when she did finally understand what it all meant, she did not utter a single word. She locked away her young soul inside herself.

No one knew what went on in her heart. But outwardly it seemed— grant that the same be said of all daughters of Zion!—that she had all the best qualities. Perhaps she was a little too pale; for some reason her eyes were always cast down. What of that? In the beginning, it was accounted the charming bashfulness of a bride; later it was said that this was the way God had created her. In any case, she was a beauty, a ravishing creature. Moreover, she went nowhere without her mother-in-law, she was not given to whims, she ate whatever she was served, drank whatever she was offered, and wore whatever dress she was asked to put on. She was always neat, quiet, and pretty. On the Sabbath, when she put on her black satin dress, set off with a golden brooch, clasped a string of pearls around her alabaster neck, while diamond earrings dangled from her ears, the women passing her in the street would stop and gape, murmuring, "A princess." And she, as if she were not the one they meant, continued quietly and daintily on her way, walking between her mother-in-law and sisters-in-law in the direction of the women's section of the synagogue. There she stationed herself next to her mother-in-law near the grating and lowered her silken eyelids. With her white hand, she opened the silver clasps of the gilt-edged prayer book, and her lips began to tremble.

And what of the rest of the week? How did she spend her evenings?

"Where would you like to go for a walk today, Malke?"

She would not say where. Wherever they went, she would go. And if they passed shopwindows with jewelry displays, everyone would stop to look, except Malke. She stopped because they stopped, but her eyes stared into the distance.

So they said to each other, "What does she need jewelry for? She is a jewel herself." This was especially true since her husband felt bereft of his soul without her and cherished her like the apple of his eye.

And so she was in every respect—on the surface, as polished, sculpted, and pure as the finest crystal.

But inside lay the tavern with its singing and dancing and merrymaking. In Malke's heart, separated from the outside world, there fluttered the image of the young nobleman. No sooner did she close her eyes, be it in the synagogue near the grating, or at the end of the Sabbath during the prayer "God of Abraham," or during the blessing of the Sabbath candles, than the passion in the blood erupted within her, and she danced—may God forgive her—with the young master in the middle of a circle in the tavern after the harvest. Or she went riding with him on the milk-white horse, chasing through forests and valleys. But above all, when her husband drew near, in that instant she would screw her eyes shut, throw her arms around his neck, and kiss the young nobleman whom she adored.

Her young husband doted on her beautiful eyes, so he pleaded with her: "My own dear life, open your beautiful eyes, which are like the gates of heaven." But on no account would she comply. If at times, determined on getting his way (he was a young man, after all), he pretended to withdraw, she tightened the grip of her arms around him like a vise. He would suddenly grow frightened and try to tear himself away, but she implored him in an ecstatic voice: "My master, my eagle."

He imagined that she was so deeply in love that she considered him to be her master, her eagle, that this was a form of peasant talk. Let her keep her eyes shut, then, if she was too shy to open them.

6

And so Malke lived one year after another. She conceived no children. She lived with her husband—and yet not with her husband.

To what can this be compared?

To an apple that hangs, seemingly healthy and fresh, on a green branch of a golden apple tree. The skin of the apple is as red as the eastern sky before sunrise, and a fresh breath, as if from paradise, lies fragrantly and enticingly upon it. But in reality, the skin alone is healthy and fresh. Inside, the worms have devoured everything.

Exactly the opposite destiny befell Yekhiel-Mikhl's elder daughter, Nekhama. Yekhiel-Mikhl's own fate underwent a reversal, and as often happens, the bread fell with the butter side down.

Having celebrated and danced his fill in Prague, Yekhiel-Mikhl returned home with only a few coins in his pocket. As he approached the outskirts of the village, he saw all his belongings, including his bed, and the tables and benches of the tavern, lying in the open field, while one of the peasants from the count's court stood guard over them.

The guard would not let him drive into the village. It turned out that while Yekhiel-Mikhl had been dancing at his younger daughter's wedding, another Jew had outbid him for the tavern, offering to pay a much higher rent, and the young nobleman had convinced the old count that he should accept the better offer. The new tenant was already settled in the tavern.

Yekhiel-Mikhl's wife and daughter started to cry and to faint. Yekhiel-Mikhl begged the guard to let him drive on, so that he might at least speak with the old master. The guard swung the rifle off his shoulder and warned that he would be forced to shoot.

The guard was an acquaintance, and there were tears in his eyes, but if his master commanded it, he would undoubtedly fire. Yekhiel-Mikhl saw that there was no hope. He did not have the resources to drive back to Prague, the wedding having left him with little more than a few gold coins. Nor did he want to shame his married daughter with his poverty. So he took his wife and his daughter Nekhama and drove with them to the village of another nobleman that was located farther away from Prague. There he asked permission to open a store where he could sell salt, bread, and other foodstuffs to the villagers. He then left the store in the care of his wife and daughter, while he himself set out to launch legal proceedings against his former landlord for breach of contract and to bring suit in the rabbinical court against the Jew who had taken over his property.

But such things are sooner said than done, especially when one's pockets are empty. A few years went by. He lost the case against his former landlord, and was obliged to spend time in jail, since he could not afford to pay the court costs. He did, at long last, win his case in the rabbinical court against the man who had usurped his property, but the latter could by no means be made to submit to the judgment; and in the meantime the saintly rabbi of Prague, who would have had the power to force compliance, had died. Prague's Jews looked everywhere for a rabbi, but could not find one who was suitable. There was therefore no judge and no justice.

After a few years Yekhiel-Mikhl returned home exhausted, emaciated, and ill. He took to his bed, and after lying bedridden for a few weeks, he died. His wife did not long outlive him, and Nekhama was left an orphan, all alone in the village, as solitary as a stone. Business was bad; there was nothing to sell. From the time she was orphaned, the young male peasants gave her no peace; they taunted her, angered that she, who was nothing more than a Jewish pauper, would not let them touch her.

She wrote first one and then a second letter to her sister in Prague. But the sister lived, as we have seen, in a world of confusion and did not read letters. So the forsaken orphan never received a reply. Undeterred, she rose one night, locked up her empty store, and stole out of the village on foot. She entrusted herself to God's care, certain that He would lead her safely to her sister's house in Prague. A sister, after all, is not made of stone.

7

Taking along a piece of bread to eat, she left the village and walked until she reached a forest. Since she feared wild animals, she did not venture too far into the forest, but climbed the first suitable tree, hoping to remain hidden among its branches until daybreak. There she lay for a while, but just as she was in the middle of reciting the evening prayer, she heard the excited yelping of dogs. The sounds of running and barking grew nearer, and she realized that noblemen were hunting animals in the forest. She tried to press her body more firmly against the branches, but the sounds of the hunt drew nearer and nearer, until a pack of dogs surrounded the tree, barking ferociously. Two horsemen approached at a quick gallop to see why the dogs were barking and circling the tree. The two horsemen were young noblemen. They climbed the tree and forcibly dragged the girl down, after which they built a fire and contemplated their catch.

They found her to be a very pretty Jewish girl, rather lean with hunger. So they assured her that they would do her no harm, because she lit up the dark like a morning star, that if only she were properly dressed, she would be as radiant as a queen and as redolent as a rose. These words naturally caused her heart to tremble. In the meantime, she heard how the two young noblemen fell to quarreling over her. Each wanted to take her for himself, arguing that she belonged to him, because it was his dog that had first discovered her. They resolved to settle the matter with a duel; whoever survived would have her. They took up positions facing each other and were about to shoot, when they thought better of it and decided instead to draw lots. The winner pulled her up next to him on the horse, and as he galloped off with her to his palace, she fainted.

8

The next morning, when she regained her senses in the nobleman's palace and realized that he held her on his lap while he kissed and embraced her, she understood that all was lost and that she was beyond salvation. Still, she pleaded with him:

"My dear master, I am in your hands. You are too strong for me to struggle against, and I no longer have the means to defend myself. So I have only one request to make of you. Take pity on me and promise me this one thing: You have corrupted my body. That cannot be helped. Do not corrupt my soul as well. Leave me my religion and my thoughts. Let me think and believe what I please."

The nobleman did not really understand what she meant by this, but since he had truly come to love her, he gave his word. He thought: "What harm can it do?" He had, in any case, no intention of marrying her. Once he even bought a prayer book from a Jewish bookseller in Prague, and made her a present of it. She accepted the prayer book with joy, but soon let it fall from her hands onto the table. "My hands," she said, "don't deserve to hold such purity."

The young nobleman wondered at this in silence.

In the nobleman's court, Nekhama led a life that was the exact opposite of that which her sister led in Prague. Both sisters kept their eyes cast down and walked about estranged and dreamy. But whereas Malke's soul sinned from within a pure body, with Nekhama it was the opposite: she abandoned her body to sin, but kept her soul pure.

When her nobleman drew near, she shut her eyes and thought, "My mother is kissing me." It was her mother who kissed and embraced her while teaching her to recite the prayer "God of Abraham."

He wanted her to love him.

She did love—loved passionately—her mother. She hugged her mother. "Repeat it one more time, dearest mother: *Torah tsiva lanu . . .*" she whispered.[3] But her sinful lips did not even dare to pronounce the words. Instead, they fluttered in her soul and there illuminated the deepest recesses of her being.

9

No one lives forever, and neither sister was allotted a full life.

When their souls parted from their bodies, the soul of the younger sister, Malke, was thoroughly stained with sin. It flew out like a black crow from her white body and lost itself in the abyss of hell. But the clean white soul of the elder sister, Nekhama, had no sooner freed itself from her sinful body than as silently and lightly as a dove it rose to the heights of the most lofty heaven, where it paused in trepidation before the gate. But God's pity showed itself to the soul, opened the gate for it, consoled it, and wiped the tears from its eyes.

Of all these things, however, people on earth knew nothing. The well-to-do matron of Prague had a large funeral; she was handsomely eulogized, and it all cost a fortune. She was laid to rest in a place of honor next to the graves of the other virtuous women. On the first anniversary of her death, they erected a tombstone on which were inscribed all her many praiseworthy qualities.

But when the nobleman sent the body of the older sister to Prague for burial, no one from the funeral society was willing to touch the sinful corpse. Ordinary porters were hired to wash the body, which was then wrapped in an old sack and thrown into a pit somewhere near the fence.

10

Sometime after, when a part of the old Prague cemetery was incorporated into the city in order to broaden a street, the graves were dug up so that the bones might be transported elsewhere. A gravedigger opened Nekhama's grave near the fence and found nothing but her skull. Of her body and the other bones, there remained not a trace. When the gravedigger unwittingly jostled the skull with his foot, it rolled away and was lost. And so it was never buried.

However, the gravedigger who opened Malke's grave found her body completely intact and fresh, with a hint of a fresh smile on her white face.

"That is what it means to be a virtuous woman," people said. "Even the worms have no power over her."

Because that is how people think and talk. Their eyes see only what lies on the surface. They never comprehend what goes on in the heart, nor grasp the true state of a human soul.

1904 (translated by Goldie Morgentaler)

A CHAPTER OF THE PSALMS

▼

This story comes down from the mighty scholar, the great light in Israel, "the Sojourner Among the Living," so called, like many others of his kind, after the name of his most famous work.

Early one cold and windy morning the Sojourner sat with his colleagues and pupils in the study house. They had just finished the morning prayers and each of them had picked up a sacred book for study. Scarcely had they settled to their task when they heard from outside a voice proclaiming, "Charity averts death," and the ringing of a charity box—the immemorial accompaniments of a Jewish funeral.

No one was surprised, for before the prayers it had been announced that Yokhanan the Water Carrier had died and was being buried that morning. But what *did* occasion surprise was the rabbi's response. He called for his street hat and for his cane and announced that he would attend the funeral.

If the Sojourner goes to a funeral, everyone else goes. Assistant rabbis and pupils closed their books and left the study house. If the rabbi and his assistants and his pupils go to a funeral, everyone in town goes; and before you knew it the synagogues were emptied, the shops were closed, and the entire population streamed in the wake of the rabbi to the cemetery.

But what is the meaning of this? How comes Yokhanan the Water Carrier by such a magnificent funeral? Yokhanan was—God forgive us—a very ordinary person. True, he was most attentive to his prayers, and in the evening he would distribute water free of charge among the students in the synagogue. But such a funeral? After all, he was just a psalm-sayer, and not a distinguished one either. He could not say two lines without three mistakes; and when he came to a difficult word, his pronunciation was so comical that listeners had to bite their lips not to laugh. It had to be said for him, of course, that he was a man who lived by the labor of his own hands and took no charity except from God. But even so!

And the Sojourner went on, street after street. The ways were slippery underfoot; a fierce wind blew. The rabbi went on, the crowd with him. They left the town. Near the cemetery the rabbi himself put a hand to the coffin; and in the House of the Living, as we call it, he participated in the last rites of purification. He himself, again, lowered the remains of Yokhanan into the grave; then he took the spade from the gravedigger's hand and threw in the first spadeful of earth. He listened to the saying of the Kaddish and responded with a loud "Amen."

By this time it was clear to all that the matter went very deep.

The funeral took place on a Thursday. Friday is filled with preparation for sanctity; the Sabbath is filled with sanctity. When the Sabbath was drawing to a close, a delegation of godly house-holders came to visit the Sojourner; not, heaven forbid, in order to pry into the secret meaning of the great funeral, but just by way of courtesy. And the talk was of everything but Yokhanan—talmudic problems generally, a recent case that had set the work of Jewish scholars on its ear, and the like. And since all discussions wind up with the subject of death, the matter that tormented the curiosity of the visitors lay at hand. The rabbi smiled, knowing what was in their minds, and the visitors confessed to it. "True, Rabbi," they said. "What else? Such a tremendous incident!"

"Gentlemen," said the Sojourner, "know that in Yokhanan the

Water Carrier there died a Jew who had a gift of the spirit for recognizing true scholars, a gift that the Sojourner does not possess. A Jew, moreover, who was able to achieve with an ax in his rough fist what the Sojourner could not achieve with the will of his mind."

Jaws dropped in amazement. No hint of this had occurred to anyone; not a word of it had come from the Sojourner.

"It was a secret," said the Sojourner. "The man refused to be revealed while he lived. To anyone. But something happened that compelled him to come to me for help. He had me promise that as long as he lived I would not speak of it. I knew, and one more, also no longer among the living—the former beadle. He too kept the secret. Now there is no longer reason to keep it."

The visitors drew their chairs closer, pricked up their ears. The Sojourner went on.

The incident of which he told them was a quarter of a century old. He himself had only just arrived in the community; indeed, he still remembered his very first visit to the big synagogue and study house.

He came to evening prayers and saw at the pulpit, ready to lead the congregation, a scraggy little man who, they told him, was one Yosl Dvoshe's—that is, Yosl, Dvoshe's husband, a good, honest householder. And Yosl Dvoshe's led the prayers at a gallop, to the distress of the Sojourner, who thought, "He hasn't the prayers in mind, but the hot meal waiting for him at home." He was about to protest, by rapping on his lectern, as the custom is, but bethought himself, being of a deliberate nature. And sure enough, in a very little while the voice of the prayer leader penetrated to his heart— something was amiss. When the time came for the Prayer of the Eighteen Benedictions, the Sojourner turned east with the rest of the congregation, and there, on the eastern wall, he saw written in chalk, "Let healing and recovery come for the lad Yekhiel, son of Dvoshe." Thereupon he understood that the Jew was hastening through his prayers to return to the sick boy, and he repented of the sin that he had committed in the secrecy of his heart, accusing the innocent man of gross inclinations. And when he came to the passage in the Prayer of the Eighteen Benedictions, the Sojourner put great feeling into the words "Heal us, O Lord, and we will be healed," directing the power of the prayer toward Yekhiel, son of Dvoshe. That same night the boy passed the crisis successfully.

This, however, the Sojourner told only by way of introduction, so as to fix the evening in his mind. The substance of the story followed.

Prayers being ended, the beadle made the rounds, distributing candles, one candle each for those who were remaining in the synagogue to study. And the heart of the Sojourner swelled with happiness when he observed how great a number of students there were. The lights burned in the synagogue like the constellations in heaven. Would that it were so in every corner of the Jewish world!

And as he sat there, waiting for the beadle to bring him a certain tractate of the Talmud, and listening meanwhile to the pleasant humming and chanting that rose from the eager students, he saw a water carrier circulating in the synagogue and carrying cold water to the lecterns. And the man's behavior and manner were most edifying. When he came to a lectern, he would stand there until the student saw him and stretched out his hand to the pail and cup; he would never break in. When the student perceived the water carrier, he smiled, took a cupful of water, and made the benediction, to which the other would respond with a hearty "Amen!" adding, "Thank you very much." He would bestow a loving and reverent look on the student and go to the next lectern.

Touched by the bearing of this simple man, the Sojourner asked who he was, and received the answer: "Yokhanan the Water Carrier." Still watching him, the Sojourner was suddenly startled by a fantastic and inexplicable incident, which no one else seemed to notice. Over against the eastern wall sat a pale young man, absorbed in a volume of the mystic kabbalah; so much the Sojourner could perceive at a distance, from the diagrams on the printed page. Yokhanan the Water Carrier made as if to approach this student too, but seemed unable to reach him! It was as if an invisible hedge surrounded the student. A most extraordinary thing. In his deliberate way the Sojourner kept his counsel, and when the beadle brought him the tractate, he asked who the student of kabbalah was. The beadle answered, not without pride: "Ah, Rabbi, that is our *porush*, our recluse. A great kabbalist, a great one for fasts and self-mortification, and he always studies alone." To which he added, in a low voice: "He lives outside the town, in an old ruin. At night strange voices are heard there, and strange melodies."

What was the Sojourner to think? No doubt the kabbalist was lifted, during his studies, to such spiritual exaltation that the simple water carrier could not break into the charmed circle. But then another astonishing thing happened. Yokhanan gave up the attempt to give the recluse water and went his way with a strange, unfriendly gesture. A little while later there came another water carrier, quite unlike Yokhanan: he too served the students, but without love and reverence; he did not listen to their benediction or answer with

"Amen"; his face and manner were coarse; his motive in the performance of the good deed was low. Yet this water carrier succeeded where Yokhanan failed. He had the power to break through; he approached the lectern, spoke to the recluse, and gave him the water, which the latter drank so quickly that the Sojourner could not even tell whether he had uttered the benediction.

"Very strange indeed," he thought. Perhaps Yokhanan had a hidden hatred of the recluse, and this hatred prevented him from performing a kindness toward him. Who could tell? The Sojourner meditated on all this awhile; then other, weightier matters drove the incident from his mind and he forgot about it until another strange thing happened.

One day, preceding a new moon, the Sojourner arrived at the synagogue before the hour of prayer. The upper windows were open, and swallows darted in and out. Down below near the pulpit stood a solitary figure: Yokhanan, absorbed in the reading of the Psalms. The Sojourner passed by him, but so sunk was Yokhanan in devotions that he did not notice him. Standing a little distance from him, the Sojourner heard Yokhanan's quaint mispronunciations of the Hebrew words and was himself tempted to smile, when suddenly he became aware that the words issuing from Yokhanan's lips, mangled and distorted as they were, were alive! It seemed to him further that the words ascended from Yokhanan's lips to the rafters, and that the drawings of King David's musical instruments up there responded to the contact: an echo came from a flute, from a drum, from the string of a violin, but so softly that only the ear of the spirit could catch it. From the rafters the words floated to the windows, and there the swallows caught them on their wings and carried them heavenward; other swallows, returning, brought other sounds and words with them.

This time the Sojourner was so troubled and puzzled that he made up his mind to get to the bottom of the mystery.

He did not speak to Yokhanan there and then; but late that evening, on returning home from prayers, he sent for him.

"Yokhanan," he said, "I wish to speak with you." And he motioned him to a chair.

Yokhanan would not sit down in the Sojourner's presence.

"I command you to," said the Sojourner, and Yokhanan sat down on the edge of a chair.

"Yokhanan, I heard you at your recitation of the Psalms today."

Yokhanan sighed, and murmured that he wished he could read Hebrew better. The words were said so simply, so unaffectedly, that the Sojourner wondered whether he had not been under a delusion in the synagogue. But he remembered the incident with the *porush*, the recluse, too vividly. "Yokhanan," he asked, "what is there between you and the *porush* that you do not serve him water?"

Yokhanan turned pale, his manner became confused, and he did not answer.

The Sojourner repeated the question, and Yokhanan answered hoarsely:

"Rabbi, I may not tell you. It is a secret."

"But if I command it?"

"Then I'll have to."

"Then I command it."

"Rabbi," began Yokhanan, "I must tell you first that the Lord of the World, in His unending goodness, blessed me with a gift of the spirit, a kind of sense of smell, with which I can recognize a true scholar and a pure-hearted student of Holy Writ. I myself am no student, I am an ignorant man. But this gift of the spirit tells me at once, and from a distance, if a student is impure of heart."

"How did you come by the gift?"

"As long as I can remember, Rabbi, I have made myself a servant of the wise. It is the purpose of my life. But I was always afraid that I might, in my ignorance, make myself useful to one whose wisdom was false and corrupt. I therefore prayed to God that He save me from this kind of error, and my prayer was found acceptable. From that time on there was in me this gift, to perceive the essence and the inner spirit of the student. There are some scholars from whose study a fresh odor arises, as of newly baked bread: those are simple students, innocent in heart; and there are some of higher degree from whom a perfume comes of new apples; and still others who remind me of the flowers of the field; and the highest are like precious spices."

"And what comes to your spirit from the *porush*?"

"Pitch! The burning pitch of hell!"

Unable to believe, the Sojourner was silent. Yokhanan continued:

"Rabbi, perhaps it is best after all that you should know. You are the teacher of this community. Someday you will need me, and you will find me useful."

The Sojourner was dumb with astonishment. Later, when Yokhanan had withdrawn, after asking permission, the Sojourner reflected: "This must be looked into," but again he let the matter slip from his mind.

Then, after a time, it returned to him; and one evening he decided to make a test. He came into the synagogue after prayers and found the students already bent over their books, with the recluse, as usual, isolated in the corner. The Sojourner passed that way and observed that the man was occupied with the study of practical or magical kabbalah. The Sojourner went so far as to brush the lectern. But there was no effect.

The Sojourner was plunged into doubt. How could such a thing be—that Yokhanan the Water Carrier should perceive something in the vicinity of the student, and that he, the Sojourner, should be aware of nothing? Surely there was a mistake. So thinking, he sat down to study, but studying was impossible. He went home to eat, but eating was impossible. So after washing his hands he ate one mouthful of food, to justify his benediction and his grace after the meal. Then, feeling some confusion in his mind and uneasiness in his body, he said his night prayer and lay down to sleep. He fell asleep toward midnight and was visited by a frightful dream.

He dreamt that someone was waking him, and on opening his eyes he saw his dead father standing over him, saying:

"Your congregation is in flames, and you do not put the fire out." And therewith the dead man vanished.

This time he really awoke, and jumping out of his bed, he ran to the window. In the distance, beyond the town limits, and in the direction of the ruin that according to the beadle housed the recluse, he saw flames rising and bending over toward the town. It seemed to him also that one fiery tongue reached as far as the roof of the synagogue; sparks were flying over the houses. The vision lasted awhile, then vanished. The Sojourner was seized with trembling.

Now he understood that the vision was a signal to him; some dreadful evil was being perpetrated in the ruin, and he was being called upon to take action. Perplexed as to what was expected of him, he bethought himself suddenly of the words of Yokhanan the Water Carrier: "Someday you will need me, Rabbi, and you will find me useful." Very quietly, so that his wife should not hear him, the Sojourner slipped into his clothes and tiptoed down to the room where the beadle slept. Three times he had to ask the man where Yokhanan the Water Carrier lived, so strange did the question sound. Finally, the beadle came to, picked up a lantern, and conducted the rabbi through the tangle of lanes to the hut of Yokhanan. They approached the window, to knock on it, but the door opened suddenly and Yokhanan came out.

"I was waiting for you, Rabbi," he said. "It is time to put out the fire."

At that moment the clouds overhead were split, and by the light of the moon the rabbi saw that Yokhanan was carrying an ax. "Yokhanan," he said, "what is that for?"

"It will be needed," answered Yokhanan.

They made for the ruin where the recluse lived, and when they drew near, the rabbi beware aware of the smell of burning pitch; and the closer they drew, the thicker the fumes became, till they were almost suffocating. Light shone through narrow cracks in the walls, and wild sounds reached their ears: women's voices singing, the playing of musical instruments, the rhythm of feet on boards.

The beadle shook like a leaf. "Hold on to my belt," said the rabbi to him. But the beadle was so far gone in fear that his knees gave under him and he collapsed in the street.

"Rabbi," said the water carrier, "leave him there. Let us hurry into the ruin, or we will arrive too late, God forbid."

The Sojourner asked him if he knew where the entrance was, and Yokhanan answered that he would find it with his sense of smell.

"What shall we do there?" asked the rabbi.

"Each of us will have his task," answered Yokhanan. "You, Rabbi, will use your brain and your willpower; I will use my ax. You will hold them off with your conjurations—and the rest you will leave to me."

At that instant he found the door and opened it. And this is what they saw:

The interior of the ruin was ablaze with light, and some fantastic wedding ceremony was being celebrated. The four walls were adorned high up with skulls, from the eye sockets of which darted red fire. At one end of the room stood an orchestra, playing on black instruments, and the sounds that issued from the instruments were accompanied by flames. Naked wenches, their black heads crowned with red poppies, danced in a circle, and streams of sparks flew out from under their goats' feet. They sang, and the voices that issued from their lips were accompanied by flames.

A wedding jester sprang up from somewhere, crying, "Sabbath! Sabbath!" And in the middle of the circle of naked wenches there was a bridal dance. The dancers were the recluse and the demon Lilith, bridegroom and bride; they held the opposite ends of a white kerchief, and the bridegroom, singing, "Come, my bride, come, my bride," drew Lilith nearer and nearer, till soon they were dancing hand in hand.

"Sabbath! Sabbath!" cried the wedding jester. The instruments played ever more loudly, the dancing became wilder and wilder, the flames fiercer; and just as Lilith was about to fall on the bridegroom's breast, they all became aware of the rabbi and the water carrier standing at the door, and for an instant all life and motion were suspended. Then tumult, screams of rage, grinding of teeth—and the assembly broke and turned with clenched fists on the unbidden guests.

But the rabbi, by the power of his conjurations, held them off, so that they stood with uplifted goats' feet outside of the invisible circle of four paces. Their faces blazed with hatred, their fists were stretched out, but they could not break through.

"Help! Help!" screamed Lilith, calling to the world of demons.

They came, like a storm wind: they circled the ruin, seeking an entrance; the old walls trembled; a million voices filled the air. But the door and the walls held, and the reinforcements could not enter, because of the conjurations of the Sojourner. The place filled slowly with incantations and the air became unbreathable for the demons inside, so that their tongues began to protrude from their mouths. Step by step the demons drew away from the rabbi, shrank into corners, withered, and crumpled, and fell.

Then Yokhanan lifted his ax and let it fly; it found its target, Lilith, and split her in two, from the head downward. In that same instant the recluse collapsed, face forward, the winds died down, the instruments burst asunder, the demons vanished, the skulls crumbled into dust, the lamps were out. Silence, then the sound of wings, and a black figure lifted the recluse and vanished with him through a window. Outside, the dawn was breaking.

"Thus it was, gentlemen," said the Sojourner with a sigh. "The recluse, the false student of sacred lore, disappeared. Who knows whether it was granted him to be buried in Jewish soil? Here, in the town, it was believed that he had gone forth to take on himself the vow of exile and homelessness.

"We went out and found the beadle where he lay. We got him and led him home. Not a living soul had seen us. My wife knew nothing: she had not seen me leave; she did not see me return. And Yokhanan made me promise that the incident would remain a secret.

"Now you may see that a simple Jew, with his gift of the spirit, can perceive that which the Sojourner cannot perceive. And that which the Sojourner, with his learning, his will, his pure purposes, cannot achieve, the simple Jew, ax in hand, can achieve, aiming without hesitation and finding his target.

"All this with the power that is in a chapter of the Psalms."

1905 (translated by Maurice Samuel)

A PINCH OF SNUFF

▼

Satan, the Evil One, the Enemy of Mankind, the Tempter and Destroyer, sat one day in his private office, idly examining his account book. He sat at ease, one leg dangling over the other, a kindly, complacent smile on his lips; and his fingers turned at random the leaves, which bore the names of all the living souls on earth.

And then suddenly his complacency vanished and he clapped his palms together: he had come upon the page bearing the name of the rabbi of Chelm, and it was as blank as blank could be.

At the sound of the clapped hands a host of demon flunkies came running and crowded the door, their tongues hanging out while they waited for a word of command.

"Send someone up," said Satan, "and find out whether the rabbi of Chelm has many years to live."

The demon flunkies vanished as swiftly as they had come. A quarter of an hour later the report was handed in from the upper chamber. The days of the rabbi of Chelm were numbered; the thread of his life, worn thin to invisibility, was about to snap. It might happen tomorrow, it might happen the day after.

"Send for the recorder."

Enter the recorder, a bald-headed little goblin, light-footed and merry-eyed. A bow, a scrape, a smirk, and he seated himself cross-legged, Turkish fashion, on the sulfur-smoldering floor; from one side he drew a bottle of blood-red ink reeking of sin and a new crow's feather, from the other a sheet of parchment made from the skin of an atheist. The recorder spat in his palm and threw a submissive look at his master. "Ready!"

Satan uncrossed his legs and leaned forward in his armchair. The Recorder stuck out a fiery tongue, the quill flew over the parchment, a report and claim were indited to the court of heaven:

"Whereas we are told in Holy Script, 'No man liveth who shall do good and no evil,'[1] and whereas there is among the living the rabbi of Chelm, who stands with one foot in the grave, and the debit side of his ledger is blank; therefore, in order that the Torah of Moses shall be true and shall remain true, let the Rabbi of Chelm be delivered into the power of the Evil One."

Back came the answer: "See the Book of Job, Chapter 1."

That case Satan remembered without difficulty: it meant he could do whatever he wanted with the rabbi of Chelm save that against the man's life he could not put forth his hand. Such as the rabbi's days were, few or many, they had to run their course.

But how was he to do with the rabbi of Chelm what he once had done with Job? For Job had been a mighty man of substance—and the rabbi of Chelm? A widower, alas, his children all married; and it is written in Ezekiel, "The fathers shall not die in place of the sons."[2] Nothing doing there. As for "flocks and herds of cattle"— the poor man hadn't even a goat for milk. Nor could Satan afflict him with boils—he had them already. What trials and torments could you visit on the rabbi of Chelm?

"Some little lust of his," murmured Satan, licking his chops. "Some tiny desire, some obscure appetite!" He stretched out his hand, lifted the bell, which was made from the skull of a sophist, and rang. The room was filled with demon flunkies.

"Whom shall we send to tempt the rabbi of Chelm from the true path?"

"Me! Me! Me!"

The competition is fierce, and no wonder: promotion awaits the demon who can pull this one off. There is almost a riot. Finally, they draw lots: a couple of minor imps get the lucky numbers, and they are off amid a chorus of "*Mazel tov!* Good luck!"

The sun shone brightly that day on the marketplace of Chelm, crowded with Jews who had nothing to do. They stood about in groups, buying and selling the skins of rabbits and hares that hadn't been caught yet, cases of eggs that hadn't been laid, timber from trees that hadn't been felled. Suddenly, the earth beneath their feet began to tremble, a crack of nearby thunder split the air, and a wagon burst into the marketplace, scattering Jews right and left. A strange and unknown wagon—and stranger still its behavior. High up in front stood the driver, a ragged cap on his head, a red belt about his loins, pulling like mad at the infuriated horses; behind him stood the passenger, in decent black gabardine and fur cap, holding the whip in his right hand and cracking it over the heads of the horses. The driver pulled the horses back, the passenger urged them on! Now and again the passenger drove his left fist into the driver's back; now and again he put his fingers to his lips and emitted a piercing whistle, which made the horses start as if they had been shot.

And meanwhile the driver was wailing at the top of his voice: "Jews! Have pity on me! Save me, Jews!"

But before anything could be done, the wagon had passed through the marketplace, followed by a stream of sparks. The onlookers stood paralyzed, murmuring, "God have mercy on us!"

The wagon drew near the slaughterhouse, where the huge dogs that hung about the place sprang at the horses' throats; the muscular butcher boys came running out, grabbed the reins, and were on the wagon in a trice. The crowd drew near.

What's the meaning of it all? Nothing much—just a little difference between the men on the wagon. The "passenger" in the decent black gabardine gasps that the driver has gone mad. He wants the horses to dawdle and graze when it's a matter of life and death to get to the next market town without delay and sell the package of diamonds. At the mention of diamonds the crowd falls back respectfully. But the next instant confusion returns. The "driver" begins to yell that he is not the driver at all. The other man is the driver. They've come a long way. In the middle of the night, the real driver put a knife to the real passenger's throat and forced him to give up the package of diamonds—and here they are! The passenger denies every word of it! He is the passenger; the other man is the driver.

Who's to make head or tail of it? The crowd pulls the wagon around and leads it with "passenger" and "driver" to the rabbi's cottage. Let him find out.

And the rabbi of Chelm interrogates each man separately and privately. The plaintiff first, the man dressed like a driver. And he talks like a driver too. And looks like one. Coarse, massive, ignorant. A man of the woods. A voice that no kheyder chant has ever tempered.

But that is not enough for the rabbi of Chelm. He cross-examines.

"What's the value of your package of diamonds?"

"Rabbi, don't ask me. I'm an ignorant man. Can't sign my name, can't add up a column of figures. But God has been good to me, and so I'm a dealer in diamonds."

"How much money is there in the bag the other man took from you?"

"Rabbi, I never count my money. You know—it's bad luck."

The man is sent from the room. He's a wealthy merchant. Unbelievable! But the rabbi of Chelm sighs a heartbroken sigh for the wickedness of the world and asks that the other man, the "passenger," be sent in. And what a difference! From top to toe the man of learning. The rabbi feels him out with half quotations; the man caps them instantly, Talmud and commentaries. "Rabbi!" cries the man. "What's the good of all this? I'm in a hurry! Here!" And opening the bag, he pours out on the table a heap of diamonds mixed with gold coins—blazing diamonds and flaming gold. "Half yours and half mine, if you say it's all mine."

A faint scream from the rabbi's lips: "Robber!"

The crowd breaks in the door. Where's the "driver," where's the "passenger," where the diamonds and the coins? Gone like wisps of smoke! And all Chelm mutters: "Magic! Or a nightmare! God have mercy on us all!"

Meanwhile, below, Satan is furious:

"Imbeciles! Clumsy dolts! Maybe he's not beyond being bribed, but not that way. Not in the open, with a chance of being found out. Do you take him for an idiot?"

The two stupid imps are sentenced to a year of their own sulphur and brimstone. A second meeting is called. This time there is less enthusiasm, no yelling of "Me! Me! Me!" An elderly demon with a clear head and a long record accepts the assignment.

Autumn days in Chelm, between the New Year and the Day of Atonement: the penitential days, the time of the soul's reckoning and of decisions in heaven. The mud lies knee-deep in the streets of Chelm, the skies above are disconsolate. And a beggar man, all skin and bones, God help us, comes into the town limping on crutches and drags himself from house to house, from shop to shop. At every tenth door he gets a crust (and he has no teeth), and at every twentieth door a battered and faded kopeck, which almost slips out of his palsied fingers. Not that Chelm is uncharitable, but it is amply stocked with paupers of its own, paupers of standing, respectable paupers, the kind who starve in silence, widows and orphans of rabbis, relics of teachers and beadles and saints.

The newcomer crawls from house to house the first day, the second, the third. The cold and wet go through him; the soaked and dripping lining sticks out of his tattered coat; his eyes sink deeper and deeper into their sockets. And then suddenly he falls down right in the middle of the marketplace, foaming at the mouth. A crowd gathers about him. One person dashes water in his face, a second brings a cup of raisin wine, a third brings a knife to force between his teeth. Meanwhile, there are some who scream, "Chelm is Sodom and Gomorrah!" The beggar man is obviously dying.

God in heaven! They can't let him die in the street! On the other hand, who's going to take him in? Householders shrink back—every room in every house is overcrowded. And just then the rabbi comes up. And you have just one guess where the beggar man winds up.

So they carry him into the rabbi's one-room cottage and there he lies, in a trance. The rabbi sits at the table, a sacred book open before him. Every now and then, he casts a glance at the sick man. Outside the cottage a number of Jews linger uneasily—who knows whether help will be needed? Night draws on, and the rabbi is about to begin the evening prayer when he hears a stirring in the bed. He bends over the sick man compassionately, ear to lips.

"Rabbi," the sick man breathes, "I have been a great sinner. I cannot die without confessing."

The rabbi makes a gesture as if to call in witnesses. The sick man stops him. "God forbid. Just we two."

And he tells the rabbi that all his life he has been a mendicant—and a fraudulent one: he begged for bread in the name of wife and children, and never had wife or child; begged for dowries for the marrying off of aging daughters; collected funds for talmudic academies and for institutions in Palestine, but not a kopeck of that money was ever seen by a poor scholar or by a needy resident of the Holy Land. He peddled Palestine soil, which the pious put under their heads in their own coffins, and he had dug it under the nearest hedge.

And he draws from under his ragged kapote a linen bag, saying, "This is what I've collected and saved!" He opens it: wads of banknotes. "Take it, Rabbi. Distribute it among the poor. Do with it as you think fit."

The rabbi of Chelm leaps to the window with a joyous shout. He is suddenly fifty years younger. "Jews! Charity money! Come in and count!"

But when the Jews enter, the beggar has vanished. So has the sack of money. Magic again! Another nightmare!

Down below, Satan mutters: "This time it was not in the open; no chance of being found out."

The black folk are in despair! Then Lilith, the demon-woman, springs to the front. "I'll bring him in—the old ways are the best."

So it came to pass one day that the rabbi of Chelm, feeling some disturbance in his health, sent the beadle for the barber-surgeon, thinking that it might be well to do a little bloodletting. Meanwhile, the hour arrived for afternoon prayers, and the rabbi was stationed at the Eighteen Benedictions, which the worshiper must repeat standing motionless and facing east. The door opened and a young woman came in carrying a fowl. Obviously, a ritual question. Is the fowl kosher or unkosher? The rabbi is absorbed in his prayers; the young woman will wait. And waiting, she begins to hum to herself, absentmindedly as it were. And what a voice! The voice of womanhood itself! Need I tell you that the rabbi of Chelm doesn't even hear it? So the young woman, seemingly bored, sits down and begins to rock herself in the chair. The rocking and the humming fill the room. What of it? If a snake were to enter the room and bite the rabbi of Chelm, do you think that his attention would be deflected from his prayers?

The rabbi finishes the Eighteen Benedictions, takes the three ritual steps backward, spits ritually on idol worshipers, repeats the closing prayer, seats himself at the table, and says in his quiet, good-humored way, "Let's see the fowl."

The young woman leans forward to put the fowl in his hand; in the same good-humored voice the rabbi says: "Put it on the table. A grown-up Jewish girl should know better than that." She begins to tell where and how she got the fowl and makes a long story of it; she can't sit still, and begins to wander about the room as she talks. The voice fills every corner with music; the white teeth flash, the white body shines through the dress, her sleeves are rolled up, a perfume as of precious spices rises from her flesh. She stands behind the rabbi and leans over; she breathes on him. And it's all wasted. The rabbi listens, examines the fowl, puts it back on the table, and says: "Kosher! And you, young woman, had better see about getting yourself a husband."

Maid and fowl disappear through the window. The rabbi smiles. He knows all about it.

Again an assembly of the black folk below. Some say this and some say that. A young and untried demon, without a feather in his hat, without a tooth dangling from his neck, asks:

"But hasn't the rabbi of Chelm a single weakness?"

"Stripped clean of weaknesses" is the answer.

"No enjoyments?"

"Maybe the ritual steambath on Friday afternoon."

The young demon persists. "But hasn't he some special custom of his own, some harmless habit or trick—like rolling bread pills after a meal while he says grace?"

"Nobody's seen him eat. Probably has no such habit."

But then Lilith recalls that when the perfume of her body assailed the nostrils of the rabbi, he took a pinch of snuff.

"That's it!" exclaims the young demon.

Every Friday afternoon, having bathed for the Sabbath, the rabbi of Chelm used to go for a walk in the woods. He always took the same path, between a wheatfield and a cornfield; and as he walked, he repeated by heart—as pious Jews are wont to do on Friday afternoons—the Song of Songs. Now, knowing himself to be an absentminded man, and fearing that some Friday afternoon he would wander out too far and fail to return in time for the Reception of the Sabbath—a grievous transgression—he had created, for his own protection, a special device. He had measured the distance against the time it took to repeat the Song of Songs and had found that halfway through the prayer he reached a certain tree. There he would sit down, treat himself to a hearty pinch of snuff from his goat's-horn snuffbox, rest awhile, then get up and return, saying the second half of the prayer. Thus, he would get back exactly in time for the Reception of the Sabbath.

One fateful Friday, just before the rabbi of Chelm set out for his walk, a spindly-legged little fellow, dressed like a German in a derby hat and green-striped trousers, appeared on the scene, uprooted the tree mentioned above, and carried it out farther into the woods; he replanted it and sat himself down on the farther side.

The rabbi, meanwhile, arrives on the spot where he has always found the tree. He is halfway through the Song of Songs, and the tree, he perceives, is quite a distance off. He is shocked. Obviously, he has been repeating the prayer mechanically, rapidly, without absorption and contemplation—also a grievous transgression. He will do penance at once. He will refuse himself that pinch of snuff until he has reached the tree. His nose itches for the grateful tickle of the snuff, his heart is faint with longing—but no! Not until he has reached the tree. His limbs are feeble, and his steps are tottering. It takes him a long time to get there. And all the time there is this itching and longing, so that he can hardly see. And now at last he reaches the tree; he sits down and snatches the snuffbox from his pocket; but his hands are all atremble, and just at that moment a wind begins to blow from the other side of the tree (it's that miserable little German, of course, blowing) and the snuffbox falls out of the rabbi's hands. He reaches for it. The wind grows stronger and the box rolls away. The rabbi crawls after it on all fours, his body crying out for the strong taste of the snuff. The wretched German grins, and blows harder. Then suddenly he uproots the tree again, and replants it in its proper place. The rabbi looks up, wondering what has happened to the tree. He perceives that it is night; the sky is studded with stars! Sabbath has begun! The sun has set, and he has not even noticed it, so furiously has his heart been set on the pinch of snuff.

But wait, my friends. The sin of the rabbi in failing to appear for the Reception of the Sabbath was the lesser of the two sins into which his lust for snuff led him that evil day. For the demon kept blowing, the snuffbox kept rolling, and the rabbi, crawling after it in anguish, went out beyond the limits of a permissible Sabbath walk.

The brilliant young demon, returning to the nether regions, was at once entrusted with another highly important mission.

Addressing the mephitic assembly before his departure, he said:

"Gentlemen, nobody ever stubs his toe against a mountain. It's the little lusts that bring a man down."

1906 (translated by Maurice Samuel)

YOM KIPPUR IN HELL

▼

Once, on a perfectly ordinary day, without a fair or even an auction, a clatter of wheels and a spatter of mud aroused the merchants in the marketplace. Who, they wondered, could it be? It was a horse-drawn carriage. As soon as they saw it, though, they turned away in fear and revulsion. Both horse and carriage were well known. They belonged to a police informer from the neighboring town who was on his way to the provincial capital. God only knew who would be the victim of his talebearing this time.

All of a sudden, the noise stopped. Involuntarily, the merchants turned to look. The carriage had come to a halt, the horse had lowered its head to drink from a puddle, and the informer was sprawled senseless on his seat.

Say what you will, the man was a human being. People ran to help—but he already looked quite dead. An expert stepped up and confirmed the diagnosis. The members of the Burial Society rolled up their sleeves and went to work.

The horse and carriage were sold to pay the burial expenses, the informer was laid to rest, and the little devils who sprout where they are sown spirited the dead man's soul off to hell and delivered it to the gatekeepers.

The informer was brought for interrogation to the gatehouse, where the chief clerk plied him with wearisome questions and yawned as he wrote down the answers.

Taken down a peg by his surroundings, the informer answered everything: place and date of birth, age when married, length of time supported by father-in-law, number of children, year of desertion of wife, nature of profession and how acquired, and whatever other vital information pertained to his life on earth, which ended as he was driving his horse and carriage through the marketplace of Lahadam.[1]

The clerk, who was in the middle of another yawn, sat up.

"Say that again? Laha-what?"

"Lahadam," repeated the informer.

A gleam of interest flared in the clerk's eyes. "Did you ever hear of such a place?" he asked his assistants.

The assistant clerks shrugged and shook their heads, their mouths slightly open. "Never," they said.

"Would you check to see where it is?"

In hell every town has its registry, arranged in alphabetical order. Each letter has its file cabinet. The devils went through the whole *L* file: Leipzig, Lemberg, Lublin, every *L* on the map—Lahadam was not to be found.

"But it exists," insisted the informer. "It's a small town in Poland."

"Since when?"

"Since the local count gave it a charter twenty years ago. It has two fairs a year, a synagogue, a study house, a public bathhouse, two taverns for Gentiles . . ."

"Has anyone from there ever been here?" inquired the clerk.

"Not a soul," answered his assistants.

"Do you mean to tell us no one dies there?" the informer was asked.

"Why should no one die there?" he replied like a Jew, answering a question with a question. "They live packed together in squalor, the public bath can make you gag, the whole place is one big sty." The informer was beginning to feel in his element. "As a matter of fact, they have their own cemetery. And a burial society that charges an arm and a leg. Why, they even had an epidemic of plague there."

The informer received the sentence that was called for and an inquiry was called for too. Something was not right. How could a twenty-year-old town, and with an epidemic of plague no less, not have sent a single soul to hell?

Devils were sent out to investigate. Soon they flew back with their report:

"It's true, every word of it!"

There was indeed such a place, the devils explained, a town like any other, with here and there a good deed and a considerable lot of bad ones. The local economy? People managed, if not by hook, then by crook. So what was different about it? The cantor of the synagogue, that's what. Not that he himself was anyone special. But his voice! It was pure music, so tender and feeling that it could melt a heart of stone like wax. As soon as he started to pray, the whole congregation repented of their sins with such fervor that all was forgiven and forgotten in heaven above, whose gates stood open for every one of the townspeople. Just say you were from Lahadam and no more questions were asked!

Needless to say, it was a state of affairs that hell could not put up with. And it was a job for the director himself; no one else could be trusted to handle it.

What did Satan do?

He ordered fetched from the world of men a Calcutta cock with a comb as red as flame and had it placed before him on a table. Bewildered to find itself there, the rooster was too frightened to move. The archfiend crouched before it and crowed, fixing his evil eye on it until his black magic was done in a trice and the red comb was as white as chalk. Hearing a distant rumble of heavenly wrath, he quickly finished his spell with the curse:

"Begone, O voice, until he dies!"

There's no need to tell you whom he had in mind. Before the Calcutta cock's comb could turn red again, the cantor of Lahadam had lost his voice. He could barely utter a word; no sound came forth from his throat.

It was no secret who was to blame. That is, it was no secret to those Jews from whom there are no secrets, although perhaps not to all of them. After all, it wasn't something that you talked about even if you knew. But there it was and nothing could be done. Had the cantor been a man of more spiritual substance, there were measures that might have been taken, but he was a no-account, a lightweight. And so, though he went from one wonder-worker to another, none was able to help him.

In the end, he turned to the saintly rabbi of Apt. Indeed, he all but went down on his knees and refused to leave the rabbi's room without an answer. You never saw such a pitiful sight.

The rabbi sought to comfort him. "I can tell you," he said, "that your hoarseness will last only until you die. Your deathbed confession will be said in a voice that will reach to the far ends of heaven."

"And until then?"

"It's hopeless."

"But why, Rabbi?" implored the cantor. "Why me?"

He pestered the rabbi of Apt for so long that the rabbi finally gave in and told him the whole story.

"In that case," croaked the cantor as he ran out of the rabbi's room, "I'll make sure that I get my revenge."

"How?" called the rabbi after him. "On whom?"

But the cantor was already gone.

This happened on a Tuesday, or perhaps it was a Wednesday. Thursday evening, when the fishermen of Apt went down to the river to haul in their catch for the Sabbath, their nets seemed heavier than usual. They pulled them out of the water: in them lay the drowned cantor!

He had jumped off the bridge. And just as the rabbi of Apt promised, his voice was restored in time for his last confession, since Satan's curse lasted only until his death. Yet since the confession could not be said under water, his voice remained trapped within him—which is, as you will see, exactly what he had counted on.

The cantor was buried behind the graveyard fence, as is the custom with suicides, and the devils whisked his soul off to hell. When asked by the clerk at the gate for his life story, however, he refused to answer. He was prodded with sharp lances, with burning coals—not a word.

"Then take him away!"

As if they didn't know all about him anyway! In fact, they had been eagerly awaiting him. But as he was led off to a cauldron of boiling water that was being stoked just for him, he tapped his throat with his thumb and burst out:

"Yisgada-al! . . ."[2]

The Kaddish—and in the special melody of Yom Kippur!

He sang—and his voice sounded far and wide, as good as ever, no, even better, sweeter and so much more tender. The cauldrons, which had reverberated with howls and groans, grew suddenly silent; then, from within them, voices took up the prayer. The cauldron lids lifted, heads peered out for a look, scorched mouths began to sing along.

The devils attending the kettles did not join in, of course, but rather stood there dumbstruck, mouths agape, tongues hanging out, faces contorted, eyes red as coals, some still holding a log to stoke the fire with, others gripping an iron poker or trident. A few even threw themselves epileptically to the ground while the cantor went on singing. Beneath the cauldrons the fires died down. Here and there a dead man began climbing out.

The cantor sang on and hell's inmates sang with him, fervently, with all their hearts, their bodies made whole again, the flesh healed on their bones, their souls cleansed of all sin. When he reached the prayer in the Shimenesre that praises God the Resurrector, the dead came back to life and answered "Amen" in one voice. And when he sang the words "May His great name be blessed," there echoed back such a chorus of voices that the heavens opened on high, and the repentance of the damned reached the seventh heaven, where God's own mercy seat stands, and the moment of grace was so great that the sinners, now converted into saints, sprouted wings and flew out of the jaws of hell and through the open doors of paradise.

No one was left behind but the devils, writhing on the ground, and the cantor, who never budged from his place.

As in his lifetime, all repented through him but he himself could not repent. A suicide!

After a while hell filled up again. New quarters were added, but still the crowding was great.

1915 (translated by Hillel Halkin)

My Memoirs

When Peretz was asked in 1913 to serialize his memoirs for the Vilna monthly Yidishe velt (Jewish World), he agreed with mixed feelings: "Only the aging are asked to write memoirs. You're saying that my granary is full and it's time to hand over the key." He did agree to provide the "key" to his public persona, but he made a distinction between the author and the private man:

> I won't tell all. Because I didn't put everything into my writing, and it's only my writing that concerns the reader. Before he prays, the pious Jew goes to the ritual bath to wash his sins away. The writer does this spiritually before he writes. (Except for the "modern" writer, who parades his sinfulness, or invents it if he hasn't got as much as the market demands, fleshing out possibilities that didn't have time to develop on their own. Often he just steals from others.)

This provocative assault on the exhibitionism of his contemporaries is a strange introduction to the ensuing memoirs, which describe, after all, the transformation of a pious Jewish boy into a modern intellectual and artist who has not seen the inside of a ritual bath since adolescence. The "ritual bath" is to be understood not as the literal mikve of observant Jews, but as its ethical equivalent, a spirit of modesty that Peretz believed the Jewish writer carried over with him into his new secular life, preserving Jewish values where there were no longer any practical Jewish commandments. The ritual bath may have come to mind because despite the inhibiting effects of his upbringing on his sexual development in particular, in telling of his self-emancipation from religious civilization Peretz never doubted that he remained morally and emotionally its native son.

Peretz's approach to autobiography was very different from that of Abramovitch (Mendele) and Rabinovitch (Sholem Aleichem), who also left distinguished accounts of their childhood and adolescence. Mendele, "the grandfather of Yiddish literature," felt that the life of the individual Jew was so organically joined to the life of his people that Jewish autobiography was a subspecies of anthropology. Sholem Aleichem wrote about himself as though he were one of his own characters, providing the romance of the Jewish writer to stand alongside (but artistically superior to) the romances of the Jewish fiddler, cantor, and actor that he had already written. Peretz probed the mystery of himself. He first recalls himself as a precocious three-year-old who spells from memory, letter by letter, the first chapter of Leviticus. He concludes the memoirs with a moment of the sharpest possible contrast: while recuperating from a near-fatal heart attack in the Swiss Alps, he heard the whistle of a shepherd boy cutting imperiously through an Alpine storm. The memoirs evoke the attempts of the Jewish boy to integrate these opposing claims of intellectual discipline and creative abandon, which formed his being.

The autobiographer warns that he is not to be regarded as a strict chronicler of events, because he does not trust much in mere facts: "Only what's genuinely characteristic of the person should be emphasized, not the accidental events of his life." Memory is stored in the subconscious, and it is from there that Peretz draws out the important scenes and impressions, very much as he does in crafting his stories and dramas. The modern Yiddish scholar David Roskies believes that the memoirs are the maturest expression of Peretz's literary theory: "Because Peretz believes that traditional mimetic methods cannot adequately communicate the complicated problematic of autobiography, he develops his own artistic theory, whose antimimetic axes are symbolism, which reveals the higher truth, and psychology, which reveals the hidden, innermost truth."

Peretz admits that he is careless about details: "If someone comes along later and adds 'the date' where necessary—that's fine. I can't do it." Taking this cue, and because the reader may be interested in the historical as well as the literary aspects of the text, we have filled in the names of relatives and friends where Peretz provided only initials, corrected occasional inexactitudes, and provided corroborative dates and information in the notes whenever it seemed helpful. Except for two very *small excisions, the memoirs have been translated in their entirety. The first seven chapters appeared in successive issues of* Yidishe velt. *The chapter "I Get Married" was published in* Dos lebn, Warsaw, 1914.

MY MEMOIRS

▼

I: CHILDHOOD AND CHILDHOOD TEACHERS

I was, as everyone said, a prodigy. I had a quick, logical mind and was very emotional. How are the two things connected? They aren't. They don't mix at all. A logical brain and a heart full of feeling are two litigating parties in the creature who the sages tell us was "born to die."[1]

Just between us, I tried to sketch myself in the poem "Monish." But I improved on my looks. Unlike Monish, I was thin and dark, though I did have large, burning eyes (sparks of which remain). The boy with the penetrating mind—"However stony the *Rambam* / he finds a cleft in the rock"—is me.[2] But when I added that I was adept as a public reader of the Scriptures, it was just for the sake of the rhyme. In fact I never really learned to chant the portion of the week. For us the thing that mattered most was the study of Talmud.

Like Monish, I heard "Maria" singing to me from the ruins, but in my case, there was more than one Maria. I'll tell about them, but I won't tell all. I don't intend to give you the incidentals. Only what affected me and my writing. But in any event, I haven't gotten to that part yet. This is still the chapter on childhood.

Thinking back, I can remember myself when I was very small: (1) among boys and girls in a courtyard; (2) on the floor in kheyder: the teacher Chaim Kelbl was a short man with a small beard, tiny eyes, and a fur-brimmed hat; and (3) under the arm of the teacher's assistant as he carried me to school during a snowstorm.

At age three I began to study Torah along with the other boys.

We began, as is customary, with *Vayikra*, which I pronounced *vayitra* because I couldn't say a *k* or a hard *g*. For years the boys made fun of the way I'd say the words, "Gad, a troop shall press upon him" (*Gad gdud yegudeni*), from Jacob's blessing in Genesis.[3]

The celebration for my commencement of Bible study took place after the Sabbath meal at my grandfather's house. During the meal my grandfather, a short man with a small, trembling head (due to age, as I realized later), lifted me and set me down in the middle of the table. My mother was frightened and quickly snatched a fork away from under me. Around the table sat the entire family: a son, two daughters, two sons-in-law, and a widow (my great-aunt, whom, without exaggerating in the slightest, I turned into the saintly "rabbi of Skul's wife" in my *Impressions of a Journey*), as well as my grandfather and grandmother. Why they set me up there I don't know. I liked it. There was a vase on the table, but when I tried to see if I could put my hands around it, my grandmother took it away and asked me if I would be able to deliver the commentary later.

"Tan" (Can), I answered, ready to get down off the table. I couldn't sit long in one spot. I was held there by my uncle in the black fedora who was already a bit of a modern, and who later valued my juvenilia enough to collect them and hide them away.[4]

"*Vayitra*—" he mimicked me. "Can you spell it?" I didn't know what spelling was, so I asked, "What?"

"How do you write *Vayikra*?"[5]

I assumed he was joking. Annoyed, I answered, "You don't write *vayitra*. *Vayitra* is a verse in a chapter of the holy Torah."

They finally got me to understand what was meant, and I suddenly saw the chapter suspended before my eyes, word by word; I read off one letter after another, except for the name of God.

My mother's eyes grew moist (incredible how I saw everything), something made her blink, and she got up and went over to the oven in the corner. My grandmother watched her and smiled: "She still gets embarrassed."

Grandfather lifted me from the table onto his lap and pinched my cheek. But I didn't stay there long—it was uncomfortable on his bony legs. I went over to my father, who kissed me.

I don't know or remember any more of my grandfather. I know that his name was Shloyme, and he had been a Danzig merchant. The story was told that he once came home on a Friday "with nothing but his whip." He went to the bathhouse, then to Sabbath services, and he proceeded to celebrate the Sabbath day as always, with no sign of distress. Only after the Havdala service, once the

Sabbath was over, did he convene all his creditors and say to them: "Gentlemen, I've come back without a penny. Take whatever we have in the house." Turning to his wife he said, "Chanele, give them what we have." Then my grandmother took off her jewelry and laid it on the table, opened the cabinets with the silver and gold, and brought in all the household valuables from the next room. But no one touched a thing.

My grandmother owned a shop. During the years that followed they lived off her earnings, paid off the debts one by one, with interest, and had enough to provide their children with dowries.

I can't guarantee how much of the story is true. But I do know that my grandmother was capable of doing this. All I remember of grandfather is that time at the table when I performed. I see his eyes, bright and generous. How or when Grandfather died I don't know either. I was probably kept away when it happened, or I wouldn't have forgotten it. I heard that when he was sick the doctor told him to take a hot bath, and that he died in the bathtub.

I will leave family matters for the time being and return to my teachers of childhood.

I started studying Gemara when I was six, according to the custom of the time.

I remember my Gemara teacher, a thin little man called Berishl. He was an angry little man, but he couldn't beat us because his hands shook when he got angry. So he would call out to his wife, "Henne! Grab the poker and split this dumbbell's skull!"

Henne never budged. She sat next to the oven, plucking feathers or knitting a sock. If it concerned me, she said, "Don't you dare touch Leybushl, do you hear, or I'll go and tell Rivele." Rivele was my mother. The teacher's wife was a peddler of onions and other produce, and we were among her steady customers. She loved my mother, and I suppose that her affection extended to me too. "Rivele's a saint," she would say. "She denies herself and her family so that she should have enough for charity. She really *gives* to charity! And this criminal wants to beat her Leybushl."

"All right, all right," the teacher grumbled, "but don't forget to tell her what a jewel of a brat she has."

She would tell my mother—that I was a jewel.

Anyway, my father would not have let the teacher beat me. He was opposed to corporal punishment. Years before, when he was still being supported by his in-laws, the word went out that the government would be drafting men into the army. He was a liberal, and something of an anarchist, and when people got frightened, his advice was not to be frightened and not to comply. People should just refuse to go.

They said, "We'll be whipped."

He said, "They can't whip the whole world."

"They will take us away in chains."

"There aren't chains enough!"

"They'll put us into prison."

"Only if they make the world a prison."

He slapped me only twice. The first time was at my brother's circumcision party. From the time I was born I hated sweets. I wouldn't touch them, and I was teased for it. "You want people to think you're smart" (according to the proverb, fools eat sweets). My grandmother used to bake all kinds of goodies: sponge cake, honey cake, torte, cookies dipped in honey; she used to put up jam for herself, for her children, for the sick in the poorhouse. All her grandchildren got tummyaches from time to time—you're given a little, you take a little on your own. I was the only exception. To this day I don't eat sweets.

On the day of the circumcision party the poor came for cake and liquor, and gathered in the central hall of the house. In the room to the right was my mother, who had just given birth. On the left were the prominent guests. We had hired a servant for the occasion— he will have to pardon me but he was a son of a bitch and that's what everyone called him. I can still see him as he was, uncommonly tall and thin, with a bloodless pallor. He was a childless widower; he'd had several wives but no children. After the last wife had died, he gave up on life and made himself a shroud. They said that at night he patrolled the courtyard in his shroud, frightening people. He bore a special hatred for the poor.

This son of a bitch was carrying a tray of cakes high above his head from my mother's room to the respectable company across the hall. I happened to see a sickly girl looking up at the tray with ravenous eyes. I was nimble enough to leap up, grab a piece of cake, and hand it to her. My father, whom I didn't notice in the doorway of Mother's room, saw the leap into the air, but not what I did with the cake when I landed. He came over and slapped my face.

The next day he complained about me to my mother as we sat at the table. "This actor pretends not to eat sweets, but he grabs cake from the tray!" At that point the servant girl, who probably heard this from behind the door, came in with the soup and told him what she had seen me do with the cake.

My mother lowered her eyes. She always hid her feelings, even from us. Father turned pale, and his eyes grew moist. He got up and went into the next room. This left me feeling guilty. I wanted to follow and ask his pardon for not explaining myself before, but I couldn't do it. To this day I can't defend myself or ask anyone's pardon.

The second time I earned a slap, I was no longer a child but "a young man" (all of fourteen, at least!). I had already developed philosophic inclinations, and was studying Maimonides' *Guide to the Perplexed*. My time was spent in the higher spheres, in a state of melancholy, dreaming and thinking about the tragedy of the world. What was the purpose of the human race? Of the world? Why do we have knowledge and free will? What is the origin of grief and pain, and what is their purpose? The premature passage into manhood of Jewish males certainly played a role in this, but I was also in a dark state of mind, and looked for solitude so that I could scratch away at my soul in private.

One Friday I disappeared for the whole day. I don't even remember where I was. I returned to the study house right before Sabbath services, still in the weekday coat and cap I had worn for my walk, my boots smeared with mud from the fields outside town. My father's face flushed when he saw me. As long as he was in public, he restrained himself, but at home, over the blessings, he couldn't take his eyes off my gloomy face, and suddenly, putting down the wine goblet, he slapped me across the face. "What lovely Sabbaths he prepares for me!" And he left the room. My mother murmured, "As if a child doesn't have his own troubles." It didn't occur to her that the things troubling me might not be childish.

I was slapped just twice.

My father certainly would not have allowed a stranger to lay a hand on me. Reb Berishl knew it, and so did his wife who sat next to the oven doing her knitting while we studied. Above her head on the ledge of the oven lay their cat, a big, lazy creature. If ever the wife, lulled to sleep by the sound of our chanting, nodded off while knitting and dropped her ball of wool, the watchful cat would leap off the ledge and chase the ball under the bed, as if it were a mouse. We would burst out laughing, waking the wife, and throwing the teacher into a rage.

For this laughter (mine was the loudest) he once wanted to beat me in earnest. But just then my father happened to come in. The scene suddenly changed. "Ah, Reb Yudl! How are you? Sit down, Reb Yudl." The teacher's wife asked after my mother, but my father turned right to me: "Why are you sweating like that, Leybele?"

"What do you mean?" the teacher broke in, worried that I would tell on him. "The holy Torah warms us up, thank God, and it's a summer day."

My father was struck by a liberal idea. "Do you know what, Reb Berishl? Why not let the children go outside and play for an hour every day?"

Reb Berishl looked as though he had been struck by lightning. "What do you mean?" he stammered, eyes popping. "Let them go out and mess around in the clay?" Another story was being added to the house, so there was clay heaped up outside.

"Why not?" replied my father.

Reb Berishl yielded somewhat. "Well, if you say so, I'll allow your Leybushl to go out."

"Me too! Me too!" cried my cousin Yekhezkl.

"I can vouch for Reb Mordekhai too," said my father. Mordekhai was Yekhezkl's father.

And so the two of us got permission to play outside for an hour a day. With a shovel that we found somewhere we dug valleys and ditches in the clay, and built a fortress. This work of ours helped us to do a kind deed. Some time after this the fortifications around Zamosc were pulled down. The walls were demolished, and laborers were hired to dig up the ramparts and fill in the moats with the rubble. They were paid by the cubic meter. The group that showed up to do the work included a few Jews—elderly, worn-out men who were no longer fit for any other kind of work. Since this was close to our schoolroom, we would run to the ramparts for that hour, and work for the old men. What I learned from Reb Berishl I no longer remember.[6]

After two terms my cousin and I moved on to Mikhl the Melamed. He didn't beat his students either.

He was a strange man, this "Blond Mikhl" with his yellow beard. He was both a teacher and the study-house sexton, and he knew mathematics and geometry. He was never seen studying Torah except with us in kheyder. In the study house he never spoke up at all, and if asked about our studies, he would answer only if the passage concerned mathematics or geometry, at which point he was transformed into another person and spoke with real love of his subject.

Ordinary study was no great concern of his. He would look pityingly at a dull boy, "the poor blockhead." He was indifferent to the good student; when he said to him, "You'll be a scholar," his tone implied: "So what? What does it matter?" Sometimes he even said with barely concealed contempt, "Well, you'll be a rabbi some-day!" As no one ever saw him praying, they said he was "a secret Kotsker." (The Kotsker Hasidim did not believe in prayer.) But if he was a Kotsker, he would have had to keep it secret; our city was anti-Hasidic, and the study house too. To give you some idea of local feeling, I recall the following incident. Beside the reading stand prayed a shrunken man named Reb Azrilekhl, an innkeeper, known for his fanaticism, who was so old and frail the merest breath could blow him away. Once during the evening service a very tall, stout stranger joined us to say the Mourner's Kaddish. When he blurted out the words, "Let there come the Redemption,"[7] from the fragment of the prayer that only Hasidim used, Reb Azrilekhl, old as he was, leaped over tables and benches to the front of the study house and slapped the mighty stranger's face.

So Reb Mikhl might well have been concealing his Kotsker affiliation when he wandered around during the service in his prayer shawl and phylacteries without moving his lips. He never laid a hand on his students. I was the special favorite of his wife, whose sister was a servant at our house. I still recall with amazement how the two sisters resembled one another. In my absentmindedness, I would often say to the teacher's wife in kheyder, "Chana, hand me a glass of water," and to the servant at home, "Pardon me, Rebetsin. . . ." Both were modest Jewish beauties, at least in my youthful judgment: pale, oval faces with delicate, transparent skin, and long lashes guarding the soft glance of their almond eyes. That's all I remember, and I don't know what became of them. Nor do I remember what I learned from Blond Mikhl. If I did no more than copy his silence, I must have absorbed from it the good-hearted sorrow that I recognize in some of my writings. Maybe those meditative eyes passed on to me a little of his Hasidism?

My cousin and I next moved on to the more advanced Gemara teacher Reb Yudl. With him we also learned to chant the portion of the week.

Reb Yudl loved two things: lashing our fingers with switches, and the *pirogen* that his wife would make for him on special occasions—leaving the house soon after because she couldn't stand "the greedy way he eats them with the fat running down his chin."

This rebetsin had nothing to do with the students and wasn't a friend of my mother's, so there was no reason for her to protect me from the teacher. By this time my father was a merchant, rarely at home. So Reb Yudl enjoyed himself, and I went around with swollen fingers, like everyone else, and waged ongoing war against him along with the others. The second term, when we went from *Baba Kama* to the more difficult tractate of *Yebamoth*, our warfare sharpened accordingly. We were often punished for no reason at all. Reb Yudl had poor eyesight, and since he could never see who was responsible, he whipped everyone alike. He would lovingly choose the supplest switches from the new broom that his wife bought from time to time (or perhaps she even sold brooms for a living) and whip us with pleasure and at length.

But we didn't spare him either. He had a long white beard that we once tried to glue to the table. It was evening, and he had dozed off after the *pirogen*. We melted down some sealing wax in the flame of a candle and set to work. But someone's hand must have trembled and accidentally pulled a hair from his beard. Reb Yudl woke up and whipped us all. However, on the next holiday, we caught the rebetsin's laying hen and set her on the bowl of *pirogen* that had been placed under the pillow to keep them warm. The teacher came in, set the bowl in front of him, peered at it with his blind eyes, and smiled with pleasure: "Look at all those fried onions!" Then he bit into one of them.

Once, we lured him out onto an ice rink that stretched in back of the study house. Between the afternoon and evening services we had covered it up with snow, and then we sent in one of the boys to report that we were skating, which was of course forbidden. He came out, stepped onto the rink, and flipped over. He was a heavy man. Each time he tried to get up, he fell down again. We roared with laughter, and started to scatter. He pleaded with us to help him get up, and swore that he would never whip us or punish us again. We helped him get up, and he kept his word. But we got our punishment anyway, because for the third term my cousin and I were transferred to a *really* angry teacher.

This one pinched. He was a *mohel* who performed ritual circumcisions, and he applied the long fingernail of his trade to our flesh as well. Here too we retaliated. He wore a wide-brimmed hat, so we filled the brim with snow. When he sat at the table, the water poured down over his face.

He loved tea. Every day his wife boiled water in a small tin samovar and poured in a few tea leaves. He always grumbled, "It isn't dark enough." She paid no attention, though the tea was really very watery. So once we took some axle grease and poured it into the samovar. When it boiled, he poured himself a glass of tea as black as ink. What pleasure he anticipated! He threw his wife a grateful glance and set the glass in front of him. But as he was about to raise it to his lips, we got scared that he might poison himself, God forbid. Someone gave the table a kick, and the tea spilled into his lap— boiling hot. . . .

The most spiteful thing we did was something else entirely: we were studying the section *Eyzehu neshekh,* and he tormented us with hair-splitting questions, digging out the answers with his long nail.[8] We knew that he was no great scholar. Neither the questions nor the answers were original. So sometimes on a Sabbath afternoon we would go to the study house and look up all the commentaries we could find on the topic for the week ahead. On Sunday mornings we would pepper him with questions. He was round and fat, and as he sat there mute, squirming like a worm, his eyes flickering in panic, we burst out laughing. He resorted to his usual weapon.

On Friday he would give everyone a beating, which was supposed to be in fun: it was an old custom to make frisky boys remember to keep the Sabbath day holy; but it often hurt.

And yet, sometimes we liked him, liked him very much. On a holiday the boys would bring change (two, three, at most ten groschen) and use it to have a feast. The teacher's wife would set out her goods: herring, cookies, and hot lima beans. His only daughter, a sad, pale girl with big, misty eyes, would join us for the meal. The teacher would stroke her golden-yellow hair, and tell us stories from the *Eyn Yakov* and from the Talmud. He was quite another person then, friendly, pleasant, and with such sweet tenderness in his voice that his normally stern rebetsin at the separate table across from us wiped the tears from her eyes. How we loved him *then*!

After that I suffered exile: I was sent to study with a teacher in Shebreshin, three miles away, and thereafter privately, at home.

2: MORE HAZY YEARS

More hazy years, the unformed years of childhood. . . . At times I was a piece of wax kneaded by various hands, with the impress of their alien fingers on my soul; at other times I felt the stirrings not of will, I suppose, but of willfulness, of desires, and I would pull off what they called wild stunts.

My inner self, as a child, was very feeble. I was a sponge, and whatever I soaked up became part of me without my knowledge, as if I hadn't been present. The eye saw, but I was not looking; the ear absorbed, but I was not listening. And it all got mixed up together. No sooner did some kind of structure begin to take shape in me than new childish whims blew it down, like houses piled on top of one another, with something protruding here and there—a rooftop, a weather vane, a chimney.

I had a nasty aunt, Yekhezkl's mother. The Yiddish writer Dr. Shloyme Ettinger based his portrait of "Serkele" on her.[9] She was a tall, thin woman, pale and sickly, forever yelling, "Give me strength!" and drinking almond milk to "soothe her throat." She used to bake cheesecake (the only sweet thing I like), which she ate herself, but hid on a high shelf in the cupboard so that the children should not get stomachaches, God forbid. Because I loved cheesecake, and to defy her, and just to pull off the stunt, I would jump up, hang on to the ledge of the cupboard, and stuff myself with cake until I really did get a stomachache. Then came grouchy old Dr. Skrishinski, who would later keep me from being drafted, and he prescribed something bitter and salty, a white liquid in a small bottle. The minute his back was turned, I poured out the mixture, replaced it with a little milk and water, and took a teaspoonful every hour, extracting the promise of presents as compensation from my parents, and making such a face you would think I was swallowing poison. As soon as I got well, I waited for Skrishinski at the window—he lived just opposite us—and when I saw him I stuck out my tongue. He grabbed a stick and ran over to our house to give me a thrashing. I was alone in the house. When I heard him on the stairs, I threw open the door of our red cupboard and jumped in, landing one foot in a pot of eggs.

Near our house was an overgrown ruin, probably a property under litigation. Quite often in the evening I used to play there with little girls at bride and groom. I of the fiery eyes was the bridegroom, and the bride was my cousin, who wore long braids. When we got to the part of the game where the newlyweds quarrel and argue over the presents, I threw a stone, hitting her just under the eye, and leaving her with a scar that she carried to her real wedding.

I also played general, with a whole troop of kheyder boys under my command. At that time there was a shortage of banknotes and not enough small change, so the government allowed merchants to use their own credit notes as currency. My father prepared some notes; I helped myself to a few, and exchanged them for wooden swords with cardboard scabbards, and for braided cord to tie them around the hips of my brave warriors. We prepared for a war with the "foresters"—our name for the boys of the suburb a couple of miles outside Zamość. The battle was to take place midway between the two, on the other side of the graveyard that served both communities.

Meanwhile, I enjoyed the easygoing talmudic commentary of Rabbi Nissim, and I was bothered by the excessive strictness of the *Pri-Megadim*. I worked up ingenious interpretations of my own and tried them out on the charity boys who spent their days in the study house.

In the mornings I had no breakfast, only coffee, and, following the teachings of *Duties of the Heart*, I brought my buttered bagel to Avigdor the Teacher's orphaned son, who frequented the study house. When I prayed, I said the Eighteen Benedictions in the manner prescribed by Maimonides, standing erect like a soldier at the front, with my arms along the seams of my trousers. I also knew from Rabbi Gershom that the Prophet Elijah didn't really fly up to heaven, and that according to Maimonides miracles are not really miracles at all, not "radical alterations."

In the study house I introduced all kinds of innovations in checkers and chess. We drew the board in chalk in front of the holy ark—it was cleaner there! The white checkers and chessmen we kneaded from white or rye dough or carved from potatoes; the black pieces we left in their skins.

Often I would go to pray in the *shtibl* of the Belz Hasidim. I was drawn by their intensity and rapture, the way they cried out and banged their heads against the wall during the standing prayer. Other times, because of its peaceful atmosphere (as I would say nowadays), I went to the *shtibl* of the Ger Hasidim for their final Sabbath meal.

I found my way on the one hand to the classic work of Jewish rationalism, Maimonides' *Guide to the Perplexed*, which lay on the uppermost shelf (who uses it, anyway?), and on the other hand to the classic of kabbalah, *The Tree of Life*, which might someday take me all the way to the Zohar itself. Sometimes I pulled down *Oracles of the Prophets*, that difficult tome which sharpened my wits like a whetstone.[10]

These are the facts of not quite three hazy childhood years. What am I to do with them? On what sort of narrative chain shall I string these little stones and glass beads, and the few genuine pearls? One theme that ties them together is my discovery of four-footed creatures. That is something I can tell about properly.

The city into which I was born, hemmed in by ramparts so that it would never change or grow in size, I didn't really see until I was sent to Shebreshin, three miles away, to study there for a term. And if I wasn't aware of the city, I certainly wasn't aware of its inhabitants. Zamość was a small, quiet place without any premonition of the wandering and emigration yet to come. Hardly anyone died, hardly anyone was born. Once, though, when I was part of the "night watch" at the bedside of a woman in labor, I was almost frightened by "the tiny red mousekin" they showed us when it was delivered.[11]

I remember the explosion, the resounding barrage when they blasted the walls of the fortress, and the terror of my teacher and his wife lest it crack the walls of the houses. I also remember the panic when a fire broke out in the clock tower above the city hall. People prepared to evacuate. It was during a snowstorm. When the tower began to sway, there was fear that it would fall and crush the houses to the right or the left, sending the whole city up in flames. While they were packing at home, I ran to the synagogue to save the Scrolls of the Torah.

It was only much later that I began to notice people, in Apt, in Tsoyzmer, in my travels through Poland, in Warsaw. Meanwhile, as I mentioned, I struck up an acquaintance with animals.

I became acquainted with cats as far back as Reb Berishl's kheyder, and we had one at home for a while, but it was gotten rid of so that I wouldn't play with it. I knew where milk and cream came from, also cheese and buttermilk, and there was goat's milk for medicinal purposes now and then, but I didn't actually see any cows or oxen. Bleating and mooing I heard only when my friends did animal imitations. Cows and oxen were brought to our slaughterhouse—"ours" because my grandfather held the lease on the farm where it was situated—but they went by the main road that circled the city. No firstborn bull calf such as I read about in the Scriptures and later in literature ever grazed in Zamość, which cultivated the reputation of being "Little Paris."

I knew horses well—also from the proper distance. In the "little courtyard," before a large, square, old house facing four intersecting streets at the edge of the city near the Lemberg road gate, right across from my teacher's house, the peasants would congregate on market days with their wagons. It was from one of those wagons that we got the grease to put into our teacher's samovar. I made whips out of horsehair, but I didn't pull them out myself, partly out of fear, partly because I didn't want to cause the animals pain.

The officers of the garrison kept horses, and when they left, mounted Cossacks took their place, or sometimes uhlans and hussars.

At the parting ceremony in the square for the soldiers who were leaving for the Turkish War, there was a young general on a beautiful mount with a coat of satiny sheen. It was braided with ribbons, and its charm brought to mind the passage in the Song of Songs, "Unto the horse in Pharaoh's chariot do I compare thee."[12]

Israel Zhdanover boasted that he had "steeds like lions" to hire for anyone who wanted to get somewhere in a hurry instead of poking along in a peasant's wagon.

Zhdanov, three miles past the Lemberg gate, had been founded some years back as a Jewish farm colony. To attract Jews to agriculture, the Polish government offered certain inducements: long-term credit, and more important, exemption from the draft. The colony's founder, Dr. Shloyme Ettinger, had worked the land himself, along with his children, but that was before my time. In my day the good doctor was long since dead, and his son built churches, growing richer from day to day. Out of jealousy people said, "You can still smell the manure on his hands."

The only survivor of the colony was Israel, who wasn't making a bad living at all. He ran a dairy farm; his wife delivered milk to town, and on Shavuot also butter and round cheeses, providing stiff competition for the dairy farmer in Shutanietz, at the other end of town, who also hired out "steeds like lions."

Now for the acquaintance I struck up with dogs.

At first, I only heard about them. An old German-Jewish woman died. She was said to have been a sinner who wore her own hair and had other blots on her record as well. They said that her soul had entered a dog, a black dog with tangled fur that prowled the roof of her house night after night. The teacher's helper, who worked for us on Fridays preparing the fish, saw the dog with his own eyes. During the penitential days before the High Holy Days, when I walked to prayers with my father in the early hours before dawn, I strained to see the dog on the roof—despite the fear that I would—but there was never a trace of him. His soul must have been granted its release.[13]

My friends in kheyder and the study house, and other young men as well, had a lot to say about dogs. The dogs were a major impediment. They didn't let anyone out of town alive.

Past the Lemberg gate, past the cemetery, and another two miles beyond the suburb, was the village of Yatutov. The inn there served a mead that was famous in the region, attracting even the local landowners. It also appealed to our young married men.

Apparently, in the old days, Jews used to go to Yatutov on Fridays in the summer, after the ritual bath and bloodletting, to fortify themselves with a glass of mead before the Sabbath.[14] But now it couldn't be done because of the ferocious dogs kept by Gentiles along the way. One of the local young married men, who was still boarding at his in-laws', bet that he could get past them. "Do you have a magic verse to ward them off?" he was mocked by his friends. No, but an old peasant told him that dogs have a fatal weakness for bread soaked in human sweat. He would knead a piece of soft bread until it was saturated in his sweat, and toss it to the dogs. His friends laid bets on the outcome. He went, and returned—without his pants, if you will pardon me, and without a hunk of his thigh. When they got wind of the story at home, his in-laws handed him a divorce.

I've mentioned the dairy farmer in Shutanietz, the village beyond the Lemberg gate and the slaughterhouse. He kept a small dairy inn where in the summertime he sold sour cream for three cents a bowl—straight from the cellar, and kept wonderfully cold by the earthenware—and hard cheese with caraway seeds. But there were also fierce dogs in the village. You could try to stop on the road, and call out his name, "Yusl!" and maybe he would come out with his whip and chase off the dogs. But suppose he wasn't there? The dogs would be the ones to hear you, and their barking was bad enough.

You couldn't even get as far as the slaughterhouse, where the slaughterers roasted the udders of the animals and were prepared to offer you a taste. The dogs with their bloodshot eyes got along fine with the butchers, licking the blood from their hands and their blood-spattered boots. But the slaughterers were not always safe. Unlike the butchers, who wore coveralls girded with a rope, the slaughterers dressed in long kapotes that were most unpopular with the dogs. We were sure that when the Jews left Egypt they were also dressed in kapotes, and of the many miracles associated with that occasion, the greatest is that "not a dog whet his tongue against them."[15]

Behind the officers' quarters was a green valley, prettier than the meadow by the riverside. There were flowers, and it was a pleasant place to take a walk. Where the demolished fortress had been you could find stacks of shells and bullets, still a bit frightening, except that it was now safe to examine them, point at them, or even touch them with your hand—"Isn't this interesting?" The fortress was no longer a fortress; the walls were razed and three-fourths of the ramparts had been dug up. But the passageway was blocked for us by the colonel's dog, a huge black shaggy dog (apparently the model for the German Jewess's metamorphosis) that was big as an ox. He was chained up, but what if he tore loose? It wouldn't take much for a dog like that to break his chain, especially at the sight of a Jewish kapote. The only one who dared to go there was my wealthy relative Yehoshua Margulies, who owned a house in town, a farm outside of town, and a second house in Warsaw where he spent several months of the year. He was a contractor. He frequented the club, and often had the colonel over to the house on business, or went to his house for a game of preference. In fact, he kept his own dogs at the farm, and knew how to handle them. Most important— he dressed pretty much like a Gentile.

Even pedigreed little dogs hated Jewish children, and this was a problem when we went swimming in the river in the summer. There were meadows all around the site of the fortress. Its inspector, who was apparently left to fend for himself when it was demolished, laid claim to the hay of the meadows, and didn't want Jewish kids to go swimming because instead of sticking to the path that led to the river, they scampered and chased each other all over the grass and the hay. And the direct path—if you didn't want to make a long detour through the Shebreshin gate, across the main road, and left through the ditches—led right between one of the ramparts that had been left standing and the inspector's window. Actually, the inspector himself wasn't much of a problem. He played cards all night at the club (people wished themselves the money that our rich Margulies lost to him every night), and as he liked a nip of the bitter drop, he spent the day drinking and sleeping. He wouldn't have heard us, even though he slept by the open window in summer ("There's a Gentile for you"). Besides, we slipped by quietly. We took off our boots and shoes and tiptoed past the house holding our breath, listening to the pounding of our hearts and the inspector's snores.

So it should have been all right. But he had a wife who didn't play cards or drink. She was renowned, the inspector's wife, for her appearance, "tall as a pole, skinny as a twig, flat as a board, pockmarked like a grater, with a pointy head full of straw like a broom." They composed a song about her, to which I added my bit.

She wouldn't have been a problem either. In the first place, she was kind and good-natured and she loved children with all her heart, even Jewish children in kapotes. If you let her, she would grab you and kiss you in the street, probably because she had no children of her own. In addition, when she wasn't running about town shopping, which took three-quarters of the day, she played patience in her room; she was so absorbed in her game that the world could turn upside down without her notice. Once, several years later, she heard a tremendous thud in her husband's room, like someone falling out of bed. She came in a little too late—after finishing her game of patience—and found her husband stone dead.

So we would have had no trouble getting past her. But she had a dog—a rare breed, with a real pedigree. When she was later widowed and our barber-surgeon won the grand prize in the lottery, he bought the dog from her for a small fortune—some six hundred rubles. Along with it he bought two houses, a house in town where he opened a bookstore stocked with "books in all languages" to educate the public, and a smaller house outside town. He gave the city house with the store to his sons, and he himself, by then a widower, retired with the dog to the small house outside town to live in solitude and contemplation. I had a lot of trouble restraining my friends from taking revenge on the dog that was now Jewish for the sins it had committed while it was still a Gentile dog.

But in the meantime it was still living with the inspector's wife, and I have still to chronicle its sins. The dog was delicate, black, and shiny, with a white spot between the eyes like a patch, and legs so thin and bowed that it seemed to walk on its knees. It was highly sensitive, with a high-pitched little bark. When it tired of sitting on the lap of the inspector's wife as she played patience, it would trot to the door for a breath of air and, catching sight of us Jewish boys, begin its high-pitched yapping. That woke the inspector, who knew what it meant, and he sent his people after us to take away our clothes while we swam in the water. We felt humiliated by our nakedness, and heartbroken to know that our Jewish ritual undershirts were in the hands of Gentiles. We had either to buy them back, or to cry and plead until they took pity on us, or until someone else came to bail us out.

But my parents said: "Thank goodness for the inspector! If it weren't for the lesson he teaches them, would they stay in kheyder through the summer?"

Another source of dog lore was the nanny of my invalid brother. The third child, he was sickly and needed someone to look after him. Father was away doing business with the gentry and mother was busy in the store. My little sister was still playing with jacks or in the sand in front of the store. So they hired a peasant woman from the village to look after him.

She was a frail old woman with thinning white hair and a wrinkled face. Her eyes were small, calm, and moist, half-sodden. Drinking, which she loved, brought out all her sweetness and tenderness. Back in the village she had a husband she longed for. Whenever she got very lonesome for him, she would steal away to see him and return bruised, swollen, with her clothes in tatters, half-naked. This would make her even more attached and devoted to us. She would carry my little brother around, crooning to him and telling him stories. I didn't understand much Polish, but I guessed at their meaning. Sometimes in the evening I would sneak into the room and lie down on the bed pretending to have a headache, and listen till my mother came to bring us dinner. According to my studies, she was only a woman, but I was attracted by her stories and songs. When she would sing the Christmas carols with their many stanzas, I waited eagerly for the refrain, "Hey, *kolende, ko-len-de.*"

At the same time I felt the most awful pity for this poor, neglected, pockmarked woman. These were more than lullabies, I knew; these were her pleas, her prayers, and who was there to hear them? Her prayer just melted into the air. Even their church was sinking by a hairsbreadth every day. (How I wished I could find a way of measuring that hairsbreadth!) Pity made me want to "open her eyes" to the errors of her ways. Besides, it was my duty to save her. Wasn't Jonah punished for refusing to warn Nineveh? But I had to wait until I knew Polish better—and by the time that happened, the nanny was no longer with us and I had lost my zeal.

Once, when she was half-drunk, she began to tell about a Gentile angel of death—a female who flies around with a white handkerchief. When she waves it at someone, he dies. If she waves it at a city, there is an epidemic. Here again she had fallen into error. I knew for a fact that the Angel of Death was a male with a thousand eyes.[16]

My favorite stories were about familiar animals, especially dogs of the village and the big estates. She would make these stories vivid, mimicking the barking of the dogs, the chase, the catch.

The dogs owned by the gentry were swift hunting dogs. They were taken out on long leads. At the sound of the bugle, they were released, and they flew wildly as the wind, giving chase. These dogs were so brave they would not only catch the hares and foxes that were their natural prey, but attack even wild boars, and bears, and wolves. I didn't mind about the pigs—that was fine! But I pitied the hares. Although I had never seen one, and knew about them only from the Scriptures, where they were reckoned among the unclean animals, the hare was a trembling thing, according to her description, soft and sensitive. As for the foxes, that was fine too. She said they strangled chickens by the neck, and I knew that they ran through the ruins of the Holy Temple.[17] I also knew from the Song of Songs that they had ruined the vineyards in the land of Israel: "Seize for us the foxes, the little foxes that injure the vineyards." Of course, the foxes were clever, as I had learned from the Proverbs of the Foxes, but what good was their cleverness if they put it to evil use?

The dogs of the peasants were also brave, guarding the farms from thieves. They suffered greatly. The police forced them to be kept on chains most of the time, and the thieves tried to poison them. Yet they remained utterly loyal to their owners! They would bark and rouse the village at the first sign of fire. In the winter, when wild animals were driven out of the woods by hunger and invaded the town in search of food, they immediately sounded the alarm. The peasants would wake up, and, arming themselves with sticks, poles, and pitchforks, they would surround the animal and beat it over the head until they broke its skull.

So why were the dogcatchers always so eager to round up the village dogs and take them off in their wagons?

Not long after this, I myself was destined to make the acquaintance of dogs of the gentry, with whom, as I mentioned before, my father used to do business. One winter day he had to call on the landowner in Stabrow, and it occurred to him to take me along. He drove into "the little courtyard," straight to the kheyder, to pick me up. Incidentally, it wasn't the usual thing to drive through the city. Why should anyone know where you were going, and on what sort of business? Why suffer the risk of competition and the Evil Eye, which could put the trip in jeopardy?

Even my aforementioned wealthy uncle Margulies, who strolled about town with his hands folded behind his back, and had his own horses sent up from the farm—even he would never leave through the marketplace, but walk through the courtyard to his carriage and drive off through a back alley. Others went to even greater lengths, and had their carriages wait for them outside town, where they made their way on foot. So when my father drove straight into the courtyard, it made a great impression. People followed him up the stairs. This had to be important! Once he opened the door, the crowd wouldn't let him shut it. A man stood gaping at him from the doorway, and several women behind him. The kheyder was astounded, especially when he explained the purpose of his coming. For some time now my father had "also" been considered a deviant from the straight and narrow—"also" because I was considered a lost cause altogether.

"Reb Yudl," the teacher tried to reason with him, "how can you interrupt the boy's learning?"

My father laughed. It was common knowledge that Yekhezkl and I were free five days out of the six each week. My father, in his easygoing manner, listened to us repeat the lesson first thing Sunday morning, while the teacher was busy with his matchmaking or arbitration, or chewing the fat with his friends. I didn't have another lesson until Friday. Fridays, because of some matchmaking he had done, the teacher got "a special deal" on beans from Moyshe-Yitzkhok's canteen. Before the beans we had our first practice for the passage to be recited the next day, and after the beans, I had my only lesson for the week. While the teacher was wiping the grease off his mustache and brushing the crumbs off his beard, I ran the kheyder as I pleased.

So my father took me to Stabrow. Yekhezkl wanted to come along, but my father was afraid to take him. Were the boy to catch cold, God forbid, he could never make it up to Freydl, his mother.

We headed into the open fields, and I was greeted by a white expanse such as I'd never seen before. My father was preoccupied by his business with the Stabrow squire. I was blinded by the snow diamonds, by a purity and cleanliness such as I tried to describe in the play *What the Fiddle Knows*, when Yoel speaks of its redemptive powers.[18] I looked up at the sky and grabbed my father by the sleeve: "Father, look at the frozen sun! Just like our citron box at home!" We had a pale silver box at home of circular shape. But Father wouldn't let himself be distracted: "Don't talk nonsense! Sit still."

Next I noticed the broad shoulders and the comical-looking fur cap of the driver. I looked straight ahead and watched the horses trotting. They were swift little horses, raising puffs of snow with their hoofs. The driver sat motionless as a slab of salt—exactly like Lot's wife—with no need of the whip that lodged beside him. Should I take the whip? What would the driver say? I knew I shouldn't give in to temptation, but my hand reached out anyway. Father impatiently said, "Don't!" I drew back my hand. I was getting cold, but I didn't tell my father because I was angry with him.

Meanwhile, we had reached the manor house, which was exactly like a house in the city, except that dogs leaped out from somewhere. I counted one, two, three, four—with mounting fear. They were big dogs with tongues lolling out of their mouths, some barking, all of them jumping at the sleigh. My father took no notice. He jumped down, took off his sheepskin, and, after wrapping me up in it, went

toward the house. What a brave man, my father! Some of the dogs
followed him, barking—he was definitely a hero!—but two stayed
behind, one on either side of the sleigh, on their hind legs, resting
on it with their forepaws and sniffing inside as if to ask: "Isn't there
something good inside?" The driver, after putting the feed bags
around the horses' necks, took something to eat himself, and tossed
pieces of bread and scraps of lard to the dogs. To my dismay, they
didn't touch the bread, but they gobbled up the lard!

A great change took place in my life.

One Sabbath I was put through an examination by Reb Moyshe
Wahl, the rabbi of Zamość, a sweet-tempered man who was very
fond of me.[19] He told my father, "Your son needs a new teacher."

"Where can I find him?"

"Send him to Shebreshin, to Reb Pinkhesl." (I will tell you about
Reb Pinkhesl in due time.)

"What will Rivele say?"

"You know what, Yudl? Try leaving him here, in the study house,
for a term. He can study on his own."

It was agreed. This happened to be the end of a term. I promised
to be good, pious, and diligent—and with that I was set free! With
great relish I took to philosophical speculations and volumes of
kabbalah, and even more to running around. I got into all kinds of
trouble.

My father concluded that this would never do, and that he would
have to find a proper teacher. To keep me from running around,
my boots were taken away on the weekdays. I ran around the
courtyard in slippers. When I felt closed in, I swung my legs to
catapult the slippers onto the roof, then climbed up barefoot by way
of the porch to the roof of our two-story house to retrieve them.
The first sight of our city from on high did not make much of an
impression on me. Taller, three-story houses blocked the view. I
remembered having heard that from the balcony of the clock tower
above the city hall you could see not only the entire city but for
miles around in every direction. This was a sight I felt I had to see.
So I scrambled down from the roof, and for days on end I went
around plotting how to steal back my boots, and how to get to know
the old clockmaker who went up every day to wind the clock, and
persuade him to take me along.

Word had it that I had calmed down somewhat. I smiled to myself
and kept working on my plan. One day, as I was standing on the
porch, I saw my father come out—too preoccupied to notice me—

and shout across to the maid in the kitchen: "Mirl, could you do me a favor and send a messenger to Israel in Zhdanov? Tell him to come immediately with a horse and wagon."

Mirl answered, "All right, all right," but it would take her a few minutes to get dressed. So I postponed the clock tower for the time being and made for Zhdanov. I ran down the street in my slippers, with people staring and calling after me, "Lunatic!" Some of them tried to stop me, but I twisted loose from their grasp like a snake. I outran everyone who tried to catch me, and I made it to the village. I knew enough Polish to ask a peasant where Israel's house was. He pointed me *tam*—over there. I assumed that I knew where he was pointing, and ran straight to his neighbor's, a well-to-do German colonist. The minute I passed through the gate, I was attacked by a dog; he jumped up on my chest and put his paws on my shoulders, and his clever red eyes looked straight into mine: "You must be a thief!" The dog was trained, and waited for someone to come out— I can't describe my panic. My blood froze, and I couldn't even scream, my throat was so tight with fear. Luckily for me, someone in Israel's house had been looking out the window as I went by. Instantly, a young girl jumped over the fence, pulled the dog off, and, flinging it away from me, led me out the gate to Israel's house. She was his daughter.

She was a young girl with a rosy complexion, bright and clever eyes, and a circlet of glistening black hair. She looked as if she had stepped out of the Song of Songs. And what courage! She might have come straight out of the lions' dens.[20]

Sometime later, when I nearly tumbled into the well, I was sorry that an older woman—not she—kept me from falling in. Every night I would dream of her, but it never occurred to me to go out to Zhdanov to see her.

Instead of that, I thought I would show my own courage by grabbing a big yellow dog by the tail. The dog pulled away, hunkered down, and leaped at my shoulder. I bear the scar to this day.

With that my parents' patience finally gave out, and they sent me to Shebreshin to study with Reb Pinkhesl.

All in all, that's how a bit of nature forces its way into the soul of a Jewish boy—or at least how it happened back then.

3: ZAMOŚĆ—SHEBRESHIN—ZAMOŚĆ.
MY LAST TWO TEACHERS. DREAMS.

"You, as an artist, don't react to things that are actually happening now. You deal in memories. The best you can offer is an epilogue to a story acted out behind the scenes a long time ago."

This was once said to me by a man I met during my travels. As it turned out from further conversation, he had read very little of what I had written, and then only in German and Russian translation. He smiled and added, "Maybe *you* eat the fruit right off the tree, but all you give us is the extract. Thanks at least for the aroma of fresh fruit."

The truth is, even in my personal life I take little notice of everyday occurrences. The facts are mostly too trivial for me; the motives behind them are tangled, the colors are harsh, the tones strident, the lines coarse.

But memory can refine everything and improve it. All I ask from life is that this wave too shall pass. Until it does, I watch it approaching with mystical resignation and philosophic calm, not letting myself be crushed, protecting my private self from the slightest incursion. All hell may break loose, but I keep myself dry. And after the waves have ebbed, and the same events emerge in memory, I am pleased to reclaim them from chaos. Once they have surfaced from "the depths of the unconscious," they are pure as gold, clear of sand.

What brings the dead back and restores them to life? For me it's mainly contrast. I find contrast the most effective way of associating ideas. It's an elevator forever on duty. If ever reality, the thesis, comes to a standstill, it can be reactivated by its antithesis. Think of a scale. The reader can lean his sympathetic weight on the right side or the left.

Born and raised in Zamość, I had to be exiled to Shebreshin, three miles away, in order to *see* my city. Shebreshin was a wooden town. In those days the only brick building was a combination inn and tavern with shops in the middle of the marketplace where the gentry used to gather. In that squat town with its straw and shingle roofs, I yearned for my city. Zamość rose before my moist eyes in all its three-storied, metal-and-tile-roofed glory, a city that did not stretch lengthwise like a rotting fish, but was impelled upward to the sky by its ramparts.

I had to see the clumsy wooden miscarriage of a town clock in

Shebreshin to appreciate the height and splendor of the clock tower at home, a skyscraper, as it then seemed to me. And as for the inspiriting blessings of nature around Shebreshin, "the meadows clothed with flocks"—that green tablecloth splattered with yellow and red manure, and the footbridge to the water and the dilapidated mill beside it, blackened by age and whitened by flour—the scene made me appreciate the contrasting charm of what lay "beyond the fortress" in Zamość.[21] I was later able in some of my stories to render those luscious fields, to describe the shadowy lanes along the hidden "escape route" between the ramparts, and to make use of the dewy meadows with their froggy swamps, bedecked with wild berries and hillocks of slim, golden-yellow primroses.

These things that come back to me as I write, these clear visions of the home that I actually saw with my own eyes, mingled with things I had only heard about the Zamość of the past.

From the moment that I was seated in the wagon, I was like unto them that dream.[22]

I was handed over to a Jew from Shebreshin who promised to deliver me safely to the home of Reb Pinkhesl. I couldn't see him because my eyes were misty, but I felt that he was thin (he left me so much room on the seat) and bony (when the wagon jostled us, our elbows bumped) and tall (his voice came down at me from above). I didn't see who came down to the wagon to say good-bye, but I heard the man saying to my mother, using the familiar second person (he must have been a friend of the family!), "Don't worry, Rivele, I am responsible for him." Then he turned to the driver: "Let's get going."

The wagon began to move. Voices, young and old, called out, wishing me well, and among them my father's: "Behave yourself!"

The wagon clattered over the cobblestone street, passed through the shadow of the church, and veered left into the darkness of the Shebreshin gate, then out into bright daylight, where it was immediately quieter. We were on the highway. So now it was a fact: I was on my way to Shebreshin to study with Reb Pinkhesl. I had no idea who he was or what he was like. For all I knew, they might have been sending me to prison. There was a bitter taste in my mouth, but I heard a voice inside me say, "It can't hurt you!"

I knew a little about Shebreshin. The Shebreshin Jews were sarcastically called "the Shebreshin rags." I didn't know why, just as I didn't know why the people in the suburb were called "foresters" or why we were "the Zamość gluttons." After all, not everyone was like my Aunt Freydl, baking one cheesecake after another. The staples of diet in our house were plain kasha and soup.

In fact, I had heard a lot about Shebreshin, because there was considerable commerce between us. As I mentioned, Zamość had been a fortress, confined by ramparts that kept it from spreading out. The post office of Zamość is in the suburb to the present day, and at that time the old courthouse was in Shebreshin. This was the seat of the district judge, who had under his jurisdiction both civil affairs and criminal cases involving life and death. Thieves who were arrested in Zamość were taken there in chains. Smugglers intercepted at Tomaszow, near the border, would also be taken to Shebreshin, but first the border guards in their green-striped uniforms would stop with them and their contraband at the government office in Zamość to file an official report.

It was there, in the courtyard of the government office, that Dovidl the Thief, the abandoned orphan of Avigdor the Teacher, stole a confiscated bolt of silk right from under the guard's nose, and used it as a bribe to free a Jew from prison—a married man, and the father of eight children. After that, the community forgave him everything. Jews patted him on the back for his clever trick, and more than one family invited him over to "pick out a shirt for himself."

In civil matters litigants who wouldn't accept arbitration, or the ruling of a rabbinic court, went before the civil judges of Shebreshin. These were stubborn and vengeful people, not very savory types.

My friend Isaac's father, Fayvl Gelibter, often traveled to Shebreshin. Fayvl Gelibter had a considerable reputation as a learned man—"almost a scholar"—and as a heretic of the highest order. No one would have given two cents for his share in the next world. This inclination he had inherited from his father, who was also one of "them": a fine Hebrew grammarian, and unparalleled in his chanting of Scripture; one of a circle of Enlighteners that included Alexander Zederbaum, Jacob Eichenbaum, and other progressive Jews.[23]

It was he, the grandfather, who introduced me and my friend Isaac, his grandson, Fayvl Gelibter's son, to Maimonides' *Guide to the Perplexed*. We had been browsing through the bookshelves and happened to pull down the volume when he was there. "It's not for you rascals, you won't understand it." That was enough for us. We wouldn't let the book out of our hands, and insisted that he quiz us on its contents.

His son, Fayvl, was even more notorious. All sorts of stories were told about him, so much of it sheer fabrication that it is hard to know whether any of them were true. I could ask my friend Isaac, who is presently a physician in Zamość, but I don't want to. Because although he would undoubtedly tell me the truth, the fable is always truer than the fact, just as the invention of the folk is truer than what passes for reality. Man bends his will and hides his true face behind a mask of propriety. But people have a sense of the person behind the mask, and they tell what he would have done had he been true to himself, what his fate would have been had random obstacles not interfered.

The stories of the holy martyrs are also shaped in this way. Once the accidents and nonessentials have been forgotten—those things which were done out of economic necessity, or in anger, or for a momentary settling of accounts—the soul emerges in its nakedness. This time it can be fitted out in its authentic attire, so that the persons who emerge are whole and forceful rather than the tentative shadows they were in their lifetime.

This is also the magic and truth of folktales, and, indeed, of art in general.

Let's return to Fayvl Gelibter. As mentioned before, he was a heretic, which is to say he committed the following transgressions: he failed to spit three times after the concluding prayers, omitted mention of the angels when the shofar was sounded, and remained standing when everyone else prostrated themselves at the words, "and we bow down." And do you know what he would do at home? He'd be saying the morning prayers in his shawl and phylacteries, and in his hurry to leave for Shebreshin, he would polish and shine his boots. There would be bread and butter and coffee on the table, and if the knife was dull he would sharpen it on the leather straps of his phylacteries. On Yom Kippur he did not perform the expiatory sacrifice with a chicken, and on Sukkot—following the example of the prophets—he did not whip the willow branches. Yet he knew chapter and verse, all of the Scriptures, by heart.[24]

He had a brilliant mind, and he had educated himself into a real scholar. Once he happened to buy a Polish code of law from a drunken peasant for a few kopecks, and taught himself jurisprudence and Polish at the same time. And in an attic somewhere he found a French mathematics text that went back to Napoleon's time (back to the days of red foulard neckerchiefs and expressions like *ça m'est égal* and *quel malheur*) and he taught himself French and mathematics and geometry all at once. So what if the newly arrived instructor from Warsaw laughed at his expense because French isn't pronounced as printed on the page? People laughed at the instructor. He could babble in French with the druggist's wife, but Gelibter really knew his geometry!

He didn't really put the mathematics to much use. When there was a difficult problem in the tractate *Zeroim* that made even Mikhl the Sexton stammer and blink, they would run to Fayvl Gelibter for a clear answer (and a quick look at his carryings-on).

Once, after such a visit, they told how Gelibter had extracted a bad tooth. He didn't go to the dentist because he didn't like to waste money. Instead, he took a large nail, pounded it into the table nearly up to the head, tied a short string around its neck, and drove in the nail the rest of the way. Then he wound the other end of the string around the bad tooth, leaned over the table for a moment, and suddenly threw his head back. The table jerked, and out came the tooth. "He didn't even rinse the blood from his mouth. He just picked up the Mishna where he had left off and went on studying."

Once he made use of his knowledge of mathematics and geometry in a public debate. In the controversy between Gavriel Yehuda Lichtenfeld and Slonimski, he published an open letter supporting Lichtenfeld's position.[25]

Mathematics mattered to him, but law was more useful. It earned him a living, though not all of it; his wife had a store of some sort. He took up many legal defenses, wrote up the briefs, and traveled to Shebreshin to present the cases. His persistence before the court resulted in many acquittals. He felt that the truth must out, and never took a case where he knew that the client was guilty. He was honesty itself. It was said that he had spent twelve years on a lawsuit over a pound of butter. The court costs reached six hundred gulden, "as much as the barber-surgeon paid the inspector's wife for her little dog." I never found out which side had had to pay the court fees.

Anyway, my friend Isaac would often tell me that his father was away, and more often that he was "away in Shebreshin."

Fayvl Gelibter lived a simple, natural life. "A Jew," he said, "should be healthy as a peasant." People said the comparison was appropriate for a man who got up at night and polished off a poppy-seed cookie (implying that he ate a whole khallah) without even washing his hands! He believed in hand-washing only for the grace after meals—since that was a religious obligation.

He would walk the three miles to Shebreshin on foot.

"But Reb Fayvl, three miles at your age . . ."

"I walk only a mile."

"And then?"

"Then I walk another mile, and another, and so on until I arrive."
He walked barefoot like Abba Hilkiah, carrying his boots on a
stick over his shoulders.[26] There were sharp stones on the road. He
reasoned that a bruised foot heals on its own, while a torn shoe has
to be sent to the shoemaker. So he'd go striding on, marching like
a soldier, calling out the drill commands: "*Raz-dva!* One-two!" He
advised people to sound off when they marched. "The nations of
the world know what they are doing."

Sitting in the wagon, I realized that I was traveling along Fayvl
Gelibter's road. And the moment I had this thought, I saw him. I
was amazed at how clearly I saw him. There he was, keeping pace
with the wagon, deep in thought, no doubt calculating some figures,
or just doing mental arithmetic for the love of it. His long, blond,
spiky brows protruded so that I never saw his eyes. I never knew
their color. Not that he hid them—this thoroughly open and forth-
right man—but his brows were so thick they kept his eyes in shadow.

Years later, at his funeral, when he lay at the edge of the grave,
I suddenly felt a wild urge to see his eyes. "If not now, when?" At
that final moment, just as the gravedigger was about to jump into
the open grave, I felt I had to uncover him. But there was a bit of
silver beard peeking out from under the white shroud. I was about
to touch him, but a hair trembled.

In the meantime, there he was marching alongside the wagon. A
short, thick-set man, with his coattails rolled up and his arms swinging
rhythmically, left, right. But since he was not sounding off his own
commands, I began to do it for him: "*Raz-dva, raz-dva.*"

The voice of my tall neighbor broke in: "Shame on you! A boy
who's going to study Torah with Reb Pinkhesl! Do you know who
Reb Pinkhesl is? He's an old Kotsker Hasid."

That interested me. I fell silent, and Fayvl Gelibter vanished. I
wanted to hear about this. The old Hasidim of Kotsk were a strange
sect: they were learned, yet they didn't believe in formal study; they
were devoted to God, yet they didn't pray. However, the tall Jew
had nothing to tell or wasn't able to tell it. He just offered a few
words with a hoarse sibilance: "Pss—sss—what a man, Reb Pinkhesl.
Pss—sss—a Kotsker."

I dozed off, and now, instead of Fayvl Gelibter, Reb Leybush
Tsimeles was walking along the road: tall, short-bearded, a pale Jew
with lackluster eyes and a pipe fixed between his tobacco-stained
lips. This silent, lonely old Hasid of Kotsk (as I described him in my
sketch "The Heretic") would pace back and forth in the study house

between the holy ark and the little window where the sexton's wife sat. Sometimes he would stop there, tap softly at the window as if he hardly dared to expect anything, and receive from her a shot of whiskey with an egg cookie. He would drink up, nibble at the cookie, and resume his pacing. Even the biggest pranksters left him alone. We knew that he was the orphan of his generation, that he had nothing in common with us and nothing to talk to us about. There was one other Kotsker of his age in the city, but he was a rich man who kept a tavern of dubious reputation. The two men didn't mix.

Now here he was walking along the road. Where to? I assumed that he was on his way to Kotsk, to visit the grave of the rabbi. Why, then, should he be on the road to Shebreshin? He was clearly lost. I wanted to call out to him, but no sound came out of me. I found I had slipped down, so that my head and shoulders were on the seat.

What a crazy idea! I had dreamt that I was on my way to Shebreshin! But why should I be sent into exile? Would my father let me go? Didn't my mother love me anymore? I must be at home, lying on the sofa near the window, watching people go past on their way to the ritual bath on a Friday afternoon. The attendant was a poor fool, married to a moron like himself. When the Sabbath ended, we would send him a concocted "rabbinic message" from some town or other, and watch him run home to his wife to ask her permission to go there.

But why was I lying on the sofa? I must be sick. My shoulders ached so! It couldn't be serious because my father had gone off calmly to the study house to welcome the Sabbath and my mother was about to bless the candles. We had two lovely pairs of candlesticks at home; one tall pair, decorated with blossoms and coronets, was particularly handsome. Mother was earnest as she blessed the candles—she was so very devout! But I was sure that although she never looked at anyone when she covered her face to recite the blessing, here she was looking at me between her fingers and smiling. Then she went over to the other window to watch for my father.

In honor of the Sabbath she was wearing her Turkish shawl; her long earrings trembled on her ears. She was about to wipe the mist from the windowpane, but then, remembering that she had already ushered in the Sabbath, she checked herself. It was dark outside, but she would recognize my father's walk. When she saw him, she would blush with pleasure, then quietly seat herself in a far corner of the room with her head facing the wall. But why was my father so slow in coming? The candles were burning down. He was probably involved in a conversation, or else he had stopped to invite one of the strangers in town to join us for the Sabbath meal. . . .

At last the door opened. "Good Shabbes, good Shabbes!" Father's voice was cheerful, that of the guest somewhat harsh and coarse. Mother answered with a gentle "Good Shabbes, a good year," then crossed the room to stand beside me. I didn't reply; my father had not offered me any greeting, had not even looked my way! He ought to have remembered at least to ask after me. But he didn't. After he had made Kiddush over the wine, he looked over at where I lay, but didn't say anything, apparently under the impression that I was asleep. He looked at me with great compassion, and he would have sighed, but the Sabbath requires us to be joyful. I must have gotten worse. That was why mother was standing by my bed. Why didn't she reach out to put her hand on my forehead? I hoped she would do it; she would have to do it or I would cry!

In the meantime, they were about to wash for the meal—first my father, then the guest. The guest took hold of our large double-eared copper rinsing cup in one hand, emptied it over the other hand, and then, switching hands, filled the cup again to the brim and repeated the process. This he did three times, each time with a full cup. Our water carrier was Ayzikl, a tiny, frail man who supported a wife and eight children. He was paid by the week, not by the pailful, refilling the barrel whenever it ran low. My mother, who was standing beside me, spoke softly to herself, but I could hear her words distinctly: "Pious at Ayzikl's expense."

My father's "They can't put the whole world in jail" and my mother's "Pious at Ayzikl's expense" were the two precepts that, once implanted in my youthful soul, took deep root there and later bore fruit in everything I wrote.

For the moment, however, they were eating the Sabbath meal without me. Was I really that sick? Then I wouldn't be going to Shebreshin! They would never send me off if I was sick. My shoulders were aching so badly. Why go to Shebreshin at all? Reb Zalman the Tavern Keeper had his reasons for going: he went to the brewery, to order yeast. He had hired Israel Zhdanover's wagon and then reconsidered because of government regulations. Unless you had your own horses, you had to take the mail coach or pay a fine for not taking it. "Oppressive government," he sighed, telling about it. He had sent to the city hall over in the new town for papers certifying that these were his own horses. But if the guard were to check the seal and signature, or ask point-blank if they were forged, the blood would turn to water in Reb Zalman's veins. So he sent his messenger

back to the new town and bought a permit to travel on a hired
wagon. But then when he remembered "oppressive government,"
he reconsidered again, sent to the new town for the third time, and
arranged to take the mail coach. And that was him now on his way
to Shebreshin. The coachman was trumpeting: "Tra-tra-tra." And
then, "Whoa-a!"

We had reached our destination.

The tall man grabbed his bag and disappeared into a shadowy
arcade of shops and stalls where women were calling out their
wares. It turned out that Reb Pinkhesl was not at home. One of his
daughters who was nursing a baby had arrived from the village to
see a doctor—there was something wrong with her breasts. She had
taken his bed, so he had gone to stay with his son-in-law for a few
days. Like all Kotsker Hasidim, he hated pain, sickness, and misery.

The rebetsin took me and my box from the wagon. She was a tall,
swarthy, hairy woman. (By the way, you don't have to take that
literally. I don't sketch the person as he was; I sketch the image I've
retained of him, which is rarely the same. As far as I'm concerned,
the contour and shadings of the soul are superimposed over the
lines and colors of the body. The rebetsin may have looked altogether
different from my description of her.)

Regardless of her appearance, she lifted me down with the box
of my belongings, and barely managed to clear a path for us through
the circle of women who had gathered around. Words flew at me:
"Reb Yudele's and Rivele's son, their eldest . . . they've sent him
. . . he's probably a problem . . . sent him to Reb Pinkhesl. He'll
straighten him out!"

"But just look at those eyes! Look at them!"

I lowered my eyes. The rebetsin led me away, into a dark room
where the door and the single window opened onto the shadowy
covered arcade. I could barely make out an oven and chimney, a
table with a long bench and a few chairs, and some sacks against the
walls—gray walls, so damp that drops of moisture ran down them
like tears. (The perfect contrast to my own bright and freshly-painted
home!) The sacks were filled with potatoes, some spilling out on the
floor, and there were piles of onions and carrots. She pulled me
along into an even darker room, which received its only light from
the doorway to the first. Beyond it was the closed door to the alcove.

"Reb Pinkhesl's alcove. My daughter, poor thing, is occupying it
right now. With God's help, she'll be well enough to go home in a
few days. Reb Pinkhesl will come back then, and you'll study Torah
with him in there."

Even her voice was black and hairy, and she didn't forget to add, "You'll buy candles, child, won't you?" She smiled a bleak little smile in the dark: "Your mother gave you some pocket money, didn't she, child?" And then urgently: "Well, didn't she?"

"Yes! Yes!" I wanted to say, but since I couldn't get the words out, I jingled the change in my pocket.

"That sounds like a lot. Well, sit down, child. You must be worn out from traveling. Right here. This chair doesn't shake."

She sat me down. "You see that place by the wall between the cupboard and the water barrel?" (There was a groan from the alcove and she called out, 'I'll be right there, my dear, I'll run for the doctor this minute!') That's where your bed will be. I'll make up a nice bed for you. Meanwhile— (Another groan. 'In a minute, I'm coming in just a minute. The boy is hungry.') You see, child, here's a plate of sliced onions that I prepared for you. I knew you were on your way. And some radishes that I've salted for you. Eat, eat! I'm just running over to the doctor. I'll bring you a glass of milk. And here's an egg cookie, instead of bread, so that you won't have to wash and say grace." With that she disappeared.

I was suddenly hungry and I wanted to distract myself from the groaning in the alcove by eating. As I ate, a gush of tears ran down my cheeks and into the dish. Why had I been driven from my home? Were my sins so awful? I tried to concentrate and to remember, but I couldn't think of anything that might have warranted this punishment. Not quite realizing what I was doing, I finished the whole dish of salted radishes, and it aroused a terrible thirst. By then my eyes had adjusted to the darkness, and I saw a glass of milk on the table. I thought that the rebetsin must have returned and brought it for me, and that somehow I hadn't noticed. So I gulped it down, and when the rebetsin came in a moment later with the milk, she discovered me with the glass in my hand!

"Oh no! Oh my God! I can't believe it!"

Two glasses fell to the floor, the one in my hand and the one in hers. There was a double crash of glass and a bloodcurdling scream from the alcove. It turned out that I had drunk the glass of milk drawn from the infected breast as a specimen for the doctor.

After what seemed like a very long time, the rebetsin said, "When they tell you he's crazy, believe it!"

And so now Shebreshin discovered that I was crazy and dreamy and did everything backward. In the study house anyone could amuse himself at my expense. He could take a piece of chalk and draw a circle on the table with a dot in the middle, then write around the perimeter of the circle all the fine qualities that a person can have: a good head, a good heart, a good eye—and in the center, beside the dot, the word "crazy." Lest the point remain obscure, he would explain, "It doesn't hurt to be a little crazy, but if craziness is at the center, it makes everything else crazy."

After a time the daughter recovered, and when she went home to the village, Reb Pinkhesl returned to his alcove.

I had to pay for the candles to light the alcove. Reb Pinkhesl didn't press me for the money; she did. And whenever she took my money she said, "Reb Pinkhesl would chew my head off if he knew." I was so delighted that this rhymed that I forgave her. But I rarely got to study in the alcove. During the day Reb Pinkhesl was usually busy with arbitration. Sometimes he spent the day hearing a dispute in a neighboring village or town. And at night he insisted on his solitude in the alcove, where he paced back and forth or sat over his commentaries on the Torah. Reb Pinkhesl was an author! People were convinced that someday the world would recognize a great light from the holy community of Shebreshin. That day never came. When Pinkhesl died in due time, the commentaries were not to be found, and though I later inquired about them, no one knew what had happened to them—not even the rebetsin.

Anyway, I studied without him. He assured me: "The most important thing is independent study, sharpening your wits on your own. You should come to the rebbe only when you have a problem, a really difficult question. And the best time for study is at dawn."

So thanks to my candles he worked in the alcove for nights at a time, and he found a friend for me to study with at dawn in the study house. I didn't write home about these conditions. First, I was too lazy to write letters, and I still am. Second, it would be informing! Third, if "they" had banished me to this place, then it was no concern of theirs. There was also a fourth reason, the most important: I was thankful for the friend.

I loved this older friend with all my heart. At four in the morning I would get out of bed joyfully and run to wait for him with my young heart pounding. We studied *Zevokhim* together, and I grew to love the tractate for his sake. The young man reminded me of my uncle Shmuel-Leybush, with throbbing blue veins at his temples, who also loved to study at dawn. Once I had lain sick in the big room of my grandmother's house, and every morning at dawn I listened to his soft chant as he read the Torah. My friend studied with the same intensity. His soft and tender voice went straight to my heart. He had lustrous black sidelocks, which he sometimes put in his mouth when he was lost in study; full red lips; milk-white teeth. Today I would say that his eyes were moist with yearning, but in those days, when sorrow seemed to me synonymous with goodness, I thought of them as "good, good eyes." His cheeks were a bit sallow, but they, too, seemed to radiate in the shadow of those "good" eyes.

One day when I was rushing to the synagogue before dawn, I saw a ghost. It was suspended from an upper-story window, and swaying in the air. I knew there was no such thing as a ghost, but I saw it clearly! Despite my pounding heart, and the throbbing of my blood, I ran right past it, not because I thought I would find refuge in the house of study or in the tractate *Zevokhim* but because I was drawn by the eyes of my friend. Later it turned out that someone had hung out a shirt on the line to dry, but what mattered was my fear and the reward that it earned me—his tenderness.

A few years later, this young man came to Zamość looking for a way to make a living. His father, who had always been poor, saw to it that his son married money. His father-in-law was rich. He held the lease on a mill. But the property had changed hands, and the new lord of the manor demanded higher rent, while the business went from bad to worse, until the miller became destitute. So the young man came looking for a way to support himself and his wife and child, as well as his aging father-in-law and *his* household. He was a different person. His face was gaunt, and you could see the anxiety in his eyes, all that terrible worry about making a living. I felt sorry for him, but I avoided him. In my heart was the picture of a person I loved. Every time I ran into him, the image darkened. So I stayed out of his way to keep my treasure as it was.

As I said, I would wake at four in the morning. At night I slept badly because the water barrel was chilly against my head. When I wanted to turn the bed the other way around, my black rebetsin clasped her hands and screamed: "Such madness! He wants to sleep with his feet to the door!" She was certain that for a living person to adopt the posture of a corpse by lying with his feet toward the door was to invite imminent death. So between sleeping and not sleeping, I heard everything that went on around me. I heard Reb Pinkhesl pacing back and forth in his alcove. I heard the scrape of his quill across the paper, or when he climbed on a stool to rummage in his bookshelf. I was a bit "touched" by then, and I wondered: Is he searching for a strict or a lenient text? But all he aspired to publish was a book of guidance for bar mitzva boys and bridegrooms. And that, as I mentioned, was lost.

The rebetsin complained, "If only he would help me with my work once in a while." He would answer in the third person, "Tell her that when I finish my book, I'll buy her pearls."[27]

The swarthy, hairy rebetsin with a wart on her forehead (which I noticed then for the first time) flushed with pleasure. Her eyes lit up. A Jewish woman loves pearls—and Torah too, of course. To hide her feelings, she turned to the wall, my mother's very gesture, but performed so clumsily, and while blowing her nose into her apron!

I'd often hear the rebetsin negotiating till late in the night with neighbors whom she had taken into partnership on some good deal or other. The discussion would begin softly, like the hissing of little flames or little snakes, I thought, although where I got the comparison, I really can't say. "Psss—the child is asleep." Or else, "Don't wake the crazy boy." Or, "Reb Pinkhesl is writing commentaries." Suddenly, there would be a strong word, followed by a coarser one, until the shouting erupted in cries of "Thief!" "Gangster!" "A curse on your mother's . . ." All of this directed at my rebetsin, who tried to shush her accusers.

Generally, she gave in. She would concede the money—they could risk their souls. Just so they shouldn't disturb Reb Pinkhesl or "the precious brat": he might write home about it.

Then it would get quieter, and after the business transactions there would be ordinary conversation punctuated by yawns. The rebetsin, who was seated next to the oven, not far from my bed and the door, did most of the talking. She talked about the string of pearls she would have someday, and the portion that would be hers in the world to come—thanks to the pious Reb Pinkhesl. Whenever the conversation turned to me, I was particularly alert. This interested me. I was made aware of a great many things that I had done and reminded of others. I did many things unconsciously, and there was even more that I forgot. While the rebetsin spoke, she knitted a sock or darned an old coat, and her cronies likewise; they never left their homes without some work to keep them busy. They were all interested in me, the bratty boy, the crazy child with the large, fiery eyes that one of the women compared to Havdala candles (an image that pleased me so much I included it in the description of Monish.) The rebetsin recounted my antics: I ripped all my clothes, I scuffed the heels off my boots, I even tore my hat to shreds.

"Is it any wonder! It's because he runs around all day long. Reb Pinkhesl is always distracted, busy being the devoted scholar! Before he has a chance to look around, the boy has vanished." (Lies! He never noticed that I was missing, and rarely bothered about me at all.) "And where do you think we find him? Out in the fields, by the river, stretched out full-length, either staring at the sky or with his nose in the grass. Or else he sneaks over to the waterwheel of the mill." (It belonged to my friend's father-in-law.) "What if he rolled down? Or if a cow grazing in the meadow caught him on her horns? Who would be held responsible, huh?"

And on and on, with a mass of details. "He was running like a demon down the arcade, so wouldn't you know it, he got his button tangled—on the braid of Menakhem-Mendl's daughter! A cry went up: 'Congratulations! Mazel tov, bride and groom!' Women's tongues are like swords and they're careful not to let them rust. So what does the boy do? He takes the girl's face in his hands and says, 'Why not? She's a lovely girl.' Did you ever hear anything like it?!"

And then to my family tree, with a touch of pride: "Do you think he's just anybody? A foundling on someone's doorstep? On his father Reb Yudl's side they were steeped in learning, in wealth, in breeding, going all the way back to Rabbi Heshl."

Then a leap, because she wasn't too knowledgeable about that side of the family. But she made up for it with a more detailed account of my mother's ancestry in Zamość. I learned, if, indeed, it was true, that my great-grandfather on my mother's side was called Reb Leybush "the Lord." I was named after him—"Crazy Leybush"— but it didn't weaken my self-esteem. They called him "the Lord" because he acted like a lordly governor. He had a house of his own— not just a corner in someone else's—with tables and chairs painted red. He wore silk stockings and spoke German fluently; Count Zamoyski, who built the city, spoke to him face-to-face, and not "Listen here, Jew!" but with great respect.

My great-grandmother had a large dry-goods store where she sold all kinds of merchandise, including goods from abroad, and imports from Leipzig. The uncle I mentioned earlier, the one in the black bowler hat who collected my juvenilia, inherited the store. "And just listen to what a saintly woman would do!" My great-grandmother set aside two drawers in the store, one for raisins, one for almonds, entirely for the poor. The entire income of those drawers went to charity. If a child of hers ever reached for a raisin, he would get it across the hands if he didn't drop in a coin into the special little till for the poor.

When the talking stopped, I would drift into a deeper sleep and see before me my city as Zamoyski had built it—"Little Paris"— mingled with the older Zamość of which I had heard stories in my childhood. I saw Zamość still a fortress in all its might and fearful splendor, its ramparts not yet razed and dug up and neglected, but standing firm, with moats of clear deep water between the walls. Once a homesick soldier from a village deep in Russia deserted from the barracks and tried to swim across the water, but his boots were too heavy and he drowned. Around the walls there were heavy artillery pieces, and shells piled in triangles and squares, and if you so much as pointed at them with your finger, the armed soldier who patrolled the walls would shoot you with his rifle: bang!—no questions asked. You had it coming to you.

The gates were still military gateways to the city. Reveille was sounded in the morning and the gates were opened. The playing of taps marked their closing in the evening. The Lublin gate faced the windows of the study house. Among the guards at the gate there was a cantonist, one of those Jewish soldiers drafted when he was just a boy to fill the Jewish quota for the tsar's army and forbidden to be a Jew. All day long he would gaze up at the windows of the study house, trying to catch every sound. After taps, when the guard changed, the cantonist would steal into the study house to learn Torah.

Once he was caught, and there in the open space between the wall and the study house he was made to run the gauntlet. His blood flowed, but he didn't so much as groan. His stubborn silence threw the presiding officer into a rage: "Dirty Jew!" he shouted, spurring the soldiers on to put more life into their work. "Let him have it, boys!" (This scene is in my story "Three Gifts.") People fainted in the study house. The wailing of the women who had flocked there was beyond anything heard on Yom Kippur, the holiest day of the year.

He received eighty lashes. Then he was sent into exile and never seen again.

Suspended from chains over the waters of the moat were three iron drawbridges that were lowered and raised with the opening and closing of the gates.

Suddenly, the scene changed, and I saw the branding of a criminal in the marketplace. I was still a child, on my way home from my first kheyder, but such a thick crowd had gathered to watch— "They're going to brand him!"—that I couldn't get through. On a table in the middle of the marketplace stood some sort of a can with a flame inside it. The half-naked convict stood on the table beside it, and next to him the dogcatcher, who also served as the executioner. He grasped the condemned man with his left hand and with his right the wooden handle of the branding iron that glowed in the fire. A terrible word was inscribed on the iron—THIEF or MURDERER. I don't remember exactly. The soldiers of the garrison band stood in a semicircle around the table playing music, and behind them pressed the crowd—the Jews of the city, Gentiles from the surrounding suburbs, even peasant men and women who happened to have come in from the village. People watched from the windows, from the pharmacist's porch. Little heads were visible on the rooftops and the surrounding chimneys (this too I included in "Three Gifts"). Dovidl the Thief crawled out on a tin gutter to watch. Someone noticed him and yelled, "It's going to fall off!" He leaped off like a cat.

Suddenly—silence, like the silence before the blowing of the shofar. The dogcatcher pulled the rod from the fire, the band sounded a drumroll, and the brand was pressed once against the forehead of the criminal, and then against his naked arm.

I suddenly felt cold. I pulled the quilt over my head, shivering like a leaf. Someone's hand—a hard hand that must have belonged to the rebetsin—felt my forehead. "Pinkhesl! Pinkhesl, he has a fever!"

I got well, and since there wasn't much time left in the term, I was sent home. Besides, Reb Pinkhesl had to travel around to supervise the koshering of mills for Passover, and he could do without a student like me. Nothing was said about my sickness, but they made sure to send along a bundle of complaints. "It's impossible to cope with him. He's absolutely crazy." I don't remember exactly what they said about me, and even at the time I didn't care. Every word of it was false, but I wasn't about to defend myself. If my father yelled at me a bit, well, he would get it off his chest and then the shouting would be over. My mother almost cried, but when she saw how calm I was, she held back her tears. I think she knew that I was not so bad.

At first, there were some comments in the study house, but they were more interested in Reb Pinkhesl than in me. I didn't know what to say about him. Of what little I had seen of him, nothing stuck in my memory. "What did you study with him?" I don't think I studied anything. In any case, I didn't care to remember. I was just happy to be free of it all.

But it didn't last long. "You'll study at home." (Bad!) "A few hours a day." (Better!) "With Reb Abraham Joshua." They arranged for me to have a study companion, and we did actually study together for a time, though I can't remember him at all, neither his name, his face, or what we learned. There are still whole chunks of the Gemara buzzing around in my head, but I can't recall when or with whom I studied them.

Reb Abraham Joshua had served as assistant rabbi. When I asked why he no longer held the post of *dayan*, no one would give me a straight answer. He didn't fare much better as arbitrator, because people lacked all confidence in him. They called him a scatterbrain, one of those scholars who are forever explicating the text and in love with their own insights. On the surface he was very pious, but no one trusted it. I remember him as a nearsighted man, with a long, narrow face and a tobacco-stained beard, who wore a high fur cap with dangling earflaps.

In our house there were two portraits on the walls that my father happened to pick up at an auction, one of Napoleon III, and the other of his beautiful wife, the Empress Eugenie. My friend and I decided to switch the empress to the side where our pious teacher sat. He glanced up, but as a pious Jew is forbidden to look at a woman, he quickly turned his head away and for the rest of the session kept his eyes fixed on the opposite wall, where we had hung Napoleon. The next day Eugenie was back in her regular spot, and he was burned again. From then on, he didn't look at the walls at all.

When he got the chance to show off his knowledge, his boasting knew no bounds. Languages? Why waste time on them? If he wanted to know a language, he would get a dictionary. Within a month, he would have it memorized and know the language. And as for modern science, that too was a joke.

"But, Rebbe, how can you find out, for example, how far it is from here to the sun?"

"It's simple. You take a candle and measure the length and the width—all the dimensions of the flame. Then you move the candle away from you, very slowly, let's say to a distance of four ells, and then you measure it again. So you know that at four ells the flame gets smaller by that much. Then you divide the distance to the sun into four-ell measures, that's a simple matter of division, and you double by the amount that the flame diminishes. A matter of simple multiplication."

We burst out laughing. "But, Rebbe, how do you measure the distance to the sun?"

That was equally simple—but first he took a pinch of snuff. "Simple arithmetic, but you do just the opposite. You know how big the sun is and how small it looks. The rest you can measure with your eye." We burst out laughing again. He was insulted, and rather than answer us, he would turn back to his study.

4:HASKALAH. A LIBEL.
ABRAHAM MANIS. HASKALAH AGAIN.

"The flowers appear on the earth; the time of singing is come, and the voice of the turtle is heard in our land. . . ."[28] The Jewish Enlightenment came to Poland, and outside of Warsaw, Zamość was the most natural place for it to take root. We boasted that even winter radishes ripened sooner in Zamość than everywhere else, and so did all the other garden produce. (Come to think of it, that must be why they called us "the Zamość gluttons.")

When the Haskalah appeared among us, it did not take the assimilationist route. The dawn may have come, and maybe the dramatist Abraham Goldfaden was right to make his rounds, pounding on our shutters and crying, "It's a new day! We Jews should be out in the street!"[29] But when we emerged, the nations of the world weren't out there waiting for us. For the time being, the fabled arm of friendship did not lock arms with us in a neighborly stroll or comradely dance.

Our "Little Paris" was a world of its own. It never occurred to us to mingle with anyone else; there wasn't anyone to mingle with. There was a market square the length and breadth of the town's two cobblestone streets. The back streets were added later. If you stood at the intersection facing the city hall with its clock tower, you were at the center of a self-contained, peaceable kingdom of Jewish householders. Directly before you was the narrow lane leading to the market, and from there, a second lane from the market to the Lublin gate.

To the right, somewhat farther back, was the Lemberg gate. The once-short trip to Lemberg now required a permit to travel abroad. So we made do with Tomaszow, a thoroughly Jewish town just this side of the border to the east.

Between the two gates and beyond the ramparts were the army barracks—big, solid red-brick buildings with metal roofs.

To the left was Brukovane, the paved street to the castle. Its garden, fronting on the street, was backed on three sides by the officers' quarters, and between the buildings in both corners were narrow paths leading down to the moat, the guild hall, the artillery and ammunition, and then along to the stockade beside the Shebreshin gate, in the rear. Following the same semicircle in the other direction, the narrow path led to the inspector's house, the river, and the Officers' Club, where the local bigwigs assembled. In front of the club was the riding academy, and beyond it the embankment, the government buildings, extending all the way to the Lemberg gate. And that's it. We had come full circle.

Who were the Poles in our city? The druggist dispensed medicine (mostly mineral water and bitters) with the airs of a nobleman who had come down in the world. When he had the time, he would sit on his porch overlooking the market square and leaf through a picture book of the old Polish kings. Through the open glass doors wafted the sounds of a piano. The performance of his wife and two daughters was as hideous as their appearance, three black nights of unending gloom. His only son, who would one day inherit the pharmacy, was still off somewhere studying.

The chimney sweep lived in a small house with a large garden near the riding academy. Childless—at least there were none around—he spent the winter nights playing cards with his wife. In the spring he would plant and tend his garden, and in the summer he showed up in the market arcade with his eyes ablaze, cheeks flushed, and feet awobble as if he were walking on springs. People tried to avoid him. His weakness was that he liked to kiss everyone. It wasn't his fault so much as his wife's—a reclusive woman who brewed him powerful vishniac from the cherries in their garden. He knew a number of Yiddish expressions.

Old Dr. Skrishinski, dubbed "the Intellectual," was a kindly man with an unconvincing temper. He too had a wife and three daughters, and they too were black as night. The doctor was a cynic: From the day he finished his medical examinations he never again opened his books. He had memorized enough to keep him going in his professional duties. Arriving at the hospital, he would walk between the two rows of beds, glance at a patient, ask to see his tongue, go down the right aisle of the ward and up the left, then back into his office with his aide the barber-surgeon at his heels. He would scrawl thirty or so prescriptions at a shot, and hand them over: "Here, son of a bitch!"

Developments in medicine since his graduation were not his concern. When my wealthy aunt with the diamond earrings and pearl-studded collar fell sick, and the attending specialist, brought in from Warsaw for a consultation, held a stethoscope to her heart, Skrishinski couldn't repress his merriment. He slapped the palm of his hand to his mouth and laughed aloud: "Doctor, don't tell me you believe in that black magic!"

If there were other Gentiles in the city, I don't recall them. Was there a Shabbes goy? Actually, I believe we had a Shabbes goye, an old, gray-haired woman, a little touched in the head, who was called "the Paw" because of the way she roamed around town not on the flat of her feet but on tiptoe. She had watery eyes and two crooked teeth in a sagging mouth, and she kept her head cocked, as if she were addressing a mute complaint to heaven: "Why did you create me? To scrub floors?" I am not certain, but I suspect that "the Paw" may have been of Jewish descent.

Who else was there? Along the wooden arcade sat old peasant women selling thin black sausages and lard. Set back on the left side of the arcade near the city hall was a Christian home for the aged. Sometimes the old women would appear (the men never did), hunchbacked, half-blind, dressed all in black with black bonnets and black rosaries around their necks. They would stumble and grumble and mutter as they made their way to the church and back.

A frequent visitor in town was a man we called Grandpa, a mason from the new town. Tall, always needing a shave, with a rough yellow face like a field of stubble, he would pass through the arcade with glazed eyes, looking for something in the air right in front of him. His clothes were in tatters. His long bandy legs tripped over whatever lay underfoot, his arms knocked over bagels and fruit, and his mouth foamed as he cursed—no one knew exactly whom. Some said he was cursing his wife and child, who had robbed him of his savings and his house and his bit of land and had thrown him out when he started drinking.

We didn't have a local nobility, only Count Zamoyski, who was never around. It was rumored that from time to time he paid his respects to his ancestors in the white church; their remains lay down in the crypt encased in sepulchers of iron, silver, and bronze, and their portraits—in long cloaks and fur-brimmed hats and yellow boots—hung up high in the alcoves. The farmers who leased his fields often came into town. (Jews who reportedly had held these positions once had all been pushed out one by one, except for Yehoshua Margulies.) They drove into town on their carts and wagons to buy provisions, the men in the hardware stores, the women at the grocers' or in the fashionable women's store, run by a Jewish widow with two strapping daughters. There was talk that army officers also frequented the place. Sometimes the visitors would eat a meal at K.'s wineshop on Brukovane.

That leaves the peasants, who came to market on Sundays and to church on all the Christian holidays. They were quiet, submissive folk, just released from serfdom. The older ones still longed for the fleshpots of Egypt. The young, still unsure of what to do with their freedom, submitted to their elders, who slapped them when they failed to fall on their knees before the landowner, cap in hand and face to the ground. In the city they were at loose ends, restless and uncomfortable, tripping over the stairs. They became dangerous only once they reported for induction. Freed from the regimen of the village and not yet subject to the military, they would break loose: cut the sidelocks off a Jew, grab a bagel from a stall, smash a window in the tavern. After their binge they subsided and deferred once again to the Jew, who had served during the years of serfdom as the intermediary between them and the landowner. In the village they still depended on "Moshke"—their generic term for the Jew. They didn't go to a doctor without first consulting him, or to a lawyer without first asking his advice, and sometimes "Moshke" himself was their arbitrator.

Obviously, we weren't about to assimilate with these people. The only other Gentiles were the military. Recruits were not even permitted into the arcades. "Troublemakers; they've got theft in their eyes." Noncommissioned officers, the sergeants, were better behaved. They sat in Mendl's tavern in a room specially reserved for them and let themselves be tempted by roasted giblets. Then they would have their brandy and try to get Mendl's daughter to convert—it was all Mendl could do to pry her away from them.

It didn't make sense to socialize with recruits and NCOs.

With the officers we did have some contact. After a night of carousing in K.'s wineshop they would smash their glasses and use their diamond rings to carve their names into the big mirror with the mahogany frame. They lent Russian books to K.'s daughter, a blond, studious girl. And often they flirted or "just dropped by to say hello" at the aforementioned dress shop of the widow with the two daughters.

The officers were not alone in this quest. There were yeshiva boys who fantasized thus: "If I were traveling alone in a wagon with one of them in a deep frost, she would have to cuddle up to me closer and closer in the cold." The widow also had a son, Yointshe, whom I haven't yet mentioned. He was an unkosher piece of goods—

stocky, red-faced, shorn clean of his sidelocks, forever picking at the pimples on his shaven face. He was a lackey for the officers. He carried notes for them and spent his time with servant girls.

"Frightful!" But we were a little jealous of him.

The Gentiles and the Jews were of two different worlds. Even so, something of a connection was forming between us. Not, God forbid, in any alliance against the Poles! We were flaming Polish patriots ourselves. How long had it been since we prayed for the success of the second Polish uprising?[30]

Actually, during the uprising of 1863, our city never saw a Polish army or even a single Pole in arms. A secret message came from Lemberg (the rebel mail drop was a hole in the wall of the arcade) telling us that Zamość had been captured. But there had been no siege. Even from the balcony of the clock tower, which gave a clear view for miles around, there was no armed regiment to be seen. So we Jewish schoolboys became the Polish army! Our tsarist foe consisted of a single boy who had just arrived from Bialystok to stay with an uncle. He was blind in one eye, and we nearly scratched out the other. Once we beat him up so badly that he was laid up for months and barely managed to recover.

Not only that. Who was the district supply officer for the Polish rebels? Who sent supplies of bread and clothes and even some ammunition stolen from the local base to the partisans in the forest? One of us—Yosef Morgenstern's renegade son! Once, the father was seized in the forest on his way home from Warsaw. His Polish captors found a Russian passport in his pocket, and in his boots a contract to supply the Cossacks with hay and oats. This son was able to rescue him from the gallows. He happened by just in time.

Despite our Polish sympathies, Jews were suppliers of the Russian garrison. There were contacts in the riding academy. Jewish girls had their charms. An officer would lend a Jewish girl a Russian book. Even I began to take Russian lessons, but that didn't last long. After Hebrew conjugations and Ollendorff's German primer, I felt I had to escape from Gretch's Russian grammar and from my tutor, a regimental clerk whose mouth stank of cheap whiskey.

So there were threads connecting us and the Gentiles, but suddenly the fabric was torn apart. The Jews were slandered! A wall arose between us and the officers that seemed to grow with each passing day.[31]

In the garden of the castle where the officers were quartered was the regimental stronghold. It was guarded, of course, by a soldier armed with sword and rifle, ready to open fire if anyone approached.

One morning at daybreak, at the changing of the guard, the soldier on duty was found tied up in a sack along with his weapons. The safe had been broken into, and the metal cashbox was gone. Later the same day, outside of town, a peasant found the cashbox broken and discarded in the grass.

Everyone knew what this was about. The colonel was an old man with a long, pointed mustache, a shaven head, rheumy eyes, and a leg that dragged behind him, but his wife was young, with a face all peaches and cream. She was a live wire who liked to ride horses and drink champagne, to travel to Lublin and to Warsaw, and to disappear for days at a time on picnics in the woods. She had three young officers trailing after her, accumulating debts and signing promissory notes that they renewed at the due dates and then renewed again until finally they had to be paid.

It was easy to see how the soldier on duty, a fresh peasant recruit from the village of Kostroma, would be intimidated by these officers. The whole city knew of this, but the colonel and his staff were in the dark, especially since one of the three Romeos was the auditor of the regiment, presumably above suspicion.

First the hero of Kostroma was dragged into the stockade under a hail of blows with swords and rifle butts that left him gasping and half-dead with fright. He had besmirched the honor of the regiment! Of the whole army! The castle tried to figure out what to do. They put the soldier on "bread and water" for two days, minus the bread and water. On the third day the auditor turned up with a detail of men armed with rods. After the beating the auditor put his questions and recorded the answers.

The soldier said Jewish thieves . . . came at him all of a sudden . . . barefoot . . . threw the sack over him from behind. . . . He'd never seen them before . . . but they were Jews with beards and sidelocks . . . and . . . He collapsed and died. He could not have signed his name anyway, so the auditor did it for him and sent the document to the colonel, signed and sealed.

The colonel sent for the soldiers who had administered the flogging:

"Did you hear him confess?"

"Yes, sir!"

"What?"

"He wrote it all down."

"What did he write down?"

"We don't know."

"Do you mean, you couldn't hear it?"

"Correct, sir."

"But could the auditor hear?"

"He's different, sir."

Angry by this time: "Did he hear?"

"Could be. . . ."

"Spit it out! Speak up!"

"Yes, sir!"

"Will you swear to it?"

"If we're ordered to. . . ."

"On your honor?"

"Yes, sir!"

So that was the story: "Jewish thieves."

An order was dispatched to the city hall: since the stronghold was plundered by Jewish thieves, the police magistrate was to produce immediately the names and addresses of all the Jewish thieves in the city. The magistrate replied that there were none! There had been a boy, Dovidl, but he was gone. And another boy who robbed a grocery store, but he was in prison in Shebreshin. Unless, possibly, there might be some thieves in the new town. The order came promptly: "OK. Try the new town." The magistrate drew up a list and sent for the men. They were brought from the new town in chains and thrown into the black, dank stockade.

Instantly, their wives and children came wailing into town. They were reassured by the local residents that this wasn't the old days: "The truth will out like oil on the surface of the water."

"But they weren't even around that night!"

"My husband was on a heist at . . ." She swallowed the name of the place.

"My husband was in the village working for the landowner." So much the better. They would say so and bring witnesses. In the meantime, since the men were thieves, it didn't matter if they were locked up for a while.

But a week went by, and then another, and suddenly there was an outcry: "They've confessed!"

"Impossible!"

Then we heard that the confession had been forced out of them. They were made to walk barefoot on hot iron grates; matches were lit under their fingernails. Their toenails were torn off with pincers. Hairs were plucked out of their eyelashes.

The wailing of the wives and children resumed. This time the Jews weren't silent. Our lawyer, Fayvl Gelibter, wrote formal appeals to the government. First he wrote them in Polish, and they were returned to him. Then he wrote them in Russian, a language he barely knew, and these too were returned to him: *"Po niegramotnosti."* They found him illiterate.

So they summoned my teacher. He didn't want to do it. He didn't dare to do it. After they had poured him one glass, then another, then a third of mixed drinks, and a fourth with something added to the mixture, he broke into tears and began to kiss us all. He would write the appeal, he loved us more than his life, he was prepared to go to Siberia to save the life of a Jew. He wrote out the appeal.

The next day he was gone—and we never saw him again. But the appeal worked. An order came down from above: the prisoners were to be reexamined by the magistrate, but this time in the presence of the rabbi.

But the thieves repeated their confession in the presence of Rabbi Moyshe Wahl! Yes, they had thrown a sack over the head of the guard, robbed the stronghold, broken into the cashbox, and then discarded it. Reb Moyshe Wahl asked, "And where did you put the money?"

The auditor called the rabbi's attention to the fact that according to the order, everything "must be done in the presence of the rabbi," but the rabbi had no authority to reexamine the witnesses. He read the deposition aloud and asked, "Is this in order?"

The prisoners answered, "Yes."

And Rabbi Moyshe Wahl had to sign it. When he returned from the city hall and was asked about the condition of the prisoners, he cried like a baby.

Something had to be done, and quickly. The first thing to be established was how they had so managed to frighten the men. As soon as Yehoshua Margulies returned from Warsaw, he would launch an investigation. But in the meantime, there were public meetings with lengthy deliberations, and mounting concern.

Suddenly, there was a new development. It was rumored in the city—no one knew where it had started, but they were certain of its truth—that one of the Jews had died in the stockade! People remembered the death of the young sentinel; no doubt this man had also been beaten to death. He was said to have died a few days earlier. The body had not been released for fear that it would show how he had been tortured. They wanted him to rot first. Or they were going to throw him into a cave or into the river. He would not even be granted a Jewish burial! The identity of the victim became known: Moyshe! The cry of his name went up in the streets, and in one spontaneous impulse men and women, old and young—everyone—set out for the stockade hollering, "Moyshe! Moyshe! Give us the body!"

They were greeted at the stockade by an officer who shouted, "Moyshe is alive!" He called into the stockade, "Tell him to show himself!" Moyshe's head appeared in the narrow stockade window high above. He was alive.

The crowd could barely believe it, so people called up to him, "Move your mouth, move your eyes!" He did, but the crowd wanted more assurance. "Say something to us!" Although he moved his lips, no one could hear what he said. He didn't have the strength to speak. But as long as he was alive, everyone went home happy.

That same day a report was sent to Lublin: "The Jews staged an uprising, attacked the stockade, attempted to take it by storm. Forced us to show them the thieves. Wanted to free the prisoners by force. Prevented from doing so by Officer So-and-so. . . ." The officer on duty was promptly congratulated and decorated for bravery, while the city was placed under martial law. Public gatherings were forbidden. No more than two people were permitted to walk together. Shutters were to be closed at sunset, after which no one was permitted outside. There were to be no meetings, either in the synagogue or in private homes. Mounted Cossacks patrolled the streets armed with metal-tipped whips. At night the patrols were doubled. Anyone seen on the street was driven with whips to the stockade. People were stopped and searched in broad daylight, and if anything suspicious was found on them, they were beaten and dragged to the stockade. Fear gripped the city.

The men rushed to the study house to pray for deliverance—and were driven back by the whips. Women ran to the synagogue to tear open the doors of the holy ark and plead before heaven. Mounted Cossacks bore down on them, ripped off their bonnets and shawls, and galloped away. In the new town people went to the cemetery to ask the dead to intercede for them. Silently, in the darkness of the night, they fell to the earth and pressed their stifled cries against the tombstones. When word of this reached "the House of Pharaoh"—the officers of the castle—they surrounded the cemetery and had the Jews arrested one by one as they emerged through the gate. The army was apparently afraid to intrude on the dead.

It was a dead town. Our one and only hope, Yehoshua Margulies, was still away, and while some said that he was sick, others hinted that he was afraid to return. We were reminded of the wisdom of the Psalms: "Put not your trust in powerful men."[32]

Then the news broke through the dead stillness of the town: "They are setting up a field tribunal." A few days later: "They confessed again!" And then: "They've been sentenced to hang!" At the point that the verdict was sent on for confirmation, the town suddenly remembered that there *were* Jews with influence who could help—who would have to help!

But how could we get to these influential Jews? The gates were under double guard and there was no hope of obtaining a travel permit. Telegrams would not be accepted, and anyone who tried to send one would end up in the stockade.

We needed someone willing to risk his life: to steal across the border at Tomaszow, travel the three miles from there to Lemberg, and speak to a preacher named Levenstein, who would telegraph to Moses Montefiore in London, or to Isaac Adolphe Crémieux in Paris.[33] Was there anyone who wanted to earn himself eternal life in the world to come?

There was such a one, Abraham Manis, known as Ronyakhes after the name of his wife. Who do you think he was—a man of substance? An overseer? A community benefactor? A scholar? An enlightened Jew? Nothing of the kind. He was an old man close to eighty, who had been planning for a long time to go to Eretz Yisroel, to Palestine, to die there. But his mate, Ronya, long life to her, refused to accompany him because she couldn't bear to leave her ancestors, who were buried in the cemetery of Zamość. Without her dead family, she would be an orphan in the restored Temple of Solomon. And Abraham Manis wouldn't go without Ronya, because whoever heard of a Jew traveling to the Holy Land without his wife?

(Two years later he persuaded her to go, but as soon as she'd left him in good hands in Safed, she rushed right home. As long as Abraham Manis was in good hands, she could fall joyfully to the earth in the cemetery, and kiss her holy soil again and again. The townspeople could hardly tear her away.)

In the meantime, we could hardly imagine how Abraham Manis could get along in Palestine without her. He was so attached to her. Take this episode, for example: He was our shofar-blower during the Days of Awe. Once he went home after morning prayers to take a nap, and when he returned he was wearing his wife's blouse, which he had mistaken for his white prayer robe. "It's all right," he said when his error was pointed out to him. "My Ronya is such a modest woman, a saint, that I may safely sound the shofar wearing her blouse."

What else distinguished him? He was a dedicated Hasid who had kept it secret for many years. He had been a ritual slaughterer. When he grew older and his eyes were weak, he retired from his profession, and only then—when he couldn't be fired for it—he confessed that he was a Belzer Hasid. So he wasn't a very learned man. In fact, he was a bit ignorant even about Scripture, and every now and then he made such clumsy mistakes that we'd laugh until we ached.

Yet this was the man who undertook the mission, and saw it through. The message to the preacher Levenstein, which I had a role in drafting, was sewn into his shirt. He made it safely through the gate and across the border without a passport. Three days later we had news: the verdict was annulled! The officers involved were later seen in Warsaw, stripped of their epaulettes and their boots. "Are you from Zamość?" they begged. "Can you spare a few groschen?"

So our troubles were forgotten. We saw Abraham Manis off to Eretz Yisroel with great ceremony. And in time the Enlightenment began simmering again.

Only simmering; in "Little Paris" it never came to a full boil. And when my friend Yekhezkl and I showed up one fine day in the arcades dressed in "the German fashion," in pants and short jackets, or when my friend Yekhezkl entered the newly founded junior high school instead of a yeshiva, there was no excessive reaction against Enlightenment.[34]

The Enlightenment was to proceed fairly smoothly in Zamość. There were no painful birth pangs; the Daughter of Heaven, as the Enlightenment was known, did not have to be delivered with forceps: the infant's head was not all that large, and it wasn't a first birth.

5. HASKALAH. RABBI MOYSHE WAHL.

In Zamość we didn't go to extremes. Zamość had always been a city of sages and scribes, a center for the study of Torah, and "where there is Torah, there is wisdom," as everyone knows. Was it any wonder that I was a prodigy? When I described myself as Monish, all I did was to move my experience a little back in time:

Those were the days
of the worthy men of old:
brass-rimmed spectacles,
tfiln housed in silver,
talis crowned in gold,
and their minds were as towers.
Other times,
other powers.

In those days the study house was full of sharp minds and so tightly
packed that people overflowed into the entry hall and onto the steps.
At least that's how they tell the story—not to me, but I always make
sure to listen. Whenever any kind of story was being told, I would
suddenly be there listening with my mouth agape "like a golem."
The grown-ups couldn't figure me out. "He has the mind of a
genius. Why does he waste his time?" My friends, who called me
"Quicksilver"—I could slide even through a page of Gemara—
wondered how I could sit still for stories. I didn't understand it
myself. But stories so enchanted me that to hear one I was even
prepared to forfeit playing bride and groom in the ruins. (Unfortunately, this soon came to an end of itself; since girls mature faster
than boys, they were soon being married off in earnest. Somehow I
never ran into my bride of the ruins anymore, even though we
shared the same doorway.)

I had a natural love of stories, and it was nurtured in the study
house. Among study-house regulars was a pair of identical twins, as
alike as two drops of water. We wondered how their wives could tell
them apart, how their children recognized their own father, if,
indeed, there were not occasional mistakes. They were inseparable.
They ran an inn in partnership on Brukovane Street, and they sat
side by side in the study house, both facing the ark, with their backs
to the lectern. One would never leave before the other, and when
they lingered together after the prayers, they would coo like two
gray doves about olden times. I was always there at the lectern, with
my ears cocked between their gray heads.

"Zamość was really something in the old days. What a mind of
steel he had, what a genius!" Their voices and their laughter were
identical, as well as the way they covered their mouths with their
hands in the French manner (like Dr. Skrishinski) to avoid spraying
people when they laughed. The anecdote about the rabbi with the
mind of steel they had already told a hundred times:

One summer day, when the sage's door stood open, a maid came in with a freshly roasted goose, still warm, on a platter. She'd found something wrong when she was slicing it, and wanted to know whether it was kosher. The girl was barefoot, so the sage didn't hear her come in, nor did he see her set down the "problem" in front of him. He was thoroughly absorbed in his book. Naturally, she didn't want to break his train of thought, so she moved back to the door to wait. The rabbi, with his sharp sense of smell, sensed the presence of the goose and thought it must be mealtime. "Ay, my rebetsin! She spoils me!" And without lifting his eyes from the page, he began tearing off pieces of the goose and stuffing them between his beard and mustache into his mouth. The servant girl was struck dumb with fright. Before she came to her senses and could cry out to the rebetsin in the kitchen, and before the rebetsin could get there, the goose was gone.

"*Sha, sha,*" he tried to calm his wife. "If I ate it, it's kosher." When the rebetsin blinked her eyes in disbelief, he reassured her. "Please tell her that the utensils were kosher."

This sage was also expert in the sciences. It was said that when he engaged in disputations with the priest, his opponent left the scene "mourning and with his head covered," blackened like a chimney sweep.[35]

"And then there was the sexton of the synagogue—a poor man, with a house full of children!" No one suspected what a brain he had. This man had devised a way to calculate all the eclipses of the sun and the moon a hundred years into the future. His correspondence with the French Academy was said to have been discovered after his death, though how true this is, or what became of the papers, no one knows. Rumor had it that at midnight this sexton and Reb Israel Zamość (the author of a text on natural science, if I am not mistaken) would meet at the house of "the mind of steel" and carry on scientific discussions from after the midnight prayers until daybreak. Whether they did or not, Reb Israel Zamość was someone you didn't talk about. He was a follower of the reformer Moses Mendelssohn, and it was safer not to speak of him at all, either good or bad.[36]

"And there were wealthy men in those days, Jews who leased huge estates. But this was oppressive Poland, and at the whim of Polish nobles, Jews were driven off the land."

"The Jews took it to court. The landowners had connections there: the estate managers testified as the landowners told them to, and if a Jew refused to leave voluntarily before the termination of his lease, they seized his assets. There was such a case. . . ."

"Reb Yosl!"

"He died in town, penniless."

"He left an orphan daughter, who never married. . . ."

I knew part of this story myself. I knew the orphan, Reb Yosl's daughter, a tall, thin creature. She dragged her feet, and her eyes watered. Her hair was white as flax, like a peasant's. But she was admired for her fluent Polish. We bought three things from Reb Yosl before he died: the pair of portraits on our walls of Napoleon III and his Empress Eugenie with which I tormented my last teacher; the red clothes closet—"big as a house"—where I knocked over a pot of eggs trying to hide from Dr. Skrishinski; and two long curtain rods with brass knobs that my mother objected to flaunting in the house—"My enemies should live so long!"—and therefore relegated to the attic. My father, whose passion for bargain-hunting I inherited, had bought these three items when Reb Yosl's furniture was auctioned off in the village.

"The Jews who leased land were driven into town, one by one."

"Only Yehoshua Margulies was left."

"Well, he is an exception to every rule!"

But these lessees had already picked up the ways of the landowners, and when they came into town, they brought with them some of the habits and customs of the nobility, just as the Leipzig merchants returned from Leipzig a touch Germanized themselves. (Like the German woman whose soul transmigrated into a black dog!)

"It's quite a distance to Leipzig!"

"Highwaymen stalked the roads."

"People would write wills before they took the trip and leave writs of divorce, just in case. . . ."[37]

"Those were different times!"

Our times were not so bad either, coming as they did after Jacob Eichenbaum, Alexander Zederbaum, and other Enlighteners had already left their mark on our city. Jacob Reifman, the notorious freethinker and student of antiquity, came to Zamość and stayed at the house of Yehoshua Margulies.[38] My uncle, the one who later collected my juvenilia, dressed in the modified German fashion, coattails down to the knees. ("Pure German" referred to jackets so short that they barely covered the buttocks when you sat down.) The Brody Singers came to town. They too stayed at the house of Margulies and performed there. In a glassed-in bookcase in his library Margulies kept the small volumes of a noted former resident of Zamość, Dr. Shloyme Ettinger—his play *Serkele*, his fables, and *Kugl*, his Yiddish adaptation of Schiller's *The Bell*.

And then there was old Reb Zalman's house. Reb Zalman was a corpulent Jew of the old school. Dressed in his wide greatcoat, he would proceed through the town collecting charity, carrying in front of him a walking stick with a silver handle, and trailing behind him the sexton with a silver charity box. His wife, whose name I have forgotten, had "a three-story goiter." Since her ears were not pierced, her long diamond earrings dangled from her headband on silk threads. They had a garden in the center of their courtyard, a wooden porch around the entire house, and curtains in the windows. Behind these curtains, or when the weather was mild on their porch, and in summertime on the garden bench around the lone tree, surrounded by flowers, sat their widowed daughter with her two little girls—one blond, the other brunette—studying French from Ollendorff's grammar, or reading German as if they were born to it. They had a large library, from which I recall having borrowed, some years later, a book on physics.

Then there was Abraham Luxemburg, who dressed in "the pure German fashion" and lived at the edge of town near the Officers' Club in a self-contained house with a large garden surrounded by a high wooden fence. The house was on the narrow path to the river, and whenever we went swimming, we'd look through the crack between the boards and see his only daughter wandering through the garden picking flowers, or reading a book. She was hunchbacked and was ashamed to show herself in the street.[39] The garden had apple and pear trees, but we didn't climb the fence out of respect for the educated girl with the hunchback, and for the inspector's yelping dog.

K. owned the wineshop where the officers drank and the landowners ate or stocked up on wine and food. In his house there was a blond girl, like a china doll, with long, silken braids (I will return to her later), who read books that she borrowed from the gentry and the officers.

In Margulies' house, where high-ranking officers played cards and the renowned heretic Jacob Reifman served as tutor, a prayer quorum gathered every day. This was not so much for the sake of the master, who was in Warsaw most of the time, as to maintain the piety of the children. A local hatmaker led the congregation, and the choir was composed of his brothers, hatmakers like himself. They were not very religious. One of the brothers was a bit of a freethinker, a teacher of calligraphy who wrote Yiddish poems in the manner of Ettinger. When another of the singers died, people said that before his death he made a point of eating a wormy plum, precisely because worms are unkosher. When they whipped him in the afterlife and called out the reason for each sin in turn, he would know that it was all over when they called out the last punishment for the last sin he had committed.

When they read the Hebrew prayers, they did not use the Lithuanian pronunciation. For the Polish Jews of those days, the Lithuanian Jew—the Litvak—was considered half a Gentile, and said to have a crucifix in his head. The story goes that a Litvak, when his friend says, "Come on, let's convert to Christianity," replies, "Wait, I just want to finish the afternoon prayer." Litvaks were actually quite scarce in our region. There was one in Zamość, quite a fine young man, the son-in-law of Reb Zaynvl. Unhappily, he died; his widow said she didn't want to remarry.

So they prayed with the Polish-Yiddish pronunciation. For the festivities of Simkhat Torah, Yehoshua Margulies' wife wore her diamond earrings and pearl-embroidered collar, exactly as in her portrait in the salon. Smiling sweetly, she offered us refreshments: cake (baked, if I am not mistaken, by her sister, with my grandmother's help), nuts, beer, and brandy. Instead of synagogue melodies, the cantor and his choir entertained us with songs! The lyrics were rather comical: "The Message of the hammer / Is knocking at our chamber," or Goldfaden rousing us to greet "the sun that has arisen and the nations of the world that await us."[40] Exactly where in Zamość were these nations of the world? But we enjoyed the singing.

The congregation skipped the long devotional lyrics. During the Yizkor service for the dead, the young men and women whose parents were still living left their separate prayer quorums and mingled in the hall to flirt a little. On Yom Kippur, the Day of Atonement, they offered one another valerian drops, but first you had to show your tongue to prove that you were really fasting.

Among those in the quorum was an old bachelor named Kinderfraynt, a clean-shaven man who used a prayer book with German translation. He was familiar with the philosophic writings of Moses Mendelssohn, his *Phaedon* and *Jerusalem*, and once he stopped me to ask, "What is your credo, my dear sir?" Recalling the reply of Rabbi Hillel to such a taunt, I answered, "Love thy neighbor as thyself." "No," he said. "Love yourself. That is the foundation of life."[41]

A certain Raphael Esigmakher joined this congregation, a stammerer who owned a vinegar factory, as his name implied. He had just returned from abroad, where he had undergone surgery, and said that he had seen a horseless carriage with his own eyes. People laughed so hard and made so many jokes at his expense that he was finally forced to retract his remark, and to "admit" that he was fooling. But though he hadn't been able to convince them, it was a start—a seed of the new age had been planted.

I remember also a poor old man who used to hang about town, a blond, gangling, broad-shouldered fellow, the perfect candidate for Torah honors during the reading of God's curses.[42] This Yoel, whose family name I never knew and whose nickname isn't fit to print, had a son somewhere in Russia—"a full-fledged military man" who sent him money by post: another sign of the times.

So all in all there wasn't much left for the Haskalah to do in Zamość. Elsewhere, there was sound and fury: Hasidim who attacked modern Jews for their use of biblical concordances; modern Jews who spent part of their time writing Hebrew lyrics on the Enlightenment and the Four Seasons, and odes to the munificent government for its bounty to the congregation of Israel, and the rest of their time denouncing the Hasidic black-hats. There were wars against the communal leaders, against the Hasidic leaders, among the Hasidic sects, among the rabbis. . . . But there wasn't a sign of this in Zamość.

True, I did complain in an early poem that it cost "twenty-eight groschen for a pound of meat" and to make it rhyme, "fit for none but dogs to eat," and I did groan: "A pound too little found too late / all stones and bones and false weight." Later, too, in *Stories in Verse*, which I published with my former father-in-law, G. Y. Lichtenfeld, the heroine of the poem "Chana" is raped by the rich man's son, and the father uses his influence, and so on and so forth. It wasn't original; it was an imitation of Heine, only in poorer taste.[43] Actually, we got our meat from a dairy farm, and though we had to pay taxes on it as in Mendele Mocher Sforim's dramatic satire *The Meat Tax*, there was none of the thievery or trickery that he describes, and the whole system was dismantled after a while. In Zamość the ideal head of the community was—and until very recently has remained—a Jew so inarticulate that he wouldn't blab at the city hall, so illiterate that he couldn't sign anything without the community's knowledge (the official seal was kept at the home of one of our notables); a husband who got slapped by his wife for giving his time to the community instead of marrying off his daughters.

To avoid controversy, Hasidic rebbes were kept out of the city. If

Zamość got word that a rebbe was on his way, the police were asked
to set a guard at every gate, and the community provided a Jew to
stand by him.on watch. When the wagon appeared, it was challenged:
"*Kudie?* Where to?" "*Nazad!* Go back where you came from!"

Reb Gershon Henekh, nicknamed "the Blue" for his connection
with the Belz Hasidim (they wore blue ritual fringes as a sign of
their "truer" piety), tried to move to Zamość in spite of the obstacles.
A man used to getting his way, he bought a house in the city,
assuming that no one would drive out a homeowner. To be doubly
sure, he stole in at night. But by morning word had gotten around,
and he was unceremoniously escorted out.

Our Hasidim were few in number and had no voice in local affairs.
They were still licking their wounds from the time that the Gaon of
Vilna had issued his ban of excommunication against them, and they
had received their punishment at the hands of the local misnagdim.[44]
One young man, a son-in-law imported from elsewhere, had felt the
need to visit his rebbe and sneaked out of town. They sent out riders
after him and nabbed him. He was paraded through the streets,
given a good whipping at home, then hauled up before the rabbi,
who divorced him from his wife and sent him packing. When a
Hasid was discovered in our midst, his family pronounced him dead
and observed the week of ritual mourning. If a secret congregation
was caught, they were taken to city hall, where the Gentiles cut off
their sidelocks and half their beards. People still remember it all.

Nowadays, thank God, things are peaceful. That is to say, the
Hasidim have reason to thank God. Not too long ago, when the
rebbe of Ishbitz attempted to overrule a decision of one of our
rabbis (not such an illustrious man), we "Germans" excommunicated
them—his Hasidic disciples!

Our rabbi, Moyshe Wahl, my examiner and the "Reb Zishele" of
my fiction, deserves a place of honor in this narrative. He was a
student of the rabbi of Lissa, who referred to him as "my illustrious
student" when citing his opinions. The son-in-law of a wealthy man,
he had tried being a merchant, but lost his money, and became rabbi
of Zamość. "A man of truth hating covetousness," he had held the
position for fifty years, and still refused to take an increase in salary.[45]
He construed it as a bonus, and refused to accept it, saying, "Don't
spoil me with riches." Any money that he received as a judge he
divided among the assistant rabbis and arbitrators who were present.
He ate only what his wife prepared. At celebrations he would take

a sip of wine in order to make a blessing and eat a morsel of dry bread for the sake of saying grace.

He was a sweet little old man with a silvery beard, and his eyes were really gentle as a dove's. Children were the love of his life. Whenever he appeared in the street or in the study house, he was immediately surrounded by youngsters, and stood barely taller than them, like a slightly older kid. His childlike, trembling voice was like a fine silver bell. When he chanted the Kol Nidre prayer, as was his privilege on the eve of Yom Kippur, his ringing voice poured into the great stillness and out to the farthest corners of the women's section above and the men's section below. All year long he was lenient in judging ritual matters, forever finding things kosher. This was a poor congregation, after all, that had to go without because of such high prices. Passover was the exception. He trembled like a fish for fear of the punishment of excommunication, meted out to those who did not keep the Passover laws.

He based his decisions directly on the Gemara. When someone, and mind you not just anybody, pointed out that other noted commentators had ruled otherwise, he replied with a smile, "In my time and in my city, I'm the final authority." That was it. No more was said.

Everyone, from the rich to the Hasidim and including the minimally observant, was in awe of this diminutive, smiling man. Plainly, heaven was on his side, whether because of his own merit or the merit of his ancestors. You may recall what happened to the protagonist of my story "Shmaye the Hero," who defied the rabbi and boasted that he would tear the hat off his head. If not, go read the story.[46]

The Trisker Hasidim do not deny that on his account their rebbe had his comeuppance. This is the story (and it was from this time on that Hasidic rebbes were kept out of the city): The rebbe of Trisk once came to Zamość, which as far as he was concerned was one of *his* cities. So he sent for the rabbi. Rabbi Moyshe Wahl smiled and said, "Tell him the honor of the Torah demands that *he* should call on me first. I am the rabbi of the community." But the Trisker Rebbe refused, and left town. He did not live out the year.

The Hasidim of Trisk, quoting Ecclesiastes, said, "It was like an error which proceedeth from a ruler."[47] They added, preening a bit, that in the case of such a righteous pillar of the world as the Trisker rebbe, the error had to be punished according to the strictest severity.

When Jacob Reifman came to Zamość as tutor or teacher for the family of Yehoshua Margulies, someone had him excommunicated—a Hasidic ploy. Rabbi Wahl announced that anyone pronouncing such a ban without the knowledge of the local rabbi and his court was himself excommunicated. That same year one of the younger Hasidim died, so it was as plain as day that he was the person responsible, and that this was his punishment.

The tsarist government began drafting young men into the army. My father's advice, not to go, since the authorities "can't imprison the whole world," did not carry much weight. As the draft date approached, it was clear that those who were called up would need financial support for themselves and for the families they left behind. Rabbi Moyshe Wahl set up a charity box in a separate room of his house, and announced that all householders should contribute a tithe of their earnings. Although the donations were made anonymously and in private, everyone was so afraid of an error in calculation and of the rabbi's "decree" that they found 789 rubles in the box! It was an astonishing sum.

And the way the women obeyed him! The fishermen tried to charge the market women an extra groschen, anticipating the pre-Sabbath demand. But when Rabbi Wahl, fearing that the poor would not be able to afford the inflated price and have to go without fish for the Sabbath, sent around his sexton to say that no one should buy, then the women ran from their barrels and fish pails as if from a fire.

Then there was our richest man, Yehoshua Margulies himself. The rabbi got along very well with him, and called him "Yeshayele." Nevertheless, when he once summoned Yeshayele to the rabbinical court, and was told that the presence of guests—government officials—prevented his coming, Rabbi Moyshe Wahl sent back the reply that God is everywhere, and anyone who has no time for God may find that God has no time for him. The summons was hurriedly obeyed.

As for the unobservant—late one Friday night Rabbi Wahl started from his sleep, awakened by a shuffling sound. A thief was removing the windowpanes. A head appeared, not Jewish. So he thanked and praised the Almighty that Jewish thieves were not desecrating the Sabbath. Meanwhile, the thief entered, looked around, and caught sight of the Sabbath candlesticks. Knowing that some Jew would buy them, the rabbi gave up his claim to them. For one week the rebetsin made the blessing over brass candlesticks, and, being a woman, she shed a few tears. The following Sabbath eve, the candlesticks were returned. They had been picked up by two Jewish fences: one had lost his wife, the other's child had died of diphtheria.

Everyone knew that for the last thirty years Rabbi Moyshe Wahl had not held a holy book in his hands. He knew the entire Mishna and Gemara by heart, and if asked to complete any quoted passage, he could recite whatever followed for as long as he liked without glancing at the text. He did read secular books, however, which he picked up I know not where. Once, when the rabbinical court was not in session, Rabbi Wahl was alone in his study house with one of the assistant rabbis, a simple man. After pacing back and forth, engrossed in a little book, he stopped before the assistant to ask, "What do you think? Can a man walk barefoot on broken glass?" He was referring to one of the characters in Eugène Sue's *Mysteries of Paris*, which he was reading in Hebrew translation.

So you see, Her Royal Highness the Jewish Enlightenment didn't have a stitch of work to do in Zamość. It was mostly a romantic sentiment. Youngsters strolled around the marketplace by moonlight declaiming the Hebrew verse "Zion, Zion . . . the Beloved . . . the Turtle Dove . . ." while casting their longing eyes toward the shops where the marriageable girls spent their time. Occasionally, an enlightened Jew would drop an ironic comment on local poverty as he passed through town. "Jews don't eat. Jews do without food. You should see how the nations of the world gorge themselves!" And in compliance with Haskalah directives, people began to shorten their coats in the modern style.

Just the same, I fell victim to the Enlightenment.

The stairwells of Zamość were all narrow and dark. I shared one such staircase with three sisters.

One day, prodigy that I was, who thought of nothing and knew of nothing except his studies, I came running or rather flying down the stairs with three buttered bagels in my pocket for the poor boy in the study house. I heard the patter of light footsteps coming toward me. All at once, I saw the shimmer of bare white arms and flashing eyes. The white arms threw themselves around my neck, and a hot breath pressed my face with a heartfelt plea: "Leybushl, let's be in love." When I drew back at this—my first offer of love— confused and afraid, my little temptress Lilith, the middle sister of the three, was terribly offended. She warned me sharply: "Oh, really? Well, then, I'm going straight to Yointshe at the riding academy!"

She had to be in love with someone, and she knew where to find Yointshe. Frightened now for her sake, I called out to her, "God forbid! Don't you dare go to him, you wild goat! He's a good-for-nothing!"

"Well, then *you* be in love with me!"

So I had to do as she said. We kissed in a childish way with pretenses of passion. She shut her eyes, but her arms as she threw them around me were rather cool and slack. I suppose she *had* to be in love, but not with me.

Still and all, we continued to meet and kiss by agreement. Like the Lilith in my poem she demanded vows of love, and like Monish I pledged her my troth, though not by all that's high and holy. I didn't go as far as the hero of my poem "Monish," and so it didn't end with me on a broomstick in the sky flying to the devil. And in any case we soon began to meet less and less frequently.

Before the week was out I ran into the eldest of the three, my bride of the ruins. We stood stock-still, both of us overcome by innocent and childish love. Shyly, we looked into one another's eyes. She broke the silence first. "You know, Leybushl, you should learn"—she hesitated, and concluded—"Polish!"

In a strangely quiet voice, for no apparent reason, I replied, "I can already read it." I had learned to read Polish in the study house from a Polish book that happened to be on the shelf, as randomly as I later learned to read a little German and Russian. She asked me if I could understand the language.

"Of course!" What else is there to say when a girl puts such a question? She offered to lend me Korzeniowski's *Collocation*.[48] If there was anything that I didn't understand, I should come to ask her about it. I felt warmed by this invitation.

"Naturally. I'm sure I won't understand everything!" And I added joyfully, "And I'll teach you Hebrew." "Good!" She blushed and there was another silence. This time I broke it. I said even more quietly than before, hardly recognizing my own voice, "Are you mad at me?" As if she didn't know what I was talking about, she asked me why she should be mad at me. "Because of the stone I threw at you when we were playing bride and groom." She brushed this aside. But the scar was still there, and she brought her cheek closer to show me. It was dark and hard to see, so I touched her cheek very, very lightly with a trembling finger. She blushed. "You can kiss me on that spot if you like," she said innocently. I pressed my lips to her cheek, but they trembled more than my finger. Drawing back her head, obviously moved, she said, "You know, had you struck me just a tiny bit higher, you would have knocked my eye out." "God forbid!" "Yes, yes! My father and mother both say so!"

With a sad smile she added, "And who would have had me with only one eye?" "I would," I cried, "I would!" This made her somewhat thoughtful. "And would you love me if I had one eye?" I cried out, "Forever, as I am a Jew!"

I put my arms around her and drew her tightly to my heart. At the same time I wondered what I was doing, what I was saying, and where this tenderness came from. Why was my voice trembling? And why was she trembling? How could her eyes shine so brightly in that darkness?

The third sister, the youngest, was "a young goat," the Zamość expression for a teenage girl. She had tuberculosis, though I didn't know about it till later. She was slender and slightly stooped, and her eyes were very warm, with exceptionally large pupils that seemed always thirsty for light, always curious and probing. Looking back, I think they may always have been taking their leave of the world.

Whenever we passed on the steps, she would stop and press up against the wall and stand there with her hands behind her against the railing. Involuntarily, I would slow down, and she would follow me with her big eyes until I had passed her and gone all the way down to the bottom. When I dropped over to their place or she to ours, she would sit in a dark corner looking at me quietly, her eyes opening steadily wider. It aroused in me a bittersweet pain, though I didn't know what her expression signified. Sometime later her older sister, my bride of the ruins, whispered into my ear that the poor thing was sick, and told me what the sickness was. It pained me even more.

Then she fell seriously ill. Whenever I dropped by, I saw the same look and felt the same sweet pain. I happened to be there just before she died, and she suddenly asked everyone but me to leave the room. When we were alone together, she motioned me over to her bed. "Come closer," she said. I bent over the bed.

"You know," she said very softly. I seemed to hear leaves rustling as I listened not with my ear but with my heart. "You know, I love my father and my mother and my brother . . . my sisters . . . and I love you most of all."

She asked me, in an even softer voice, to kiss her on the forehead. Before I understood her meaning, she added, "Don't kiss me on the mouth. My saliva is contagious!" I kissed her on the lips.

Here I skip ahead in order to conclude the story of my love for three sisters. The youngest died. The middle one I neglected for the eldest. She complained that I had betrayed her, "breaking our vows." She was angry; she wrote me vindictive letters. So I avoided her. She sent the servant girl with secret messages: "How dare you? What is the meaning of this?" Overcome by my playful muse, which I don't even begin to understand, I replied in rhyme:

> I kissed you, so you complain.
> I must have been insane.
> A dybbuk must have inspired it,
> I couldn't have desired it.
>
> A dybbuk must have besieged me.
> It wasn't your magic, believe me.
> It may come again and soften my brain,
> But meanwhile, I am sane.

This "sin of my youth" I later discovered in my uncle's house and revised and unfortunately published in the Jubilee edition of my works. As for losing me, she quickly found comfort elsewhere.

About the eldest, the innocent one: Before I had a chance to teach her Hebrew, she got engaged to be married, but not to me! To a young man from Russia.

The engagement was signed in Ustile, midway between Zamość and the young man's town. I wasn't at home when she left. My father had suddenly (and perhaps deliberately) taken me along with him to where he was felling trees, in a forest not far from Ustile. He persuaded me to accompany him. "You'll see the forest, and if you like it and if the work suits you, you can stay there." It turned out that I wasn't suited to lumbering, but I made my first acquaintance with the forest and with the Bug River.

At first, the trip was boring, up hill and down dale. The Psalmist rhapsodizes, "They went up the mountains, they flowed down the valleys," but it wasn't so very pleasant.[49] On either side of the road were flat, harvested fields. Their black, spiky stubble reminded me of the badly shaven jaws of Yointshe and "Grandpa."

But little by little, as we approached our destination, we heard a rushing noise that kept getting stronger the closer we came. I asked my father if it was a waterfall. "No," he said, "it's the forest coming toward us." Those were his words. I was astonished. "How can a forest make noise?" "With its branches, and leaves, swayed by the wind."

"Aha!"

As soon as we entered the forest, I was under its spell. The trees were gigantic, so heroic they made me feel insignificant.

"How old are those trees?"

My father didn't know. "They're very old."

"What sort of trees are they?"

"Pines. Out of tall pine trees like these they make the masts for ships. The logs are shipped very far away."

"How?"

"They are floated downstream on the Bug, which you'll soon see, down to the Vistula, and from the Vistula to the open sea at Danzig, and from there—to other seas. But this piece of forest hasn't been sold yet. Meanwhile, I'm felling oaks a little farther on."

When we got to the oaks and I saw a short peasant grab an ax and chop it into the tree, something gave a stab at my heart. I rushed into the bookkeeper's cabin, choking back tears, in a state of shock and agitation. I threw myself down on the bed, buried my face in the pillow, and lay there shivering until fatigue overtook me and I fell asleep. When I woke, it was morning. I asked for my father. The bookkeeper smiled behind his mustache and said that he had gone to Ustile and would be back in the evening. "Do you want to go into the forest?" I shook my head. "No." Whenever the wind carried the echo of the ax blows from the woods, it made me shudder.

My father returned at dusk. "*Mazel tov!* Congratulations!" He looked at me tentatively. My bride of the ruins was now properly engaged, but as I said, not to me.

It was not a tragedy, less like the crash of a steel bar than of a bundle of moonbeams. I grew accustomed to the forest. I went down the Bug River and down the Vistula as far as the town of Rakhev.

Here I have to add a postscript about something that happened between me and Rabbi Moyshe Wahl, a personal incident I failed to include when I was presenting his portrait.

All year long Rabbi Wahl prayed in his own house in the room used for the rabbinical court. He came to the synagogue only for Kol Nidre and on the eve of every new moon. Once he arrived too early, when the synagogue was still locked. So he went up into the study house and stood there reading a holy book beside the eastern wall, next to the ark. This was exactly where our simpleton stood, the one we called Yehoshua the Ox, who always waited and hoped for a rabbinic message to carry. As I mentioned, we pranksters would send him with phony summonses to the rabbi, and he would run to his wife to ask whether he should go, whether the trip was worth his while. He wore the same kind of fur-trimmed hat and satin coat as the rabbi, and when I came into the study house, I thought, "Well, there he is!" I snuck up to him quietly and gave him a gift of my hand—not a slap to hurt him, just as a joke, and who should turn around but Reb Moyshe Wahl. I was stunned.

He said to me, smiling, "Who did you think it was, boy?" Tears sprung to my eyes. "Are you sorry for what you did?" What a question! But I couldn't speak. "Do you want me to forgive you? Do you want to make up for it?" Still choked for words, I barely managed to nod my head. "Promise me that you'll never again lift a hand against anyone." I offered my hand. "No," he said, "no sealed promises."[50]

I kept my word. Except for one single time when it would have taken a superhuman effort to control myself, I haven't raised my hand against anyone, not to this day, not to return a blow or even to defend myself.

6: THREE SPANS ABOVE THE STREAM OF ENLIGHTENMENT. PASSIONATE LOVE OF LIFE. PROBLEMS OF DEATH. THE LIBRARY KEY.

Jewish children grow up quickly. If only their bodies ripened as quickly as their hearts and minds! Were this an artist's crayon in my hand instead of a pen, I would draw the following caricature of how I looked as a boy: small and wiry, with arms and legs like sticks, a big head, not much of a forehead, and great, aching, questioning eyes.

I would be in a little boat. The boat is held aloft, three spans above the Stream of Enlightenment, by a small hot-air balloon. The boat is at the wind's mercy. I am sitting inside the boat with a butterfly net in my hand, waving it about in the air trying to catch problems. And thus, busily catching problems, I sail willy-nilly into the Bay of Sexual Awakening.

Three spans above the Stream of Enlightenment. The Enlightenment—Haskalah—meant education: knowing "how to say 'boots' in several languages," plus a few poems about the four seasons of the year; Schiffman's Hebrew declensions; Stern's German lessons (*Wie haben Sie geschlafen?*—How did you sleep?); the distinction between the participle—*prechastia*—and the gerund—*dieprechastia*—

according to my Russian teacher's text. Along with this, it meant declaiming Hebrew verses by the light of the moon. Of my friends only one, Isaac, finished junior high school at home and went off to study medicine.

I was taken up with the great questions of existence and creation. Why had God created the world? Despite Aristotle and all the Greek philosophers who argued that the world had no beginning and no end, I could prove that it was a creation out of primal matter. It was there in Scripture, in black and white, that the world was created *ex nihilo* when the Creator spoke the words, "Let there be light!"

Fine, but why did He create? So that man, the goal and purpose of creation, should serve Him? But why does a God require the service of man? According to Rabbenu Tam, Rabbi Jacob ben Meir, so that He should be able to reward the human being rather than shaming him with gifts.[51] But that applies only to dealings between one person and another. If I take what I haven't earned from my employer, he's out of pocket. Surely that can't apply to God. There was more sense in the kabbalistic notion of Creation as the spontaneous emanation of the Sephirot. Yet it seemed to me that this made less of God's will, and that was a shame. I was afraid of the way it raided the borders of God's omnipotence. His power was unending yet limited: he could not, after all, make a square of a triangle. Later I grew afraid of sinning before the Almighty. Like the doomed sinner in one of my plays who is chained to the wall in the synagogue vestibule for having fallen in love with a betrothed young woman, I was afraid that for something that had once happened God would not alter His judgment by even so much as the dot of an *i*.[52]

What does life in this world signify, and what does it mean to leave the world—to die?

The problems that absorbed me sprouted like wild mushrooms in that restless, ominous chaos of the subconscious where the sexual instincts awaken. Without my knowledge, and irrespective of my will, the male animal emerged and colored all that had once been black and white in a rainbow of shades, mostly bloodred and purple.

I sank into melancholy. On account of that melancholy my father slapped me that Friday night, and my mother murmured, "As if a child doesn't have his own heartaches." I was lonely—who do you talk to about such things?—and made my way through the misty net of people and objects, loosely contained in time and place, who seemed either to swirl dizzily in gray fog or to shimmer through columns of sundust. Dream and reality merged.

· · ·

There is very little nature in what I remember. I saw very little of it in those early years which are expected to nourish the mature man.

I was a Jewish child born in a fortress, walled in from forest and field by gates and ramparts. I had already been deeply moved by the Sabbath hymn in praise of God the Creator of Nature and by other biblical passages of nature description before I even saw a living blade of grass. I knew that there were such things because I had learned that angels stand over each blade of grass with whips in their hands, urging it to "Grow! Grow!" Thus are the tender shoots forced to break through the hard ground and sprout into life.[53]

I had already penetrated the entire mystery, in its depth and exaltation, of the burning thornbush in the desert before I knew what the steppe was or had seen a single thorn or stalk of anything that grows. Only once, on a hot day, when I went down to the damp cellar to cool off, did I see things sprouting from the potatoes.

I suppose that nowadays you can't easily imagine a childhood or adolescence like mine. You would find incredible this creature with his head full of the sweetest-smelling scents of "the field that God has blessed," of mandrakes and Mount Lebanon, of the rose of Sharon and the lily of the valley, who hadn't raised a single living flower to his nostrils. Yointshe's sister, the regimental chaplain's daughters, and some of the officers' wives wore nosegays over their hearts. The wives of the engineers who lived in the enclosed garden outside the city sometimes came into town wearing white dresses bedecked with tiny flowers, and strolled around the castle. It was not exactly easy for a child or a young man to creep around sticking his nose into their blossoms. . . .

And, anyway, how could I stoop to satisfying my appetites? After all, I was the softhearted boy raised on *Duties of the Heart* who got his satisfaction from self-denial, from sharing his breakfast with the poorer boys in the study house. I was the boy who had only two desires for himself—"from his father in this world an additional scallion, and from his Father in heaven, to restore the moon's lost parity with the sun."[54]

My pure, childish heart was still locked. Whose hand was to unscramble the combination, open the door, and kindle the flame—holy or profane—on the little altar? For the time being, in our childhood games I was the girl and my bride of the ruins—the boy! Yet my outsized head had already been exposed to all the economic, judicial, and sexual entanglements of relations between "Adam and Eve," from the refusal of a woman to keep to a marriage that had been imposed upon her while a minor to a widow's claim on her brother-in-law after the death of her husband.[55]

And I suffered for the exile of the Shekhina, of God's Divine Presence. Why does falsehood triumph over truth? Why do mistakes determine fate? And why does the Redeemer—as it says in Lamentations—"keep ashes in his mouth and remain silent"?[56]

Then there was the problem of being in exile for real.

In gala uniforms, with musical instruments that glittered in the sunlight, a division of troops paraded one gala day from the officers' quarters at the castle down the length of the cobblestone street to the barracks at the Shebreshin gate. They were accompanied all the way by a gang of kids. Except for the druggist and his three dark ladies, everyone ran to their windows, or to the doors of their shops. As the band exploded in a triumphant, joyful march, I felt stricken: "Where is my army, my martial music?" Tears rose in my eyes.

In my mind's eye, I already owned a large part of the world, all of ancient Israel, that land flowing with milk and honey where every man sat under his vine and his fig tree.[57] True, it was a mistaken geography. Just recently, when I wrote the story "Devotion unto Death," I had Lake Kinneret lapping the shores of the holy city of Safed. But what a piece of the world that was! A land with cities (including Jerusalem), villages, rivers and seas (the Dead Sea in their center), mountains covered with vineyards. All I actually saw with my own eyes on the other side of the fortress was Stabrow, the village I mentioned earlier.

I don't remember just when it was, but once I was filled with a powerful desire to climb to the balcony of the clock tower. So I stole away from my parents' house, climbed the slippery, narrow, dizzying tower stairs, and emerged on the balcony, from where I could suddenly see two or three miles of unimpressive, flat land around the city, "buildings like houses of cards, people like grasshoppers," and a few scattered dwarf trees. To my intense dismay, I concluded that the higher you are, the farther you see—but not necessarily the better.

Gradually, my little world began to expand. It reached out beyond the city and annexed the engineers' garden, from which the ladies with blossoms on their skirts came into town to stroll about the castle.

Here is the story of that garden: For many years the fortress had not served its purpose. The ramparts were no longer awesome, the cannons and piles of ammunition had been removed, the water had dried in the moats, and the frogs had moved to the swamps in the meadow. The garrison was gone, and it had been replaced in the barracks with uhlans and Cossacks. The major general with his bristly mustache had said farewell to the city, drunk a toast, taken his gift, and gone. There was no trace of the three drawbridges, and the moats had been filled in to serve as roads to the highway. The supervisor stayed on to keep Jewish boys from swimming, and everyone forgot about the engineers who lived in the garden outside town. They were still doing the calculations for the proper dismantling of the fortress, and in the meantime, the garden where they lived in a large white house that shone through the trees was a locked Gentile paradise.

Sometimes, walking along the highway, I would get down into the ditch near the engineers' garden and look in with longing. I would stick my head as far as it would go between the fence posts and stare. There were lots of trees and garden paths and the gleaming white house among the green trees, and the fluttering white dresses, bedecked with flowers, of the engineers' wives. On a side path I sometimes saw an angelic little girl on a swing. Her laughter rang aloud. Her golden locks flew in the wind as her father the general pushed the swing himself.

In the festive evenings brightly colored Chinese lanterns swayed in the leaves over the length of the main path to the house, casting strips of rainbow light on the ground below. The regimental band would play in front of the house. New guests kept arriving from the officers' quarters. There was dancing and drinking, and the occasional echo of a toast before it was swallowed up in the music of the brass.

Sometimes on quiet evenings you could hear piano music inside the house. Mikhl, the leader of our Jewish band of musicians, who later served as the model for one of my stories, would stumble through the ditch—he was seldom fully sober—and thirstily strain to hear the music. From these melodies he was said to improvise moralistic songs for the veiling of the bride, processionals to the wedding canopy, and other dance music for Jewish weddings. Boys who loved music, among them members of the synagogue choir, gaped with their heads between the posts. When we were noticed, we were chased away—why should Jewish children be permitted to enjoy themselves? The guard dogs would be unleashed against us, and in tearing our heads from between the fence posts to flee we would leave behind pieces of our skin.

Then suddenly someone remembered the engineers, and they

were summoned to begin their work. The paradise opened up, and my child's world expanded. Much later, when I fashioned my fictional garden for the wealthy Jew of Safed, I joined it to sections of Saxony Park in Warsaw and the rabbinic gardens of Strukov and Biala.[58] But on that first occasion when I entered the garden, my heart was pounding as if I were one of the four great sages of the Talmud entering that mysterious orchard from which only one of them would emerge intact.[59] I had entered the garden whole. But having already begun to "cut the plants in the garden of faith," I wondered whether I would emerge unscathed.

I walked along the long, dark garden path thinking about death. Why did God create death, and what happens afterward? The soul flies to heaven or to hell. Maimonides maintains that something of the dead person's mind continues to exist at the highest level to which his soul had been educated on earth. But what of my little brother who died so young that his reason had no time to develop? What about infants in the cradle or stillbirths? The Baal Shem Tov tells us that we will continue to lead the same life that we led here on earth, but pleasurably or miserably according to our merits. The rich landowner remains a rich landowner and the teamster a teamster—a kind of reward and punishment of the imagination, a chimerical settling of accounts, as if the Almighty were deceiving us. There was a crazy middle-aged woman in town who had been divorced or thrown out by her husband, along with her clothes and jewelry. All day long she wandered around the streets with her bundle. I don't know where she spent the nights. She would stop in the market, open her bundle to spread out her things, look them over and smile, try on her jewelry, one piece at a time. She took off one wig and put on another. She also tried to change her clothes in the middle of the market, as though this were a holiday in the middle of the week. Her emaciated face and her eyes beamed with joy. Does another such paradise await her? Here the police came and dragged her off to jail. Up there, in the imaginary world, where there are no police, she may be able to change her clothes ten times a day.

As for the body, it was but dust and ashes. "The spirits speak" was only a symbolic expression, whereas "The dead don't know that they are dead" was literal truth. But I could not imagine how anyone lies in the grave without feeling the confinement, the dampness, the dark, and the worms eating his body. What if there remains a bit of awareness, a touch of feeling, God help us? All my limbs went icy.

And why die at all? Where was the justice in that? Because Adam sinned by eating of the Tree of Knowledge. Was knowledge sinful, or the fact that God forbade it? And if eating of it were a sin, did it merit eternal punishment for all subsequent generations? "I will visit the sins of the fathers on the children to the third and the fourth generations," says the Bible, but it doesn't say forever! And why was the fruit of the Tree of Life forbidden? "Lest he live forever." Well, why not? "They will be equal to me." What's wrong with that? Later He did demand just that—"I am Holy, thou must be Holy too," and "Be thou merciful also." He wanted us to be like Him after all.[60]

And then how very harsh and terrifying was the punishment, the agony of death.

Now comes Maimonides again, the wise and profound philosopher who divides the world thus: everything from the earth to the heavenly spheres is subject to the law of Aristotle; everything above the spheres is subject to the law of Moses: "He is true and His Torah is true."

Maimonides says it's all a textual error. There is no pain, no suffering, no agony, no death. None of it exists, just as the darkness doesn't exist. There is only light. "He formed light and created darkness" is only a figure of speech in prayer. It was light that God created! Darkness is only the absence of light, what remains when God takes the light away. And He has the right to take it away because He didn't have to give it to us in the first place. By the same reasoning, there is no illness, only health. Health is real, the gift of God. Its absence is called illness, but the word doesn't signify anything real.

God created life, and when He takes it back, there is death. We cannot complain. He does not bring death, He takes back only what is His. Beruria, wife of Rabbi Meir, was right when she told her husband not to weep. "Our two sons haven't died, Meir. The Almighty has taken back only what He entrusted to us."[61] "The Lord gives and the Lord takes." Job understood it, and so clearly! I have this same sense from the words that Leah speaks in my play *The Golden Chain*: "Snow is clear, ice is clear, everything is clear—everything but life."

But my young heart resisted this cold logic, and pumped the hot, rebellious blood through my veins until my temples throbbed: "What is death? Why do we die?"

You might be interested to hear of my own brushes with death. When I was still a child, I barely missed meeting the Angel of

Death face-to-face. One day I was on my way to my grandmother's store to get my weekly allowance of six groschen. As I entered the shop, I felt weak and dizzy. I tried to lean on the wall, but my hand wouldn't hold. I fell, and felt myself falling into a deep chasm.

When I regained consciousness, I was in the big room of my grandmother's house, in a big bed, and it was before dawn. I heard a soft, pious chanting. Slowly, I opened my eyes. My uncle Shmuel was studying in a corner of the room by a lamp, his face obscured by a holy book. I could hear the chanting, but I couldn't make out the words. In order to hear better I tried to move to the edge of the bed, but my body would not obey me. My bones ached. I was frightened, and realized I must be sick. I didn't want to ask about it lest I interrupt his learning. My illness might have been the reason my uncle Shmuel Leybush was chanting in such a heartfelt way, so that the merit of his study would help me. I lay there motionless. My head felt heavy. I touched it, and found it wrapped in a kerchief. There was a sour smell in my nostrils—the kerchief had been soaked in vinegar. I glanced toward the window. A white night shone into the room and bottles of medicine stood on the windowsill. What was wrong with me? When did I get sick, and why was I here? I plied my weak head with questions and remembered how I had gone to my grandmother's store and collapsed there. I must be seriously ill. That was why my uncle was so absorbed in his studying. In the marketplace, which the windows faced, a wagon drove by, and dogs began to bark. "Dogs bark; the Angel of Death has come to town." Things were grim. But no, the dogs must have barked because of the wagon that passed. Meanwhile, I was getting hotter and hotter with fever. I was bathed in sweat and my body seemed to be on fire.

When I woke again—I think it was the same day—before I opened my eyes, I heard voices around my bed:

"He is *ours*"—the voice of my grandmother.

"The yellow bottle . . ."—my aunt Yente.

"And I say it was the cupping"—my aunt Temma.

My mother only laid her hand on my forehead.

"Back from the other side, really from the other side!" This was a man's voice that I didn't recognize. I heard his footsteps as he left the room and closed the door behind him.

"A close call—a very close call," I thought.

But I had an even more frightening brush with death at the well.[62] In the middle of one corner of the market there is a well under a wooden roof supported by four heavy posts. The well is surrounded by a wooden railing about as high as a grown man's chest. The water is drawn in buckets on a rotating iron chain that winds around a roller when you turn a gigantic, spiked wheel.

It sounds like your ordinary town well. But it was very, very deep, and when you pressed up against the railing (children had to stand on tiptoe) to look down inside, you could see a little wheel of light flashing over the black surface of the water—a liquid smile is how I might describe it today. If you looked into the well long enough, your head began to spin and you were seized by a marvelous attraction to that smile. It drew you so magnetically that you had to hold on tight to keep yourself from jumping in. There was magic in the black well water and its liquid smile.

That's not all. Boys and girls said that on really dark nights when all the lights went out in the houses, and the city was asleep, cats would gather at the well, white cats and black cats, and arranging themselves along the points of the wheel in alternating fashion— black cat beside white cat—they would yowl in unison. As they yowled, their motion along the wheel would set it turning, until the buckets would come up and down, faster and faster. The night watchman who patrolled the marketplace, a Gentile said to be in his nineties, would hear the yowling of the cats and the creaking of the wheel, and the buckets going down, slapping the water, spurting back with a little laugh, and then the buckets rising again, turning over by themselves, and splashing the water back into the well. He would shudder and make the sign of the cross, over and over again. The old women said that the cats were not really cats at all but wandering souls, seeking their redemption in the water. The black cats were men who had scorned the ritual bath; the white cats were wives who had not attended scrupulously to the Jewish laws of modesty and ritual immersion.

It was no ordinary well, as you can see.

One Friday as I was running across the marketplace, I saw workmen taking down the railing, which was rotting with age, and blocking the approach to the well with boards. With my own ears I heard them say, "We'll put up the new railing on Monday." Then I forgot all about it. Friday night after dinner—it was a hot summer evening—I grabbed the copper jug and ran to the well for fresh water. I ran right over and tried to lean over the railing to check if you could see the water smile at night.

As I've already recalled, an old woman grabbed me and pulled me back. This was Raggedy Freydl, the tar seller who figures in my story "The Cellar Room."[63] She saved me from certain death.

She saved me, that is, for day! But death and its terrors claimed me at night. In contrast to my love of life by day, every night for a long, long time I fell into the same deep well. It got to the point where it wasn't death that frightened me but its brother sleep. I would try to keep my eyes wide open all night so as not to fall into a chasm, as I had done in my grandmother's shop. I didn't want to sink into oblivion and be torn from life.

The heavier my eyelids grew from the lead of sleep, the greater my terror and my desire to hold on to life. I would tear open the window or run outside into the marketplace. The market slept in the blue darkness of the night, its houses frozen, and the windows black. Inside, there were people breathing, animate, yet I had no sense of their lives. Why was that? Why were there walls between us, between my life and theirs?

This feeling came over me recently when I passed through a quiet, remote Swiss village at night. Suddenly, I was seized by the pain of being cut off from the life behind the shutters. People were breathing, yearning, grieving, complaining, or rejoicing there, enjoying their happiness in the silent night, while I had no knowledge, no experience, no share of it. Yet I was a person, like them. I had a tremendous urge to stand up and shout so loud that all the people would wake up and throw open the shutters, and thrust their heads out through the open windows. It was the same feeling I had when I was a boy.

People are so original in the way they die, in the different ways they choose to "depart from the world."

The caretaker of the fortress died suddenly one day. I don't remember whether I was there when it happened or only heard about it from others. He was a skinny old veteran who swept the streets and served as Shabbes goy before "the Paw's" time. He was nearly blind and always angry, a true enemy of Jewish children—like his boss, the supervisor. He would eat his breakfast in the middle of the street, pulling a chunk of black bread from his filthy shirt and smearing it with fat from a penny candle that he kept in his pocket. We were afraid of him because at the slightest pretext he would throw his broom at us, and we avoided him because he was so repulsive, and his cursing was so repulsive—real Russian cursing, especially when he was drunk, and he was seldom sober. One day while sweeping he began to shake, reached out for support, tried to steady himself on his broom, and fell with it to the ground crying, "Hear, O Israel!" And died. It turned out that he'd been one of

those Jewish boys taken away for lifetime service in the tsar's army—
a "cantonist." He was buried in the Russian Orthodox cemetery,
where he will lie till the resurrection of the dead. We didn't steal
him out of there: no one did that sort of thing anymore.

His death hardly affected me. It took only a moment. How much
could he have suffered? Here one minute, gone the next.

There was an old clockmaker in town, Reb Hershl if I remember
correctly, who was also a city employee. His job was to climb up to
the clock tower every morning and evening and wind the wooden
mechanism of the clock, which was balanced by suspended weights.
He was a hoary little man in a long coat and a hat with earflaps, a
fashion long since out of date. A quiet, self-effacing person, he had
never been seen to laugh or cry, and I had never heard him speak.
One day he came down from the tower and said good-bye to
everyone he met in the marketplace. "What is it, Reb Hershl?" "I'm
going to die tonight." "You're imagining things—better wish it on
your enemies. . . ." The next morning the clock had stopped. The
clockmaker never awoke. That's the way death ought to be!

Simon the Hatmaker, who helped out at the reformist services,
died a strange death. Just before he died, he asked his wife to buy
him a half pound of carp, cook it, and serve it to him in bed. He
wanted to take leave of his worldly pleasures, of which carp was
foremost. He also wished to compare it to the feast of Leviathan in
the next world. And to test out the old, world-famous joke, he ate
a wormy plum for dessert, so that when he was whipped for his
transgressions he would know when it came to this final punishment
that he was about to taste of the heavenly feast. Unpleasant, but
witty.

But my uncle Lipa's death was different. He drowned. This uncle
of mine was a wonderful man with a heart of gold who would give
away anything and everything to the poor. Aunt Yente had to keep
an eye on him at her dry-goods shop, and even at home, for he was
worse than a thief. Once, just before Passover, she went down to the
cellar to check on the turkey that she was fattening for the holiday—
and the turkey was gone. Of course, she knew the culprit. Another
time a poor man came into the shop when Yente wasn't there. My
uncle tried the cash drawer where she kept pennies for charity, but
it was locked. So he gave the man the shirt off his back. Once he
gave his pants away. Their life was unusual, to say the least. Aunt
Yente was learned and knew the limit of how much a Jew was
permitted to give to charity. When he exceeded it, she threatened
to drag her husband to the rabbi, and she had a sharp tongue. The

entire market heard the curses that she heaped on his head. She even threatened to claw him with her nails, and had she not been afraid of God, she might have done it.

Once my uncle Lipa went to bathe in the river before morning prayers. He sat down under the falls and let the water gush over him, and they pulled him out of there dead. They said that a rock in the strong current had knocked him unconscious, and when he had opened his mouth, he had swallowed water.

According to the precepts of death that I had learned from *Guide to the Perplexed*, I should not have been upset. But it was sad to lose such a good uncle. As for drowned people, I had already seen one. A young man had been pulled out of the river. According to local lore the river demanded its annual sacrifice, and it had to be a human being, no drowned cat would do. He was swollen, and they kneeled on his belly to force the water out of his mouth, but the corpse obviously felt nothing. Having seen this, I didn't rush to the river to see my uncle Lipa.

But the funeral was not so matter-of-fact. As we followed the body to the cemetery, my aunt Yente did not so much walk as drift in the air with a fixed smile on her face, her eyes roaming around, then sending out mysterious flashes. She moved modestly on the tips of her toes, as though performing the bridal dance. I walked right beside her among the women, and heard them crying out to God, wringing their hands, "Father of the Universe, let her cry at least. Bring just one tear to her eyes!" As she walked along, she murmured (I used this in a sketch called "After the Burial"), "Eat, Lipale, eat. It'll do you good." Suddenly, she tore off her wig, pursed her lips, and let out a piercing whistle.

When K., the owner of the wineshop, was dying, I was drawn there irresistibly. I had to see how people died. He lay in a large room in terrible pain. His daughter, the porcelain beauty, lay in another bed, white with terror. Her mother, a tall woman, was curled up in an armchair, with her face hidden. I made my way through the throng of people to the bed. The dying man grimaced horribly and howled uncontrollably as he said his confession, but suddenly, in a completely altered voice, he said, "Tell my wife that the key to the second cellar is . . ." I didn't stay to find out where it was. I ran out to the engineer's garden, deeply offended by this deathbed scene. For shame! This man deserved to die—otherwise he would never tear himself away from the key to the second cellar.

Night was falling. I walked along the highway just beyond the town, and saw the sun setting behind the engineers' garden as if I were seeing sunset for the first time. There were purple flames among the branches and, opposite, a pale moon rising and growing brighter as it rose in the sky. I stood there leaning against a fence, wondering why I should be discovering this as if for the first time. Surely the sun sets every day, the moon rises every evening.

The moon, meanwhile, kept moving higher and higher in the sky. A pewter poorhouse plate? A silver tray as a wedding gift? Was it the radiant face of Joshua as described by the sages?[64] Maybe I should ask Joshua why people die, whether it serves any purpose.

Suddenly, someone touched me on the shoulder. It was Mikhl Fidler. I had been standing by the fence of the house where he lived in solitude. He had shuffled out to see me, very quietly, and there he was with his sad, watery eyes, holding a book in one hand and a lantern in the other.

"They say you're a prodigy. Can you tell me what this means?"

He pointed to a passage in a kabbalistic text, the name of which I've forgotten, that had to do with the transmigration of souls. I read the passage, understood it, and explained it to him.

"You really are a prodigy. Wait here."

He disappeared into the house. It occurred to me that this passage on the transmigration of souls might be the best answer to my questions, but before I could think this through, he came out again with the lantern, and this time instead of the book he had in his hand a large, rusty key. It was the key to the library in town.

"You deserve this."

With trembling hand, he gave me the key. His voice was toneless and hollow. I raised my eyes and wanted to say something to him, but I couldn't open my mouth. By the light of the lantern I saw the face of a waxen corpse.

A corpse was handing me the key. I took it and left with it in silence. The key was to open a new world of books for me and a new chapter in my life. When and how Mikhl Fidler died, I don't remember.

7: THEIR STUDY HOUSE.
RUINS OF THE MIND. I TRY TO LEAVE. MY MOTHER.
I BECOME ENGAGED.

You don't just suddenly rush from the Jewish to the Gentile study house. Mine was a Jewish heart, after all, and in a muddled way I felt that I was tearing myself away from someone and something dear and familiar to me. I didn't sleep nights, and spent the days wandering around outside the city gates. Actually, I had already "jumped the fence," and there were many things I no longer believed in, many aspects of religion no longer sacred to me. But all of this had happened within the confines of my home and the study house beside the synagogue.

I see myself before I finally did it, gripping the big, rusty key in my fist inside my pants pocket as I walked through the Lemberg gate. I stopped at a point midway between our cemetery and theirs, and listened to a debate between my good and evil inclinations, much as I presented it in the poem "Monish," though there I spiced it with a bit of wit à la Heine. Whereas the fictional Monish was drawn to the ruin by Maria, beckoning to him from the windows, leading him on with her song, my "Maria" was out at the riding academy, strolling with Yointshe every evening, and my "bride of the ruins" was busy with her trousseau. Seamstresses sat in her house sewing linens, while she ran to the tailors to be fitted for clothes. Neither of them called to me. It was knowledge that summoned me. All I had learned told me not to go, but as with Monish, the evil inclination prevailed.

I see myself in a black cap, wearing a Bismarck coat and boots smeared with white clay—I had just begun to notice colors—crossing the cobblestone street from the red barracks to the green castle (it was springtime), and coming to a halt in the lane in front of the castle to stare at the house with the locked library in its attic. I forced myself to step over the threshold. Beads of sweat formed on my forehead. I didn't know this house. No Jews lived there, either coincidentally or because of its proximity to the castle. It was a new house, at that time the newest in town, and its well-lit stairway was the only one of its kind in Zamość. I climbed up, encouraged by this propitious sign—the way was lit! The light illumined my way to the first floor, and the second. At the landing to the attic the daylight was extinguished, and I grew a little uneasy. But as Proverbs has it, "Those who enter will never return." There was no going back.[65]

My hand shook a little as I groped for the door and the keyhole. I would first take a look. I bent down and peeked in. The place was dark. Opposite the door was a window shuttered from inside, but a ray of shimmering dust forced its way through to a pile of books on the floor.

The pillar of cloud and the pillar of fire! Both were to lead me through the wilderness!

I turned the key. It scraped in the old lock, and my heart did a turn, but by then the door was already open. I tore open the shutter, and there I was—in "their" house of study.

At the time, it didn't occur to me that we have a share in all the study houses of the world. But there were so many books! They lined the four walls and they were strewn underfoot all over the floor. I determined to read them all, starting with the first, straight through to the last!

I didn't read them all. There were books in three languages: most were in Polish, including many translations from other languages; some were in German, and a few in French.

I didn't know any French, not even to read. To take advantage of the library, I would soon begin to memorize a French grammar from cover to cover, but it was a pointless exercise. I forgot every bit of it. I postponed learning German, figuring that I could get by on the little I had picked up from my teacher Stern. My thirst for knowledge was too great for me to sit down at that point to pick out successive syllables. I began with the Polish books, and true to my word, I proceeded in order, starting to the right of the doorway— as it says in Ecclesiastes, "A wise man's understanding is at his right hand."[66] The books had been shelved at random, with novels, scientific works, and serial romances all mixed up and scattered, especially the translations from the French—Alexandre Dumas, Eugène Sue, Victor Hugo, and so on. There would be a tenth volume of Sue, followed by a ninth volume of Dumas, or a third volume of Hugo. But I read on anyway. I wasn't looking for plot, and I didn't bother with the nature descriptions either. They told me nothing, stirred no corresponding images in me. I had so little acquaintance with nature. One exception was Hugo's description of the green meadows in *The Toilers of the Sea*. There were meadows like that around Zamość. Another was the description of a sleigh path by a Polish author—Korzeniowski, I believe—since I had seen snow before! But what really appealed to me were the dialogues, "the passages between the dashes" as I called them, where people talked. Each dash seemed to me a crack through which to look into a human soul. This fondness for dialogue, for characterization through speech, has remained with me. I never learned to tell a story properly. The most I've managed, as one of my critics noted, is "a tale within a tale." Maybe that's why even my best work, "The Three Weddings," is clumsily constructed along those lines.

As I read, all the stories mixed together in my head, and I couldn't and didn't want to disentangle them. The library was like a market full of people who had come to the fair, people from every station and walk of life. They stood around in groups, talking among themselves, each group with its own concerns. And I strolled around the marketplace, eavesdropping on them all, taking in snatches of conversation and figuring out what was going on.

Soon after, I came across the Napoleonic Code in Zavatsky's translation. I read it and was delighted by what I understood. I may have read superficially, maybe even mistakenly, but I was amazed! Here were principles of law without the Talmud's ubiquitous Reuben and Simon! Not even Maimonides in his codification of Jewish law had achieved quite this clarity. Then I came across Buckle's *History of Civilization in England*. Before I properly understood it, the style and the way of drawing inferences reminded me of the philosophic commentary on the Bible by Rabbi Isaac ben Moses Arama.[67] I also discovered physics. God Almighty! The blanket does not warm me, my body warms the blanket! We human beings can make snow and thunder! Lacking mathematical background, I skipped the algebraic calculations the way the Polish kheyder teachers skip the bits of grammar in the commentaries of Rashi,[68] and fell back into the sea of novelistic and romantic dialogue, then swam to the shores of "natural science." The descriptions of limbs and torsos or plants and animals made no impression on me. It was the same old problem: they called up no familiar associations. I had seen dogs, horses, and cats. In summertime there were birds in the sky, but you could hardly single out one specimen of the flock for observation! Sometimes they would fly down in a bunch to forage in the dust and mud for a kernel of seed from a peasant's wagon or the crumb of a boy's breakfast, then fly away fast. An occasional crow perched on the top of the clock tower. I knew nothing of these creatures.

It was different when I came upon the descriptions of the way of life of the different species, with details about their instincts and understanding, their habits, their adaptation to the environment through color and form, the way they built their nests, raised their young, gathered food for the winter, flocked together in the blue sky; and then the serenading of the male birds, their display of colorful feathers, their battle over the females—this struggle for life and for love swept me up in its magic.

Dear God, how immense was the world, how various, with how many kinds of intelligence, and how much spirit!

Then suddenly came the revelation of Hartmann: "Everything is matter!" One pamphlet after the other insisted, "There is no free will!" And Carl Vogt to boot: "The brain produces thoughts much as another organ of the body produces urine."[69]

Something in me froze, something died. I could no longer believe in the mysteries of the Divine Creation of heaven and earth or the mystical speculations on the Divine Chariot. There was no heaven. The blue that we see was the limit of human vision. And there could be no divine reward or punishment if there was no free will.

To whom could I talk about all this? To whom could I pour out my lament for the ruins in my mind and the corpses in my heart? To the people around me? I lacked the very language to speak to them. I couldn't express these things in Yiddish, because I had no words for these ideas in Yiddish. I couldn't even talk about them to myself when I tried.

Only Shimon Khodok could save me. First, let me draw his portrait—not exactly his portrait, because I didn't really know him. You look into a person through his eyes. Shimon blinked and was shifty-eyed. His pupils moved constantly back and forth as if afraid of being trapped. But I can offer you a sketch. He came from a poor, harassed family in Lithuania, and had never learned to look people in the eye. He came to us as an instructor of religion after having finished the government school for rabbis in Zhitomir, and taught us "biblical history" from a small Russian text. He kept his distance, and spoke nothing but Russian, but the community turned to him when they needed him. Once, the magistrate had the idea of clearing the square of peasants' wagons and consigning them to the outer market. He had decided to run streets through the market-place, dividing it into four equal parts, and to plant it with trees and flowers as a public garden. The merchants with stores fronting on the market were afraid of losing the peasants' business, and wanted to appeal the ordinance. So they turned to Khodok, since he was presumably close to the government.

He wrote them a petition on government stationery, with genuine black ink in lovely calligraphy, thus: "If there are to be public gardens, trees will be planted in them, and in time these trees will grow tall and spread their leaves and branches. Since the city lighting is poor, and the nights are often dark, the shadows of the trees will conceal thieves, bandits, and murderers. This will constitute a menace to the safety of the population. Also, on summer nights when nature wakens love [here followed a nature passage] the shadows will entice lovers to sin, thereby undermining the morals of the city and corrupting the youth and spreading venereal disease through half the populace, if not through all of it, may God forbid."

If that doesn't describe him, here is more: He lost his job as instructor of religion, for some reason I can't remember or never knew, and without the city's knowledge he persuaded the governor to appoint him rabbiner, governmental rabbi of Zamość. As soon as he got the nomination, he completely changed his behavior. He wore a skullcap at home, quit smoking on the Sabbath, and began attending synagogue for morning and evening prayers.

So the Hasidim conferred and sent him a message: "Listen, Mr. So-and-so. If, like most appointed rabbiners, you intend to take three hundred rubles from the city for no work, that's fine with us. You would be no worse than any Gentile who takes Jewish money for nothing. But if you take your work seriously and try to make changes, we will tear you up by the roots." They advised him immediately to resume his non-Jewish behavior—stop coming to prayers, remove his skullcap, and smoke on the Sabbath with his head uncovered. All of which he did, and a little while later he resigned from the post of rabbiner to become censor in Warsaw.

But at the time I am describing, he was just starting out, at the first stage of his career. When I came to him, he listened, blinking his eyes all the while, and then said, "*Niczewo!* Don't worry." I must make something of myself by going away to study, in Zhitomir or Vilna. All my doubts would be cleared up, everything would straighten itself out. He was prepared to help me.

Maybe he was right. I hung around the front steps waiting for my "bride of the ruins" so that I could ask her advice. At first, when I intercepted her, she was frightened to death. I hadn't stopped her like this on the stairs in quite a while. Besides, she was preparing for her wedding. But when she heard what it was about, she took me by the hand and in a sisterly fashion led me down to the courtyard and through the little back door to the riding academy, where we sat on a bench and talked. We talked with our hands clasped, in quiet earnestness.

"Yes, go!" she said, with a hint of tears in her voice and her eyes. "You should go. Tell me when you're leaving, and I'll come down to say good-bye."

Shimon Khodok pawned his gold chain to cover my travel expenses. It was decided that on a certain day I would steal away at dawn. The wagon was ordered, and I packed in great secrecy. The night before my departure I pretended to go to bed early, with my pack under the pillow, knowing that I wouldn't shut my eyes. A whistle from the street was to be my signal. I put out the light and took leave of everyone and everything in the dark house. My heart was heavy, but I felt I had to go. As I lay there, I heard a rustling in the next room. The door opened, and my mother came in very softly, in her bare feet. I could barely make her out by the weak light of the moon in the window. Silently, she approached my bed, sat down facing me, and looked at me with pain. I couldn't close or avert my eyes. I had to see the tears running down her face. She was saying good-bye to me. Who had told her my secret?

She kept watch at my bedside. Her tears kept watch over me. I decided not to go.

My father was not at home at the time. He came back a few days later with the news: "I have arranged a match for you with the daughter of Gavriel Yehuda Lichtenfeld.[70]

I gave in. I saw no way out. I was the victim of my mother's tears. Khodok never recovered his gold chain from the pawnbroker. The wagon that had come for me returned empty to the suburbs. My "bride of the ruins" who had come down half-naked at dawn to see me off, all for nothing, caught a heavy cold. In a short time I did leave home, to get married.

I refused to observe the Jewish custom of fasting on the day of the wedding. But the marriage took place according to custom, out of doors. When it started to rain during the ceremony, I dashed inside the house. They followed me with the wedding canopy. Gavriel Yehudah Lichtenfeld laughed. His daughter cried. I could not account for my behavior.

Thus ends the first volume of my memoirs. The feelings of childhood and youth vanished with time. The treasure-house of homy narratives and images was locked away. After that, whatever I encountered in cities and towns, on highways and byways, I observed with a critical eye. I no longer felt things with the same immediacy. Had my soul hardened to the point that it could no longer penetrate another, and return enriched, enlightened? Do we have any access at all, apart from sensual experience, to the unfamiliar world that follows childhood?

In any case, the chapter of childhood has come to an end. The

misty gallery of figures and faces that drifts by whenever I shut my
eyes has begun to dissolve and disappear.

8: I GET MARRIED

As I got older, my cloud of melancholy lifted. I was less tragic.
And when I became engaged, I felt even easier, knowing that I
would be with Gavriel Yehuda Lichtenfeld, my fiancée's father,
a mathematician and philosopher and reputedly a man of great
knowledge. He would explain everything and answer all my questions
about God and the world. I stored them up in my memory in
anticipation of meeting him. I didn't think about my bride-to-be, I
didn't care what the engagement contract stipulated, but I looked
forward to the wedding as if the Messiah would be there—the
redeemer from doubt.

In the meantime, I played with the gold watch and chain I was
given as a present. I was still boy enough for that. And when one
of my study-house friends, a Hasidic young man my age, boasted
that he had received an embroidered satin tfiln bag as well as a
watch, I smiled and said with an oh-so-clever air, "Who knows
whether Gavriel Yehuda Lichtenfeld even puts on tfiln any longer?"
The young man persisted, "Will he give you a prayer shawl and a
white robe for the wedding?" "We'll see," I answered.[71]

And in the meantime I lived a double life. Outwardly, I assumed
the airs of all other respectable betrothed young men. I ate more
sedately, took more leisurely strolls, and joined some of their serious
discussions. I'd soon be their peer.

One Sabbath my father, my uncles, and I were invited to the
afternoon meal at a rich man's estate some distance away (a Sabbath
boundary was put up to allow walking the distance). Along the way
I joined in the talk about important issues: should we follow Paperna's
example in writing *hadrama*?[72] Would the two parts—the foreign
word "drama" and the Hebrew definite article—sound right to the
Jewish ear? Some said yes, others no. I suggested *ha-drame*, joining
the Hebrew definite article to the Yiddish word for "drama." When
a purist in our midst asked, "How would we pronounce it?" the
question seemed crazy to me. Did he mean how would it be read
aloud? At the time, it hadn't occurred to anyone to *speak* Hebrew.
Leaving grammar behind, we went on to other matters.

We were walking along the footpath between the fields of wheat and rye, and I was drawn to the blue flowering oats among the golden stalks. One of the young men picked a flowering bud and put it to his nose. There was no smell. He placed it in his buttonhole. One of the elders chided him: "It's Shabbes." We joked about it. "He forgot that you aren't allowed to pick flowers on Shabbes." "He forgot that he's a Jew." Taking the part of the young man, I wanted to pick a blue flower too, but my hand wouldn't obey me. It wasn't used to desecrating the Sabbath. I defended my inaction to myself by calling it pity for living things, by the (non-Jewish) notion that everything is animate. This and other such foreign ideas, a profusion of feelings and images and newborn longings from the books I'd read in my secret library, tumbled and seethed inside me. Every so often the cauldron boiled over; smoky tongues of flame would shoot into the open in the form of impulsive gestures, distracted expressions, and wild outbursts, to everyone's amazement, mine included.

I would compare myself as I was then to a field of crude oil, dry on the surface, but instantly ablaze with smoke and flame at the touch of a lighted match. I did crazy things. Once, in the presence of the whole study house, I took down a well-known collection of rabbinic responsa from the shelves of the eastern wall and, with a blue pencil (of a kind that only I possessed) and in full view of everyone, crossed out two or three lines where the author expressed his dissatisfaction with Maimonides' *Guide to the Perplexed*. As people made a rush for me, I leaped up on the dais, and striking the pose of a hero who was prepared for martyrdom no less, arms crossed on my chest like Napoleon, I stared down at the congregation. This made an impression, because they slowly backed off, muttering, "Crazy."

It occurred to someone that my future father-in-law ought to be informed of this incident. But the idea was scoffed at: "You picked the right person! He would probably reward him with a fine present!" And I felt proud of myself, though privately I was no longer interested in the *Guide*, or in Aristotle for that matter. I had crossed them off my list of priorities.

The wedding was to take place in a village midway between Apt and Zamość. (I don't recall the name of the village; we didn't sign anything there and picked up the license subsequently in Shebreshin.) As the day of the wedding approached, my sleep grew troubled and I had terrible dreams. Suppose the bride was blind in one eye? Or lame? This wasn't a bride I had fallen in love with or picked out for myself. Suppose that during the ceremony of veiling the bride I was to discover a freak of nature? Jolted from my sleep, I would lie awake for hours thinking: Why did it have to be a bride from Apt? Why didn't I choose a bride for myself in Zamość? True, Zamość had no Gavriel Yehuda Lichtenfeld. And any suitable family with whom my father could have made a match would not have had me as a son-in-law. Didn't they know all about me? But why not fall in love, and run away, and live in a four-by-four hut in the forest, as the books tell us; "The smallest hut / is ample space," according to Schiller and others.[73]

But whom would I have wanted from home? I sifted through all the girls I knew in the city. They stopped before me, one after the other—the dark-haired beauties, lively redheads, fetching blondes— all the daughters of Zamość as if on a stroll around the riding academy. I said no to them all. The only one I would have said yes to belonged to someone else and was eating at her in-laws' table. Too bad. A great sorrow came over me, and when I finally drifted off to sleep with an aching heart just before dawn, I made up my mind that no matter what happened I wouldn't fast on the wedding day, and for all I cared, the bride could cross the threshold before me. It was all nonsense! And I would absolutely forbid them to shave the bride's hair, whatever the color.[74] She would wear neither kerchief nor wig but her own hair in long or short braids or curls. Half-asleep, I smiled into my pillow, thinking that Gavriel Yehuda Lichtenfeld would be pleased with me. Even his opponent Chaim Zelig Slonimski, who was, after all, a man of learning, would approve of my behavior.

I finally fell asleep at daybreak, but my childish-adult heart remained alert. Below the windows I heard two wagons pulling up, and the drivers cracking their whips, one after the other, to let us know it was time to go to the wedding. I jumped out of bed, and before I had even poured the water over my fingernails, I repeated to myself, "I won't fast, I won't let them cut the bride's hair, I won't even break the wineglass under the canopy—come what may![75] And maybe I'd go even further than that and refuse to have the bride circle me seven times! Why seven? It was probably an idolatrous custom anyway.

But when I poured the water over my fingernails, I felt a leaden heaviness in my heart: "The main thing is, what does she look like?"

Meanwhile, I was seized from behind by our closest neighbor, Aunt Yente, if I remember correctly, with a bar of green soap in her hand. "Good God," cried my aunt, "look at that neck!" As the servant girl set a basin of warm water in front of me, she forced my head down to the water and scrubbed my neck while my mother laid out my underwear. For the first time I became aware of packs of clothes and food on the floor all around, and of the heap of butter cookies that were just being packed into a fresh sack. "Oh, no!" cried a second aunt, who was helping with the packing. "We forgot the salt! The way we forget about death!" My mother answered, "Put it into the sack with the butter cookies. Wrap it in a napkin and tuck it in there."

"Time to pray! Time to pray!" my father commanded.

After a while we set off. The road passed through flat land between fields that stretched right and left, harvested land that looked tired, sunk in melancholy—despite the very festive blue of the sky overhead.

"Well, it certainly won't rain."

"Because the groom doesn't eat sweets."

"And evidently, neither does the bride!"[76]

I sank into my own thoughts. I was squeezed in the straw of the women's wagon with my mother and my aunts. My father and uncles were in the wagon up front. I didn't have anything to say to the women, and I'd soon had my fill of the monotonous blue of the sky. There was nothing to look at. The flat landscape stretched endlessly. There were still green crops in the fields (I had no idea what was growing there) and here and there a few spots of gray and white, the peasants in their homespun linen working in the fields, much like those I saw every Sunday at the market in town. Suddenly, I remembered that I was fasting, and it made me angry. I pulled out the sack of butter cookies, and ignoring the very agitated glances from my aunts while my mother pretended not to see, I took out a cookie and bit into it. Pure salt! The bundle had come apart during the ride and the salt had spilled. The cookie wasn't fit to eat, but I made do with it anyway. Now I certainly wouldn't be able to say confession at the afternoon prayer!

Then I began to have regrets. Why should I be having regrets? I thought hard, but couldn't figure it out. All at once, we started to move uphill. The steep road made a tremendous impression on me, greater than Switzerland when I saw it later in life. The horses' collars rose above their heads. The driver jumped down and so did I, and we walked, he with the reins in his hand, and I picking gold and orange stones from the walls of the cliffs on either side of the road that cut through this mountain.

"They mine metals from this mountain, don't they, Father?" My father was immersed in a conversation about a business for me. He had asked my father-in-law for a full year's support for me, and I was to have six rubles a week from the dowry plus a business. Quite proud of himself, he said, "You'll see, he'll straighten out!" So I put the stones away. I would show them to Gavriel Yehuda Lichtenfeld, who would surely know what they were.

By then we were heading downhill. The cliffs on either side gradually fell away and vanished, and we were in a brand-new landscape with much more greenery in the field and what seemed like an even bluer sky. Among the colorful chessboards of ploughed fields of all kinds, there were peasants dressed in livelier colors—red, green, and another color that I couldn't identify. Like the peasants we had seen before, they were bent over in some kind of activity that I knew nothing about. It hurt me. "Why doesn't one person know what the other is doing?"

One of the peasants straightened up and noticed us passing. "There go the Jews!" he yelled, and because he knew our superstition about appearing to be too many, he began to count us aloud.[77] We rode by in silence and passed silently into a thick cloud of dust. Then we cut through a herd of cows, and "Thank God!" said my father. "We're here!" "May it be in good fortune," said my mother.

We drove into the village. The host of the place where we'd be staying came running up to us, dressed in his Sabbath best, followed by his broad-shouldered wife, also decked out. She was holding the hand of a barefoot little girl, who clutched her mother's skirt at the sight of these strange people and screwed up her dirty little face, uncertain whether to laugh or to cry.

We climbed down, prepared to walk the rest of the way. "Has the bride's family arrived?" we asked. "Not yet," we were told. "With God's help they'll be here soon." My father said, "Tell Chaim"—the host of the place where the bride's family would be staying—"to let us know as soon as they get here, and we'll have the veiling of the bride and the wedding ceremony right away." "The man is always in a hurry!" my mother murmured, unhappy with all the rush. And my Aunt Yente protested, "And when will we wash and dress?"

I shuddered for my neck, which still burned from the earlier scrubbing. They all went into the house and forgot about me for the time being. I stayed outside and pulled the little girl with the dirty face away from her mother's apron. She had flaxen white hair and her blue eyes were frightened, but ready to smile. I lifted her up and tossed her several times high into the air. The little girl laughed and laughed, and her laughter sounded full of joyous life and wonderfully free.

Then Chaim appeared, out of breath, from across the way, crying, "They're here! Bless us, they're here!"

I've already recounted that when the wedding ceremony began there was a slight drizzle, and that I ran from under the canopy to the porch of the house followed by the bride, musicians, candles, and canopy, and the gently smiling Gavriel Yehuda Lichtenfeld.

The next day the bright autumn sun forced its way through the small village window between the tangled leaves of yellow flowerpots. It woke a crawling gray thought in my brain. "Is that it? Is that all there is to it?"

My newly acquired better half lay there with the covers over her head, still asleep—or maybe not. She might have been having the very same thoughts, but being shyer than I was, she may have felt greater heartache. Maybe she was crying softly to herself. I was suddenly seized by a muddled kind of pity for us both, two fish caught in the same net. So was that it? Was that all there was to it?

"As if they were frozen"—that talmudic phrase was truer than all the books and pamphlets in the attic library. Something had been born in the heart, but it was some creeping thing without fabled golden wings or glowing eyes. It was something colorless, voiceless, tentative . . .[78] I wasn't able to think the image through. One of my uncles knocked on the door to call me to morning prayers. It was my modern uncle. I was needed for the minyan. I got into my clothes quickly—"Coming right away!"—and ran out to the entrance hall. My uncle had disappeared. There was an open door leading to a small village garden, and suddenly a strong-scented autumn breeze wafted over me. I escaped from the sounds of prayer in the house, turning left and right into a strange little garden full of color. The chirping of a bird made me forget all at once that deaf and dumb creature in the dark chamber of my heart. I sucked the unfamiliar free air into my narrow city-boy's chest and drank in the bright village colors. I was overjoyed that I could recognize poppies, which I knew from the market, and I shook the flower heads next to my ear to hear the rattle of their little black seeds. Next I ran to the flaming red roses, which were fluttering in the slight breeze. "Don't tremble, little red flower, my hand isn't used to plucking." Then there were skinny stems with pale blue leaves like the ribbons on my mother's Rosh Hashana bonnet. "What's your name, ribbon stems?"

They rippled in silence. But some were beginning to sprout, and the stems of what might have been radishes or carrots were reaching upward toward the blue sky. I suddenly felt constricted and sad in this small garden with so much that was strange to me, and I leaped out into the road. Which way to the house—right or left?

"Moo!" At this sound, I noticed a little peasant boy who was standing barefoot on the ledge of a well, drawing up water and pouring it into a watering trough. Cows with large, dull, melancholy eyes stood at the trough lapping the water and lifting their heads to the sky between slurps. "Moo-oo!" It was hard to tell whether there was joy or grief in the sound.

The peasant boy let go of the empty bucket. It swung wildly in the air, then jerked and quivered to a complete stop. The boy's tanned chest was visible under his gray linen shirt, and his feet were smeared with clay. Jumping down, he picked up his whip from the ground and gave a loud, bold whistle. The cows raised their heads. He cracked his whip and they were on their way, away from the village, across the harvested field where a peasant was harrowing and a number of peasant women were stooped over in their work. The mooing grew fainter in the distance. A bird cut the sun-golden air with a sudden, piercing shriek, and after that it was quiet. But this quiet was unfamiliar and frightening. It was not the familiar quiet of Sabbath or holidays at home. I moved along in this stillness with uncertain steps, as though on alien ground.

And I saw Gavriel Yehuda Lichtenfeld coming toward me. There he was in some kind of embroidered jacket, a bathrobe, and bedroom slippers, all smiles. It occurred to me how much he resembled Rabbi Moyshe Wahl, with the same natural goodness and the same soft, starry eyes. I would ask him about everything, and he would be sure to know the answers. As we approached one another, the bitter questions rose from my heart to my mouth, where they grew confused like a tangle of threads. In the meantime, he was asking me, "You aren't at morning prayers?"

Everything suddenly collapsed in me like foamy egg whites at a cooling breath. Everything hardened and shrank into a knot, and instead of the airy philosopher it was the yeshiva student who sprang forth with a counterquestion: "And you?" We walked along together for a while in silence, with compressed lips and eyes on the ground, until he asked again: "Do you write poems?" "Yes, I do." "What do you write?" I was beginning to tell him when suddenly, as if out of the ground, my uncle appeared, the modern one who collected my verses, and asked what we were talking about before we had prayed.

"Does he write?" "Yes, he does. He writes and loses the pages, writes and tears up the result, writes and burns his manuscript. Fortunately, I am around to steal things from under his hands. I gather up the scraps. He's developing into a writer." "Do you have anything with you?" Lichtenfeld asked me. At that moment we heard the sound of music way off from the house. It was time for the wedding breakfast and then the trip home.

It was over and I hadn't asked Gavriel Yehuda Lichtenfeld a single thing. I had gotten no answers to my questions; the questions had lost their vitality and their sharp tang. Like late crabgrass they shrank and wilted and gathered somewhere in a dark recess of my heart, where they were to lie for a long, long time until freshened by dew and light from the outside. But even when that time came, the questions were to remain unresolved, with no answers expected, with not even a lingering hope of response from anyone on earth or in heaven.

We said our good-byes. I took sincere and heartfelt leave of Gavriel Yehuda Lichtenfeld, of whom I would never ask any questions. I would only learn some mathematics from him, and we would publish a book of Hebrew verse together that I blush to remember. Then we headed back home. An apartment had been rented for me and my better half with a window looking out on the market arcade. I heard about it only as we said good-bye. My father told Lichtenfeld about it as we were climbing into the wagons—there would be a room for him to stay in when he came to visit.

I sat there on the wagon, a married man next to his wife, facing an aunt and uncle. They were exhausted from dancing all night, and as they dozed off, their heads kept bumping together and moving apart. I was ashamed to laugh. My better half took advantage of their nap to ask shyly, "Are you really such a good student?" "Yes." She gave my hand a grateful squeeze. "Are you going to sit and study?" "No!" She dropped my hand. But after a while she asked, "And suppose I ask you to?" Her hand moved back; the driver answered for me, "Giddyap, you bag of bones!" waking my uncle and aunt from their sleep.

We were on our way back through the flat, boring landscape. My uncle and aunt nodded off again, and apparently so did my better half. The silence and the napping were interrupted from time to time by shouts from the wagons behind us, where they seemed to be having a jolly time. And by "Whoa!" whenever the driver stopped the horses, jumped down to fix something on the ancient patched harness, put one foot up on the wheel and another on the seat, and urged them back into motion: "Giddyap, you bag of bones!"

The horses weren't insulted or frightened, as long as he didn't use the whip. Lightly, they trotted along the hardened dirt road, and the sound of their heaving chests under the gracious spread of sky was like pebbles bouncing in a sack. Suddenly, a whip whistled over the horses' backs. The driver turned around toward us, and as if easing his conscience for his harshness to the animals, he said, "It's going to rain."

He turned back, and hunched deeper into the collar of his sheepskin. Hearing "It's going to rain," my uncle woke up and looked around warily. I did too. It was true. The sky was thickening, the air was full of moisture. A wall of rain was heading for us from the left. The sun was like a white mirror dipping into batches of white cloud, cotton batting or silver, then disappearing into clouds of gray smoke.

"Are you cold?" My uncle addressed my aunt with protective concern, and, not waiting for an answer, adjusted the scarf around her shoulders and buttoned her up to the neck. "No, Joseph!" She replied very softly, and her big, moist eyes, quivering in gratitude, caressed my uncle. I noticed her large eyes and thin blue lips and how fragile she was, and realized for the first time what everyone else had long since known, that she was sickly. Then a breeze came up, the clouds rushed in faster, and the sun disappeared. It was growing dark and chilly and some drops were falling.

"We shouldn't have gone," my uncle grumbled.

"It won't hurt," my aunt answered.

"Will it be a heavy rain?" My uncle addressed the driver, tapping his broad shoulders as if he were knocking on a door.

"It's getting windy," said the driver, whipping the horses on. "Maybe we can make it to the inn."

My uncle glanced searchingly back at my aunt and she answered with a reassuring look, and I felt that their glances were embracing and kissing as they joined in the air. And yet this couple were so old!

There was the inn! We reached it just in time; it was starting to pour. My uncle Joseph jumped down at once and helped my aunt from the wagon and inside. I was also on the ground, and I thought I should help my better half as she stood up and placed her foot on the wagon step, but—I have wooden hands, those same hands that aren't used to plucking flowers, and I didn't reach up to her at all.

Someone else came up from the other wagon to help her down. Soon we were inside, and rummaging in our sacks for something to eat.

"Tea! Tea!" my uncle Joseph called out.

It was a Gentile inn. My aunt insisted she wouldn't drink anything. Who knows what kind of utensil they use to boil the water?

Uncle Joseph hurried out to the kitchen and came back with the news that it was all right. "They use a samovar!"[79] The women unpacked and served whatever they had had time to pack.

"Leave half the table for dairy," said my mother.

"For the salty cookies?"

"Who needs to wash up?"[80]

There was great commotion as some washed up and others paced the room balancing glasses of tea in their hands. I walked around by myself and whistled. Something of the barefoot peasant's whistle sounded inside me, free and easy, and the cloud of my melancholy lifted. It was all so much nonsense! Whistle and be done with it! Of course, my mouth like my hands would not readily comply, but a spirit of abandon took hold of me then that was to see me through many years—through Zamość, Apt, Tsoyzmer, Warsaw, Great Poland, and back to Warsaw—until something new stirred my heart. That wanton whistle has the power of warding off everything that invades us unexpectedly, giving us time to shut our doors and gates to protect ourselves from strangers. I introduced it into quite a few of my early writings. . . .

I was walking thus about the inn, whistling to myself, when my better half stopped me and said with a dissatisfied expression, "Where were you this morning during prayers?"

"I was listening to someone whistle."

"What?" she asked angrily.

So I told her about the little barefoot peasant, his cows and their eyes, and about his whistling. She listened, her anger softened into a smile, until finally she asked me whether I too knew how to whistle.

I have just been reminded of a whistling that I heard only a few years ago that affected me even more deeply than the first. It was in Switzerland, where I was recuperating in the mountains from a serious heart attack. One evening I was resting outside, listless and indifferent to everything that went on around me. My eyes and ears were open, but I had no desire to put them to use. Farther down the mountainside, where a herd was grazing, the occasional cowbell sounded, and here and there in the grass thick reddish backs emerged, or a heavy bovine head was raised to look dimly around. Then the cowbells clanged as the animals moved to a juicy clump of grass. Down below near the foot of the mountain, sounding softly through the bells, was a bubbling mountain stream, and on the other side of it stood a row of bright whitewashed houses with open green shutters and crystal windows that seemed to be laughing cheerfully out at God's green earth. From the little windows came the sound of piano music and from the mountains in the distance the sound of yodeling, reverberating in echoes. All these intermingling sounds came through the scented air to my ear, and a suffused blend of colors—green, white, and the gray of the mountain rock with the deep blue of the arching sky—soothed my dulled eye.

Suddenly, from among the white mountain peaks there was a clap of thunder, followed by a second, warnings of a storm on its way. A cloud rolled toward us. The wind roared in as if loosed from a leash. The cows trotted downhill, their bells sounding fearful. A small shepherd boy who was barefoot and hatless like the boy of my first wedded morning drove the cows with a very long whip. Down below shutters slammed, the piano fell silent, the yodeling stopped. I dragged myself down the mountain, bone-tired, and I saw the small shepherd herding the cows into the barn, one group at a time, and barring the door behind them. But he himself did not take cover. He climbed back up the mountain in my direction, without noticing me. There was a deep, rumbling noise. Through the distant mountain peaks veiled in heavy mist broke bolts of lightning and thunderclaps, and then a downpour, a flood from the sky, turned the Swiss paradise into a darkening, terrifying hell.

In the midst of this streaming rain the little half-naked boy jumped onto a boulder, and throwing back his head, all windblown, he put the flat of his hands against his mouth and whistled for all he was worth. His whistling cut the darkness, the rain, and the thunder like a knife, and it kept growing bolder and clearer:

"I'll make you listen to me! You will have to hear me!"

1913–15 (translated by Seymour Levitan)

▲

A Night in the
Old Marketplace

A NIGHT IN THE OLD MARKETPLACE

DRAMATIS PERSONAE

Theatrical Staff

Director
Stage Manager
Narrator
Poet

Living People

Wanderer
Fiancé
Fiancée
Prostitute
Stocking Knitter
Egg Seller
Fruit Seller
Lamp Snuffer
Jester
Recluse
Noson the Drunk
Folk Poet
Someone
Night Watchman
Hungry Worker, Shopkeepers, Housewives, Youngsters from the
    Study House, Circle of Girls, Two Young Ladies, Speakers at
    Meeting.

Souls from Purgatory (dressed as in life)

Water Carrier (with bottomless bucket)
Woodcutter (with ax and rope)

Pious Woman (poorly dressed, with an old shawl on her head)
Shopkeepers (they resemble the living and are on their way to a
    fair with their suitcases and travel clothes)
Wealthy Jew
Two Paupers
Two Coachmen
Cultured Jews
Kabbalist
Blind Typesetter
One-Legged Prisoner (dragging a chain)
Hussar Killed in Action (wears a uniform with torn buttons and a
    black wound in the chest)
Tanner
Hanged Man
Cantor
Beadle
Frozen Woman
Public Speakers
Martyrs
Musicians

The Dead (dressed in shrouds)

Adulteress
Old Man
Butcher
Informer
Old Maid
Philosophers
Hasidim
Workers
Brody Singers
Bride (wearing a bridal dress, she is about 14–15 years old)
Men and Women of various ages (the condition of their shrouds
    testifies to the amount of time they have been dead)
Small Boys and Girls

Other Characters

Gargoyle
Stone Statues of Knights, Priests, and Bishop
Churchbell
Tin Rooster

STAGE LEFT (from front to back)

1) The synagogue or shul. An old, low building with gray walls. Its windows, rounded at the top, are mostly broken. On its heavy, oddly misshapen roof is a weathervane in the form of a tin rooster with tattered wings. Stairs run down from ground level to a heavy iron gate.

2) The synagogue street.

3) The study house. It is entered by a door in a peeling old wall facing the street. Its old, freshly patched roof slants toward the marketplace. Its windows are long and rectangular.

4) The ruin. Half a gate hangs askew in its entrance. Its windows are boarded up. On its roof is a black chimney that is missing its top.

5) The factory, whose red roof with its many smokestacks looks down on the marketplace.

6) An old courtyard with a two-story building. A wooden balcony that creaks with every step runs around the second story. Steps lead up to it from the marketplace. At the rear of the balcony are apartments with windows and doors. On the ground floor are shops.

STAGE RIGHT (from front to back)

7) The tavern. On it is a sign with the motto, spelled out in little lightbulbs: "To The Last Drop!"

8) The church street.

9) An old house. By its entrance hangs the shingle of a barber-surgeon with its symbol of a brightly-lit red cross and three brass bowls. A separate entrance leads to an apartment via a wooden porch. The building has a new second story with large windows and a balcony with glass doors.

10) Across a back street stands the church. It has two towers, one with a bell and one with a gold cross. Both look down on the marketplace, throwing their converging shadows over it as far as the door of the synagogue.

11) The town hall with its clock tower. In the niches of its walls are stone statues of old Polish knights and priests. On the clock tower, overlooking the marketplace, is a statue of a bishop holding a cross and a sword.

STAGE CENTER

12) The marketplace. In the middle of it stands an old, partially filled-in well. Its gargoyle of old, green-patinated stone is in the form of a monster that is half-man and half-woman, with a horn in its male side.

13) A street in the background, running out of town to the cemetery. It is flanked on either side by shops.

14) The cemetery.

The time is from evening to dawn on an autumn night.

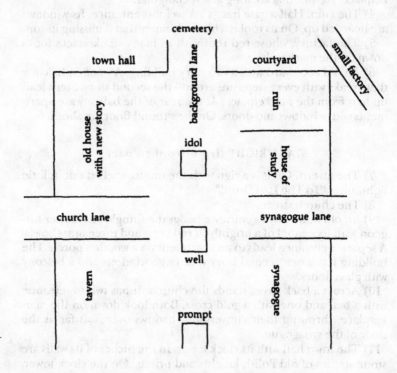

cemetery

town hall   background lane   courtyard

small factory

old house with a new story

idol

house of study

ruin

church lane   synagogue lane

tavern

well

synagogue

prompt

PROLOGUE

There are two curtains: a front one, which is already raised, and a scrim of black gauze behind it that gradually grows more diaphanous until, by the end of the prologue, the entire stage is seen through it. The DIRECTOR *and* STAGE MANAGER *enter from opposite wings. The* STAGE MANAGER *is followed by the* NARRATOR.

DIRECTOR (*to* STAGE MANAGER):
  Ready?

STAGE MANAGER:
  Almost.
  There's just the fence to put around the well.

NARRATOR:
  In which once, long ago,
  The drunk musicians drowned . . .
  But what about the gargoyle
  Whose magic power lured them into it?

STAGE MANAGER:
  It's all in place—
  A huge thing,
  Half-man and half-woman,
  With a horn in the half that's a man.

NARRATOR:
  A long-forgotten god
  From days before the synagogue and church . . .

DIRECTOR:
  . . . which will awake and start to spout . . .

STAGE MANAGER:
  . . . a river of red water from its mouth,
  As though it were a cow that dreamily
  Lifts up its head from drinking
  To cast a magic circle with its eyes
  In a zealous, red-beamed light,
  Exactly as the stage directions call for.

DIRECTOR (*to* NARRATOR):
  You'll introduce each act—
  Just make it short and snappy!

STAGE MANAGER:
  Or else it's curtains for you!

DIRECTOR:

> Before Act One you'll walk around the stage
> And explain the set.
>
> >(*To* STAGE MANAGER)
>
> Make sure you spotlight everything he points to.

NARRATOR:

> Who'll summarize the plot?

DIRECTOR:

> That's the playwright's job.
> And here he is . . .
>
> >(*The* POET *enters.*)

NARRATOR:

> He has no color in his cheeks,
> But his dark eyes burn bright.
> Look how he keeps his right hand on his heart.

DIRECTOR:

> He doesn't even see us!
>
> >(*He exits peevishly.*)

NARRATOR:

> He's lost in thought . . .
>
> >(*To the audience*)
>
> This is his play.
> He wants to tell us something.

POET:

> >(*Bowing to the audience from the right wing*)
>
> A fevered dream by night
> On a sickbed in a swamp that will not drain!
> Half-scared to death,
> The frightened heart keeps vigil.
> From far away,
> From the black wastes,
> From fields and forests spattered by the night,
> Wild peals are borne on air
> Of howling, bloodthirsty beasts,
> Of cackling devils
> And tittering ghosts,
> Far-off, a will-o'-the-wisp,
> Toadstool or dogskull,
> Dances and prances

With a horrible gleam,
While above,
Hushed as a dove,
A pale sky spreads itself out . . .
Not a shimmer,
Not a glimmer,
Not a dark eyeball's sheen
Or the white of an unseeing eye . . .
The world is asleep, in a fever of
Silence hushed as a dove,
While a madcap fool
Weaves a net of shadowy beams
At the foot of the old gargoyle.
      (*He paces back and forth.*)
Ah, shades of the past,
Whose fountainheads scarce are behind us!
Ah, beams intertwined
With the net's bare hope of a haul . . .
And the anguished heart asks:
Is it over once and for all,
Or is there more still ahead?
And if so, how soon will the thread
In the weave be made tight?
Who can know on a fever-night?
The jackal, or else the hyena . . .
      (*Having reached a wing, he suddenly exits.*)

STAGE MANAGER:
      Powerful!
            (*Nudging the* NARRATOR)
      Set the scene!
            (*Exits*)

NARRATOR:
      An old marketplace.
      Over there is the town hall.
            (*The town hall is lighted up.*)
      In the niches of its walls
      Are statues made of stone:
      All kinds of old nobility;
      A pair of pious, pensive priests;
      And up above, as you can see,
      High on the clock tower
      (The clock itself no longer tells the hour),

A bishop with a cross and sword,
Both held above his head
To fight for the true faith:
One is for blessing, one for striking dead . . .
In that street on your left, you see the church.
  (*The church is lighted up.*)
Commanding the whole square,
It stands there with a supercilious stare,
Its Jesus gold, its marble white,
Throwing its long shadow all the way
To the synagogue over on your right . . . .
  (*The synagogue is lighted up.*)
It's just a shul like any shul,
Peering out through cracked old spectacles,
An old building damp with tears
And full of grief,
Stooped beneath a heavy roof,
From which it glances at the church in fear:
Look here,
I hardly take up any room,
I'm colorless, I make no sound,
My steps go down into the ground—
And you're so dazzlingly tall and bright!
Why don't you let my windows have the light
Your shadow takes from them
And stop your poking in my soul. . . ?
  (*The study house is lighted up.*)
Poor but cheery—that's the study house.
Despite its old, ramshackle frame
Its large windows are aflame
With youngsters learning Torah:
Their cheeks are pale,
Their curls are dark,
Their glowing eyes could win your heart—
Like birds they sing!
Like bells they ring!

STAGE MANAGER (*muttering from the wing*):
  We're running late!

NARRATOR (*hearing steps, he breaks off and says nervously*):
  Someone's there!
    (*The WANDERER appears, walking slowly and looking* 1
    tired.)
  An unfamiliar face . . .

DIRECTOR (*leafing through his notebook*):
>I can't find him anyplace.

NARRATOR (*regarding the* WANDERER *with astonishment*):
>He walks
>As though to leave his footprints in the air;
>A knapsack on his back and heavy travel wear;
>A walking stick carved with a faded rose
>That drops its petals as he goes . . .
>Look how he bites his lips!

STAGE MANAGER:
>I'd better let them know.
>>(*Exits*)

NARRATOR:
>A sickly smile;
>Eyes young but sorrowful
>Beneath a wrinkled brow . . .
>>(*He cups his hand to his ear.*)
>Sshhh, he's talking now!

WANDERER (*looking about*):
>The same stars, the same sky,
>The same earth . . .
>How much these ears have heard,
>And yet they would hear more!
>How little do these eyes
>Feel they have seen their fill
>Of color or of form!
>What's near still drives me on;
>What's far still draws me to it:
>On and on and on . . .
>My legs feel like lead.
>My pack
>Sits heavy on my back . . .
>>(*He begins to remove it.*)
>And beside the weight of my own clothes,
>I bear with me the dust of many lands and roads . . .
>>(*He sits down by the synagogue wall.*)
>Come closer to me, night, drift close around me!
>Your breath is pure,
>Your shadows soft . . .
>Where am I coming from? Don't ask.
>Before these shadows flee, I must be off.
>Where am I going to? Don't ask again.

Maybe Someone Up There knows,
But I myself
Have grown old but hardly wise
From seeing set and seeing rise
The sun that I've been following so long.
Nowhere a stranger and nowhere at home;
Driven by the same unknown hunter
Who drives us all but me a little faster . . .
No matter where I sleep, I dream in a strange bed,
And with the crack of dawn I'm up.
Night, let me lay my head down in your lap!
I won't bother looking at the town—they're all the same . . .
Be good and spin for me a dream
That gently rocks my weary heart to sleep:
Spin red, spin black,
Spin gray—
Mix the colors any way—
But spin!
Spin life,
Spin death,
Spin out what's in between . . .

(*He falls asleep. The scrim now seems so thin that the entire marketplace can be seen clearly, along with all the characters on stage. The synagogue is dark, the study house brightly lit; oil lamps burn smokily in the backs of the shops in the old courtyard. The shopkeepers are getting ready to put out the lights and close for the day. On the wooden balcony overlooking the courtyard women sit looking down, some at the study house, others at a group of girls standing in a circle in the marketplace, still others at the shops below. Behind them the windows of their homes are like red, burning eyes. In the street in the background leading away from the marketplace stand two young ladies. One holds a letter up to the light of a streetlamp. The* LAMP SNUFFER, *his instrument in his hand, is about to start work. The town hall is shuttered from within. A rainbow-colored light plays over the edges of the shutters. On a corner near the church street a boy and a girl are holding hands. They are about to stroll into the marketplace. The* NIGHT WATCHMAN *leans against a wall by the tavern door, from which he has apparently just emerged, ready to begin his rounds; around his neck is a whistle on a chain. The gargoyle in the* middle of the marketplace is a somber green. The cobblestones gleam in the paved streets. The flames of the streetlamps quiver in the damp air.

   The characters are all in place, motionlessly waiting for a sign to begin.

   The STAGE MANAGER returns with the DIRECTOR and the POET. They walk on tiptoe.)

STAGE MANAGER (pointing to the WANDERER):
   He's fast asleep.

NARRATOR:
   As if in some deep fog.
   The things that happen in the theater!

DIRECTOR:
   Come on, let's get him out of here.

   (The DIRECTOR, the STAGE MANAGER, and the NAR-
   RATOR drag the sleeping WANDERER offstage, leaving his
   things behind.)

POET (suddenly inspired):
   Hold on!
   I've just glimpsed one of his dreams:
   That's the play we'll put on!
      (He gathers the WANDERER's things.)

   (Curtain)

ACT ONE

[The curtain rises.] The stage is full of noise and movement. A singsong of Talmudic study comes from the study house. The tavern is boisterous. Through the brightly lit windows of the new second story on the house across the street from it, one can hear the hubbub of a public meeting. The shopkeepers are locking up, their old keys grating in their locks. In a window of the courtyard a light goes out; soon after the STOCKING KNITTER steps outside and continues working on a stocking by the light of a streetlamp, to which she holds it up to make sure she hasn't lost a stitch. Eyes on each other, the FI-ANCÉ and FIANCÉE walk hand in hand toward the synagogue street, passing the circle of girls. Their place is taken by a young PROSTITUTE, who stands against a wall, surveying the marketplace with darting, sickly-bright eyes. She coughs. The FRUIT SELLER gives her a fearful look as she walks *past, wearily crossing the market with her unsold goods in the direction of the* STOCKING KNITTER. *The* NIGHT WATCHMAN, *unsteady on his feet, searches groggily for the whistle around his neck before beginning his rounds. In the background the* LAMP SNUFFER *is at work. The two young ladies move away from him to a streetlamp in the marketplace. The circle of girls revolves dreamily, humming softly. Men and women step out on the balcony to cool off from the heat. Voices rise above the din.*

A YOUNG VOICE FROM THE STUDY HOUSE:
> . . . If she's a *mukas ets*, the rabbis think . . .

A HOARSE VOICE FROM THE TAVERN:
> Drink, you bastard, drink!

A LOUD VOICE FROM THE BALCONY (*shouting across the marketplace to the public meeting*):
> There's no two ways about it!

A SHOPKEEPER CALLING UP FROM BELOW:
> You still don't have to shout it!

A SECOND SHOPKEEPER:
> Cut out that racket overhead!

A HOUSEWIFE ON THE BALCONY:
> It's you down there who'll wake the dead!
> (*The noise dies down a bit. The circle of girls comes to life.*)

Andante

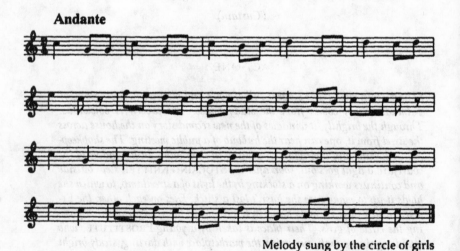

Melody sung by the circle of girls

FIRST GIRL:
>Eenie, meenie . . .

THE CIRCLE:
>. . . minie, mo . . .

FIRST GIRL:
>. . . catch a weasel by the toe . . .

SECOND GIRL (*pointing to the couple holding hands*):
>Sshhh, keep it low!
>Look who's coming . . .

FIANCÉE:
>. . . And on the walls, red wallpaper . . .

FIANCÉ:
>Your wish is my command, my dear!

FIANCÉE:
>We'll need a lamp . . .

FIANCÉ:
>The very best
>One from Trieste!

FIANCÉE:
>And a gramophone for guests!
>Won't that be swell?

NIGHT WATCHMAN (*beginning his rounds after finding his whistle*):
>Ten o'clock and all is well!
>Watch out for fire!
>>(*He walks through the marketplace, half-asleep.*)

JESTER (*hugging the wall of the study house, to the* RECLUSE):
>What was it that I was about to say?
>It was important, that's all I remember . . .
>I've spent too many days
>In that old ruin talking to the spiders.
>Why, it's right on the tip of my tongue—
>If only I could think for a minute!
>That ruin has the weirdest shadows in it,
>All kinds of holy spooks . . .
>I think I hear them cry and try to speak.
>They put the bats on edge and rile the crickets.
>And here—this study house, those children . . .

That woman on the balcony up there . . .
That bar . . .

A WOMAN ON THE BALCONY:
How greedy some men are!

JESTER (*pleading with the* WOMAN):
If only you'd be quiet for a minute!
I tell you, it's important!
And very aggravating . . .
(*To the* RECLUSE)
There has to be a word
For changing, for remaking everything . . .

RECLUSE (*raising a hand toward the sky*):
His handiwork!
(*They exchange defiant glances until both look away simultaneously, though remaining where they are.*)

THE YOUNG LADY WITH THE LETTER (*having finished reading it, she shows it to her companion*):
Look, it's wet with his tears!
(*She kisses it, then hides it in her bosom. More proud than in love, she sums up its contents.*)
I am his star that shines!
Each time he looks into my eyes
They make him thirst for more, like wine!
He calls me his darling. "Beloved of mine . . ."
(*She walks past the circle of girls.*)
He kisses my blue eyes each day . . .

GIRL IN CIRCLE (*incredulous*):
Her eyes—are gray! (*The young ladies quickly leave via the synagogue street. The* LAMP SNUFFER *enters the market and sets to work there.*)

SECOND GIRL (*imitating his walk*):
Flip-flap! Flip-flap!
Waddling about.
He reaches up and gives a tap—
Poof! The streetlamp's out.

(*The shopkeepers drift into the marketplace, waiting for each other there. The* PROSTITUTE *steps forward. The first shopkeeper notices her. Their eyes meet.*)

HOUSEWIFE ON BALCONY (*looking worriedly down at her husband*):
Your supper's getting cold. You're late!

SHOPKEEPER (*embarrassed*):
> I'll only be a minute . . . wait . . .
>> (*He takes out his pocketwatch as though to check it against the clock tower.*)
>
> I can't make out the time from here . . .
>> (*To two other shopkeepers who join him*)
>
> What does it say?

SECOND SHOPKEEPER (*amused*):
> That clock stopped running back
> In King Sobiecki's day!

FIRST SHOPKEEPER (*unwilling to lose face*):
> My watch is fast . . .

THIRD SHOPKEEPER (*coming to the rescue*):
> Well, I sold that wagon of old clothes at last!

SECOND SHOPKEEPER:
> Will I see you tomorrow at the fair?

FIRST SHOPKEEPER:
> I wish I had the cash . . .

RECLUSE (*timidly walking toward them from the study house*):
> Oh, take me there!
>> (*No one hears him.*)

FOURTH SHOPKEEPER (*arriving in the marketplace, he stares at the* PROSTITUTE):
> Well, I declare!

SECOND HOUSEWIFE ON BALCONY (*sternly*):
> Yeshaya!
>> (*The shopkeepers disperse, some up the steps to the balcony.*)

STOCKING KNITTER:
> Will we ever be sent the Messiah?

RECLUSE:
> The world's so full of sin, so—

CIRCLE OF GIRLS:
> Eenie, meenie, minie, mo,
> Catch a turkey by the toe . . .

STOCKING KNITTER (*pointing to the* PROSTITUTE *and speaking with growing passion to the marketwomen who have gathered in the square*):

My dears,
If this had happened long ago,
She'd have been whipped, I promise you,
Decked in feathers,
Smeared with tar,
Shown who her betters are,
And ridden out on a rail!

FRUIT SELLER:
Why, I could tear her . . .

EGG SELLER:
. . . head from tail!

GIRLS IN CIRCLE:
Drunk Noson'l! Drunk Noson'l!

> (NOSON THE DRUNK *staggers out of the tavern, through the open door from which singing is heard.*)

FOLK POET (*from within the tavern*):
Sing!
Drink!
Hug and kiss!
Love makes you young,
Wine brings you bliss!

CHORUS FROM THE TAVERN:
Love makes you young,
Wine brings you bliss!

FOLK POET:
Raise high your glasses,
Toast the new morn:
It's now or never—
Take life by storm!

NOSON THE DRUNK:
Before death takes you without warn—
    (*He staggers and falls.*)
—ing . . .

> (A HUNGRY WORKER *appears from the street in the background and tries helping* NOSON *to his feet as he passes by.*)

NOSON (*uncooperative*):
But I'm already where I like to be:
Flat on my back.

HUNGRY WORKER (*from a low gate on which he has meanwhile sat down to rest*):
> Swine!

NOSON:
> How sweet, how fine
> The damp earth smells,
> Like milk and honey!
> It has no hands, but it fondles me like a mother . . .
> It has no tongue, but it talks to me like a brother . . .

>> (*The study house falls silent. Its young students have put out the candles on its tables and stands. Holding colorful paper lanterns, they emerge into the street.*)

GIRLS (*opening the circle*):
> Come!
> Games without boys are no fun!

BOYS (*still in the synagogue street*):
> What is a man? What is his worth?
> Ashes and dirt! Dust of the earth!
>> (*They enter the marketplace.*)
> Today in your room—
> Tomorrow your tomb!

>> (*They fall apprehensively silent as they approach the gargoyle. One by one, the girls drift over to them.*)

BOY (*looking at the gargoyle*):
> Is it a he or a she?

SECOND BOY:
> It's both, can't you see!

GIRL:
> My mama told *me* . . .

FOLK POET (*overhearing them as he steps out of the tavern*):
> Love!

RECLUSE (*silencing him*):
> Blind sin!
> But within
> You can choke
> On the fire and smoke!

FIRST BOY:
> Sometimes in the middle of the night

It wakes without a sound,
Opens its mouth wide,
Makes its eyes round . . .
A jet of water shoots out from its mouth,
The eyes glow red—
And anyone stepping inside
The magic circle it's made
Will lose his mind right away
And never find it again,
Because the well sucks him down . . .
That's how the musicians drowned.

SECOND BOY:
Let's hope it doesn't get us like it got them!

GIRL:
Do you think that they're still down there at the bottom?

BOY:
They dredged for them and never found them.
This fence was built around it at the time.

FOLK POET (*striding over to the balcony*):
I even put it into rhyme!
  (*He ascends the balcony and declaims from there*):
Why, haven't you heard of the terrible tale,
Of the terrible tale of our musical band?
Exactly at midnight it finished its stand,
It finished its stand at the nobleman's ball.
Hatless as goyim it came to this place:
Fiddle, and trumpet, and snare drums, and bass.

A band of musicians come from the ball,
From ladies so lovely in dresses so fine,
From goyishe feasting and goyishe wine,
Drunk with desire and goyishe ale.
Exactly at midnight
The monster awoke,
And plucked them and sucked them down into the well!
One after another they leapt in the water . . . (*He breaks off
with an angry glance at the* JESTER.)

BOY (*looking at the* JESTER *in fright*):
Was he there too?

SECOND BOY:
You bet he was . . . and saw it all . . .

JESTER (*angrily pulling a red handkerchief from his breast pocket*):
Ha! The things they learn these days in school!
(*He chases them with the handkerchief.*)
Go on, scat!

> (*The children run up the balcony and into their houses with frightened laughter.*)

HOUSEWIVES AND SHOPKEEPERS ON BALCONY:
—An odd one, that!
—It's all the monster's fault!
—Why doesn't someone smash it?
—It was a god once, don't forget that!

LAMP SNUFFER (*finished in the marketplace, he heads for the church street*):
Good night!

JESTER (*coming back into the marketplace*):
Good night!

VOICES:
Good night! Good night! Have a good night . . .

> (*People retire into their houses. One after another the lights in the windows go out.*)

JESTER (*pleased*):
Ah, that's better now . . . all eyes are blind . . .
(*Holding up the handkerchief*)
With this cloth I make a wind
That blows the lights out in each home.
Let it be darker than the grave,
More silent than the tomb!

> (*He waves his handkerchief at the last lit-up houses, whose lights go out at once. He waves it, too, at the second story where the meeting is in progress, but this time to no avail.*)

YOUNG PEOPLE (*on their way to the meeting, they speak quickly, self-absorbed*):
—What shall we discuss?
—The Polish parliament!
—No, Palestine!
—A people, like a person, needs a home!

JESTER (*still waving his handkerchief at the second story*):
Or else a dream!

HUNGRY WORKER (*jumping to his feet*):
>   Don't you want more than that? Don't you?

PROSTITUTE (*to the young people, who scatter in alarm*):
>   Won't one of you come with me? Won't you?
>> (*They run off. She notices the worker and smiles at him boldly.*)
>   You're the best-looking of them all, mister!

HUNGRY WORKER:
>   Sister!
>   How can you do this to yourself?

PROSTITUTE (*regarding him suspiciously*):
>   Have you anything to eat?

HUNGRY WORKER (*insinuatingly*):
>   I haven't even got a bed . . .

PROSTITUTE (*turning sharply away*):
>   No. You've got a big fat mouth instead!
>> (*She heads toward* NOSON THE DRUNK)

HUNGRY WORKER (*shaking his fist at the roof of the factory*):
>   Go on, suck us dry!
>   Throw our sisters on a sty!
>   Make everything that's holy hell!

NIGHT WATCHMAN (*rousing himself from his stupor*):
>   Eleven o'clock and all is well!
>   Watch out for fire!

PROSTITUTE (*shaking* NOSON THE DRUNK *disgustedly*):
>   Hey!

NOSON THE DRUNK (*half-opening his eyes*):
>   My little Sheyndele!

PROSTITUTE (*impatiently trying to sit him up*):
>   Sheyndele?
>   It's all the same to me.
>> (*She lets go of him, out of breath.*)
>   Are you heavy! Whew!

NOSON THE DRUNK (*looking at her, startled*):
>   Who are you? Who?
>> (*He collapses again, sobbing.*)
>   Believe me, Sheyndele, I swear
>   I've never seen her anywhere!

JESTER (*to the* PROSTITUTE, *with compassion*):
　　Will you come with me, then?

RECLUSE (*alarmed*):
　　Get behind me, Satan!

　　　(*The* PROSTITUTE *jumps back, frightened by them both, and
　　　bumps into* SOMEONE *coming out of the pharmacy with a
　　　large bottle of medicine in each hand. He drops the bottles,
　　　which fall and shatter. A shudder runs through the market-
　　　place.*)

SOMEONE:
　　O come into my arms!
　　Your eyes blaze in the night . . .
　　Your body smells of holiness . . .
　　Above you doves fly, white.
　　　(*The* PROSTITUTE *tries breaking away.*)
　　Stay, stay in my embrace!
　　Quietly let yourself go . . .
　　　(*He holds her more tightly, not letting her speak.*)
　　Your lips are to kiss, to kiss!
　　Don't ask—I don't want to know!
　　Knowing lames me,
　　Scares and shames me,
　　Sets me back . . .
　　The chance, silent encounter is bliss!
　　Concealed deep within it,
　　Flames, blossoms the mystical rose:
　　Eternity in a minute!

PROSTITUTE (*barely managing to tear herself away, she jumps back and
　　regards him with loathing*):
　　You're thin as a spider,
　　You croak like a frog—
　　Say who you are!

SOMEONE (*snatching her back in his arms*):
　　I can't!
　　I don't know who I am.
　　I only know what I want.
　　　(*He drags her into a doorway, where they disappear.*)

RECLUSE:
　　O Lord, chastise!
　　　(*From within the shuttered houses are heard soft murmurs of
　　　prayer.*)

BEDTIME PRAYER:

    Send Thou sleep to our eyes,
    O Lord who reigneth in the skies,
    And rest to our brow.
    Hear our prayer now,
    And give us sweet, pacific dreams
    Of comfort and salvation.
    Be our soul's destination,
    And shelter it beneath Thy wings
    Till morning comes . . . till morning comes . . .

> (*The prayer is broken off. The shutters of the tavern are shut from within. Only the letters of the tavern sign remain lit. The* FOLK POET *steps out on the balcony with a nightlamp, which he sets on a table.*)

FOLK POET (*staring at the sky*):
    On the horizon's western rim
    A secret hand is fashioning—

RECLUSE:
    The sky is full of sorrow!

FOLK POET:
    . . . Gray mists are spun there,
    Smoky threads run there,
    Nets are woven there, nets . . .

RECLUSE:
    For every little soul—a star!
    The heavens shut their eyes . . .

FOLK POET:
    A silvery moon
    Sends quivering beams.
    Each golden star
    Glitters and gleams . . .

RECLUSE:
    Each tear! Each tear!

FOLK POET:
    Far and wide . . .

RECLUSE:
    Evil spreads its nets on every side!

FOLK POET:
>The bright stars are fading.
>They're quaking, they're waking . . .

RECLUSE:
>Evil has them in its clutches now!

FOLK POET:
>Sleep, my town and marketplace.
>Bless them, God, with Thy kind grace!

JESTER (*with barely suppressed joy*):
>Out! Out! Out! Out! Out!
>Each window's black, each house is blind!

FOLK POET:
>It's not a night for humankind.

RECLUSE:
>It's one to go out of your mind!

FOLK POET (*departing with his lantern, to the* JESTER*'s quiet satisfaction*):
>Watchman,
>Watch till the cock crows!
>Make sure your eyes never close!
>(*He exits.*)

RECLUSE:
>There's horror in the air.
>(*He enters the study house.*)
>Watchman, keep guard!

NIGHT WATCHMAN (*half-sitting, half-leaning against a wall*):
>I've had as much of this as I can stand.
>(*He looks first at the synagogue, then at the church.*)
>If one of them can't do my job, perhaps the other can!
>(*The sign on the tavern is extinguished.*)
>The tavern sign has gone out too . . .
>(*Drowsily*)
>My head feels like it weighs a ton.
>(*He falls asleep and snores.*)

JESTER (*shaking a fist at the sky*):
>And in Your image You created man!

>(*Curtain*)

ACT TWO

The curtain rises, revealing the front of the stage.

NARRATOR:
> Night!
> One mad fool alone still mans the watch.
> The old gargoyle's about to cast its spell
> And resurrect its long-forgotten might . . .
> There'll be a play of shadowflares,
> Of feversick electric glares:
> The heart is dead from fright!
>
> The night is lost
> In darkness, silent as a dove.
> From somewhere comes a sound of brutish laughter . . .
> The fevered heart,
> Recoiling, gives a start:
> Nightmare-tossed, it
> Is exhausted.
>
> And where can we turn in our need?
> All faded
> Are the roses,
> The lilies, posies—
> Dead.
>
> Madness, with its fist raised at a sky
> At which its blasphemies are hurled,
> Wakes from their night-enshrouded tents
> Old, long-abandoned worlds . . .

JESTER (*kneeling before the sleeping* NIGHT WATCHMAN, *he removes the whistle from his neck and goes over to the gargoyle*):
> Hey, you old monster, you:
> Open your eyes!
> Let's look in your mouth!
> Give us some light!
> Let's see you spout!
> Heaven's shut down;
> The night is our own!
> > (*The stone statues descend from the church and stroll over with a horrid gait.*)

A KNIGHT:
> He's waking the monster!

A PRIEST:
>Just let him try!
>The churchbells are primed;
>God in heaven's standing by.
>>(*The monster wakes and does the* JESTER*'s bidding.*)

BISHOP (*from the clock tower*):
>It is the time of the Antichrist!

JESTER (*putting the whistle in his mouth and blowing it in all four directions and up at the sky*):
>You can punish me tomorrow—
>But since You're sleeping now,
>I'm generalissimo!
>So follow me
>From all the quarters of the night,
>From forest, field,
>Cave, cleft, and dell,
>From the pillaries of Hell:
>Come, you shadow-dwelling clan,
>Of dream and foam
>Together spun!
>His beloved Name's a sacred swindle . . .
>To be alive you must believe and kill!
>So let me wish you happiness and health:
>Come, one and all, to the old marketplace
>To do my will!

A KNIGHT (*protesting*):
>To think this is happening here!

SECOND KNIGHT:
>The very idea!

JESTER:
>I'll be the leader of God's world!
>I just hope I remember where to take it.

>>(*Shadowy apparitions from Purgatory appear in the marketplace. They move about with a ghostly unreality. Those who drift to the front of the stage can be heard by the audience.*)

>Who is that fellow with the bucket?

WATER CARRIER (*like all the apparitions, he freezes in place as soon as the* JESTER *looks at him*):
>Whew, is that place hot!

In the study house sit
Scholars and sweat,
Their tongues hanging out.

> (*He hurries over to the gargoyle, places a bottomless bucket beneath the jetting water, and calls over his shoulder, as though to the scholars he has left behind in Purgatory.*)

I'll be right back!
I won't make you wait.
I'll bring you water,
Fresh and sweet.

JESTER:

May you live to greet
The Messiah
Because of your good deed!
> (*The* WATER CARRIER *exits hurriedly.*)

A PRIEST (*looking piously upward*):
O cleanse this unregenerate
In the blood of the Lamb!
Let him not fetch water in vain,
Holy Father of mine!

WOODCUTTER (*transfixed by a look from the* JESTER):
It's freezing down there!
The little orphans are naked and bare,
Shivering, seated all day
In a school that's unheated . . .
> (*He chops at the air. As though to the orphans*)
I see your pain, I see your tears—
Soon, soon, my dears,
I'll bring you wood to make a fire.
There's a log! And there's another!
In no time I'll have stoked the oven!

JESTER:

For which, when this is over,
You'll get to hear the Messiah's shofar!

A PRIEST (*indignantly*):
Listen to the lying loafer!
The trumpet sounded long ago.
Christ's death redeemed all men.

A PIOUS WOMAN (*transfixed by the* JESTER *too*):
Not, God help me, that I had the yen!

I'd never go to the bathhouse
In such bitter weather
Just for me and my husband
To sleep together.
So bless my womb, dear God,
And the loins of my Yeshaya . . .

JESTER:

They shall bring forth the Messiah!

WOMAN (*running off joyfully*):
Oy, what good news! Am I a
Happy woman!
That was an angel's voice—
There is a God, there is!
I'll tell my man about it right away.

(*Two coachmen appear, cracking long whips.*)

FIRST COACHMAN:
My grandpa always used to say:
If you value your horses,
Put oats as pure as diamonds in their hay.
(*He gives his whip a crack*)

SECOND COACHMAN:
God bless his soul, but those were different days.
I feed my nags bran and sunflower pips,
Sit myself down with a crack of the whip—
And heigh-ho,
Off we go!

JESTER:

To meet the Messiah!

(*The coachmen hurry anxiously off toward the church street.*)

KABBALIST (*calling after them*):
Where to?
To the fair?
Take me there! Take me there!
I do mystical ciphers and mystical sums,
And I must find Elijah, to ask him the num—

JESTER:

—ber of years left until the Messiah comes!

SHOPKEEPERS (*hurrying after the coachmen*):
—Where is your carriage?

—Why not go by train?
—The price of fresh cabbage!
—I wish it would rain!

(*They exit. A stout,* WEALTHY JEW *appears, accompanied by two thin paupers.*)

WEALTHY JEW:
Are you gentlemen acquainted with my house?

FIRST PAUPER:
Are you serious?

SECOND PAUPER:
It takes up half the block.
And the interiors!

FIRST PAUPER:
And the foundation!

WEALTHY JEW:
Right down to the middle of the earth!
There's brandy in the basement,
The attic's full of wheat—
You should see the noblemen who eat
Out of my hand. This world—d'you hear?—
Can be a treat!
After my bath I have a glass of beer,
And when the Sabbath's out, if it's not late,
I have the cantor over to my place
For a private concert . . .
Managing my real estate
Is high finance!
My underwear's from Leipzig,
My tobacco comes from France . . .

JESTER:
Die! (*The* WEALTHY JEW *staggers and starts to collapse.*)

FIRST PAUPER:
Why, he's white as a sheet! Just look at him!

SECOND PAUPER (*catching the* WEALTHY JEW *as he falls and dragging him into the marketplace*):
Who knows a prayer from the book for him?
(*They exit. Enter some cultured Jews.*)

CULTURED JEWS (*reading the shingles in the marketplace*):

—Thank God for modern times!
—There's been progress, that's a fact.
—Doctors, dentists, lawyers . . .
—The clock can't be turned back!
(*They notice the red roof of the factory.*)
—That building over there, what's that?

HUNGRY WORKER (*jumping up*):
It's a factory,
You jackasses,
And it bleeds us dry!

(*Shocked, the cultured Jews exit. Enter a group of workers. Led by a* HANGED MAN *with a rope around his neck, they march toward the factory. Among them is a* BLIND TYPESETTER *who can't keep up and stops. Behind her limps a* ONE-LEGGED PRISONER.)

HANGED MAN:
The closer you get to the sky,
The freer you grow!
Eyes opened wide,
You see the whole world
Stretched out below . . .
(*He walks off toward the factory.*)

JESTER (*to the* BLIND TYPESETTER):
Is this as far as you go?

BLIND TYPESETTER:
I'm blind! Would you like to know why?
For years I worked in a dark cellar.
I was in the underground, get it?
Never stopping to rest . . . and all that lead dust around . . .
And the type so small you hardly could set it.
It's no wonder that I lost my sight.

ONE-LEGGED PRISONER (*catching up with her, he takes her by the arm, with a suspicious look at the* JESTER):
Come with me, you'll be all right!

BLIND TYPESETTER:
You're limping.

PRISONER:
Did you forget?
I sat in chains for twelve long years.

When my leg was too gangrened to keep any more,
They sliced it off with a rusty old saw.
It didn't even get a decent funeral!
And yet the road leads onward, after all . . .

(*A* HUSSAR *riddled with bullets encounters a* TANNER *who
stumbles around with his head in his hands.*)

HUSSAR:

Are you mad at me?

(*The* TANNER *fails to answer. The* HUSSAR *takes the head,
places it on the* TANNER's *shoulders, and asks more loudly.*)

Are you mad at me?

TANNER:

I . . . I really can't say.
Why should I be?

HUSSAR:

But it's a fact
That I hacked
Off your head!

TANNER:

How come you did?

HUSSAR:

I felt like it!
You held a red flag in the street.
"Ready Arms!"
Was the command—
A soldier's hand
Obeys its orders . . .
I hope you didn't mind.

TANNER:

I never even saw your sword!

HUSSAR:

After that, they shot me too.
It took a while for me to understand.

TANNER (*pleased*):

Well, then, it did us good, both me and you!

HUSSAR:

Let's have your hand!
(*They exit hand in hand.*)

JESTER (*disappointedly left by himself*):
> All that chitchat—
> And for what?
> They never got anywhere!
> One minute, though—
> I think I know
> That fellow over there.

CANTOR (*stepping forward*):
> Always the same dumb dais
> And fat audience—
> No scene could be sorrier!
> But then the curtain starts to rise,
> And I look out at those sweet eyes
> And break into an aria:

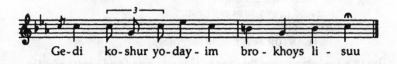

Ge-di ko-shur yo-day-im bro-khoys li-suu

> (*Sings*)
> *Ge-di*
> *Ko-shur yo-day-im*
> *Bro-khoys li-suu* . . . uh-hu uh-hu . . . uh-huuuuu huuuuuuu
> huuuuuu . . .

FROZEN WOMAN (*stepping forward*):
> Uuuuu . . . ooh. . . . ooh . . . ooh! Uuuuu . . . ooh . . . ooh
> . . . ooh!
> I'm frozen through and through!
> What shall I do, what shall I do . . .
>> (*She halts, transfixed by both the* JESTER *and the* CANTOR.)
> He makes me feel I'm full of icicles!
> Just watch him twitch his fingers when he sings . . .
> And the notes that spout
> From his big fat mouth—
> It stinks!
> His voice could turn you over in the grave!
> And look at how his bottom lip hangs out . . .
> Brrrr!
> A real monster!
>> (*Exiting*)
> Oy, I'm frozen through and through!
> What shall I do, what shall I do . . .

CANTOR (*to* JESTER):
>   Is she alive?

JESTER:

>   As much as you!
>   (*Compassionately*)
>   I don't want to play games with you.
>   Go!

CANTOR:

>   Where?

JESTER (*pointing to the synagogue*):

>   There!
>   Go try again . . .
>   Go down on your knees
>   And beat your breast,
>   Sing and pray your very best . . .
>   Just beat it!
>   (CANTOR *exits toward the synagogue.*)

BEADLE (*appearing from the street in the background and heading for the synagogue*):

>   Into the shul, into the shul!
>   Everyone pray for our martyred souls!
>   The drowned and the raped
>   And the burned at the stake . . .
>   Everyone into the shul!

>>   (*The apparitions gather in the marketplace, looking to the JESTER for instructions. On the balcony appear old Jews with prayerbooks and burning candles. Behind them the shopkeepers bring stools to sit on. They all sit down.*)

MIDNIGHT PRAYER:

>   See, O Lord, our devastation
>   Since You turned away Your face.
>   See our daughters' violation,
>   Sons dragged off from us in chains.
>   You withdrew in righteous anger
>   And hid Yourself in a thick cloud . . .
>   Now the Sea of Evil rages:
>   Jewish towns have been destroyed.
>   Synagogues are set on fire,
>   Torah scrolls are scorched on pyres . . .

HUNGRY WORKER (*jumping up*):
> Bless the hands that torch them higher,
> Smashing
> And dashing
> To pieces
> Whatever
> Won't let us be free
> And makes a god
> Of robbery!
> It must be shattered
> And ground to dust!

JESTER:
> It must?
> Is that the word?
> Dust?
> > (*He notices the apparitions beginning to move toward the syn-
> > agogue.*)
> Stay where you are!
> *I'm* field marshal,
> Why listen to that imbecile?
> You are my troops—
> I've weapons for you
> Somewhere near,
> Stashed away
> Not far from here.
> If only I remembered where!
> Let me think for a while.
> In the meantime let's drill:
> About face!
> March in place!
> Left . . . right! Left . . . right!
> I have to think about dust for a minute . . .
> > (*The apparitions fall all over themselves.*)
> You're out of step—
> You need some music to get in it!
> > (*To the gargoyle*)
> Cough up the musicians, monster!
>
> > (*To the musicians, who, rapidly wiping off their instruments,
> > tumble out of the well all wet and covered with weeds*)
>
> Hey, old friends, strike up the band:
> Give us a march for our regiment!

This isn't just one of your weddings or balls—
It's a command!
The enemy's at hand . . .

> (*From the synagogue comes the sorrowful sound of the mid-
> night prayer, which mingles in a single mournful cry with
> that of the vigil on the balcony. The* JESTER *grows agitated.*)

But who's that crying?
> (*The musicians gradually take up the melody of the prayer.*)

RECLUSE:

The shul is weeping and sighing!
It says:
Woe to the Father
Who has exiled His son
And is now all alone,
And woe, woe to the son
Who is banished from his Father's table . . .

FRIGHTENED VOICES OF SHADOWS:

—The shul is sighing!
—The shul is crying!
> (*Pointing at the church*)
—The foe has frightened it!
—How wan and white it is!
—The church reaches up to the sky!

MANY VOICES:

We have been made a mockery!

> (*The meeting hall on the second story is suddenly lit up. Out
> of each of its three windows leans a speaker.*)

FIRST SPEAKER:

We need a home in Palestine!

SECOND SPEAKER:

We need a voice in Parliament!

FIRST SPEAKER:

No, a homeland, a new home!
One not spattered with our Jewish blood.
One where Evil has not trampled Good.

THIRD SPEAKER:

Old Mother Israel weeps and would
Stretch out her hands to you, her children . . .

(*The* HUNGRY WORKER *jumps up. At the sound of his voice, all the workers regroup.*)

HUNGRY WORKER:
> Shut up, you old sods!
> (*The lights go out. The three speakers disappear.*)
> *Our* will will be done.
> A new hero will junk
> Your world and its gods!

BLIND TYPESETTER:
> I hear his voice from afar!

HANGED MAN:
> From above
> I see his galloping horse!

TANNER:
> Why, of course.
> Would anyone care for a head?

> (*He takes off his head and stumbles toward the exit. There is laughter on one side of the stage, angry muttering on the other.*)

FOLK POET (*storming out of a room onto the balcony*):
> Cut out that laughter—and those grumbles!
> He's coming, the new man, he's on his way.
> His eyes flash lightning and the thunder rumbles
> In his mouth. He'll keep strange hands and our hands
> away—

JESTER:
> From what?

FOLK POET (*pointing stammeringly at the synagogue*):
> Those holy walls.
> (*Once more ecstatic*)
> Behold the day!
> And there shall come to pass
> Great heroes and great doings . . .

JESTER:
> It already has. They're stranded in the ruin.
> (*Calling out to the ruin*)
> Hey, you New Maccabees,
> Let's have a look at you:
> Come show yourselves!

(*The ruin is enveloped in a deathly pale blue light, in which the martyrs are seen groping their way out into the street.*)

MARTYRS (*boastfully lamenting, they hobble toward the synagogue*):
>Our ribs are cracked in two!
>We're full of holes like sieves . . .

JESTER:
>O grand new times!
>Heroes of a brand-new kind!

MARTYRS:
>With our blood we have made signs
>To show the way—

JESTER:
>—which way to go!

AN OLD MARTYR (*simpering foolishly when all the others are silent*):
>Like bits of hail we felt the blows . . .
>I turned my head this way and that
>To catch them on each cheek,
>First the right one, then the left,
>Just like a clock:
>Tick-tock, tick-tock!

FOLK POET (*his head in his hands*):
>What the poor man has been through!

JESTER:
>But can you tell me what it's been for?

RECLUSE:
>Far and wide, all over the world,
>He sowed Redemption's holy seed
>And crowned and sanctified
>The Name of God.

JESTER:
>And God?
>What did *He* have in mind
>When He chose you for His people?
>Was that His punishment?
>Has He run out of miracles?
>Why doesn't He say: Stop!?

A VOICE FROM THE SYNAGOGUE:
>He spoke to Job

From the whirlwind!
O Man
Your life is a brief span,
Your time
A twinkling of the eye—
What makes you gird your loins and try
To question me and argufy?
Do you believe that you can read my signs?
Can you probe the Void's bottomless pit?
Where were you, Man,
When my great hand
Spanned the heavens over it?
Where were you, dwarf,
When I raised up mountains,
And fashioned the Earth,
And fenced the Sea,
And made the Land be
So wide and so long?

CHURCHBELLS (*interrupting angrily*):
Ding-dong! Ding-dong!

> (*The synagogue windows darken and fall silent. The shadows
> flee.* NOSON THE DRUNK *jumps to his feet. The* JESTER *falls
> flat on his face with his hands over his head to protect himself
> against the hammer blows of the bells.*)

STATUES ON THE CHURCH (*in a chorus*):
Bing-bang! Bing-bang!
They've had it coming for ever so long!
Revenge is sweet!
See how it sweeps
Down over their heads,
Stunning them,
Making them run!

> (SOMEONE *reappears from the house he dragged the* PROSTI-
> TUTE *into. The chorus of bells and statues fades. Little by lit-
> tle, the stunned apparitions return. The* JESTER *slowly lifts
> his head.*)

SOMEONE:
I heard the pandemonium,
And so I've come,
You sorrowful and fearful ones,

On the wings of love.
I have devoured the holy body of my dove!

VOICES:
Did you ever hear of
Such a thing?

SOMEONE:
I have drunk from the fountain of bliss,
From magic sparks of godliness
In eyes as black as night!
I have come on an eagle's flight;
The night and fog flee from my look . . .
I can call the sun back when it's set;
Make faded summers bloom again;
Plow boulders into flowerbeds
Till poppies glow and lilies flame
And roses gleam on barren plains;
Cause hill and valley to be drunk
With songs divine and magic scent . . .
I shall bring you wonderment!
    (*Suddenly inspired*)
Listen, east, west, north, and south:
Let the graves open their mouths!
Let the dead awake!
    (*In a superhuman voice*)
Arise! Arise!

STATUES ON THE CHURCH (*uneasily*):
We'll believe it when we see it with our eyes!

(*The* JESTER *puts the* NIGHT WATCHMAN'*s whistle to his
mouth and blows three times. A shofar sounds its calls:* teki'ah, teru'ah, teki'ah. *In midair, above the road leading out
of town, a cemetery emerges from the mist. Gravestones are
pushed aside. The dead crawl out of the ground.*)

RECLUSE (*coming out of the study house and staring at the cemetery*):
How soft
This gentle wind of God's
That carries me aloft
To the Valley of Dry Bones . . .
Though no one's to be seen,
I hear a beat of wings above,
And purer than a violin,

A voice that asks:
Can these bones live?
And boldly I reply:
O most
Great God,
Thou know'st,
For I do see Thy wonders every day . . .

JESTER (*jumping up*):
As well you may!
All things are possible
When what must be is my own will!
(*There is a commotion in the cemetery.*)

(*Curtain*)

ACT THREE

(*Curtain*)

NARRATOR:
"Once upon a time"—
That's all some need to hear and they believe it . . .
And so,
Among that portion of mankind
That is too weak or not quite bold enough
To shield itself from life or live it,
We find tormented souls
Who look for comfort to the world of myth,
In whose protective lap (how great the risk!)
They hide their heads.

Without bright stars, without the sun,
The eye thirsts for the images of dreams,
And the ear yearns
For olden days and cloudy climes—
For "Once upon a time" . . .
Once upon a time—

Life was exchanged for fantasy,
Which sows not, reaps not,
Bears no golden fruit,
But only raises, sick and shadowy,

Its pale blue sprouts
Full of sweet poison for the head and heart;
While deeper yet, out of a black abyss,
Stare enigmatic eyes, man's, beast's, or winking god's . . .
Ah, irresistible hasheesh!
Once—
But listen well
To what befell
Upon a time.

Picture a world where all is shattered,
Souls tortured to the point of madness,
Bodies flayed and flogged with poison snakes!
Overhead, at the highest zenith,
So faint that few can still have seen it,
Is a creature with hair gold-streaming
And eyes as bright as the brightest star.
A single word is written on its forehead:
"Truth!"
It pales, it fades,
It vanishes in mist . . .
And now, out of the abyss,
Rises its opposite—
A ponderously cloud-gray shape
On whose plutonic brow's inscribed
The words: "Have faith!"
Through the dark night
This legendary beast keeps watch,
And Death awakes!
Graves yawn wide
And from them crawl,
In snow-white robes and prayer shawls—
The dead! . . .
Without a sound, without a word,
They slip into the synagogue
To pray and chant,
And to lament
The queenly Shekhinah's banishment:
The dead! . . .
If you want to live, stranger,
Don't pray with them: it's mortal danger!
If they call you to the Torah,
Your wife's life with you is over;
Should your house have a male heir,

Teach him quick the mourner's prayer;
If you're a bachelor, or have no son—

> (*The scrim rises. The* NARRATOR *walks off, shouting angrily.*)

But I'm not done! I'm still not done!

> (*Night. The dead walk up the back street, heading into town from the cemetery. Unsteadily gripping the cemetery fence, since they have no gravestones of their own to support themselves with, are a police* INFORMER, *his tongue in his hand, and a* BUTCHER *who sold his unwitting customers non-kosher meat and now has the tripe of a cow around his neck. Others are still crawling from their graves, rubbing their eyes and stretching themselves. The* BRODY SINGERS *climb out of a common grave in tarred sacks, embarrassed to be without shrouds. On a knoll in the middle of the cemetery stands an* OLD MAN, *shading his eyes and looking about as if searching for a sign in heaven or on earth.*)

JESTER (*to gargoyle*):
Quick,
Your magic ring!
Here come the dead—
Show them your blood-red rays!
> (*To the apparitions*)

And you, who believe you're alive—
Disappear!
Beat it, scram, get out of here!
Back to your barracks!
When the dead
Come swarming from all corners,
Be prepared
For anything!

A WORKER:
He thinks we're easy to scare!
Doesn't he know we're Reds?

CULTURED JEWS:
Jews—they'll believe whatever they're told!

FROZEN WOMAN (*clinging to the warmth of the gargoyle's light*):
I'm so cold! I'm so cold!

> (*The workers, the cultured Jews, and the* FROZEN WOMAN *remain; all the other apparitions disappear.*)

SOMEONE (*unnerved*):
>> Here they come! They're almost here—
>> And they'll expect us to decide.
>> All that talk was a lot of hot air . . .
>> I feel so empty inside . . .
>>> (*He runs off up the church street.*)

OLD MAN (*calling out*):
>> What a terrible night!
>> Someone's playing magic tricks, all right.

>> (*The dead stand in a circle. The* JESTER *clambers quickly up the clock tower and tinkers for a long time with the hands of the clock. With a squeak, they begin to move. He starts to count the hours, the clock chiming them angrily after him. Between each count and each chime, the* RECLUSE *interrupts.*)

JESTER:
>> One! . . . Two! . . .

RECLUSE:
>> God is through!

JESTER (*impatiently*):
>> Three! . . . Four! . . .

RECLUSE:
>> He'll send no more—

JESTER (*losing patience completely and rushing ahead*):
>> Five! . . . Six! . . . Seven!

RECLUSE:
>> . . . miracles from heaven.

JESTER:
>> Eight!

RECLUSE:
>> He's shut His gate.

JESTER (*angrily*):
>> Nine! . . . Ten! . . . Eleven! . . . Twelve!
>>> (*Shouting down to the* RECLUSE)
>> Why don't you learn to help yourself?

>> (*All of the dead except for the* OLD MAN *head determinedly for the marketplace.*)

BUTCHER (*grabbing hold of the* INFORMER):
> Has the Messiah woken yet?
> (*Shaking him*)
> Answer me!

OLD MAN:
> The Messiah will wake by day,
> And now it's the black bottom of the night!
> Someone's playing with black magic!
> There's not a sign of Judgment Day
> Anywhere in heaven or on earth . . .
> Wait!
> (*Calling to the dead, who ignore him*)
> You can't escape
> The long arm of God!
> You're blind
> As the wind—
> And it's an ill wind that has sinned . . .

> (*He returns to his grave and pulls the gravestone back over himself. The other dead keep walking. The closer they come to the marketplace, the more they begin to remember snatches of prayers and psalms. Their memory soon fails them, however, and they break off in the middle.*)

A DEAD MAN:
> . . . *Ashrey yoyshvey veysekho . . . va'avorkho shimkho le'oylom vo'ed . . .*

A DEAD WOMAN (*as though chanting a prayer*):
> All I'm asking is a little crust of bread!

SECOND DEAD MAN (*to the melody of the Yom Kippur service*):
> *Vehakoy-ha-ni-im . . . ah ha ha . . . ah ha ha . . .*

DEAD BOY (*singing and skipping in time*):
> O Hanukkah, O Hanukkah . . .

FIRST DEAD MAN (*reaching the marketplace*):
> God help me if this isn't the old square!

DEAD WOMAN (*peering through a window*):
> My chickadees are sleeping there!
> (*Imploringly*)
> God keep them healthy and strong!

SECOND DEAD WOMAN:
> Look at her eyes! Is something wrong?

THIRD DEAD WOMAN (*turning pensively away from the window*):
> He didn't mourn her very long!

DEAD MAN (*stepping with anticipation into the synagogue*):
> We'll pray a bit . . . read from the Torah . . .
> What a pleasure it will be to say
> To God:
> *Oy vay!*

DEAD WOMAN:
> Who has the strength left to pray?
> Who has the strength left to cry?

SECOND DEAD MAN:
> Everything's gone from my mind . . .

THIRD DEAD MAN:
> Everything's scattered like sand . . .

OLD DEAD MAN (*fervently*):
> Don't forsake the shul!
> It belongs to us all . . .
> It's holy!

DEAD MEN AND WOMEN (*as though remembering something*):
> Holy! Holy! Holy!

JESTER:
> Hey, go slowly!

> (*Some of the dead halt and stare at him wonderingly, then approach him for a better look. Those who enter the gargoyle's magic circle lose all sense of direction and wander aimlessly about the marketplace. The* JESTER *calls out.*)

> Come get
> Your tefillin bags,
> Your sukkah poles,
> Your Torah bells!

TALMUD STUDENT (*entering the circle*):
> Well,
> At least I won't suffer through any more meals
> At my father-in-law's!
> A dead Talmudist needn't bother with eating . . .

JESTER:
> He just has a little problem with forgetting!

STUDENT:
> I can't deny that it's a—

OLD DEAD PEOPLE:
> — . . . can't even do a mitsvah any more!
> —Like giving food to the poor.
> —Or visiting the dying.
> —It's a crying shame!

JESTER:
> Then you still have tears to cry?

OLD MAN:
> Not a one!
> > (*He enters the circle.*)

FIRST DEAD PERSON (*examining self*):
> I can't recall
> If I'm a boy or a girl.
> I don't even remember my name.

SECOND DEAD PERSON:
> What does your tombstone say?

FIRST DEAD PERSON:
> The letters are all worn away.
> > (*Steps into the circle with one foot*)
> Something's burning my soles—
> It's like standing on hot coals!

> > (*Unable to free the foot, he/she leaves it there and hops off to the synagogue, leaving the* SECOND DEAD PERSON *bewilderedly behind.*)

SECOND DEAD PERSON (*after pausing to think*):
> There's one thing I never understood.
> The governor—
> What made him have me flogged?
> I didn't do a thing, I swear to you!

THIRD DEAD PERSON (*laughing*):
> The things a dead man thinks he has to know!
> It was the fashion . . .
> He was a bastard . . .
> He beat me, my wife, and my daughters, too,
> Until we were all black-and-blue.

FOURTH DEAD PERSON (*desperately*):
>How long does a dead man live? I'm asking you!

FIFTH DEAD PERSON (*to the* JESTER):
>You know, right over there I had a tavern.
>I had a daughter, too,
>Whom I cared for more than anything.
>Once, when I was laid up with some complaint or other,
>They kidnapped her and made a Christian of her . . .

JESTER:
>Who did?

FIFTH DEAD PERSON:
>The priest.

JESTER:
>When?

FIFTH DEAD PERSON:
>It happened on a Monday,
>In 1841.
>The Torah reading was *Va'eskhonon.*

DEAD WOMAN (*begging from person to person*):
>Can you spare me a diaper for my dead son?
>When I died they left him in my womb.
>Goodness knows what will become of him
>Without a scrap to cover him!
>Just a little diaper—
>Has anyone a diaper for my son?

ANGRY DEAD POOR FOLK:
>—You'd think they cheated us enough when we were
>   living!
>—Look at the shrouds that we've been given!
>—They gave us smaller graves than they ought to!
>—When our corpses were washed they scrimped on water!

DEAD WOMEN:
>—I wasn't given a bridal veil!
>—Or a manicure for my fingernails!
>—They don't treat you like that when you're famous!

DEAD MAN:
>Before I even could catch my breath,

Who comes along but the Angel of Death
And wants to know what my name is!

DEAD MEN AND WOMEN (*running around*):
Where's the president of the congregation?
We should bash his rotten face in!
(*They run toward the gargoyle.*)

JESTER (*to a dead man who stays behind*):
Don't you want to join them?

STAY-BEHIND:
No, I don't.
(*Boastfully*)
I went through life with so little to eat
That I almost forgot what to do with my teeth—
But I never made any trouble.
You should have seen the funeral I got!
The president himself made sure they gave me double
And washed me not with one egg yolk, but two!
And little forks to clean each nail—
They did everything down to the last detail,
I'm telling you!

DEAD GIRLS:
Yoo-hoo! Yoo-hoo!
Our mama's not home.
Before the night's through
Let's play knucklebones!
(*They look for, and find, pebbles to play with.*)
—Here's a stone!
—Here's another!

AN ELDERLY WOMAN:
Come one, come all, and bring each other!
Let's have a wedding!

GIRLS:
—Who will the bride be?
—Sheyndele!
—And who'll be the groom?
—Our handsome Noson'l, that's who!

NOSON THE DRUNK (*getting to his feet*):
Do they mean me . . .
And *Sheyndele*?

A GIRL (*singing a folksong*):

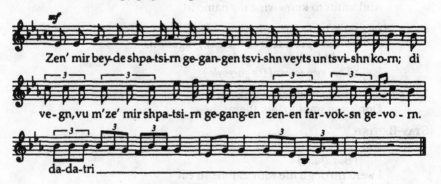

Ah, the day we both went walking
Through the wheat and through the corn!
Ah, the path where we stood talking—
Now with grass it's overgrown!

LITTLE CHILDREN (*chanting*):

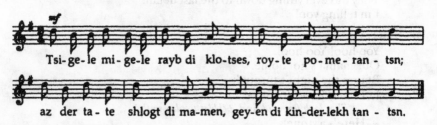

Tsigele, migele, pick up sticks,
What will be your fancy?
When papa's giving mama licks
The children will go dancing!

JESTER:

Dancing? Is that the ticket?
        (*To the musicians*)
Hey, old friends, come and be quick!
The children want some dancing
And won't take no for an answer!
Fiddle, trumpet, drums, and bass:
Let's have a ball right in this place!
        (*The musicians tune up*)

CHILDREN (*imitating the instruments*):
—El-leh pel-leh!
Pel-leh mel-leh!
—Boom-tsik boom-tsik,
Bim-bam-bo!

MUSICIANS:
We're so blotto
We can't stand.
Who'll keep time
And lead the band?

FROZEN WOMAN:
Come on, let's dance! I need something to warm up to!

MUSICIANS:
Not unless there's a conductor!

NOSON THE DRUNK:
All right, all right, I'll conduct.
No matter what happens, it's always my luck!

(*He runs over to the gargoyle, snatches the horn from its fore-head, and uses it as a baton. The musicians strike up a polka. Three circles of dancers form: one of children, one of women, and eventually, one of men. Meanwhile, the* BRIDE *arrives beneath a black canopy held by four beadles, each also holding a still-smoking havdalah candle. The dancers break off abruptly and make commiserating sounds. The polka turns into the prayer for the dead, the* el moley rakhamim. *The* BRIDE *halts. The beadles don't notice and walk on ahead with the canopy.*)

BRIDE:
Please save your sympathy
And don't feel bad for me,
Because I didn't even want the man:
He scared me, like a bug!
If ever I cared for anyone,
It was for a boy I can't forget,
Who was as bright as gold.
I wasn't sure if he really saw me—
But soon Death came,
So kind and white,
And solved the problem for me . . .
(*Looking around*)

Where is my boy,
My golden boy?
Good people, if you meet him,
Tell him I still love him!
You'll know him by his voice—
It's like the clearest, dearest bell.
Oh, I could kiss each darling curl,
Each little bone,
Each eye that shone
As gentle as a lamb!
Each look of his was like a magic charm.
Tell him, tell him that Sheyndele . . .

NOSON THE DRUNK (*throwing away his baton and falling on her*):
They don't have to! I already know!

BRIDE:
Oh!
You're so old!
So . . .
Hot!

NOSON THE DRUNK:
And you're so cold.

BRIDE:
You're all in a sweat!

NOSON THE DRUNK:
Your breath is like frost.
(*He notices a hole in her cheek and recoils in fright.*)
What's that you've got in your cheek?

BRIDE:
I thought you knew:
A little worm ate its way through.
But why are you so red?

NOSON THE DRUNK:
I drink too much . . . from loneliness . . . and need . . .

BRIDE:
If you don't stop, you'll soon turn black!

NOSON THE DRUNK (*burying his face in her breast*):
Oh, hug me! Hug me back!
(*They stand there without a word.*)

VOICE FROM THE SYNAGOGUE (*chanting to High Holiday melody*):
>   Will the groom Noson
>   Step up to the Torah
>>   (NOSON *faints and slips from the* BRIDE'*s arms.*)

BRIDE:
>   Oh, my God!
>   I couldn't stop him, he just keeled over . . .
>>   (*The* RECLUSE *runs to fetch a doctor.*)

THE DEAD (*nervously*):
>   What's happening?

JESTER:
>   Nothing you haven't already seen!

THE DEAD:
>   What a terrible night . . .
>   Stand back!
>   Make room!

>>   (*A path is cleared for the doctor, along which an invisible soul
>>   makes its way.*)

INVISIBLE SOUL:

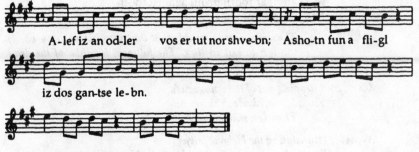

A-lef iz an od-ler   vos er tut nor shve-bn;   A sho-tn fun a fli-gl

iz dos gan-tse le-bn.

>   "A" is for Apple,
>   So juicy and red;
>   Don't wait to eat it—
>   By then you'll be dead.
>   "B" is for Baby,
>   Its life still ahead;
>   But death is the trial—

JESTER:
>   Ha ha ha!

INVISIBLE SOUL:
> . . . So try to forget!

JESTER:
> Ha ha ha ha ha!
> (*A wooden laughter runs through the dead in the market-place.*)

(*Curtain*)

ACT FOUR

(*Curtain*)

NARRATOR:
> Nothing is worse
> Than the laughter of the dead.
> It sounds like wood,
> Like a bridge that has cracked
> When the last rope has snapped
> And fallen into the abyss.
> And in this wooden shriek,
> You can hear tooth grind against tooth
> And every bone creak . . .

> (*The scrim rises so quickly that the angry* NARRATOR *barely manages to exit in time. The fatigued laughter of the dead starts turning into sobs.*)

CANTOR (*stepping out of the synagogue*):
> Yisgadal veyiskadash shmey rabo . . .
> (*There is a sudden hush.*)

WOMEN (*translating the Hebrew prayer*):
> Exalted and sanctified is His great Name . . .

ADULTERESS (*running out through a gate, behind which she has been hiding*):
> It's him!
> He's come!

THE DEAD IN THE MARKETPLACE (*sounding a lookout's whistle*):
> Tweeee-wheeeeet!

ADULTERESS (*throwing herself at the* CANTOR's *knees*):
> The night is dark,

My heart pounds hard . . .
Come away!
I have such faith in you.
My husband's asleep,
My child is too—
Let's fly from here!
Where is the wagon?
Where is the horse?

CANTOR:

Deep in the earth, my dear.
Put out the fire
And forget me. I am dead.
        (*Glancing heavenward*)
And may He too forget!

        (*They depart, the* CANTOR *rejoining the other dead, the*
        woman retiring behind the gate.)

OLD MAID (*stepping forward*):

What?
How gullible can you get?
Forget what—
The years I sat home in the dark
Playing the game they call "Wait"?
"Wait, your true love will turn up."
Well, that's all a big load of crap!
        (*Shouting at the sky*)
I can't stand it any more!
        (*She walks back to the marketplace.*)
Right outside my front door
Life went rollicking by
In a gale of desire,
And I—
I lay in a ditch like a worm!
I might as well have been tone-deaf and color-blind,
The way I lived, day after day,
Night after night, in a cloud of gray!
Not a laugh, not a smile, not a moment of fun,
Not a single warm hand on the back of my neck . . .
I never heard a good word,
Never met a stranger's eyes or looked back . . .
I bit my nails,
And gritted my teeth,
And ate out my heart that was pining away . . .

Well, now I say:
No!
No! No! No! No! No!
You can take your "Be a good girl" and stow it—
You've already used it to cut my throat!
Who'll pay me back?
I want to scream, I want to curse,
Hand me a stone and I'll—

> (*She breaks off, catching sight of the* BRODY SINGERS, *who enter in their tarred sacks.*)

FRIGHTENED VOICES:

—Who are you? What's that you've got on you?
—Tell us about the troubles you've gone through!

> (*The music changes to the High Holiday Prayer* Odom lehevel domoh, *"Man is but vanity."*)

BRODY SINGERS:

We are the singers, the singers of Brod,
And we have been punished, punished by God!
We traveled through heat and we traveled through frost,
Till we came down with plague and we gave up the ghost;
The pallbearers came without waiting a minute,
Each brought a tarred sack and put each of us in it;
With pitchforks of iron, we still were alive,
They prodded and poked us right into the grave.
And now we are asking, we're asking of God:
Why did He punish the singers of Brod?

MORE FRIGHTENED VOICES:

—Better not ask! You don't want to know!
—Better to stick to the straight and narrow!
—Better to dance!
  (*Excitedly*)
—Go ahead, dance!
—Let's see a fire in your pants!
—Let's see a gleam in your dead eyes!
—Show us you've got a spark of life!
—Shake a leg there, prance!
—Dance! Dance! Dance!
—Give it all you've got!
—Dance till you bust a gut!
—Kick up your heels!
—Pretend you're on wheels!

JESTER:

> Feel what you've never let yourselves feel!
> Live what you've never lived before!

> (*They dance apathetically. The music limps along. Still, two circles form to the right and left, one for men and one for women. They keep stubbornly revolving while philosophers, a* KABBALIST, *and some Hasidim walk up and down between them.*)

FIRST PHILOSOPHER:

> Life, death—
> I don't know what they're for . . .

SECOND PHILOSOPHER:

> What a nit you are!
> There are some things you just have to accept.

FIRST PHILOSOPHER:

> You mean the human intellect—

SECOND PHILOSOPHER:

> . . . is useless? Let it rot!

FIRST PHILOSOPHER:

> But that is not . . .
>> (*Growing agitated*)
> What is Truth
> If all's just semiotics?
> How completely idiotic
> It is to hold
> That all we know of anything
> Is what it's called!

THIRD PHILOSOPHER (*approaching them*):

> That isn't so at all!
> You can't deny that suffering is real.

SECOND PHILOSOPHER:

> It's simply a modality
> Of an unknowable reality.

FIRST PHILOSOPHER (*regretfully*):

> Well, anyway,
> Philosophy has had its ups and downs . . .

KABBALIST (*coming over*):

> There are mystical ciphers and mystical sums!
> Once—

FOURTH PHILOSOPHER:
>Just look at those bones
>All creaking away
>To a number that dead musicians play!
>Some seem quite cheeky and bold.

FIRST PHILOSOPHER:
>At least they won't catch cold!

KABBALIST:
>To get back to what—
>>(*A group of four Hasidim enters.*)

FIRST HASID (*singing soulfully*):
>My mama told me
>To pick apples from a tree . . .
>But a Jew is too small,
>And a tree is too tall,
>And I never picked
>Any apples at all.

FIRST PHILOSOPHER:
>Semiotics!
>Idiotic!

SECOND PHILOSOPHER:
>According to Ecclesiastes,
>Life is foolish, vain, and nasty!

SECOND HASID:
>If you ask me,
>Dancing's better than talking.

>>(*The Hasidim form a circle with their hands on each other's shoulders and begin to whirl around, breaking into song. The dancing circles of men and women sing along with them.*)

FIRST HASID:
>Dancing is a mighty thing!
>You don't have to think!
>You don't have to know!
>Just step out of your body and leave it below!

CIRCLE OF HASIDIM (*clapping their hands*):
>Bom-bom!

CIRCLES OF DEAD MEN AND WOMEN (*stamping their feet*):
>Clomp-clomp!

SECOND HASID:
>Dancing is a mighty thing,
>It has every advantage!
>I ask no questions when I dance,
>Because right off I'm in a trance . . .

DANCING CIRCLES:
>Bom-bom!
>Clomp-clomp!

THIRD HASID:
>Dancing is a mighty thing!
>Trust in God and kick your feet!
>Once you get into the spirit,
>All your sins become good deeds . . .

CIRCLES OF DANCERS:
>Bom-bom!
>Clomp-clomp!

FOURTH HASID:
>Dancing is a mighty thing!
>Ask no questions! Never doubt!
>Let philosophy debate
>What everything is all about!
>When we whirl
>And twirl
>And swirl,
>We only know the dance goes well . . .

PHILOSOPHERS (*joining the circle of Hasidim*):
>—Let philosophy debate?
>   We can tell you what it thinks!
>—Life is a Sphinx!
>—Death is a Sphinx!
>—Meanwhile, dance
>   And laugh all you can . . .

CIRCLES OF DANCERS:
>Bom-bom!
>Clomp-clomp!

CULTURED JEWS (*coming over*):
>—I say, did you hear that man?
>—He could make a pig's foot kosher!
>—Go ahead, then, faster, faster!

—Hippity-hop! There's no way to stop
Once you take the first step down the slippery slope!

(*The circle of Hasidim whirls away from them and keeps dancing. The cultured Jews remain behind, at a loss. Soon they
drift off.*)

JESTER (*staring at the dancers*):
They're dancing! They really are!
They feel!
Their dead faces almost look alive.
There is desire, even lust, in those dead eyes.
They hop about with so much zeal,
Their resurrection seems quite real!
(*Wistfully*)
If only the music were a bit more . . . musical,
And the ladies all wore flowers in their hair,
And scented it with rose oil, letting it flow free . . .
I can see it shining, shimmering:
Ah, every glance would be love's arrow, then!
Their marble breasts, décolleté,
Would breathe as at the balls of noblemen . . .

(*Dead figures peer out the windows of the synagogue. The*
JESTER *beckons to one of them, a woman.*)

WOMAN (*rousing herself*):
Hey, girls,
Let's make our shrouds shawls
And dance up a storm!

DEAD MAN IN SYNAGOGUE WINDOW (*shouting at her*):
You can't!
It's not allowed.

WOMAN:
Says who?

GROUP OF WOMEN (*dancing with shawls and laughing brazenly*):
Says you!
We'll do what we want!

SECOND WOMAN (*defiantly*):
Off with your bonnets!
Let down your hair!
(*To the man in the window*)
We don't give a damn for your can's and your can't's!

CIRCLE OF WOMEN:
>We can! We can!
>We don't give a damn!

THIRD WOMAN:
>Go call the men,
>It'll make it more fun!
>Tell them to come over, won't you?
>To hell with all their do's and don't do's!

BOTH CIRCLES (*now joined together*):
>We can! We can!
>We don't give a damn!

>>(*The circle begins to move faster. Several of the dead slip be-hind the musicians and play along with them in pantomime. The* BRODY SINGERS *join in too, swelling the chorus.*)

STONE STATUES ON CHURCH (*excited and aroused*):
>—Lovely women, darling girls,
>>We're smitten by a glance from you!
>—Snow-white dresses, dark-brown curls,
>>Won't you let us dance with you?
>—Cheek to cheek and close together—

JESTER (*overhearing them*):
>Come on down and join us, brother!
>In joy and sorrow,
>Be our guests—
>Everyone's equal
>Since everyone's dead!
>It's our night,
>There's no one beside us . . .
>>(*The statues obey him, climb down, and head for the dancers.*)
>Hey, open the circle,
>And let them inside it!
>They're two of our leading citizens—
>Tonight there are no differences!
>Mix and mingle,
>Hug and kiss . . .
>Ha ha ha,
>What a night this is!

STATUE OF BISHOP:
>Dead God!
>By the old monster's light,

This clown has bested You tonight . . .
It's too much for me to handle—
Ah, the shame of it, the scandal!

> (*He turns his face aside. The dance grows even faster. The en-
> gaged couple comes down the synagogue street, arms around
> each other.*)

FIANCÉE:

This must be our wedding night—
The band's already playing!

FIANCÉ:

And look at all the lovely guests—
Come and dance, my darling!

FIANCÉE:

Soon the men will bring the poles
For our canopy.
I'm so happy I feel weak—
Oh, hold me, hold me, hold me!

FIANCÉ:

Heart to heart and breast to breast,
I hold you tight against my chest!

BOTH TOGETHER:

Heart to heart and breast to breast—

STATUE OF KNIGHT (*cutting in*):

Let's see who can dance the best!
> (*He whirls the girl away.*)

DEAD WOMAN (*to the bewildered* FIANCÉ):

Come here, young fellow, dance with me:
My name is Queenie, you be my king!
> (*She tries to get him to dance.*)
Oh, come on, you silly thing!
> (*She grabs him and they dance.*)
Step lively, now!

FROZEN WOMAN (*running over to the* RECLUSE, *who is wandering
    about*):

Hey, sweetheart saint,
Let's take a spin!
My, what clammy hands you've got!
I've got hellfire in my gut
And snakes that hiss inside my brain,

But I'm glad I caught your eye,
Because I need a little warmth from somebody . . .

> (*The morning star suddenly appears in the sky. The* FROZEN
> WOMAN *lets go of the* RECLUSE. *The music stops. The
> dancers separate.*)

ANXIOUS VOICES:
   —Oy, it's the morning star!
   —The night is through!

DEAD MAN'S VOICE FROM THE SYNAGOGUE:
   I told you so!

ANXIOUS VOICES:
   It's getting light out!

JESTER (*insistently*):
   Dance the night out! Dance!
      (*The dead struggle to obey him. There is a tumult.*)
   Why be so afraid
   Just because the sky is turning gray?
   Wash your face with morning dew,
   Let the rising sun dry you,
   And go on dancing your great dance
   Into the day!

VOICE FROM SYNAGOGUE:
   You mean we may?

JESTER:
   It's up to you!
   Don't ask so many questions . . .
   Couples, don't split up!

THE DEAD:
   It's up to us—
   But are we up to it?

JESTER (*angrily*):
   Haven't you lain in the ground long enough?
   Don't you miss life enough to want more?
   If your graves are not filled in
   And your souls are not restored
   To you this minute,
   Stand up and fight!
      (*Egging them on*)

> If only you want to—
> And I see by the light
> In your eyes that you do—
> You could have blood stronger than steel!
> Why stay bare bones?
> Life must be taken by force,
> And if you don't have the strength,
> Pluck it from the cedar and the oak—
> Suck it from the juices of the grass—
> Steal it from the fire of the sun!
> Take from the lilies their white,
> From the roses—their red . . .

THE DEAD (*dispiritedly*):
> But we are dead!

JESTER:
> You are misled
> By your own false notions!
> Whatever you believe in—that alone exists.
> Whatever you deny dissolves in mist.
> Say no to death,
> Believe in life
> With all your might and main—
> And you'll remain.
> No one can move you from this place!

THE DEAD:
> We will remain!

JESTER:
> Swear it to me!

THE DEAD:
> We swear!

JESTER:
> Do you deny death?

THE DEAD:
> With every bit of strength
> That we have left!

JESTER:
> Then it is gone,
> Destroyed,
> Made null and void.
> From this day on death is no more!

THE DEAD:
>   No more!

TIN ROOSTER (*from the roof of the synagogue*):
>   Cock-a-doodle-doo!

THE DEAD (*scattering in panic*):
>   —I can't see!
>   —I can't hear!

JESTER (*to the rooster*):
>   You piece of old tin!
>   (*The rooster flaps its wings.*)

THE DEAD (*frightened*):
>   Its wings are whipping up a wind—

JESTER:
>   A tin rooster!

THE DEAD:
>   . . . that lashes,
>   And slashes,
>   And drives us ahead of it . . .

>   (*The dead in the synagogue come calmly out and begin to head back for the cemetery. The dead in the marketplace start to follow them.*)

JESTER (*with his last strength*):
>   Wait!
>   If it's too strong for you, hang on to the walls!
>   Grab each other's hands and hold them tight!
>   (*Some do as he says. To the rooster*)
>   Just a minute, you tin degenerate!
>   There's a ladder in the entrance of the synagogue—
>   You started up with me,
>   And now I'm coming up to you
>   In order to teach you a thing or two!
>   The Battle of Tonight is just beginning.
>   I'll beat the daylights out of you,
>   I'll tear you wing from wing and wring
>   Your scrawny neck and fling
>   You down
>   Into the garbage on the ground!
>   You've crowed your last crow, mister!
>   (*To the dead left in the marketplace*)

Who of you's still with me?
    (*No one answers.*)
Hey, what's happened to you all,
You Lightspreaders-and-Understanders,
You Messianic-Door-Bangers,
You Head-Against-the-Wall-Bashers,
You Futuristic-Flycatchers?
    (*No one answers.*)
Aren't there at least a few old-timers,
Roofers, sweeps, or fearless climbers,
Who'll follow me up there?
    (*He points to the roof. One or two of the dead step forward.*)

BLIND TYPESETTER (*restraining him*):
    It's not the revolution, friend. Who cares?

JESTER:
    No?
    (*No one answers.*)
    Then I'd better go.
    Alone.
    It's best that way:
    Alone.

    (*The dead remain in a state of confusion. The* RECLUSE *goes to the synagogue and waits for the* JESTER *there.*)

    (*Curtain*)

EPILOGUE

    (*Curtain*)

NARRATOR (*entering and about to speak when he hears voices behind the scrim. Walking over, he peers through an opening in it.*)
    How they weep, how they mourn,
    The wind-borne dead!
    No new life was granted them.
    Listen.

    (*Voices can be heard from behind the scrim, receding into the distance.*)

FIRST VOICE:
    There once was someone who went off

And left his image in a pool,
Shimmering in water—
Until the bucket caught it . . .

SECOND VOICE:
When the earthen jug was cracked,
Out the wine cascaded.
A single drop alone was left—
And that evaporated . . .

THIRD VOICE:
There was a song
That echoed long,
Till one last sound
Was left behind.
It hummed once more
And fell
Dead on the ground . . .

FOURTH VOICE:
After the sun has set,
A misty wake that's made
By its reflection reddens in the west—
And fades . . .

ALL FOUR VOICES TOGETHER:
There were dreams . . .
There was sin . . .
There was a wind
That carried them away
Like straw
Or spray . . .

NARRATOR:
How piteous!
(*He puts his ear to the scrim.*)
How hideous!

VOICES OF THE MARKETPLACE DEAD:
An illusion, that's all it ever was.
Now His long arm has overtaken us,
And we're to blame . . .

NARRATOR:
They're at the graveyard gate . . . they're entering . . .

MOURNFUL VOICES OF DEAD MEN:
With our heads bare . . .

VOICES OF DEAD WOMEN:
> . . . and unbraided hair . . .

MEN AND WOMEN TOGETHER:
> . . . we step into the grave.

CHORUS OF SYNAGOGUE DEAD:
> The night begins to fade!
> We, Thy humble slaves,
> Await Thy sign tonight,
> As every night.
> Do as Thou seest fit!

NARRATOR:
> They're standing by their graves.

SYNAGOGUE DEAD:
> And when the earth has covered us again,
> Thy will be done!
> We shall wait and be still
> Until Thou wakest us.
> Thy will be done!

NARRATOR:
> Now I see children.
> (*He turns away.*)
> I can't look . . .

CHORUS OF GIRLS:
> Goodbye, goodbye,
> You sweet blue eyes,
> You little flower heads,
> Goodbye . . .

CHORUS OF BOYS:
> And you, sweet pears and peaches,
> On the sweet little branches
> Of the sweet little trees . . .

BOYS AND GIRLS TOGETHER:
> Goodbye, goodbye,
> You birds who fly
> In the sweet blue air
> Of the sweet little sky!

SYNAGOGUE DEAD:
> And may our sins

Be wiped away
Just like a cloud
On a summer's day!

> (*The scrim rises, revealing the cemetery. The dead stand by their open graves. The* OLD MAN *is once again on the knoll in the middle of the graveyard.*)

THE DEAD:
We do renounce
All things!

OLD MAN:
Into the ground!

> (*The dead descend. The cemetery is cloaked in mist again.*)

NIGHT WATCHMAN (*waking and fumbling uneasily for his whistle*):
Damn!
What did I do with that whistle of mine?

> (*The* JESTER *emerges from the synagogue, his head in a bloodstained bandage. In one hand he holds the gavel used by the* BEADLE *for waking Jews for the morning prayer; in the other the whistle, which he tosses to the* NIGHT WATCHMAN. *The* NIGHT WATCHMAN *backs away with it and exits.*)

JESTER (*to the* RECLUSE, *penitently*):
I really overdid it this time—
Fell flat on my face, I did!
> (*He sees the musicians and is terrified.*)
Be gone! Back to your home of slime!
I do renounce all things!
> (*The musicians disappear. He turns to the gargoyle.*)
Turn yourself off, you wild thing!
> (*Pointing up at the sky*)
He's awake, don't you see?
Shut your eyes and mouth and listen to me!
> (*The gargoyle does as it is told. The* JESTER *turns to the stone statues, which are stumbling about in the street.*)
Back into your niches!
Stick to your own business!
Up you go, turn back to stone!
Forget all that you've heard, all that you've seen:
Last night was perfectly routine.
> (*They do as he bids them and he turns to the rooster.*)

You were right,
And your verdict was just!
O bird,
You are Symbol
And Word.
My sin is great;
I won't repeat it.
I'll lay down my life for you if you need it!
I'll wake the Jews for prayer from now on . . .

> (*He knocks with the gavel on a gate.*)

One . . . two . . .
That'll do.

> (*He walks along, knocking on gates.*)

Soon they'll all know we had a death last night.

FIANCÉE (*wandering disheveled into the marketplace*):
    And what about me? What am I supposed to do?

> (*When no one answers her, she disappears down the church street.*)

NARRATOR (*following her with his eyes*):
    I always knew it wouldn't last between those two!

> (*The* RECLUSE *and the* WANDERER *enter the marketplace from opposite ends and slowly converge without noticing each other.*)

RECLUSE:
    Vanity of vanities,
    All is in vain!

WANDERER:
    On the horizon's
    Eastern rim
    A secret hand is fashioning—

RECLUSE:
    The chain runs round,
    Link after link . . .

WANDERER:
    —bright beams of light,
    Spinning mist out of the night,
    Weaving a new day . . .

RECLUSE:
    And there was night and there was day . . .

Who but a fool could ever say
That he has lived to see new things?

WANDERER:
And in the heart's interior,
A secret hand is fashioning . . .
New music's born,
New hopes are spun . . .
O weave yourself, Desire, weave!

RECLUSE:
All's vanity . . .
(*Bumping into the* WANDERER)
Live
All you can,
Wander
All you want:
You'll see nothing new
Beneath the sun!
What was is what will be.

WANDERER (*startled*):
And yet something renews itself in me!
Something draws me out
And drives me on,
Away,
Away . . .
But to what end?

NARRATOR (*firmly*):
That isn't in the play!

DIRECTOR (*appearing in the wings*):
Watch out for the curtain!
(*The* WANDERER *and the* RECLUSE *step quickly back. The
scrim begins to drop.*)

WANDERER (*clutching the* RECLUSE):
You don't know?

RECLUSE:
No!
(*The scrim descends all the way.*)

JESTER (*from behind the scrim*):
Jews,
Go

To shul!
Jews, go—

> (*A blast of the factory whistle drowns out everyone and everything.*)

(*Curtain*)

(*translated by Hillel Halkin*)

▲

Afterword

Afterword by Hillel Halkin

▼

Every translation, if it is any challenge at all, has a dominant problem. Even before I began to work on *A Night in the Old Marketplace*, I could see that this was going to be the rhyme. If I could cope with that, the rest would take care of itself. If not, nothing else would help.

Of course, being entirely serendipitous, a matter of chance combinations of words that occur in only one language, rhyme is always a vexation for verse translators. There tend to be two schools in regard to it, one holding that it is a hopeless task that should not be attempted and the other that it is a hopeless task that must be attempted. My own sympathies, perhaps because I have not translated a great deal of poetry in my life, are with the second school, but even if they weren't, there would have been no choice but to try to rhyme *A Night in the Old Marketplace* anyway. The rhyme in it is simply too important to leave out. It is the play's heartbeat, the force that drives it on and links its parts in one flow.

This is especially true of the many rhymes that pass in it from character to character. Take, for example, the opening of Act One, which begins with a voice chanting in the study house ". . . If she's a *mukas ets*, the rabbis think . . ." and another shouting in the tavern "Drink, you bastard, drink!" (In the original text these two lines are, *Haney miley—a mukas ets* and *Trink—podlyets!*) Here and in the lines that follow, the rhyme tells us immediately, long before we have articulated this perception as a thought, that the many voices of the play, however opposed, belong to a single identity of contradictions. We can call this identity the dream of the sleeping wanderer, or the collective self of the shtetl, or the Jewish historical subconscious, or anything else that we please, but its existence is already impressed on us by the tense coupling of tavern and study house in the very first rhyme of the act.

What is also viscerally felt by us before we are consciously aware of it as readers or spectators is that the play's rhymes set the play's pace. They are a form of unwritten stage direction that almost always means "Be quick!" How is it, for instance, that in the same opening section of Act One, we know from reading the text that the written stage direction "The noise dies down a bit. The circle of girls comes to life" permits a pause in the actors' speech, while the one a few lines further down, "[Second girl] pointing to the couple holding hands," does not? The answer is that the lines before and after the first instruction do not rhyme, while those before and after the second do. A rhyme is an echo: if one rhyme word no longer still sounds in our ear when we hear the other, the rhyme is lost. This dictates that nearly all of *A Night in the Old Marketplace* must be performed without stopping for breath. The rhymes that leap the gap from speaker to speaker whip the play on like a brushfire.

In this respect, those rhymes that are purely internal to a single character's speech are less important. One cannot dispense with them—try imagining a brushfire in which all that is burning is the tips of the bushes—but one can settle for less. Consider the wedding jester's opening lines in Act One:

What was it I was about to say?
It was important, that's all I remember . . .
I've spent too many days
In that old ruin talking to the spiders.
Why, it's right on the tip of my tongue—
If only I could think for a minute.
That ruin has the weirdest shadows in it,
All kinds of holy spooks . . .
I think I hear them cry and try to speak.
They put the bats on edge and rile the crickets,
And here—this study house, those children . . .
Those women on the balcony up there . . .
That bar . . .

The original Yiddish here is:

S'iz mir epes arop fun zinen . . .
Kh'hob epes a vikhtik vort fargesn . . .
Tsu lang in khurve gezesn

Tsvishn di shpinen . . .
Un kh'volt mir dermant, kh'volt es gefinen . . .
A rege shtil un s'volt mir gerotn.
Iz ful de khurve mit alte shotn,
Epes heylike alerley . . .
Epes veynen zey, epes zogn zey . . .
Un s'tshepet zikh di feldermoyz,
Un es shtert di gril . . .
Un do—di kinder, di kloyz . . .
Di vayber oyfn ganik iber der leng . . .
Un di shenk . . .

Like most of the longer speeches in *A Night in the Old Marketplace*, the Jester's lines are built on rhyming couplets, the actual rhyme scheme being *ABBAACCDDEFEGG*. Nearly all these rhymes are full ones. In the English, on the other hand, I for the most part made do (as I did throughout the play) with half-rhymes ("say/days"), quarter-rhymes ("remember/spiders"), consonances ("spooks/speak"), and assonances ("crickets/children"), and my couplets came out differently from Peretz's: *ABABCDDEEFFGG*. Moreover, to achieve even this much I sometimes had to rephrase the Yiddish. In the latter, for instance, the Jester's opening line is not a question, but a statement that means literally, "Something has slipped my mind" rather than "What was it I was about to say?" which I introduced to rhyme "say" with "days."

When it came to inter-characters' rhymes, which had to be more forceful, I was prepared to take greater liberties. An example is in the passage further on in the act where Noson the Drunk staggers out of the tavern while the Folk Poet is declaiming inside. My translation goes:

FOLK POET:
   Raise high your glasses.
   Toast the new morn:
   It's now or never—
   Take life by storm!
NOSON THE DRUNK:
   Before death takes you without warn—
      (*He staggers and falls.*)
   —ing . . .

What Noson actually says is *S'iz farn toyt keyn mentsh bashitst*, "No man is protected against death," and he falls after he has finished speaking, not before. But *bashitst* rhymes perfectly with the last two lines of the Folk Poet (*Ven az nisht itst? Dos lebn farblitst!*) and it was vital to do as well with "morn" and "storm." I do not think that my little trick with "warning" did any harm. In fact, it adds a nice touch: Noson lurches out of the tavern, croaks "Before death takes you without warn—," is forced to give the rhyming syllable an exaggerated emphasis because of the involuntary expulsion of his breath as he slips and falls, and weakly groans the final "—ing" as he lies sprawled on the ground. Visualized on stage, it works.

I must confess that when I first read *A Night in the Old Marketplace*, it did not seem to me a stage play at all. I thought it was a book play, as purely poetic a drama as Shelley's *The Cenci* or Goethe's *Faust*. And because its poetry qua poetry did not strike me as outstanding, my initial opinion of it was not high. It was not until I began work on it that I realized how wrong I was. This realization came to me because I soon discovered that the only way to translate *A Night in the Old Marketplace* was to act it in my head. Before long my ultimate criterion for success became the question, "Can this line as I have translated it be easily and credibly said by an actor?" and the more I acted the play, the more I saw how gloriously actable it was. It was not just another stage play, it was one of the most extraordinary stage plays I had ever come across, and the fact that it had almost no history of being staged did not weaken my faith in this judgment. On the contrary, it is because *A Night in the Old Marketplace* is so extraordinary that it seems so unstageable and is indeed so difficult to stage.

Consider some of its difficulties. It has close to one hundred roles, the exact number depending on the size of the many little groups that drift in and out of it (the heder boys, the circle of girls, the philosophers, the Hasidim, etc.), so that even if the actors double or triple up in some roles, a cast of at least fifty would be needed for a full performance. It requires an enormous stage with a large and expensive set that must in part be solidly three-dimensional, since much of it—the house with the balcony, the clock tower on the church, the town hall, the synagogue—is not only entered and exited, but climbed and stood on as well. It calls for complex stage, electrical, and sound effects: streetlamps that can be lit, a statue with blinking lights, a well with a hidden catapult, churchbells whose chimes rhyme with words, moveable tombstones big enough for actors to crouch inside, a remote-control-operated mechanical rooster, etc. And it needs a director, assisted by a composer, choreographer, and choirmaster, with the ingenuity of Steven Spielberg and the organizational talents of Barnum and Bailey, since it has even more than three rings. There are moments in *A Night in the Old Market-place* when the stage is occupied by dozens of actors, often divided into four or five groups, who are singing, dancing, chanting, playing music, speaking, and miming all at once. It is little wonder that it has hardly ever been produced, and by all reports done badly when it was. How many Yiddish theaters had the means to do it at all, let alone well?

I do not know whether, in his conception of *A Night in the Old Marketplace*, Peretz was influenced by avant-garde currents in the European theater of his day, such as the productions of Adolphe Appia on the Continent or of Edward Gordon Craig in London, which aimed to put into practice what Wagner called "total theater." Presumably, in an age when serious drama was still dominated by Ibsen and Strindberg, his inspiration for such a multi-media extravaganza was not solely autochthonous. And yet, I can think of no other major early twentieth-century play in which the idea of total theater is so totally realized. And why limit ourselves to the early part of the century? How many such plays do we have later on? The closest thing to them, perhaps, is the Broadway musical, and it may well be that only Broadway could do *A Night in the Old Marketplace* properly—but for all its splendor, where in the tradition of *Showboat* and *Oklahoma* do you find the emotional rawness, the imaginative wildness, the theatrical daredeviltry, the delirious energy, the ferocious language, the human *in extremis* of Peretz's play? Put it next to even something like *West Side Story* and the latter seems soft by comparison. Still, what a pity that Leonard Bernstein did not write music for *A Night in the Old Marketplace*. I rather think that had he known of its existence, he would have jumped at the chance.

Am I seriously proposing that *A Night in the Old Marketplace* should be produced as a Broadway musical? As a matter of fact, I am. Why not? After *Cats* and *Les Misérables*, it is a play whose time has come. (I do not even speak of its content, which was far ahead of its times too. Think of the play's outspoken feminism, for example.) I say give it the works: strobe lights, synthesizers, electronic music, film projectors ("In midair, above the road leading out of town, a cemetery emerges from the mist," reads a stage direction in Act Three: what could be easier?), a snarling, wailing, driving, pleading, tenderly spine-chilling score. And no one has to write the book because it already exists and does not need to have a word changed. Let it be the 1990s' answer to the 1960s' *Fiddler on the Roof*, that charmingly mawkish sentimentalization of the shtetl that appealed to every self-congratulatory piety of contemporary Jewish life. If there is any one message that runs through Peretz's work, of which *A Night in the Old Marketplace* is without a doubt the crowning achievement, it is that nothing smells worse than unlanced piety. Go for it!

Zichron Ya'akov

Notes

▼

This Peretz reader does not presume a specialized knowledge of the culture of Polish Jewry. Explanations, definitions, and clarifications are provided in the form of notes and a glossary. The notes clarify or amplify specific items in the text, e.g., sources of biblical and talmudic quotations, dates or circumstances of historical events, folk customs, etc. The glossary explains terms and proper names that occur in one or more of the works.

Translators have used different strategies to render Jewish terms and practices in English. The glossary will therefore, in some cases, include both the Yiddish and English terms for the same thing, e.g., "tfiln" and "phylacteries." Yiddish terms are spelled phonetically except where they have more common spellings in English usage, e.g., "Torah," "Rosh Hashana."

Place-names generally appear in these translations according to their Yiddish usage. Corresponding Russian and Polish place-names appear as an appendix to the glossary.

Monish

1 / Shor shenoygakh es hapora: A popular passage of Tractate *Baba Kamma*, dealing with responsibility for an ox that gores a cow.

2 / Tsoyer: A legendary gem or window that served as a source of light in Noah's Ark.

Impressions of a Journey

1 / Baron Maurice de Hirsch (1881–95), a Belgian-Jewish philanthropist who devoted his fortune to alleviating human distress. He embarked on a project of transporting Russian and Romanian Jews to Argentina, where they would set up agricultural colonies, but he was not successful.

Baron Edmond James de Rothschild (1845–1934), a French-Jewish philanthropist and patron of Jewish settlement in Palestine. Because of his concern for all problems in the settlements, he became known as "the Father of the Yishuv" (settlement).

2 / Rabbis with the reputation of being able to perform miraculous cures were called masters of the Good Name, or Good Jews.

3 / "Guilty or innocent"—Tractate *Sanhedrin* 98a.

4 / "He issued His commands to Jacob, His statutes and rules to Israel. He did not do so for any other nation; of such ordinances they know nothing"— Psalms, 147:19–20.

5 / "If you keep account of sins, O Lord, who can stand?"—Psalms 130:3.

6 / "The Lord said to Moses as follows: speak to the Israelite people and instruct them to make for themselves fringes on the corners of their garments throughout the ages; let them attach a cord of blue to the fringe at each corner"—Numbers 15:37–8. Gershon Hanokh Leiner (1834–91), the Hasidic rabbi of Rodzin, claimed to have discovered the *tekhelet* (the color blue) of the *tzitzit*; his followers, who wove blue thread into their fringes, became known as the Blue-Thread Hasidim. Most rabbinic authorities disagreed with Leiner.

7 / "There is no justice"—Tractate *Baba Metzia* 97a.

8 / "So Jeshurun waxed fat, and he kicked. . . . He forsook the God who made him, and spurned the Rock of his support"—Deuteronomy 32:15.

9 / "Why do nations assemble, and peoples plot vain things; kings of the earth take their stand, and regents intrigue together against the Lord and against His Messiah?"—Psalms 2:1–2.

10 / "*Moj panie*" is Polish for "My dear sir."

11 / "Jacob sent messengers ahead to his brother Esau in the land of Seir, the country of Edom, and instructed them as follows: Thus shall you say to my lord Esau—thus says your servant Jacob: I have sojourned with Laban and remained there until now." Genesis 32:4–5. Rashi comments on the phrase "I have sojourned with Laban": I have sojourned with Laban the wicked, but the 613 commandments I observed, and I did not learn from his evil deeds." The maskil appears to be alluding to this comment by Rashi and implying that just as Jacob was uncorrupted by his impious surroundings, so he preserves his worldliness in his benighted surroundings.

12 / "Let the young warriors duel"—II Samuel 2:14.

13 / In II Samuel 20:19, a wise woman of the city of Abel refers to her city as the mother city in Israel.

14 / "Behold, the Guardian of Israel"—Psalms 121:4.

15 / "Then Mordekhai returned to the King's gate, while Haman hurried home, his head covered in mourning"—Esther 6:12.

16 / There is a general principle found in the Talmud (see, for example, *Kethuboth* 16a) to the effect that if someone creates a prohibition through his testimony, he is allowed to continue his testimony and nullify the prohibition.

17 / The Hasidic Rebbe Israel of Kozinitz (1733–1814) was known for his sweet devotion and ecstatic faith.

18 / Perhaps Peretz had in mind the Tosaphot in *Nedarim* 4a, *Elu Hataot ve-Ashamot*, and the parallel Tosaphot in *Rosh Hashana* 5b.

19 / "He fulfills the desire"—Psalms 145:14.

20 / With respect to Joseph's dreams, "his brothers were wrought up at him, and his father kept the matter in mind"—Genesis 37:11.

21 / "The Jews had light and gladness, happiness and honor"—Esther 8:16.

22 / "People are not held accountable"—Tractate *Baba Batra* 16b.

23 / "A man's heart knows"—Tractate *Yoma* 83a.

24 / Maimonides' "Laws of Idol Worship," 11:16 in the *Mishneh Torah*, says all witchcraft is false and nonsense.

25 / Peretz conflates two verses: "He will not have regard for any ransom. He will refuse your bribe, however great"—Proverbs 6:35; and "Wealth is to no avail on the day of wrath, but righteousness saves from death"—Proverbs 11:4.

26 / "Equal in size and power were the moon and sun created, but the moon was reduced because it complained and said, 'It is impossible for two kings to use one crown' "—Rashi on Genesis 1:16. It is believed that the moon will be restored to its full size when the redemption comes. The prayer for the moon based on Isaiah 30:26 states: "May it be Your will, O Lord, my God and God of my forefathers, to fill the flaw of the moon."

27 / "Every river has its own current"—Tractate *Hullin* 18b.

28 / Certain defects found in some of the organs of a slaughtered animal render the animal *treyf*, and forbidden for consumption. Since a fair percentage of animals suffer from lung disease, the lungs must always be carefully examined by the slaughterer and, if a defect is found, brought to a rabbi to determine if the meat is thereby rendered unkosher.

29 / "No leaven shall be found in your houses for seven days. For whoever eats what is leavened, that person shall be cut off from the community of Israel, whether he is a stranger or a citizen of the country"—Exodus 12:19. Rabbis traditionally gave two major sermons a year, the first on the Sabbath during the Ten Days of Repentance, and the second on Shabbes Hagadol, the Sabbath before Passover.

30 / "Whatever discovery"—*Leviticus Rabah* 22:1.

31 / "Blessed be the Lord"—Psalm 68:20.

32 / According to Jewish law, a blemish invalidates a sacrificial offering.

33 / The notion that each man has his own unique God-given task is widespread in Jewish literature. One classic expression may be found in the Talmud *Berakhoth* 17a: "A favorite saying of the Rabbis of Japheh was: I am God's creature and my fellow is God's creature. (Rashi comments: I who study Torah am God's creature and my fellow the peasant is God's creature.) My work is in the town and his work is in the country. I rise early for my work, and he rises early for his work. Just as he does not presume to do my work, so I do not presume to do his work. Will you say, I do much and he does little? We have learnt: one may do much or one may do little; it is all one provided he directs his heart to heaven."

34 / At the conclusion of the recitation of the Kaddish (prayer of sanctification), one takes three steps backward.

35 / Queen Esther's complexion—*Megillah* 13a.

36 / "Therefore shall a man"—Genesis 2:24.

37 / "Thou shall not insult the deaf, or put a stumbling block before the blind. Thou shall fear thy God: I am the Lord"—Leviticus 14:14.

38 / "When a righteous man departs"— See Rashi's commentary on Genesis 28:10.

39 / "The Lord God said, 'It is not good for man to be alone; I will make a fitting helper for him' "—Genesis 2:18.

40 / The morning Shema must be recited from shortly before sunrise till the end of the first quarter of the day. Tractate *Berakhot* 1:1–2. Hasidim in emphasizing their spiritual preparation for prayer often recite it later than the prescribed time.

41 / "When thou eatest the labor of thy hands"—based on Psalm 128:2.

42 / Tractate *Kiddushim* 1:7 states that women are exempt from time-bound commandments.

43 / This legend about the arrival of the Jews in Poland after their 1492 expulsion from Spain was still circulating by word of mouth at the time of Peretz.

44 / Peretz, contrasting the high spiritual inheritance of these Jews with their current misery, was himself thought to be a descendant of prominent Spanish Jews. The author of the standard work of laws governing kosher slaughter was Rabbi Alexander Sender Schorr (d. 1737).

45 / Before studying the *Chapters of the Fathers*, it is customary to recite the Mishna *Sanhedrin* 10:1, which quotes this passage of Isaiah 60:21.

46 / There is an ancient Jewish mystical concept concerning the *Pargod* ("Curtain" or "Veil") that separates God the Creator, who sits on the Divine Throne, from the other parts of the Divine world; it prevents the ministering angels from seeing the Divine Glory.

47 / "As if I were a raven"—Psalms 147:9.

48 / Probably Abraham Joshua Heschel of Apt (d. 1825), the Hasidic rebbe who recounted fantastic events he claimed to have remembered from former incarnations.

49 / "And he dreamed, and behold a ladder was set up on the earth, and the top of it reached to heaven; and behold the angels of God were ascending and descending on it." The midrash is cited in Rashi on Genesis 28:11 and is based on the Talmud *Hullin* 41b.

50 / "A scholar's waiver"—Tractate *Kiddushin* 32.

51 / Spelling Noah with seven mistakes is a common idiomatic description of an ignoramus.

52 / "There was not a house"—Exodus 11:30.

53 / The Hasidic Rebbe Yakov Yitzkhak of Pzhysha (d. 1814), called "the Jew" (Yehudi). See Martin Buber, *Tales of the Hasidim: The Later Masters*, pp. 33–36.

54 / Hasidim tied a belt around the waist to separate the upper from the lower, profane part of the body during prayer.

55 / *Hemdat yomim* is an anonymous popular prayer book and compilation of customs and practices dating from the eighteenth century.

56 / Psalm 47 was read before the blowing of the shofar on Rosh Hashana.

57 / Jewish Law required tailors to return remnants to customers, but a popular expression held that they lived off "remnants," i.e., routinely told customers to order more cloth than was actually needed.

58 / "The ignorant man"—*Chapters of the Fathers* 2:5.

59 / There will be no second flood—Genesis 9:11.

What Is the Soul?

1 / "A man is not held responsible"—Tractate *Baba Batra* 16b.

2 / "For out of Zion"—Isaiah 2:3.

3 / According to the Code of Jewish Law, nail-cutting on Friday afternoons was to begin with the left hand in the order 4, 2, 5, 3, 1, and then the right hand in the order 2, 4, 1, 3, 5. This scheme was believed to have mystical associations, with serious consequences if altered.

4 / The discussion of messianic portents in Tractate *Makkot* 24b comments on Lamentations 5:18: "For the mountain of Zion, which is desolate, / the foxes walk upon it."

5 / Delaying the reading of Torah scrolls in the synagogue was the standard recourse of Jews who had grievances to make public.

6 / Major commentaries, identical with texts named in Peretz's memoirs as the works he studied.

7 / Knives that had become ritually unclean (because of contact with meat if dairy, with dairy if meat) were buried as part of repurification.

In the Mail Coach

1 / This seems to allude to government censorship that hobbled the Jewish press in tsarist Russia.

2 / According to Deuteronomy 22:11, Jews were not permitted to wear garments made of a mixture of wool and linen.

3 / He studied with her Tractate *Baba Kama* with the major commentaries. *Maharsha* is the Hebrew acronym for the name of Rabbi Shmuel Eidels, a famous seventeenth-century talmudist.

Bryna's Mendl

1 / "When the boys grew up, Esau became a skillful hunter, a man of the outdoors; but Jacob was a mild man who dwelled in a tent"—Genesis 25:27.

2 / Charity boxes of Meir Baal Hanes symbolized longing for Eretz Israel.

3 / Talmud *Ketuboth* IIIa. "Rabbi Elazar said, 'The dead outside the land of Israel will not be resurrected.' . . . But can Rabbi Elazar maintain that the righteous outside the land of Israel will not be resurrected? Rabbi Ela said, '[They will be resurrected] through rolling [to the land of Israel].' "

4 / *Chapters of the Fathers* 3:17: "If there is no Torah, there is no food."

5 / The prayer of Takhanun was not recited after the Amidah on days when there was a circumcision in town.

A Musician's Death

1 / It was customary to measure the grave of a holy man with a string that would then be used for the wicks of candles. The burning of these candles in the name of dangerously ill persons was considered the most efficacious intervention on their behalf.

The Pious Cat

1 / Zimri as wrathful avenger in I Samuel 16:11–14.

2 / Pinkhas, son of Eliezer, Numbers 25:7–10.

The Shabbes Goy

1 / Chelm is the name of an actual Jewish town in Poland. For reasons its inhabitants could not explain, it became known in Jewish folklore as "a fools' town," and many humorous stories were attributed to the Jews of Chelm. Peretz brings this tradition up to date.

The Poor Boy

1 / A committee man is a member of a charitable organization.

2 / Two groschen equaled one kopeck.

3 / Because the consequences of breaking vows according to Talmudic Law were so dire, Jews would sometimes say under their breath "Not to be meant as a vow" after having accidentally undertaken something that they might not be able to fulfill. The "enlightened" Jew here associates this practice with religious hypocrisy.

4 / According to tradition, upon the coming of the Messiah those in Paradise will feast on the body of the monster Leviathan.

5 / Tractate *Pesakhim* 8 says that emissaries of good deeds come to no harm, either in their going or in their return. According to folk tradition, every good deed creates a good angel, just as every bad deed creates a bad angel.

The Dead Town

1 / The name of this town, Tsiachnovka, is fictional.

2 / "The more knowledge, the more sorrow"—Ecclestiastes 1:18.

Uncle Shakhne and Aunt Yakhne

1 / "A man may not wear women's clothes"—Deuteronomy 22:5.

A Conversation

1 / The two Hasidim are adherents of the Polish dynasty of Menahem Mendl of Kotsk (1787–1859) and the Galician dynasty of Shalom Rokeach of Belz (1779–1855).

2 / "You shall not return a slave"—Deuteronomy 23:16.

3 / "The man who fasts overmuch"—Tractate *Taanit* 11.

4 / "Rejoice in the festival"—Deuteronomy 16:14.

5 / "Pour out Thy wrath"—Jeremiah 10:25. The passage is also included in the Passover Haggadah.

6 / "My children drown in the sea"—Tractate *Megillah* 10b.

7 / "Israel does not rejoice in the manner of the nations"—Hosea 9:1.

Between Two Mountains

1 / The rov (teacher) is leader of the religious community, teacher of the Law, and head of the rabbinic court. The term "rebbe" came into use to designate leaders of Hasidic groups, who could also, where Hasidism gained political power, assume the status of rov. The historical struggle between the misnagdim and the Hasidim is here dramatized largely in social and psychological terms.

2 / In the formative period of the Hasidic movement, the exceptional qualities of the rebbe were spontaneously "revealed" to his followers, who recounted these events as part of the lore of their sect.

3 / Folk customs to ward off death.

4 / "From the shoulder and up"—I Samuel 9:2, 10:23.

5 / *Nivrakh aleynu*—the beginning of the prayer "May we be blessed."

6 / "The heart knows the bitterness"—Proverbs 14:10.

Stories

1 / The blood libel was an allegation that Jews murdered Christians in order to obtain blood for the Passover ritual. The approximate coincidence of Easter and Passover led to the charge that Jews used the blood of Christian children in the preparation of matza or in the seder. Peretz's story takes for granted the reader's awareness of centuries of such incidents and of tales about Jewish martyrs and miraculous saviors.

Revelation

1 / Nahman ben Simkha of Bratslav (1772–1810), great grandson of the Baal Shem Tov, was noted for his parables and stories.

2 / "By the waters of Babylon, there we sat down, sat and wept, as we thought of Zion"—Psalms 137:1.

Three Gifts

1 / On Simkhat Torah, the festival marking the completion of the annual cycle of the reading of the Pentateuch, scrolls are taken from the ark and paraded seven times. Bidding for this honor (used in financing the synagogue) was especially spirited.

Downcast Eyes

1 / A portion of the khallah dough—at least the size of an olive—must be separated from the rest and burnt. The law (hearkening back to the injunction of Numbers 15:17–21 that a portion of dough be donated to priests of the Temple) was one of the three particular commandments of Jewish women, along with lighting the candles and maintaining ritual purity after menstruation.

2 / The biblical story of Esther was part of Polish lore: the legendary Esterke, Jewish mistress of King Casimir the Great (1333–70), had been the subject of historical speculation since the fifteenth century.

3 / *Torah tsiva lanu:* "[God through Moses] has given us the Torah."

A Pinch of Snuff

1 / "For there is not a just man upon earth, that does good, and sins not"—Ecclesiastes 7:20.

2 / "Fathers shall not die in place of the sons"—Deuteronomy 24:16. The passage in Ezekiel quoting Deuteronomy is much harsher. See Ezekiel 20.

Yom Kippur in Hell

1 / Lahadam: An acronym for *Lo haya hadavar meolam* (It never existed)—a nonexistent place.

2 / *Yisgadal:* The first word of the Kaddish.

My Memoirs

1 / "Born to die"—*Chapters of the Fathers* 4:29.

2 / See p. 5 of this volume.

3 / "Gad, a troop shall press upon him"—Genesis 49:19.

4 / Moyshe and Paulina Altberg, Peretz's uncle and aunt, preserved his juvenilia and published some of it after his death.

5 / *Vayikra:* "And the Lord called"—the first word of the book of Leviticus, with which kheyder education began.

6 / The fortress of Zamość was razed in 1866.

7 / The verse *Vayitsmakh purkanye* had been dropped from Ashkenazic prayer but was reintroduced by the Hasidim from Sephardic usage.

8 / *Eyzehu neshekh*—Tractate *Baba Metzia* 5 deals with the laws of interest.

9 / Serkele, in the play of that title, is a greedy and manipulative woman who schemes to defraud her niece of her fortune. Shloyme Ettinger (1803–1856) practiced medicine in Zamość and was one of the pioneers of modern Yiddish literature.

10 / Rabbi Nissim ben Reuben Gerondi (Ran; 1310?–1375?) was an authoritative Spanish commentator on the Talmud. The *Pri Megadim* is a classic commentary on the Code of Jewish Law, the *Shulkhan Arukh*, by Joseph ben Meir Teomin (c. 1727–92). *Duties of the Heart*, by the eleventh-century moral philosopher Bakhya ibn Pakuda, is one of the best-known Jewish ethical books. Rabbi Levi ben Gershom (Ralbag, Gersonides; 1288–1344) was a mathematician, astronomer, moral philosopher, and biblical commentator.

Guide to the Perplexed by Maimonides (Moses ben Maimon, the Rambam; 1135–1204) forges a synthesis of rabbinic Judaism and Aristotelian philosophy. *The Tree of Life* (*Etz Chaim*) is an exposition of the kabbalistic system of Isaac Luria by his most outstanding disciple, Chaim Vital Calabrese (1542–1620). The Zohar is the major work of Jewish mysticism. *Oracles of the Prophets* (*Urim ve-Tumin*) by Jonathan Eybeschuetz (c. 1690–1764) is noted for its clarity and incisiveness.

11 / Kheyder boys would be called on to recite psalms at the bedside of a woman in labor to help ensure a healthy birth.

12 / "Unto the horse in Pharaoh's chariot"—Song of Songs 1:9.

13 / According to widespread folk belief, the soul of an evildoer transmigrates after his death into a lower species until its penance has been done and it is redeemed.

14 / Bloodletting for medicinal purposes was performed in the bathhouse.

15 / "Not a dog whet his tongue"—Exodus 11:7.

16 / This is one of the talmudic descriptions of the angel of death.

17 / Foxes in the Temple—Tractate *Makkot* 24b; Song of Songs 2:15. There are many animal fables about the cunning fox.

18 / The musician Yoel in the one-act play *What the Fiddle Knows* describes the sinful man from the sinful city who when he suddenly emerges onto a snowy plain is exalted by the cleansing power of God's brilliant grace.

19 / Rabbi Moyshe Wahl (1797–1873) is described in chapter 5.

20 / "Out of the lions' dens"—Song of Songs 4:8.

21 / "The meadows clothed with flocks"—Psalms 65:13.

22 / "Like unto them that dream"—an echo of Psalms 126:1.

23 / Fayvl Gelibter (1808–88) was an attorney in Zamość. His son Isaac was an ethnographer and prominent Zionist. Alexander Zederbaum (1816–1893) founded *Hamelitz*, the first Hebrew weekly in Russia in 1860, and its Yiddish supplement, *Kol Mevasser*, two years later. Jacob Eichenbaum (1796–1861) wrote Hebrew poetry and translated mathematical works into Hebrew.

24 / The sins of omission attributed to Gelibter were practices the maskilim considered superstitious accretions or irrelevant. They stressed study of the Bible.

25 / In 1874–75 Gavriel Yehuda Lichtenfeld (1811–87) published polemical tracts against Chaim Zelig Slonimski (1810–1904), a Hebrew writer on popular science and founding editor of the Hebrew newspaper *Hatsefira*, questioning his competence in scientific matters. Lichtenfeld was the father of Peretz's first wife (see chapter 8).

26 / Aba Hilkiah, an early-first-century rabbi, is mentioned in Tractate *Ta'anit* 23a, b. As part of his strange behavior, he walked barefoot carrying his shoes, but put them on when he had to cross the water.

27 / Pious Jewish males did not address women directly, not even their wives.

28 / "The flowers appear on the earth"—Song of Songs 2:12.

29 / Abraham Goldfaden (1840–1908), founder of the modern Yiddish theater, is presented here as one of the spokesmen for Enlightenment.

30 / Among Jews there was widespread sympathy with the Poles in their 1863 uprising against the tsarist government. Peretz describes below a Jewish rebel leader, Morgenstern, who is mentioned in memoirs of Polish rebels. The identical initials in Yiddish of Yehoshua Margulies and Yosef Morgenstern are the cause of some confusion.

31 / The events described here occurred in Zamość in 1870.

32 / "Put not your trust"—Psalms 146:3.

33 / Bernard Levenstein (1821–89). Isaac Adolphe Crémieux (1796–1880), French jurist and political figure, was noted for his defense of oppressed Jews. He and Moses Montefiore had secured the release of Jews imprisoned in Damascus during the notorious blood-libel case of 1840.

34 / The progymnasium, or junior high school, of Zamość was founded in 1867.

35 / "Mourning and with his head covered"—Esther 6:12.

36 / Israel ben Moses Halevi Zamosc (1700–1752), one of the founders of the Haskalah movement, tutored Moses Mendelssohn in mathematics and astronomy.

37 / In case of the husband's disappearance, the writ of divorce would prevent the woman from becoming an *agunah*, a deserted wife, and give her the right to remarry.

38 / Jacob Reifman (1818–94), a scholar of the Bible and the Talmud, was an outspoken critic of Hasidism.

39 / Rosa Luxemburg (1871–1919), one of the founders of the Social Democratic Party of Poland and Lithuania, was a leading figure in the revolutionary left wing of the German socialist movement and after 1918 of the Communist Party of Germany.

40 / Goldfaden's song "The Dawn."

41 / Rabbi Hillel said, "What is hateful to you, do not to your fellow creature." Tractate *Sabbath* 31a.

42 / Some communities called up men of lower status for the synagogue reading of the biblical passages Leviticus 26:14–43 and Deuteronomy 28:15–68, containing the curses and punishments that will be inflicted on Israel if they do not obey God.

43 / The little collection *Stories in Verse* was published in 1887. Haskalah satire attacked the community tax on the sale of kosher meat as a pseudoreligious vehicle for the rich to fleece the poor. The 1867 play *The Meat Tax* by Mendele Mocher Sforim (Sholem Jacob Abramovitch; 1835–1917) exposed "the gang of town benefactors" with special bite.

44 / The Gaon of Vilna, Elijah ben Solomon Zalman (1720–97), the leading scholar of his generation, tried to fight the encroachment of Hasidism through bans of excommunication.

45 / "A man of truth"—Exodus 18:21. The character of Reb Zishele appears in, for example, "Stories of Reb Yokhanan the Melamed."

46 / Angry with the rabbi's interpretation of a certain passage, Shmaye "the hero" goes to the rabbi's house and tears the hat from his head. Although the rabbi cries out that he forgives the insult, Shmaye feels himself haunted by guilt and dies.

47 / "It was like an error"—Ecclesiastes 10:5.

48 / *Collocation* (1847), a novel by the Polish playwright and writer Josef Korzeniowski (1797–1863).

49 / "They went up the mountains"—Psalms 104:8.

50 / Because one is not permitted to break a vow, pious Jews refrain from sealing vows.

51 / Jacob ben Meir Tam (Rabbenu; 1100–1171), is considered the greatest talmudic authority of his generation.

52 / The play is *In polish oyf der keyt*, about a sinner who is "chained in the synagogue vestibule," the Jewish equivalent of being placed in the stocks.

53 / The Sabbath hymn "Borkhi nafshi" closely follows the biblical story of Creation. The midrashic gloss on Genesis is from *Bereshit Rabba* 10:79.

54 / See pp. 42–44 ("A Little Boy?"), in *Impressions of a Journey.*

55 / The Haskalah objected to the custom of studying these laws before puberty.

56 / "Keep ashes in his mouth"—Lamentations 3:28–29.

57 / "Land flowing with milk and honey"—I Kings 5:5.

58 / The story, "Devotion Without End," can be found in I. L. Peretz, *Selected Stories*, ed. Irving Howe and Eliezer Greenberg.

59 / Four sages enter the mysterious orchard (*pardes*)—Tractate *Hagigah* 15.

60 / "Sins of the fathers"—Exodus 20:5, etc. The comments of Maimonides are from *Guide to the Perplexed.*

61 / Beruria in *Midrash Proverbs* XXXI, 10, f. 54b. Leah, the rabbi's daughter in Peretz's drama *The Golden Chain*, returns to her Hasidic family after becoming disillusioned with the iciness of the Enlightenment.

62 / It is described in "Der farsholtener brunem" (The Cursed Well), a story about the seemingly supernatural power of a well to lure victims to their death.

63 / "In keler-shtub," a study of people who live in close quarters, in a cellar apartment.

64 / Tractate *Baba Batra* 75a comments on Numbers 27:20: Moses' face beamed like the sun, Joshua's only like the moon.

65 / "Those who enter will never return"—Proverbs 2:19.

66 / "A wise man's understanding"—Ecclesiastes 10:2.

67 / Isaac ben Moses Arama (c. 1420–94) was the author of *Akeydat Yitskhak* (*The Binding of Isaac*), a philosophic commentary on the Pentateuch and the Five Scrolls, written in the form of sermons.

68 / The kheyder teachers were reputed to be ignorant of modern disciplines, including Hebrew grammar.

69 / Edward von Hartmann (1842–1906), a German pessimistic philosopher, was the author of the three-volume *Philosophie des Unbewussten* (Berlin, 1969). Carl Vogt (1817–95), a German biologist, wrote, "The relation between

thought and brain is roughly of the same order as that between bile and the liver or urine and the bladder."

70 / Lichtenfeld; see n. 24.

71 / The white robe (*kitl*) worn on one's wedding day and on certain ceremonial holidays was also to serve as a shroud. These were traditional gifts to a son-in-law.

72 / Abraham Jacob Paperna (1840–1919), Hebrew writer and critic, in 1868 published a much-discussed brochure, "General Drama and Hebrew Drama in Particular."

73 / The concluding lines of Friedrich Schiller's "Der Jungling am Bache": "Raum ist in der kleinsten Hütte / Fur ein glücklich libend Paar."

74 / These were all traditional practices and customs that the author intended to defy. Folk belief held that whoever crossed the threshold first would dominate the other spouse.

75 / The custom of breaking the wineglass was commonly interpreted as a commemoration of the destroyed Temple in Jerusalem. But the rebellious bridegroom still observed the morning custom of ritual hand-washing even as he planned his defiance.

76 / A folk belief that if the couple likes sweets, it will rain on their wedding day.

77 / Because it was feared that the jealous demons would snatch Jews from their midst, Jews refrained from counting people, except negatively: "not one, not two . . ."

78 / "As if they were frozen"—Tractate *Nedarim* 20.

79 / The innkeeper might have been boiling water in a pot used for unkosher foods.

80 / Those who intended to break bread over a meal would have to ritually wash their hands; those who made do with biscuits would not.

Glossary

▼

BAAL SHEM TOV ("Master of the Divine Name"): Israel ben Eliezer (1700–1760), founder of the Hasidic movement.

BADKHN: A master of ceremonies and wedding entertainer.

BAR MITZVA: At thirteen a boy is of age to assume full religious responsibilities as a Jew. At the ceremony marking this initiation the boy is called up to the reading of the Torah.

BEYSMEDRESH: A study house, sometimes attached to or serving as a synagogue, containing a library with tables and chairs.

BLUE-THREAD HASIDIM: Followers of the Hasidic rabbi of Rodzin, who claimed to have discovered the original blue that Jews were to include in their ritual fringes (Numbers 15:37–38).

BRIS: The circumcision ceremony.

CHAPTERS OF THE FATHERS (Ethics of the Fathers): One of the best-known parts of the Mishna, consisting of the wise sayings of great rabbis; it is often studied on Sabbath afternoons between Passover and Rosh Hashana.

CITRON (etrog): A fruit resembling a lemon, one of the Four Species used in the celebration of Sukkot.

DAY OF ATONEMENT: See Yom Kippur.

DUTIES OF THE HEART: A popular work of Jewish religious philosophy and ethics by Bahya ibn Pakuda (1050–1120?). It teaches that duties of conscience (e.g., humility, asceticism, trust in God) are just as important as practical commandments.

DVAR TORAH: Torah commentary.

DYBBUK: The soul of a sinner that, after his death, transmigrates into the body of a living person.

EIGHTEEN BENEDICTIONS: See Shimenesre.

ELUL: The Jewish month corresponding roughly to September. The shofar is blown daily in anticipation of the high holidays.

ETROG: See Citron.

EYN YAKOV: A collection of legends of the Babylonian and Palestinian Talmuds compiled by Jacob ben Solomon ibn Habib (1445–1515).

FEAST OF TABERNACLES: See Sukkot.

FOUR QUESTIONS: See *Ma Nishtana*.

FRINGES (*tzitzit*): Fringes are worn on prayer shawls and special undergarments as a reminder of God's commandments.

GEHENNA: Hell.

GEMARA: The second part of the Talmud, which consists of discussions and commentaries on the basic part, the Mishna. Sometimes the term is used to refer to the Talmud as a whole.

GOOD JEWS: Wonder-workers; Hasidic leaders thought to have magical healing powers.

GOLEM: An automaton in human form, created by magical means.

GOY: A non-Jew; a Gentile.

HAGGADAH: The text of the home service read during the seder ceremony on the first two nights (in Israel the first night) of Passover.

HASIDISM: A populist mystical movement that arose in the middle of the eighteenth century in Eastern Europe. It centered around a charismatic leader called a zaddik or rebbe, and placed great emphasis on religious enthusiasm and knowledge of God.

HASKALAH: The Hebrew term for the Enlightenment movement and ideology that had its roots in the general European Enlightenment of the eighteenth century. An adherent was called a maskil.

HATSEFIRA: A Warsaw Hebrew newspaper founded in 1862 by Chaim Zelig Slonimski; it emphasized science and technological advancement.

HAVDALA: A ceremony that marks the end of the Sabbath or of a festival. Blessings are made over wine, spices, and a braided candle, symbolizing the separation of the sacred from the ordinary.

HOSHANA RABA: The seventh day of Sukkot, when according to Jewish lore everyone's fate for the coming year is sealed in heaven.

KABBALAH ("Tradition"): The term that refers to the tradition of Jewish mysticism. The Kabbalah developed a system of symbols to try to describe the mystery of creation as a reflection of the mysteries of divine life. Its major text is the Zohar, "The Book of Splendor."

KADDISH (Aramaic for "holy"): A mourner's recitation.

KAPOTE: A caftan or long coat worn by observant Jews.

KEYN EYN HORE: "May no evil eye befall him/her." This expression was used after words of praise to ward off the envious Evil Eye.

KHEYDER (literally, "room"): A Jewish elementary school for boys, often convened in the teacher's room.

KHUPE: A wedding canopy.

KIDDUSH: A prayer over wine.

KLEZMER: Jewish band musicians.

KLOYZ: A small synagogue also used as a study house.

KOL NIDRE ("All Vows"): A prayer chanted at the beginning of the synagogue service on Yom Kippur eve.

KORAH: A relative of Moses' who led an uprising against him and Aaron (Numbers 16).

KRISHMA ("Reading of the Shema"): The prayer that fulfills the commandment of the acceptance of God's absolute sovereignty: "Hear, O Israel, the Lord

our God, the Lord is One" (Deuteronomy 6:4). It occurs in morning and
evening prayers and before retiring.

LAMDAN: A learned man.

LAMED-VOV: See *Thirty-Six Just Men.*

LEVIATHAN: According to tradition, upon the coming of the Messiah, those in
paradise will feast on the body of this monster.

LILITH: The queen of demons.

LITANY OF CURSES (*Tokhekha*): Reproof sections of the Bible: Leviticus 26:14–
43 and Deuteronomy 28:15–68.

LITVAK: A Jew from Lithuania. The term denotes someone of a rationalist,
skeptical, and anti-Hasidic temperament.

MAIMONIDES: Rabbi Moses ben Maimon (1135–1204), the greatest medieval
Jewish philosopher and rabbinic authority. His two chief works were an
encyclopedic codification of Jewish Law, *Mishneh Torah*, and *Guide to the Perplexed*, an attempt to reconcile Aristotelian philosophy with Jewish theology.

MA NISHTANA: The opening words of "the Four Questions" asked by the
youngest member of the family at the Passover seder service.

MASKIL: A follower of the Haskalah.

MATZA: Unleavened bread eaten during Passover.

MEIR BAAL HANES: A reputed miracle-worker whose tomb near Tiberias was
the site of pilgrimages. Contributions to charity boxes in his name were
thought to offer protection against certain dangers and evils.

MENORA: An eight-branched candelabrum, with an extra branch for the candle
that is used to light the others (*shames*). Beginning with a single candle, one
light is added during each of the eight days of Hanukkah, the Festival of
Lights.

MIDRASH: A form of commentary on a biblical passage, much like a homily.

MINYAN: A prayer quorum of ten adult Jewish males.

MISHNA: The basic part of the Talmud, the first compilation of "the Oral Law,"
by Judah Hanasi, ca. 200 C.E.

MISNAGED: An opponent of Hasidism, who stressed the study of Jewish law and
the rational rather than the mystical basis of religion.

MOHEL: A man who performs ritual circumcision, introducing a Jewish male
child into the Jewish covenant with God.

NEILA ("Closing"): The concluding service on Yom Kippur, the climax of the
day of prayer and fasting.

NINTH OF AV: See *Tisha B'Av.*

PASSOVER: The eight-day festival that marks the beginning of spring and
commemorates the deliverance of the Israelites from Egyptian slavery.

PEYES (Hebrew for "corners"): sidelocks worn by observant Jews in literal
obedience to Leviticus 19:27.

PHYLACTERIES: Small leather cases containing passages from Scripture that
observant Jewish males affix to the forehead and left arm during weekday
morning prayers. They are signs of the covenant between God and Israel.

PRAGA: A suburb of Warsaw, across the Vistula River, which during Peretz's
lifetime was home to many poor Jews.

PRAYER SHAWL (*talis*): A garment in the four corners of which fringes have been knotted, worn during morning prayers by observant Jewish males over thirteen.

PURIM: The holiday that celebrates the rescue of Jews from the Persian Haman.

RAMBAM: See *Maimonides*.

RASHI: Solomon ben Isaac (1040–1105). His commentary on the Bible became the basic guide for Jewish study, and accompanies almost every edition of the Hebrew Pentateuch.

REBBE: The term for a Hasidic leader.

REBETSIN: The wife of a rabbi or teacher.

ROSH HASHANA: The Jewish New Year, traditionally regarded as the day of the creation of the world.

ROV ("rabbi"): The leader of the religious community, teacher of the Law, and head of the rabbinic court.

SABBATH BOUNDARY: On the Sabbath, a day of complete rest, observant Jews are not permitted to exert themselves through walking long distances. The *Eruv Tekhumim*, or Sabbath boundary, amalgamates boundaries in order to permit Jews to exceed the Sabbath limit of two thousand cubits outside a town.

SAMMAEL: The postbiblical name for Satan, the prince of demons.

SEDER: A Passover service at home that recounts the liberation of the Jews from Egyptian bondage.

SEPHIROT: According to the kabbalistic system, the mystical hierarchy of the ten creative powers emanating from God.

SHABBES ("Sabbath"): The weekly holy day of rest, which begins at sundown on Friday and ends at sundown on Saturday evening.

SHABBES GOY: A Gentile hired through previously contracted arrangements to do certain required jobs on the Sabbath, thereby circumventing the general injunction against all work.

SHALOSH-SEUDA: The third Sabbath meal. Hasidim suffused this meal, which takes place at the Sabbath's close, with an atmosphere of religious ecstasy and yearning.

SHAMES: Sexton. The term is also used for the extra candle that kindles the Hanukkah lights.

SHAVUOT ("Feast of Weeks"): The festival of the first harvest, which commemorates the giving of the Ten Commandments on Mount Sinai, celebrated with decorative greenery and dairy foods.

SHEKHINA: The Divine Presence.

SHEMA: The declaration of God's unity and providence. See *Krishma*.

SHIMENESRE (Hebrew: *Shmona-esreh*): Eighteen benedictions recited in silent devotion at each of the daily services, also known as the Amidah.

SHOFAR: The horn of the ram (or any other ritually clean animal except the cow), sounded on Rosh Hashana and Yom Kippur.

SHTETL: Any Eastern European market town inhabited largely by Jews.

SHTIBL: A small Hasidic prayerhouse.

SIMKHAT TORAH: The feast on the day following Sukkot, marking the completion of the annual cycle of Pentateuch reading.

SIYYUM: A celebration held when the study of a tractate of Talmud is concluded or when the writing of a Torah scroll is completed.

SUKKAH: A booth or hut erected for Sukkot in which, for seven days, Jews "dwell" or at least eat.

SUKKOT: The autumn festival that commemorates the tabernacles that the Israelites inhabited in the wilderness after the Exodus. A blessing is made over the Four Species: *lulav* (palm), *hadas* (myrtle), *aravah* (willow), and *etrog* (citron).

TAKHANUN: The prayer of supplication, an especially heartfelt plea for God's . gracious compassion.

TALIS: See *prayer shawl*.

TALIS KOTN ("small talis"): A garment worn under the outer garments by observant Jewish males during waking hours. Fringes in its four corners are knotted in accordance with the biblical prescription (Numbers 15:37–41).

TALMUD: A collection of postbiblical writings based on academic discussions of Jewish Law by generations of scholars and jurists over several centuries and in several countries.

TAMUZ: The month of the Jewish year corresponding roughly to July.

TAZ (*Turei zahav*): *Golden Columns*, a classic commentary on the *Shulkhan Arukh*, the Code of Jewish Law.

TEN DAYS OF REPENTENCE: The days between Rosh Hashana, the Jewish New Year, and Yom Kippur, the Day of Atonement—a time for introspection and penitence.

TFILN: See *phylacteries*.

THIRTY-SIX JUST MEN: According to a tradition handed down in the name of the talmudic rabbi Abbaye, "There are not less than thirty-six righteous men in the world who receive the Divine Presence" (*Sanhedrin* 97b; *Sukkah* 45b). Jewish folklore is replete with legends about these anonymous saints (*lamedvovniks*), for whose sake the world is said to exist.

TISHA B'AV: The ninth day of the Hebrew month of Av, commemorating the destruction of the Temple in Jerusalem in 586 B.C.E. and in 70 C.E.

TORAH: The Pentateuch, the Five Books of Moses; it is also a term for Jewish learning in general.

TOSAPHOT: Thirteenth-century glosses on the Talmud. Their study together with the commentary of Rashi is part of the traditional rabbinic curriculum.

TUMIN (*Urim ve-Tumin*): *Oracles of the Prophets* by Jonathan Eybeschuetz (ca. 1690–1764).

YARMULKE: A skullcap worn by observant Jewish males at all times.

YESHIVA: An institute of talmudic learning.

YOM KIPPUR: The Day of Atonement, holiest day of the Jewish calendar. There are five services: Maariv (Kol Nidre, on the eve), Shakharit, Musaf, Minkha, and Neila.

YONTEV: Any Jewish holiday.

YORTSAYT: The anniversary of a death.

ZADDIK: The leader of a Hasidic community, also called *rebbe*.

ZOHAR: The Book of Splendor, the chief work of Jewish mysticism.

Jewish Place-names, Followed by Their Polish Equivalents

▼

Apt	Opatów
Biala	Biala Podlaska
Brisk	Brest Litovsk
Ger	Góra Kalwarja
Ishbitz	Izbica
Kotsk	Kock
Lashchev	Laszczów
Lemberg	Lwów
Nemirov	Niemirow
Rakhev	Rachów
Rizhin	Ruzhin
Shebreshin	Szczebrzeszyn
Tishevitz	Tyszowce
Trisk	Turzyisk
Tsoyzmer	Sandomierz
Ustile	Uscilug
Vorke	Warka
Yartsiev	Jaryczów Nowy